KT-563-467

KANYE WEST

GOD & MONSTER

MARK
BEAUMONT

OVERLOOK OMNIBUS

This edition published by Omnibus Press and distributed in the United States and Canada by The Overlook Press, Peter Mayer Publishers Inc, 141 Wooster Street, New York, NY 10012.

For bulk and special sales requests, please contact sales@overlookny.com or write to us at the above address.

Copyright © 2015 Omnibus Press
(A Division of Music Sales Limited)
14/15 Berners Street,
London, W1T 3LJ, UK.

Cover designed by Fresh Lemon
Picture research by Sarah Datblygu

ISBN: 978-1-4683-1137-2

The Author hereby asserts his/her right to be identified as the author of this work in accordance with Sections 77 to 78 of the Copyright, Designs and Patents Act 1988.

All rights reserved. No part of this book may be reproduced in any form or by any electronic or mechanical means, including information storage or retrieval systems, without permission in writing from the publisher, except by a reviewer who may quote brief passages.

Every effort has been made to trace the copyright holders of the photographs in this book but one or two were unreachable. We would be grateful if the photographers concerned would contact us.

A catàlogue record for this book is available from the British Library.
Cataloguing-in-Publication data is available from the Library of Congress.

Visit Omnibus Press on the web at www.omnibuspress.com

CONTENTS

Introduction

"That's not good. We gotta share the rap but… this video cost a million dollars, fam! I had Pam Anderson, I'm jumping across canyons and shit! Oh! Hey, if I don't win the award show loses credibility. I appreciate it, man, it's nothing against you, I've never seen your video, it's nothing against you, but heeell no, man. I love you all."

Kanye West, interrupting Justice's Best Video acceptance speech at MTV Europe Music Awards, Bella Centre, Copenhagen, November 2, 2006

Jaw stern against the spotlights, eyes blazing, Kanye soaked in the silence, the vacuum left by taped music being sucked from the room. The audience glared back at him, shocked, embarrassed, teetering on his reaction.

He raised the microphone and went to speak.

For the last time in his life, nothing came out.

The seven-year-old Kanye West fled the stage, his Stevie Wonder sunglasses hiding his tears. At the side of the talent contest's stage his mother, Donda, swept him up, stroking his costume braids. She'd watched him practise lip-syncing along to I 'Just Called To Say I Love You' for weeks. She knew that, as something of a veteran of the Chicago children's talent contest circuit, he felt he was the best act of the night. And she knew that, at the worst possible moment, the guy operating the backing track had cut the music right at Kanye's favourite part, "no New Year's Day…".

In the car home, Kanye bewailed the injustice. "I wasn't done!" he bawled, "I could have won!" Donda reassured him, "You'll win next year, honey," and a steely determination set in. No longer would he have his talent brushed off, dismissed out of hand; never again would he be denied the recognition and acclaim he deserved. And when he wasn't, he wouldn't bottle it up.

The following year, Kanye won the same contest. And the following year. And the year after that. In fact, Kanye won it every year until they changed the format, making the event a straightforward talent show where no one won or lost. Kanye's belief in himself was vindicated, along with his deep-rooted conviction that hard work and raw talent should be fairly rewarded.

It wouldn't be the last time the young Kanye fought for his own brand of fairness.

In seventh grade, Kanye decided he wanted to be on his school's basketball team. On his first attempt he didn't make the cut, but he'd been brought up by the attentive Donda to believe that he was capable of anything if he worked hard enough. So that whole summer he practised intently, clawing his way onto an amateur summer league team as a point guard and helping his team win the championship. By the eighth grade try-outs he was vastly improved, hitting every shot in the practice session. Yet when he raced to the pinboard to see who'd made the team, once more his name was missing.

"I asked the coach what's up, and they were like, 'You're just not on it'," he said. "I was like, 'But I hit every shot'." Though he'd refuse to fail and would go on to make the junior team the following year, he never forgot that coach who barred him from the team when he'd proved he was good enough. Every time he'd be snubbed for an award, not taken seriously by fashion designers or critics or put down by reviewers, it would be that coach's face he'd see, telling him he just wasn't on it.

"Where I didn't feel that I had a position in eighth grade to scream and say, 'Because I hit every one of my shots, I deserve to be on this team!', I'm letting it out on everybody who doesn't want to give me my credit," he'd say. "[When I hit all my shots] you put me on the team. So I'm going to use my platform to tell people that they're not being fair. Anytime I've had a big thing that's ever pierced and cut across the internet, it was a fight for justice. Justice. And when you say justice, it doesn't have to be war. Justice could just be clearing a path for people to dream properly. It could be clearing a path to make it fair within the arena that I play. You know, if Michael Jordan can scream at the refs, me as Kanye West, as the Michael Jordan of music, can go and say, 'This is wrong'."

So when Kanye invaded the stage during the Best Video acceptance speech from the ironically named electro act Justice at the EMAs in 2006, stared sternly out into the crowd and complained loudly that he should have won for his video for 'Touch The Sky' – the moment that his reputation as rap's biggest, most egotistical loudmouth first reared its head – he was simply following his natural instinct to speak out against slights he perceives against his talent and effort. A homage to Evel Knievel's failed jump across Snake River Canyon in 1974, 'Touch The Sky' was an impressive piece of work, a seventies Blaxploitation style clip starring Kanye as Evel Kanyevel, a motorcycle stuntman preparing for his biggest ever jump, riding a Death Rocket across the Grand Canyon. With the Booker T Washington High School marching band and news crews seeing him off, Lupe Fiasco providing a guest spot, comic interludes referencing his off-script claim that "George Bush doesn't care about black people" during a to-camera speech during the previous year's Concert For Hurricane Relief – "Kanyevel, are you concerned about the effects of your comments about President Nixon?" a TV interviewer asks him – and stars such as Pamela Anderson playing his argumentative wife and Nia Long his angry ex-girlfriend, it was certainly an expensive endeavour. In his outburst, Kanye may have mistaken the cost of production for quality and the credibility of the ceremony for commercial concerns. But as he hugged Justice and left the stage to continue his tirade in backstage media interviews – "It's complete bullshit," he said, "I paid a million… it took a month to film, I stood on a mountain. I flew a helicopter over Vegas… I did it to be the king of all videos", while admitting he'd had a "sippy sippy" – he was speaking for a minor part of a major talent, the ambition and potential of which the world was only then beginning to glimpse.

Over the coming years, Kanye would justify such acts of perceived arrogance over and over again. His albums would break barrier after barrier, both in the inventiveness of their sounds and the breadth and openness of their genre-straddling collaborations. They'd shatter, reinvent and reform rap music until it became virtually unrecognisable in tone, fashion and sentiment. Time and again Kanye would pioneer a brand new approach, make it so successful it spawned a whole range of mainstream imitators, then immediately abandon it for something even more challenging and revolutionary. He became a character with what seemed like a vastly inflated opinion of himself and his work, yet repeatedly lived up to – if not superseded – it on record.

Along the way Kanye became the most loved, hated, admired, ridiculed, celebrated, lampooned and consistently unignorable force in rap. A self-proclaimed God and a mutherfuckin' monster.

Stand well back. We're clipping free the wire.

CHAPTER ONE

The Roots Of The Roses

The West empire, you might say, was built on a quarter.

A 25 cent piece, pressed into the palm of nine-year-old Portwood Williams at the central train station in Oklahoma City one afternoon in 1925. His father placed the coin in Portwood's hand, handed a dime to each of his two sisters, then stepped onto a train without ever telling them where he was headed. Wherever he went, he never came back.

Portwood rolled the quarter in his palm, hot with sweat and significance. Though he'd never stop loving his father – none of the Williams clan would – his parting gift would grow to symbolise Portwood's determination to stand by his family to the bitter end, to live his life as a bastion of unconditional support and love to those that needed him. Portwood Williams would be no deserter. Portwood would provide.

Already making some money picking cotton as a child, in sixth grade Portwood dropped out of school to help support his family full-time. His jobs were menial and racked with racial abuse – as a shoe-shiner buffing footwear for tips he'd be spat on and sworn at and when he took up labouring work in Oklahoma's Capitol Hill area he would walk daily past signs enforcing a sundown curfew on blacks and dogs. But Portwood was never beaten out of his dignity or robbed of his ambition.

He scraped together enough money to launch an upholstery business which went from strength to strength; before long he'd be a fully-fledged entrepreneur honoured as one of Oklahoma City's Outstanding Black Businessmen. Over the years he'd come to be regarded as a man of personability and leadership, of strong convictions and good humour – they called him "the Bill Cosby of Oklahoma City". The rise of the Roses had begun.

Marrying young – his marriage to Lucille Williams would last 72 years – Portwood and his wife set up a solid and dependable family home. While still holding down jobs as a hairdresser, a domestic and a key punch operator at Tinker Air Force Base, Lucille gave Portwood four children and was endlessly dedicated to them all. The youngest, Donda, was nicknamed 'Big Girl' and showered with care, attention, religious teaching and no little spirit. When she wasn't acting out passages from the Bible or giving readings and speeches at oratorical contests, the prize orator for the 5th Street Baptist Church, she was being told by her mother to use only the 'whites-only' water fountains and changing rooms in malls on their regular shopping trips. At the tender age of nine she and her brother Portwood Jr took part in the first US sit-in demonstration to campaign for public accommodations – recreational facilities, stores and educational institutions – for Afro-Americans. Donda was raised with faith, and with fight.

She was also raised to feel rich, no matter how much the family struggled. Lucille and Portwood stretched every dime to ensure their children had all the material goods they could, and showered them in love and praise while also engendering a subtle expectation to do well in life. Donda was gifted one dollar for every report card A and a mild grilling over every B. She rarely brought home a B.

She knew early on, then, that real strength was in the mind. While maintaining a dream of being an actress, she put dating on the back burner and studied hard, eventually graduating from Douglass High School to Virginia Union University for a four-year Bachelor degree in English funded in part by the savings bonds her parents had snaffled away for her. Hungry for more knowledge, she moved to Atlanta, Georgia, in 1971 to throw herself into a Master's degree at Atlanta University, buying a two-bedroom townhouse with a $600 deposit and paying her $125 per month mortgage by holding down three jobs in town. She taught business writing at the Atlanta College Of Business, filled the secretary desk at a local law firm during lunch hours and worked the rest of the hours God sent as an assistant to the head of public relations at Spelman College. And it was while working at Spelman in 1972 that she met a photographer that the college had hired to put together its brochures and promotional material. Donda was hugely impressed by the work of Ray West.

From speaking to him on the phone, Donda was surprised to find that Ray was black. His speaking voice was clipped and prim English, the result of being brought up in a military family and attending white-dominated schools – his degree was gained at the University Of Delaware. Educated, talented and single-minded, Ray had exhibited some of the same entrepreneurial spirit that Donda saw in her own father – he'd become the first African-American photographer at the renowned *Atlanta Journal-Constitution* newspaper, had won awards for his stunning photos of the South Sea Islands and was self-employed, having launched his own photography business. Places at Spelman were highly sought after and drew a lot of applications from smart students from across the state – it was part of Donda's job to recruit the best local students to even out the intake. So she and Ray would regularly go out on recruitment drives together, until he suggested they hang out outside of working hours. Inexperienced in the realm of romance, Donda accepted coolly, but with a bubbling excitement.

The car that pulled up outside Donda's apartment for their first date didn't look like the car of a big-shot entrepreneur who was going any place besides the salvage yard. The metalwork was beaten up, the windscreen was held together with straps of duct tape and the passenger door didn't open, forcing her to slide over from the driver's side. Yet the driver was gracious; at the Greenbriar mall on the south west of town Ray held Donda's hand as they walked to the Paccadilly Cafeteria and over dinner she learnt more about him. The son of Fannie B Hooks West and her sergeant husband, James Frederick West, Ray was one of six children in a very spiritual family that was constantly on the move, criss-crossing the country wherever James was posted, even heading to Spain for a while before finally setting a solid family base in Delmar★. Though Donda would come to feel that due to his military upbringing he had never had what she'd call the "black experience", he had seen his fair share of discrimination – while travelling the country his parents had often been refused motel rooms or service in restaurants – and had developed a militant attitude. "He understood what it meant to be discriminated against because he was black," wrote film director Steve McQueen in *Interview* magazine. "He also understood what it meant to be discriminated against by black people because he talked white."

His militancy had led him as a student to become involved with the Black Panther movement, a controversial group in the late sixties and seventies. As a militant arm of the US civil rights movement dedicated to opposing police brutality against African-Americans and enforcing black rights, they were a popular rallying lobby amongst poor and downtrodden black communities, but their use of violence against police and their revolutionary rhetoric made them an anathema to J Edgar Hoover's government, a feared and dangerous enemy and a blueprint for gang culture he devoutly wished crushed. Ray had never become embroiled in the violence which sporadically broke out at Panther demonstrations but firmly advocated their 10-point manifesto calling for such legislation as an end to police brutality and decent housing, education, healthcare and legal trials for the black community. At one student meeting Ray, as the president of his university's Black Student Group, snatched the microphone from the university President to speak, such was his passion for the cause.

"My father would always... confront people," Kanye would say years later. "My father was a military brat. He would be in Germany surrounded by a bunch of white people, and he was darker than me. He'd be around all these white people so he would sound white. Now, this is the thing – black people hate black people that sound white. So he would be around black people and they wouldn't like him because he sound white. He get around white people and they wouldn't like

★ Ray's parents were so close that when, after 60 years of marriage, James died following a long illness, Fannie died the very next day.

him because he was black. So sometimes, in that situation, you got to find a place where you can fit in, where you'll be accepted. To be a part of a movement. To be a part of a struggle. So he became a part of that. Somewhere they accepted him. They accepted his energy. He would go up and grab the mic from someone at a college and be right there in the front of rallies they had. But he started to realise that regardless if this was the hate that hate made, that from his perspective it was still a hate group. But the Black Panthers weren't made to be a hate group but more to protect the community... It's not to say that any group was perfect. But think about this. It was just like the Klan almost, because they were made, supposedly, to save the good white folks from the now-freed slaves that were running around. Then they started going to the houses of black people that weren't doing nothing and began raping, killing and burning them. But originally they were formed as a self-protection group. So everything is started with good intentions. The Panthers had all their after school programmes. They did a lot of good stuff. What's so crazy is when crack... I want to know who the person was who knew that black people would love crack? That was a genius. That was a racist genius right there. Because crack not only destroyed the BPP it destroyed the black community. It took the fathers out of the community. Without fathers, families can't be raised properly. Sons end up in jail with no proper direction."

That day at the mall, Donda admired Ray's intelligence, his talent, his political zeal. She also liked his style – he wasn't one of the slick operators oozing predictable lines that she was usually dating, he was refreshingly honest, ramshackle and geeky. The chemistry between them bubbled over. As they wandered the mall after eating, she stopped by the fountain, closed her eyes and threw three pennies into the water, wishing they'd one day marry.

Three months later, on January 1, 1973, at dawn, Donda and Ray were wed in Oklahoma City, Donda in a home-made dress. Their reception was held in the church basement, followed by a breakfast of fried chicken. Eschewing a honeymoon, the pair booked their wedding night in the honeymoon suite at the Ramada Hotel, but found the room so foul they didn't stay. Instead they drove straight back to Atlanta, where Ray would give up his elegant loft apartment in Greenbriar Village to move into Donda's townhouse. They both took teaching jobs – Donda taught English And Speech at Morris Brown College while Ray took a post teaching Photography And Media Production at Clark College – and in their spare time they'd coast the streets of Atlanta browsing for houses, keen to dip their toes into property development. Before long they'd swapped the townhouse for a down-at-heels four-bedroom house in the Cascade Heights area popular with the more affluent Afro-Americans in Atlanta, renovating it themselves. Within another year they'd upgraded to another property a few blocks away, then moved to a house on four acres with a forest at the border, a garden where Ray could grow his own raw vegetables for juicing and a basement he converted into a state-of-the-art darkroom where he started producing photo essays of their neighbourhood families, developing all of the pictures himself. They got themselves a rescue dog they called JT – short for Jive Turkey – and found a kitten named Mr Smith in a parking lot.

For those first months of marriage the West household seemed idyllic, the perfect all-American family unit★, but for one thing. Neither Ray nor Donda were interested in having children. Donda had watched her sisters tied down by motherhood and wanted no part of it. The Wests would see the world, live life to the fullest, free from responsibility.

When her Masters degree was complete, Donda was given the opportunity to study for a doctorate at Auburn University in Alabama. Her keenness to reach the very highest levels of academia won her over; she moved out to study, seeing Ray at weekends until, a year into her studies, he moved out too, teaching Medical Illustration at the nearby Tuskegee Institute while studying for a Masters of his own in Audiovisual Studies And Media. The pair lived in married student accommodation a short walk away from the Auburn campus, and their more restricted environment caused friction. Several times during their time in Alabama the couple split up, only to get back together before any lasting damage

---

★ Although, according to her book *Raising Kanye*, at one point Donda suspected that Ray was tempted to have an affair with a woman she believed was called Cynthia, but wasn't sure anything ever happened.

was done – following one break-up they were shopping together for furniture for an apartment that Ray was going to move to in Tuskegee when they decided they were making a mistake. When Donda's studies in Alabama were completed and they returned to Atlanta where she was to finish writing her dissertation, they went as a couple.

And a couple with an itch. Three years into their marriage, Donda had a complete volte face on the issue of offspring. Her hormones suddenly went into overdrive, her mothering instinct became overwhelming and undeniable. She begged Ray to give her a child and, despite his reservations about his abilities as a father, within three months Donda was expecting. She ditched the dope, bought an antique rocking chair to rock the child in and began praying hard for the health and intelligence of her baby, which she instinctively knew was a boy as he wriggled so much in the womb. Her parents were a constant support and despite Ray's increasing fear of fatherhood as the months flew by, he made for an attentive parent-to-be. He helped Donda with her exercise routine and diet, trained her to distract herself from pain by thinking of calming countryside scenes and took pictures of every stage of the pregnancy.

They chose a hospital in Douglasville, Georgia for its birthing room that would allow Ray, Lucille and selected friends to be there for the big day and, like all first-time parents, nervously awaited their lives being turned upside down.

Little did they know, they were about to bring forth a hip-hop saviour. And he'd make a characteristically unexpected entrance.

★ ★ ★

At his birth, for the first and last time in his life, Kanye West didn't seem to want an audience.

June 8, 1977 and 12 hours into labour, the child was showing no sign of turning up on time. The hospital sent Donda and Ray home, telling them to come back when her contractions hit five minutes. When she did, she was told her child needed to be born by Caesarean section in a theatre rather than in the birthing room, with only Ray allowed. Still, Ray took pictures of his son's first few moments and all of the people who first held him.

They called him Kanye, an Ethiopian word plucked from a book of traditional African names, Swahili for 'the only one'⋆. And he would undoubtedly turn out to be unique.

Those first few weeks as a fully-fledged family were tough for Ray and Donda. Unable to breast-feed due to the c-section, Donda suffered post-natal depression while Ray threw himself into fatherhood with enthusiasm, but soon found the lure of his photography distracting him. With Kanye only a few months old the family planned another move, putting down $8,000 and borrowing $125,000 with the intention of buying a stunning restored home in the white-dominated west end of Atlanta. It would have made a fantastic family base, but just before they signed the papers Ray came across a warehouse space that would be perfect as a photography studio, with a loft space for the family to live in above it. Ray convinced Donda that this was a great opportunity to base their lives around both family and business – they'd set up their own company called RaDonda and build their future as a family firm.

As those first few months went on, though, Ray turned more and more of his time to the business. Fractures and stresses arose between them, what Donda would describe as "some serious differences of opinion surfaced that were seemingly insurmountable". One night a row erupted over Ray's priorities; he admitted in the heat of the argument that he was focussing on the studio over his family. They were words he'd later wish he could take back.

Eleven months into Kanye's life, his parents separated.

He was too young to know anything about his parents' issues, of course, but as Donda gazed into his eyes in a vegetarian restaurant in Atlanta when he was seven months old, she felt he had "an old soul". She saw him as a special child, God-blessed, and he was already beginning to show traits he'd exhibit all his life. He'd show intense determination to climb out of his crib and never giving up until he succeeded in attaining this seemingly insurmountable obstacle. At eight months he became a jet-setter, flying with his mother to her 10-year high school

---

⋆ Kanye's middle name, Omari, was also significant, meaning 'wise man'. Ray and Donda were pleased he'd have the initials KO.

reunion and winning the prize of two pacifiers for being the youngest child there. In the event, he didn't need them – he busily sucked his middle and index fingers until he was eight years old. He was so keen to have his voice heard that even before he could speak he'd babble wildly in his own invented language, eager to learn words so he could express himself. And by the time he was walking, talking and running around in day care, he was the centre of attention, a natural entertainer who fascinated his peers and kept a constant running commentary of his own actions and achievements. The other kids were drawn to him as a leader, following him as he ran around, but even then he'd wrong-foot his followers, ducking left when they expected him to dive right.

He knew how to play people too, to twist their emotions and expectations. When he was just over one year old and his mother left him at school right through until 10pm as she was doing essential overtime work at her $7,000 a year job back at Morris Brown College, she found him sulking so hard she thought he'd never forgive her. Then, once she'd repented enough for his purposes, he burst into laughter; he was mastering the art of manipulation.

In June 1980, with Kanye turning three, Donda attended the Kool Jazz festival in Atlanta where her friend Sheridan introduced her to a guy named Larry Lewis who was in town for a fortnight. Instantly smitten, the pair spent those two weeks together, Larry extolling the excitement and opportunities that Donda might enjoy back in his hometown of Chicago. She was sold. Applying for two teaching posts in Chicago – at Chicago State University and Roosevelt University – she was offered both and plumped for Chicago State as it had such a healthy black intake and was offering her the princely sum of $17,000 a year. Seeking a clean break, a rebirth of sorts, she also filed for divorce, requesting full custody of Kanye. Ray didn't put up much objection – their split was good-natured and friendly and he even set about helping to find her an apartment in Chicago, knowing that this time the separation was for good. The divorce was finalised on August 28, Ray's birthday.

So that August, Donda loaded up a truck and made the 11-hour drive to Chicago solo. She settled into a two-bedroom apartment on the top floor of a three-storey building on the south side of town, close to both Chicago State and the Professional Playhouse Daycare she'd chosen for Kanye to go to school. Once she'd moved in, she went back to Atlanta to pick up her son and transplant him to his own room. Though times would be tough for the two of them surviving on a single teacher's salary with no family close by for help, and though Donda's relationship with Larry would fizzle out after barely a few months in the city, she was excited by the metropolis and set out to give Kanye the very best upbringing she could. "He grew up with middle-class values and middle-class expectations," she'd say. "But we were living on my teacher's salary, so we didn't necessarily have middle-class income."

And so began the building of a superstar.

During school terms Kanye stayed with his mother in Chicago; during the summer holidays he'd visit his father. He was raised to be religious – his mother would regularly take him to Sunday school at the Christ Universal Temple and to the Hillside Church, keen to develop his spiritual side, while Ray was on the road to becoming a Christian marriage counsellor and would be more overtly religious, praying with him on the phone when they were apart. Donda, as perhaps many religious mothers do, saw a higher spiritual connection in him than in other children. Though his father would teach him to consider and question everything he was told rather than simply accept it, his religious teachings would become deeply embedded in his psyche. One afternoon, playing in the Chicago apartment, Kanye pointed to the doorway and said "look, there goes Jesus". Christ, he was convinced, was walking with him even then.

At pre-school, even at the age of three, he was showing a prodigious talent. His Crayola crayon drawings were of full figures rather than stick men, as good as many six-year-olds' and imaginatively rendered. He'd purposely colour fruit the wrong colour to challenge standard perceptions: purple oranges, green peaches. At home his mother read him history-based bedtime stories, fifth-grade tales of the nose being knocked off the Sphinx, or would show him educational slides from her work trips abroad that she couldn't take him on – to Moscow or to Bombay in India. She vowed after nine weeks away never to leave him for that long again.

Above all, she taught him to believe in himself. "When Kanye was very young, I began teaching him to love himself," she wrote. "As a black man and as a man, period, he would need to be strong." Preaching politeness, patience, morals, respect and discipline alongside non-conformism and the need to challenge things he saw as wrong, she created an understanding and reasonable child open to discussions but also a self-assured kid determined to get what he wanted, as long as he wasn't stepping on anyone else to get it. "People say Kanye and humility don't belong in the same sentence," she said, "but he's had that determination since he was three."

He also knew his own mind. On trips to the park he'd insist the ducks were quacking wrong, and whenever Donda would take him to restaurants to try out different types of food, he'd insist on burger and fries. Kanye was a child who knew how he wanted the world to be, and felt he could change it.

After a while Donda, who was working three jobs to get by, moved Kanye to the pre-school at Chicago State so she could look in on him during the day and allow him to wander the town-like campus after school hours until Donda finished work, surrounded by books to flick through and students and academics to talk to and learn from. Never withdrawn or scared to talk to people, from an early age he was having discussions about how the media manipulates society and the value of honesty, integrity and hard work. Chicago State became his University Of Life.

A year into their life in Chicago, Donda set about trying to provide a more stable environment for her son. She bought a home in South Shore Drive, an upmarket area within walking distance of Lake Michigan. The garden backed onto Rainbow Park and it was the perfect place for Kanye to invite school friends to come and stay. She'd also use the summers when he was away with Ray to try to meet new partners, only introducing Kanye to those that became serious relationships. Ulysses Buckley Blakely Jr was one such guy, nicknamed Bucky. He'd take Kanye to play in a park near his place in Evanston – Kanye would call it Bucky's Park – and even moved in with the two of them following Donda's Indian trip. There was talk of the two of them buying a house together and becoming a family but, in Donda's eyes at least, God intervened. One day, stepping onto a local bus, she spotted an advert for a campaign to stop people paying with notes and using up all of the driver's change. The slogan read 'Ban The Buck'. Donda took it as a message from on high. Bucky was history.

Kanye, meanwhile, was developing his prodigious skills. Donda set his challenges high in the hope that he'd excel, and certainly in art he was swiftly becoming very skilled. Every Saturday from the age of five he'd attend the free art lessons at the Chicago Academy For The Arts and join the art classes for children in Hyde Park, learning to draw cartoons. He became interested in computer graphics and considered a future in animation. He was also showing strong signs of a masterful way with words. "We were coming back from a short vacation in Michigan when he was five, and he composed a poem in the back seat," Donda said. "The one line that sticks with me is 'the trees are melting black'. It was late fall, and the trees had no leaves. He saw how those limbs were etched against the sky, and he described them the way a poet would."

His forthright personality was coming on too. "I've always called Kanye a totalist," Donda would say. "As a child, if he was going to dress up as a fireman, he had to have the whole outfit: boots, hat, jacket, hose, everything. He's never wanted to do anything halfway." At six, accompanying his mother to a polling station to vote, he pulled on Donda's sleeve, nodded to a man nearby and told her to check him out. When they chanced upon the same man while looking around some model homes later the same day, Kanye virtually dragged her over to him. His name was Tony and he and Donda dated for the next two years. Kanye became particularly interested in Tony's motorbikes, even though his mother would never let him ride on one.

Kanye's ultra-confidence wasn't helping him make friends at school, though. When Donda went to move him from pre-school into kindergarten – she'd chosen the premium, arts-heavy Vanderpoel Elementary Magnet School for him and pulled strings to get him considered after the application date had passed – his teachers at Chicago State told her that though he was clearly gifted they thought him too socially awkward and self-centred, and suggested that she keep him back a year until he had matured enough to fit in at kindergarten. Her friends chipped in ideas, telling her to send him to the boy scouts to help him get on with other kids. But Donda hadn't noticed him failing to bond with other children and she was convinced that what others saw as arrogance in him was actually a healthy confidence. So she ignored their advice and Kanye sat the tests for Vanderpoel, designed to select only the strongest students for its places. In one test Kanye was asked to draw a man, a request he found too simple. "I'll draw a football player," he said, but was told no, he should just draw a man. He retorted that he'd draw a man but put him in a football player's uniform. He drop-kicked into Vanderpoel.

At his new school his attitude was quickly noted. "My, he doesn't have any problem with self-esteem, does he?" one teacher, Mrs Murray, commented to Donda. She knew it was said in spite, like the other snipes she'd overheard about him being "undisciplined" or "snot-nosed", yet she replied proudly: "He does not."

In elementary school, Kanye started entertaining dreams of becoming a fashion designer, drawing sketches of clothes he'd one day love to produce. He'd always hated going on trips with his mother to shop for cheap clothes in Unique thrift stores or Payless but as his teens loomed he began pining for designer label clothes and would hide in the aisles of the cheaper shops in case anyone he knew saw him shopping there. He was never prouder than when Donda bought him his first pair of $65 Air Jordans.

And then came music. Donda's side of the family was inherently musical; on their Christmas trips back to Kanye's grandparents' house in Oklahoma City, everyone in the family would play an instrument or sing well. All, that is, except for Kanye, who his cousins remember slinking off into a corner to avoid the jamboree.* "It was weird," his

---

★ Their journeys back to Oklahoma City would sometimes involve educational lay-overs on the Greyhound bus route for Kanye to see the St Louis Gateway Arch, St Louis Zoo and the key political and informative sites in Washington DC – they toured the Smithsonian Institute, followed the route of the march on Washington and tore round the Space Museum.

cousin Tony Wilson recalled, "but he was always a genius kid, so we knew he would do something." Yet from the age of six or seven, Kanye began competing in talent shows, miming along to Stevie Wonder songs in full costume. On occasion Donda would splash out to take Kanye to Disney World in Orlando, Florida alongside his godmother Glenda and her daughter Alexis. On one visit they came across a booth where kids could record their own music video while singing along to a song on tape. Kanye did his best Stevie Wonder act and, though the tape of this first Kanye West video performance has since been lost, the bug stayed with him.

His musical idols were Stevie Wonder, Michael Jackson and George Michael, and he'd eventually move on to appreciating Madonna and Phil Collins before rap acts like LL Cool J and A Tribe Called Quest entered the frame. "When you're a little kid you don't listen to underground music," he'd say, "you listen to what your parents play and shit that's on the radio. Back then you had a choice of, like, two big songs. The problem was when people started to process pop music. I mean, there were once real pop artists: Phil Collins, Madonna, Michael Jackson. No underground artist has been able to compete with what they did." By third grade, aged eight, Kanye was rapping, dreaming of a life as a hip-hop superstar. His aunt Klaye, who made a living singing in clubs as Little Miss Klaye The Steam Heat Girl, noticed his show business ambition and sat him down to give him advice.

"People will try to bring you down," she told him, "you must never let them break you."

It was advice that Kanye took directly to heart.

CHAPTER TWO

Lost In The World

Scotty was the right guy at the very wrong time. Willie Scott was an old-fashioned gentleman, short, bulky and deep-voiced but with traditional manners and a job in academia, albeit teaching car mechanics at a high school. To Donda he seemed perfect relationship material, but for one crucial sticking point. She met him at a going away party she held in her back yard shortly before she was due to leave the US for a year in China.

It was an offer too good to refuse. In 1987 Donda was approached to take up a fellowship for two semesters at Nanjing University as part of an exchange programme between Nanjing and Chicago State – she'd be teaching English to the local students. When she heard that the trip would take up a year she came close to turning it down: she'd promised herself she wouldn't spend so long away from Kanye again after those stressful nine weeks in India. But on investigation she was told that she could take Kanye with her, and suddenly the trip took on a more vivid hue. An adventure of cultural discovery, a chance for the 10-year-old Kanye to absorb worldliness.

Straight off the plane, their eyes were opened. The restrictiveness of Chinese society under the Communist government was apparent as soon as they stepped out of the airport; everyone was cycling since only government officials were allowed to travel by private car. After hiring a couple of bikes, Donda settled them into their lodgings at the Foreign Experts building on the Nanjing University campus and began introducing Kanye to the 10 other tutors on the exchange programme, and their children. Kayne met a Mexican child called Diego who'd been there for six months with his Spanish-teaching parents already and who became the pair's unofficial tour guide for the whole time they were there. The first night Diego accompanied them to the Jinling Hotel, a Western-styled place where they could ease themselves into China with a meal of American food, and Diego began helping them understand the language, acting as translator with the waiters. Donda had started trying to learn in the weeks leading up to the trip and had struggled – she'd never really get to grips with much more than a few essential phrases – but Kanye took to Mandarin like a natural. Within weeks he was miles ahead of his mother and able to communicate reasonably with the other kids in his class at his new school, an eight-block cycle from the campus. They were first-graders; Kanye was forced to start his schooling at the earliest level due to the language barrier, making him by far the oldest in his class.

Besides being significantly bigger, Kanye was also an oddity to his classmates for his colour – kids would stare and even rub his skin. "It was weird going over there," he said. "Most of the kids had never seen a black person before, so they'd come over to me and touch my face, thinkin' it was paint or something." Much of the time Kanye used his novelty value to become popular with his classmates and teachers. He developed a love of lamb skewers that were a local culinary staple and would charge crowds of chanting kids to watch him break dance – he was an adept head-spinner – then spend the money on skewers, a born entrepreneur. But the throngs of kids shouting "Break-dance! Break-dance!" became taxing and the constant stream of stares from passers-by in the street became tiring. Kanye would start staying in to avoid the attention, and one afternoon on a trip to the Confucius Temple he snapped at a gaggle of gawkers pointing at him in a café. "Get back!" he shouted, and they scattered, terrified.

Besides being a great preparation for the glaring attention of superstardom, much of their year in China was enjoyably eye-opening.

On top of his school lessons in maths and science Kanye studied the language, took private lessons in art and cheap tai chi classes and studied in the evening with a private tutor called Ezra from Zimbabwe to keep in step with the classes he was missing back in Chicago. "My mother had to take me out and home-school me. Because I couldn't speak the language I wasn't excelling," Kanye said. "That can throw a kid off slightly. So then when I went back to school, I had to do some tests. I sent them and they thought my mother did them for me, that I cheated. When I went there, I had to take the test again while they monitored me." And when Kanye wasn't sunk in a book, they ate traditional African food with a group of friendly African students or went sight-seeing, their trips often booked for them by Kanye's babysitter, language teacher and – according to Donda – all-round "life-saver" Chang Don Bing. They visited the Great Wall Of China and Yellow Mountain, where Kanye insisted his mother take the full day's hike to the peak with him rather than ride up in the cable car, leaving her with swollen legs. They took a slow boat all the way from Canton to Hong Kong over the Chinese new year to stay in the notorious Slum King Hotel – $11 per night – then moved on to Thailand to see the red light district and Ko Samui, where Kanye was particularly taken by the nudist beaches, much to the shock of the Catholic professor to whom he discussed his trip when he got back to China.

Though Kanye understood the traditions and customs of respect in China, his forthright self-belief wasn't completely crushed. In the winter his classroom was freezing cold and the school had no heating, so children would wrap themselves in coats, hats and gloves for lessons. Everyone wore fingerless gloves except for Kanye, who preferred normal American gloves. When one teacher snatched them off him, he instinctively lashed out, kicking her and grabbing them back. Cue an apologetic trip to the headmaster's office, his eyes down out of respect, while his mother talked the school into letting him wear the gloves he wanted.

★ ★ ★

The whole time Donda and Kanye were away, Scotty was asking after her, badgering friends to find out when she'd be back in Chicago. So when the pair returned to South Shore Drive, wiser but glad to be home, Donda and Scotty reunited. Within a year Scotty had moved in and the couple were planning a wedding. Strict and with high standards, Scotty seemed good for Kanye; he brought discipline and taught him responsibility and developed his masculine front. Kanye was given chores he was expected to do well and without complaint – keeping his room tidy, mowing the lawn, taking out the trash, mopping the kitchen and cleaning the bath – and Scotty, who'd already brought up three sons and ruled over his mechanics classes with an iron fist, was angry if he didn't do a good job. As long as he wasn't abusive Donda didn't intervene, considering Scotty the strong male role model Kanye needed in his life as he approached adolescence and became a young man. Kanye, for his part, would call Scotty "almost step-dad".

Kanye would soon need a slice of Scotty's toughness. Out riding his bike in a nearby park one afternoon he was set upon by a knife-wielding gang trying to steal his bicycle. When he tried to ride away, they slashed his tyre. Donda was shocked – she'd long banned Kanye from riding on the L train along the south side of Chicago because of its crime-infested stations where people would be murdered for their jackets or trainers, but the fact that such gang violence had crept into their seemingly safe and family-friendly neighbourhood was totally unacceptable. She and Scotty vowed to move; they found a house on Longwood Drive in Blue Island and settled there. Donda arranged her shifts at Chicago State so she'd be home when Kanye returned from school, or would allow him to meet her at the university and do his homework there. At home he lived under firm but reasonable rules; aside from his chores he was allowed limited television unless it was public TV, was barred from hanging out on street corners where he might get involved in gangs and drugs, was never to raise his voice to adults and had one main job in life – get good grades.

Kanye was growing up fast. At the age of 11 he began taking great pride in his appearance and his outfits, even going so far as to do his own laundry so he'd have the right clothes when he needed them. His grandfather Buddy, a huge fan of Muhammad Ali, would tell him "life is a performance" as he showed him how to iron his shirt collars and knot a tie. One year Donda gave him $200 to go to the store and buy new clothes for school, usually enough money to get several complete outfits. He came back with two high-end shirts and one pair of jeans. He began styling the group he performed with at talent shows – Quadro Posse, an amateur dance act. Initially he put them in a unified colour; wearing all black they won a school talent competition. One time Donda caught him posing in a mirror, telling himself, in all seriousness, "I could be a teenage sex symbol." Though his teeth were perfectly straight, he insisted on getting braces, convinced he needed a perfect TV smile. His regular successes in talent shows were convincing him he was born for stardom. "I would help the other [competitors] because I just knew I was going to win anyway," he said. "The teachers used to say, 'This ain't meant to be the Kanye West show'."

When he hit 12, he went through a period of selfishness and self-obsession, not caring about anyone else's feelings – he'd moodily finish off drinks and food without asking if it was OK with Donda and Scotty. His mother became disappointed with him: "Kanye," she told him, "I love you, but I don't like you. I don't like the way you're acting. I don't like the way you have regard for no-one in this house but yourself, and you must stop it, now." Almost in tears, Kanye vowed to change, and gradually an inner maturity began to break through. On a race to the airport to put him on a cheap flight to visit his father, Kanye insisted Donda drive a different route than usual to avoid traffic, only to be held up by a freight train. When Donda started freaking out at him, angry that she'd wasted so much money on a non-refundable ticket, he cut her down: "Mom, only something that will help." Inevitably, Kanye made the plane.

Kanye was also maturing sexually. On the school run one day the topic of teenage pregnancy came up on the radio and Donda took the opportunity to give Kanye and a few of his friends in the back of the car a frank lecture on sex as well as the risks of pregnancy and AIDS. Masturbation, she told them, was better than sex at their age. The car fell into an embarrassed silence.

In fact, Kanye was already developing an obsession with sex, bordering on addiction. At a young age he'd come across one of his father's pornography magazines. "It just excited me," he'd say. "I just liked it. I liked it a lot." On his visits to see his father he'd also be interested in the girls that Ray would be dating, his photography being something of a draw for the opposite sex. "He would... use that to pick up hot females," Kanye said. "A little head shot in return for a little head shot. I remember my daddy used to have the baaad girls, when I used to go down to visit him. His girlfriends would make my wee-wee tingly, when I was 10 years old. He went out with girls that really looked like the books under his bed."

When he shifted to Polaris High School in Oak Lawn he'd be caught passing around porn magazines. On one occasion, when Donda was called into the school and told that Kanye had claimed he found the magazine in his mother's closet, she bawled him out all the way home and even slapped his face. When Donda borrowed his VCR recorder because hers was broken, she found a hardcore tape inside, which she waited several days to calmly confront him with. He'd been brought up to tell the truth no matter what the consequences, so he told her everything; it was a tape he'd been given by someone as school. Faced with the dilemma of how to punish him despite his honesty, Donda came up with a way to make his shame educational – she set him an essay to write on the effects of X-rated movies on teenage boys. He completed it with research notes and bibliography attached; it turned out to be a useful lesson in how to construct a research paper, even if he used it to undermine his mother's disapproving stance.

"I started giving examples of people I knew who saw them from when they were young – 'but this guy turned out pretty good' – so I was giving rebuttals," he said, although he would admit to pornography affecting his sexual rapaciousness. "That could be the influence of watching pornography. You see a girl walk and you instantly do the Howard Stern and undress her and shit with your eyes... it puts you in a wolf mentality. The whole goal is to find girl, get laid. I think the Devil basically put a crack in the structure – God made us find girl, get laid, have family, but the crack in the structure is find girl, get laid... and before I have a family there's another girl right here."

His sex drive, he'd claim, would ultimately turn him into a workaholic. "People ask me a lot about my drive," he said. "I think it comes from, like, having a sexual addiction at a really young age. Look at the drive that people have to get sex – to dress like this and get a haircut and be in the club in the freezing cold at 3 a.m., the places they go to pick up a girl. If you can focus the energy into something valuable, put that into work ethic..."

It certainly provided him with some early inspiration. In seventh grade, hooked on De La Soul's 'Me, Myself, And I' and '2 Hype' by Kid 'n Play, he decided to start writing his own beats, unaware that most major rappers buy theirs in from writers. "First beat I did," he remembered, "was in seventh grade, on my computer. I got into doing beats for the video games I used to try to make. My game was very sexual. The main character was, like, a giant penis. It was like Mario Brothers, but the ghosts were, like, vaginas. Mind you, I'm 12 years old, and this is stuff 30-year-olds are programming. You'd have to draw in and program every little step – it literally took me all night to do a step, 'cause the penis, y'know, had little feet and eyes."

His earliest songs would rip off Brand Nubian and hone in on the positive rap that was becoming prevalent at that time. His schoolmates would often see him wandering the corridors, rapping to himself. "I walk through the halls of the school/And it's cool to be known by many/For my rapping ability/What about the brothers who ain't got it like me/Making money off the trade/You could say I had it made/Death is on the rise/And that ain't no surprise/You can see your soul in a young brother's eyes/Hardened by the streets cos the streets is kinda hard/But here's another factor that we wanna disregard…"

His hard-working nature, sadly, didn't extend to his lessons. Within a few semesters at Polaris Kanye had slipped from being an honours student to B and C grades. Kanye's time-keeping also left a lot to be desired. His aunt Shirlie recalled coming to visit the family during a period when Kanye would always be late for the school bus. Having no time for such nonsense, one morning Shirlie threw him out of the house to catch the bus before he'd even dressed for school, his clothes in a bag. Kanye had to get dressed on the bus.

"We instilled a bullshit detector in Kanye from an early age, and as he got older, it detected the bullshit in school," Donda said. "I don't think education is bullshit, and I don't think Kanye does either, but the schools are flawed." At school he was only interested in music, art, lunch and recess and bored for the rest of the time, thinking more about his first attempts at rapping. At 13 he started a rap group called State Of Mind with his friends Lucien and Gene, co-wrote his first hip-hop tune – 'Green Eggs And Ham', named after the famous Dr Seuss book – and badgered his mother to fund a recording of it. Keen to encourage his creative leanings, Donda looked into booking a studio but found them all way too expensive, $125 an hour at most places. Then Kanye came across a studio in someone's basement advertising sessions at only $25 per hour and jumped at the chance.

When State Of Mind arrived, the neighbourhood was fairly upmarket, but the studio itself was a wreck. "It was just this little basement studio," Donda said. "The microphone was hanging from the ceiling by a wire hanger. But he was so excited, I couldn't say no." In fact, Kanye was in his element, diving into the producer's role as if he was born to work a mixing desk. Having practised the song intently with his group in the Blue Island house, 'Green Eggs And Ham' came together in a matter of hours, the first ever Kanye West production.

As low-rent as the studio was, there was a real thrill to the experience, as if stepping into a world of which he'd only ever dreamt. Sat at his first ever production desk, Kanye had found his calling.

And his obsession grew.

★ ★ ★

Five hundred dollars. Over and over he counted it. Money he'd scraped and saved over months and months, more money than he'd ever had in his life. But still it didn't add up to enough.

If his first production experience in that basement studio had opened his eyes to the possibilities of music, his cousin Tony had gone on to blow his mind. A producer and songwriter himself, and 14 years Kanye's senior, Tony had been Donda's first port of call for advice when it became clear that Kanye wasn't feeling art as much as he had, and music was his new passion. Tony helped look into the appropriate drum machines and samplers to help him on his way, and also had a friend who was producing for Oklahoman R&B act Color Me Badd. One holiday, Tony took Kanye to see his friend in his studio, a veritable sweetshop of technical gizmos.

His heart was set on a keyboard, and no cheap kid's toy. He wanted to take his writing to the next level, and for that he needed a professional instrument, but those cost closer to $1,500. An impossible amount, he could save for years and never buy it.

Then, the Christmas of his fourteenth year, his gift from Donda was a cool grand. Suddenly, he was a real-life musician.

He started making beats on his new equipment that very Christmas, his keyboard set up in his aunt's kitchen, and his keyboard quickly took over his life, sucking him into a private world of intense creativity. Rather than hang out on the streets or spend his spare time studying – around this time Kanye developed a saying: "Use school, don't let school use you" – he'd invite his friends round to his room and work on beats or listen to the latest rap records they'd picked up. "[A Tribe Called Quest's] *The Low End Theory* was the first album I bought," Kanye said. "I was like, 'Oh shit, [they] have whole albums? They don't just have the singles?' I was like, 'I'mma start buying a bunch of shit.'"

He bought into Run DMC. He bought into Public Enemy despite his parents' protests about the language – his father only let him listen to their albums because he was in favour of their black power message. He bought into the Wu-Tang Clan too. "Wu-Tang had one of the biggest impacts as far as a movement," he'd say, "from slang to style of dress, skits and samples."

He took on part-time jobs to save up for more equipment, adding a drum machine, a turntable and a mixer to his bedroom setup until he had his own minor league home studio. Then he became a virtual hermit in his room, working up beats and combining them with samples from Michael Jackson, Luther Vandross and classic R&B records.

Beats shook the house day and night. Kanye wrote relentlessly, accompanied by a revolving cast of visiting friends, only ever leaving his room to eat or go to the bathroom. If Scotty or Donda wanted to talk to him, they had to go in and catch his attention between tracks. The noise was such that Donda found it a blessing when Kanye left the house to go play basketball or catch a movie.

In 1992 he started a production team called Numbskulls with another fledgling producer and promoter called John Monopoly, whom he'd met through his State Of Mind bandmates. He was soon playing his songs to his mother, making sure to turn the volume down at the profanities so as not to offend her, recruiting his cousins to help him sell his earliest mix-tapes in the local mall and boasting about his talent at school. "He was going to be best rapper in the whole world," his physical education teacher Marilyn Gannon said, remembering telling him, "You can get in line."

Kanye's withdrawal into music may have had something to do with his discomfort with his family arrangement. One night at the dinner table Donda found Kanye in tears. Scotty's strict, almost military approach to his upbringing, working on the fear of punishment and restriction of privileges rather than reasonable discipline, had broken him. Kanye had let a piece of paper fall onto the lawn when it was his job to keep it clear, and a vicious row had erupted. Kanye had had enough; he told his mother he'd like to go and live with his dad. That was enough for Donda – she and Kanye soon moved out of the Blue Island house and out of Scotty's life. They found a place in Tinley Park, just the two of them once more.

So much was Donda on Kanye's side, in fact, that she was about to forge a connection for him that would set him on the road to superstardom.

In the early nineties the Chicago rap scene was a rough, rudimentary affair with a huge amount of promise. Operating out of basements and with no clubs or radio stations to help bring it overground, it still operated the sort of territorial rivalry that was prevalent across the genre. From K-Town in the west side of town came Tung Twista, releasing his first album *Runnin' Off At Da Mouth* in 1992 and gaining the world record for being the fastest rapper, his chopper rapping style allowing him to spit 598 syllables in 55 seconds, before eventually finding fame with the shortened name Twista. And from the south side came Common

Sense, soon to be shortened to Common, a change prompted by being sued by a Los Angeles reggae band, also called Common Sense. The son of former ABA baseball player Lonnie Lynn, he was covered by *The Source* magazine ahead of his 1992 debut single, 'Take It EZ', and the subsequent album *Can I Borrow A Dollar?*. On 'I Used To Love H.E.R.' from his acclaimed 1994 album *Resurrection*, Common would expand these local territorial differences to try to drag Chicago into the conflicts erupting around the LA gangsta rap scene by condemning the style in a story about a woman losing herself in the gangsta lifestyle, a metaphor for the degradation of hip-hop via rough-edged commercialism. Sure enough, the song ignited a feud with Ice Cube.

Bubbling under or soon to emerge were acts such as Crucial Conflict and Do Or Die and, by the end of the decade, Lupe Fiasco. These acts merged the jazzy, soulful samples coming out of the East Coast with slick West Coast production. And dead centre, the pivot of the entire scene, was a producer called No I.D., the man who'd come to be credited by Kanye himself as the godfather of Chicago hip-hop.

Born Ernest Dion Wilson, No I.D. – his hip-hop name was the reverse of his middle name – was a 19-year-old house music DJ around Chicago who was starting to get into hip-hop production. Since the age of eight he'd been friends with Common Sense, growing up together in thrall to rap and dance music. "In Chicago we were different," No I.D. recalled, "we used to just dance to good music and just enjoy the music. Pretty soon I started break dancing and all that. Me and Common had a rap group [C.D.R.] with another guy called Corey [Crawley] and we used to open up for Big Daddy Kane and Eazy-E." When No I.D. had quit making music to go to college, Common had stayed in Chicago and carried on chasing his dream; eventually No I.D. saw the error of his educational ways and came home to help write his beats for his friend's first album, *Can I Borrow A Dollar?*, under the producer name Immenslope. It was No I.D.'s beats that gave Common his biggest successes in those early stages – that the debut single from the album, 'Take It EZ', was a number five hit in the US rap chart made Common and No I.D. major names in the burgeoning Chicago rap scene. "After a while," I.D. said, "I thought 'I'll just do this'… We all just started in basements as kids with nobody, no help, no hook-up, no special connections, just 'Man, we're about to do some music'. We got this bootleg equipment, no clubs to really go and do hip-hop, no radio stations, we really pioneered a whole city on hip-hop so I'm proud... Everyone in Chicago is super lyrical and really know how to rap a bunch of good raps, lyrically. I feel we're at the forefront of cutting edge creative music."

By chance, I.D.'s mother also worked at Chicago State alongside Donda, and knowing of No I.D.'s growing reputation, Donda asked his mother if he'd consider helping her son break into the game. "Moms are always like: 'Here's someone that you should help'," said I.D.. "I understood, checked it out and it was him. He was just learning how to make music, but he was the most persistent person who I've ever met. The first song he played me called 'Green Eggs And Ham'. It was a real super-early, nineties-sounding, yelling type of hip-hop record with a computer keyboard beat that was really quite funny." What was he like as a teenager? "The same way he is now. Not too much different, just a younger kid with less responsibilities and stress. A little less chasing the girls."

"He was just one of them energetic kids, like 'Teach me everything, teach me anything!'," he remembered. "At first it was just like 'All right man, take this, learn this, go, get, get, get. But eventually he started getting good. He was always trying to prove himself, and he kept getting better and better."

Kanye made himself an endearing nuisance to No I.D.. He had a studio in town called Mellowswing which he'd use with Doug Infinite, where Kanye would regularly show up in the hope of gleaning some knowledge and experience, and I.D. humoured him without taking him too seriously as a rapper or producer just yet. He was a plucky and ambitious kid, hitting No I.D.'s sessions with Common eager to battle the star rapper. "Kanye would always have dope rhymes," Common said, "but he didn't have his style down at that time. He had good samples, but it wasn't polished." Kanye did convince Common to battle him, live on a radio station. "I was drunk," Common admitted, "I don't think he was drunk, but some people said he got the best from me."

His music, under No I.D.'s guidance, became jazzier and peppered with samples from soul records by classic acts like the Ohio Players, who were amongst Kanye's favourite groups at the time. It was a style that would eventually take over the nineties hip-hop underground world. "[No I.D.] taught me to speed up the records to save sample time and memory," Kanye said. "And that's actually how I developed the style I'm known for."

Kanye would come to consider No I.D. his mentor, but I.D. himself plays this role down, likening himself, instead, to a friend and father figure. "The mentor part came from him being a shorty with no father," he said, "and me knowing him and helping him with every aspect of life, not just music."

"I never wanted to even say that I was his mentor. I never once even said that. When you think about it, I never said, like, 'Yeah I taught Kanye West'. This is what he says. I always thought of myself as the male figure that he didn't have growing up because his father wasn't around. Music stuff was there too, but a lot of the things we've always talked about was more about life than just music. With music, we was competitive but were helping each other. It just so happens that when I met him, I helped him get to a certain level before he could help me see things… I helped him early and he helped me later. No one ever asked me that. They always say we know you did this and we know you did that. Maybe I did, but I never once used that as a platform for anything. Anything I ever did was out of pure giving at the moment, and it was never planned."

In fact, No I.D. claims the mentoring went both ways – by inviting him into his recording sessions with Common he gave Kanye his grounding in music, in technical production and stylistic guidance – and later Kanye helped forge his career too. "I'll be the first to say [my relationship with Kanye] helped me, period. If you help someone or teach someone, that doesn't mean they can't help or teach you. It's just not like that. He always gave it up to me because I've never tried to claim anything or ask him for anything or take anything for what I did do to help him. I think he went through so much with people and people felt entitled. For me, I never felt entitled to anything. I always just gave. The law of life is, you give and you receive. It didn't surprise me that I would receive. It surprised everyone that he would give to me like that. It's just the energy of the universe. Everything is what it is. I give to people when I don't even have a reason to give to people. I gave to him and never asked for anything."

I.D. certainly feels the relationship had a brotherly aspect to it. "I felt like he was a younger guy, so he wasn't like my friend like the way Common was my friend. We have a different friendship from a younger-older guy sense. He says Jay is his big brother, but I feel like a brother. I don't know if I'm big, little, equal, or whatever it is. We're more like brothers – fighting when we want to, arguing when we want to, be there or not be there, don't talk for six months or talk every day. That's my brother… It could be like when he's dating. I'm like, 'Why are you doing that?' He will voice his opinion to the fullest and sometimes he doesn't even believe what he's saying. He'll say it to test it, and then come back later to say you were right about this or that. If I know I'm right I just fall back and say, 'OK, cool. Nah, do that'. Then later he'll come back, like, 'I know, man. I just had to see'."

What's more, No I.D. saw a similar creative mindset to his own in the young production hopeful. "He always evolved, we've got the same mentality, every day is a new day, what you did yesterday don't count. So he was always working to achieve something new every day, that's kinda how I look at it too, that's how a lot of producers don't make it in the game, they get to talking about the records they did [but] it's about what you can do with this artist today."

At that time No I.D. still saw Kanye as little more than a keen young friend he was helping out, and as Kanye delved further into Chicago's rap world, he found further cohorts and hang-outs. When No I.D. sold Mellowswing to a local group with the same name, the group turned it into a barber shop and it became a local hip-hop hang-out, Kanye kept going there to have his hair cut by a guy called Ibn Jasper, make a few extra dollars by cutting some hair himself and play the rap kids – a rising video director called Coodie Simmons among them – his latest beats. "I thought, 'This dude is out of here, and I'm about to start filming him and do a *Hoop Dreams* on Kanye'," Coodie said. Coodie, who had his own public access channel in Chicago called Channel Zero – Kanye hung around the station as a teenager, hoping for airtime – would indeed start filming Kanye at work, capturing hundreds of hours of footage of him as he worked on material that would eventually become his debut album, convinced from the very start that this kid would win Grammys.

Through a schoolfriend called Birdman★ he was introduced to Really Doe, with whom he clicked and began collaborating on mix-tapes. "We'd go to Taste of Chicago to mack girls down," Doe recalled, "party and enjoy ourselves. As kids, his room was full of crates of records. It pulled a lot out of me that I was holding in musically." John Monopoly also brought a market trader and part-time party promoter called JB Marshall to meet Kanye. "This guy with braces comes to the door," Marshall said. "'Aye, my name is Kanye'. I walked into his house on 95th and he had three three-foot-high stacks of *GQ* magazines. I was like, 'OK, this is weird'." Before long Kanye would be showing up at Marshall's parties, becoming a face on the scene and forging a strong friendship. Though he went under the moniker Kanye The Influence, his baggy pants and backpacks earned him the nickname Deep House.

In 1993, aged 16, a local rapper called GLC (Gangsta Legendary Crisis), an 87th Street kid and one-time member of Chicago's Gangster Disciples gang, met Kanye through his hairdressing endeavours. A friend of his turned up one day with an odd haircut he claimed was by his new best friend Kanye West. He took GLC over to Kanye's house. "It was a lot of African artist type shit because that's what his mom was into," he said. "So I felt very comfortable. And Kanye had a lot of pornos, sex magazines, and nice clothes – he was really into girls, music, and black liberation as a shorty. We connected on all of that because it was instilled in him through his mom and it was instilled in me through my brother. We both had a crazy love for the hoes."

The pair also bonded over their admiration of their rap heroes, the hip-hop stars who'd also become entrepreneurs, building million-dollar businesses around their names. In their eyes they weren't working a day job or punching any clocks, they were living dream lives with women in abundance. "So, it was like, 'Hey, this seem like the thing to do'," GLC said. "We started making songs that weekend." GLC noticed

★ Not the same Birdman who co-founded Cash Money Records.

Kanye's fashion sense developing too – Kanye would try out Calvin Klein clothes for a month or two at a time, then retreat from it again, scorched by the jokes and ridicule of his peers. "Man, he crazy," they'd mock him, or "That motherfucker gay?"

GLC noted Kanye's serious work ethic. "Kanye applied himself. When we would be out chasing hoes, there was times Kanye would be with us, but a majority of the time he'd be in his bedroom making beats with the same clothes on for days, no haircut or nothing. That dude was focused since he was a shorty." He was insistent about his rap abilities too. When John Monopoly called his friend DeRay Davis, who had links to the Def Squad, and told him he had to speak to Kanye, Kanye kept him on the phone rapping for a full 30 minutes. "The dude did not stop spitting," Davies recalled. "He probably did a whole album back to back. I'm literally like, 'Yo, this kid is crazy'."

Between the age of 15 and his graduation year, Kanye got his grounding in production from No I.D., as much of a prodigy at the mixing desk as he was in art, and began earning his stripes around town as a rapper and producer. His cousin Devo Springsteen remembers meeting him in 1995 and soon being taken on as his assistant, finding samples, recording pieces or talking him out of his more ill-advised creative decisions. No I.D. remembers him as having a tougher edge during his development, more of a "little gangster". One early Kanye track that turned heads, now sadly lost, was called 'You On Something'. "It was the solo record we wanted to put out in '95 with him," John Monopoly said. "I still believe that record's a hit… That's a classic, never-heard-before Kanye record… 'You only call me when you want something!' That was the hook. It was a song about girls only wanting guys for money. It was cool – great record, great beat… [His production] was always dope and clean. Kind of current. He was a little influenced by what was going on. I remember, when Bad Boy was super-popping in that era, you'd hear some shakers in his production, those sounds. He always kind of mixed different sounds, always had his own thing. He's been rocking with the soul samples for a while. But he was definitely influenced by Bad Boy."

At home, Donda saw changes in him. He started wearing his trousers hanging low in the prevailing hip-hop style, brushing off her complaints by claiming, "I have a big butt, mom, I have to wear my pants low like this so it won't look so big." He even started giving his mother style tips at this time, telling her to shop at Jenny Craig. He was also beginning to act macho and thug-like, spouting the sort of profanities and homophobic attitudes he was hearing around him every day in the hip-hop community, afraid of being seen as any more of an outsider than he already was as a middle-class mummy's boy. This was the result, he'd come to believe, of the lack of a regular father figure and his closeness with his mother. "I would go see my father on Christmas, spring break and summer," he explained. "My father was my everything, but during the rest of the time, my mother was my everything. Of course there's a good side to that, but the bad side of that is that people call you a mama's boy. It gets to the point that when you go to high school and you wasn't out in the streets like that, and you ain't have no father figure, or you wasn't around your father all the time, who you gonna act like? You gonna act like your mother... And then everybody in high school be like, "Yo, you actin' like a fag. Dog, you gay?" And I used to deal with that when I was in high school.

"And what happened was it made me kind of homophobic, 'cause I would go back and question myself, like, 'Damn, why does everyone else walk like this, and I walk like this?' People be like, 'Yo fam, look at you. Look at how you act'. If you see something and you don't want to be that because there's such a negative connotation toward it, you try to separate yourself from it so much that it made me homophobic by the time I was through high school. Anybody that was gay I was like, 'Yo, get away from me'. And like Tupac said, 'Started hangin' with the thugs', and you look up and all my friends were really thugged out. It's like I was racing to try to find that constant masculine role model right there, right in front of me."

To earn extra cash he sold knives door to door for a while before he realised it wasn't for him, then got a summer job as a greeter at The Gap, where he'd be placed at the front of the store to make other black customers think the chain was more welcoming. "My job was to stand inside the door and welcome people to the store," he said. "But I put my own spin on it, I used to freestyle. 'Welcome to the Gap/We got jeans in the back/And we got some khaki slacks/And if you like that/ You'll probably like the shirts/Try one on, it won't hurt/You got red socks on/Why don't you put a red hat on?/We've got all that/And it's all at the Gap'. And to think that they fired me for rapping."

"He really didn't like the job," GLC would say, "but his mom was teaching him responsibility, like, 'Look, you want to have a nice car, you want to do this and that, you got to be able to support yourself.' He worked there for the summer and it kept him G'd up because we was wearing Gap clothes mixed with Polo."

And, night and day, the beat went on. Donda looked into the cost of getting their garage soundproofed to turn it into a dedicated studio, but it was too expensive. So for the time being she endured the endless noise and the rap friends that would traipse in and out of Kanye's bedroom studio. Every now and then, when a new beat grabbed her, she'd put her head around the door to encourage him: "Kanye, that's a million dollars right there."

She had, after all, more pressing concerns. In hand with his rising star in Chicago, Kanye's grades at school continued plummeting. Despite Donda's efforts to stay on top of his schooling by volunteering and going on field trips at Polaris, avidly making PTA meetings and editing the parent-teacher newsletter, his Bs and Cs became a D in calculus and an F in French, and Saturday detentions became more regular. He even received a suspension for falling asleep in study hall. Donda hired a private tutor who helped improve his grades, but now she was only hoping he'd graduate from high school. There was certainly still a future in his art – he'd been entering national-level art competitions since the age of 14, winning every one.

So, when he did finally graduate from high school, he wasn't entirely out of further education options. He applied for scholarships to three local art schools – the Art Institute Of Chicago, St Xavier University and the American Academy Of Art. Despite the strong competition for scholarships, he was offered all three. He plumped for the American Academy due to its courses in interior and fashion design, taking a partial scholarship and $550 a month contribution from his mother; affordable since she was now earning $70,000 as the chair of English at Chicago

State. The plan was that he'd stay at home with Donda and take the train to college every day. That way he could please his education-orientated mother by continuing his studies without dislocating himself from his home studio or his Chicago rap contacts.

It was a plan, however, that would soon crumble.

CHAPTER THREE

The College Dropout

"**M**om," Kanye said, "I don't want to be an artist."

They were the words Donda dreaded the most. She knew Kanye wasn't enamoured with his course at the American Academy; he'd been complaining about the strict nature of his assignments. He found it tedious simply drawing what he was told to draw rather than being able to construct his own work, and the idea of graduating into a life of uncreative commissions – designing corporate brochures and pamphlets to strict requirements and directions – left him very cold indeed. After just one semester at art school his portfolio was impressive and he'd had an insight into the processes of the professional creative mind, but his ardour for art had waned. The American Academy was to be the first college that Kanye would drop out of.

An evangelist of the advantages of study, Donda wasn't giving up on his education so easily. She convinced him to consider transferring to Chicago State, where she could easily find him a place at a 50 per cent staff discount on his tuition. She could also choose his courses and file all of the application forms for him; he didn't even have to so much as turn up and queue. She enrolled him as an English major studying freshman composition and learning to recognise and dissect quality writing. Dutifully, Kanye took the place, although his heart was undoubtedly elsewhere. The studio.

In the years to come, Kanye would be put down by his more hard-nosed peers and mentors for not having paid his dues hustling drugs around the projects or over cold, dangerous nights on the wintry streets. But at 18, Kanye had to do his own kind of street hustling to get noticed. "I was either going to or coming out of a Fugees concert," recalled Chicago rapper Grav, "and this young kid runs up to me like, 'Yo, I heard you got a record deal. Yo, you should let me get some beats on your album. I'm nice, I got skills. You should just come to the car and let me play some beats for you'."

Intrigued, Grav – a big name around Chicago since landing a deal with Correct Records for his first album – agreed to take a seat in Kanye's little Nissan. "I go to the car, he pops in a cassette. Fire. Fire, off the bat. I'm telling you, the boy was a child prodigy way back then. I'm like 'Oh my gosh'. First track I can remember is the 'Keep Movin' track, 'I move rhymes like retail, make sure shit sell'." No I.D. had already approached Grav to appear on his own album, which he'd signed up to make at the same time as Common, and the deadline was fast approaching. "So after I got the tape from Kanye," says Grav, "I was at Dion's crib and said 'You ever heard of this kid named Kanye?' He was like, 'Oh, man, he be on me, man, he coming like bugaboo-ish or something'. I was like, 'I don't know about that but listen to this tape, dude'. When I popped that tape in for him that motherfucker picked up the phone right then, and was like, 'Yo man, I heard the tape, it's crazy'. He was right on top of it. The rest is history."

Finally spotting the superstar right under his nose, before long No I.D. would take on a co-management role with Kanye alongside Common's A&R man from Relativity, Peter Kang. And Kanye's beats went down a storm with Grav's record label. Kanye sold his first professional beats to Grav for $8,800 – he spent the money on a Jesus piece and some Polo clothes, his first major investment in the brand of Kanye West.

Recording the first half of the album in New York City and the second half back home in Chicago, Kanye would produce a total of eight tracks on Grav's 1996 debut album, *Down To Earth*, which also featured production from Chicago's Lil Ray and Beatnuts' Al' Tariq, and it's evident from these tracks that Kanye's style was already advanced. That first beat that Grav had heard, 'Keep Movin', along with 'One Puff' and 'Thought It Was On', were spacious, ethereal and hazily narcotic takes on the 'Bad Boy' sound, full of manipulated classic soul samples that aligned them to Sean 'Puffy' Combs work on later Notorious B.I.G. records, Nas, Mase and, ironically, to Jay-Z's seminal debut album, *Reasonable Doubt*, released that same year. The megalomaniacal 'World Domination 1' and the deviant, horrorcore 'Sick Thoughts' took similar tacks but were laced with the kind of sinister, background devil yelps, trip-hop darkness and warped underworld noise that marked an early sign of Kanye's unsettling sonic edge, while 'City To City' and the title track boasted a pleasantly elastic West Coast bounce.

There was already a sense of heady invention to these tracks, a knack for otherworldly atmospherics and psychedelia and a canny ability to merge East Coast soul with West Coast gleam. And on 'Line To Line', there was vaulting ambition too. Kanye used his position as one of the record's chief producers to talk his way into a guest verse. Contrasting with Grav's lustrous tone, Kanye's voice had a menacing, impish sharpness, a sharp tooth and acid tongue, as he attacked the gun-toting gangsta image. "Yo, mad niggas got dreams of the Lexus and coupes," he spat, reeling out a warning tale of a rapper falling foul of his own notorious fantasies, "got their signing bonus and bought Tecs for the video shoot/Ayo, them shits backfired before the cameraman arrived/ He died for his image". "Kill the black-on-black crime," he concluded, but couldn't help himself falling into the traditional rap tenets of bloodily boasting of his murderous rhyming skills: "I cremate MCs and breathe they ashes in my last breath/In a life or death situa(tion) I come through with the Chi representa(tion)/And bleed you pussies that be marked like ovula(tion)".

Reviews for *Down To Earth* were favourable. "Though *Down To Earth* won't reshape the rap world, Grav shows promise on the mike and demonstrates that MCs don't have to focus on materialism to move the crowd," wrote Option, while Rap pages highlighted Kanye's style – "*Down To Earth* gives you that genuine dirty-yet-phat street sound that true hip-hop listeners have grown to cherish." "Doing that album was definitely a ball," Grav said. "It was everybody's first published works, it was a really good album, we got some really good write-ups. It's an honour to have a piece of work that's a part of hip-hop history in some way, shape and form, and associated with the things that are relevant right now."

Meanwhile, No I.D. and Kang set about touting Kanye to their record company contacts. One of their first stops was an A&R man called Kyambo 'Hip Hop' Joshua from Roc-A-Fella Records in NYC – Jay-Z's homegrown label that he'd launched to release his own debut album when none of the established labels would take him on. Joshua had just been given his job as the fledgling Roc-A-Fella label was looking to expand its roster and was introduced to Kanye on a business trip to Chicago. "Wendy Day of Rap Coalition had a convention in Chicago [or] a panel that she sent me to be on," Joshua said. "No I.D. was on the panel. No I.D. didn't really have any music but he told me, 'I have this kid that I'm working on.' I met a kid the next day [at Harold's Chicken in Chicago] – the kid was Kanye. He started sending me beats for a long time."

Kanye's beats also found their way to Jermaine Dupri though the precise details on how this happened are fuzzy. In a *Hot 97* interview, Deric 'D-Dot' Angelettie mentioned that he had hooked Kanye up with Dupri. Although both Kanye and Angelettie produced tracks on *Life In 1472*, Angelettie's claim seems unlikely as D-Dot was himself introduced to Kanye through Free Maiden, the head of Dupri's record label So So Def, so the label must already have known of him. It's more likely that No I.D. and Kang suggested Kanye to So So Def. Dupri was a producer out of Atlanta, Georgia who'd put together the successful teen duo Kris Kross – famed for their 1992 multi-platinum singles 'Jump' and 'It's A Shame' and wearing their clothes back to front – and then founded So So Def Recordings, home of Da Brat and Xscape. Between working with Lil' Kim and Destiny's Child, Dupri was putting together his own debut album, *Jermaine Dupri Presents Life In 1472: The Original Soundtrack*, and was taken with what he heard from Kanye. He invited him to contribute; Kanye produced one song on the album, '(Intro)

Turn It Out'. Featuring one of Kanye's biggest heroes, Nas, spitting a tongue-twister verse, West pulled in samples from Davy DMX's 'One For The Treble' and Willie Hutch's sumptuous soul classic 'Hospital Prelude Of Love Theme' to create a lean, crisp funk groove that would – almost – make his name.

Aged 19, Kanye had a beat on his first platinum album. And the music business sat up.

★ ★ ★

When the limo met him at JFK airport to sweep him into Manhattan, he firmly believed the Columbia deal was in the bag. Why on earth else would its umbrella label Sony fly him and his management team all the way to New York, all expenses covered, and whisk him around in a stretch? As he slid onto the plush leather, just turned 19 years old, he just knew he'd be going home with a major record deal.

Sony President Don Ienner and the head of its urban music department, Michael Mauldin, had caught wind of Kanye's releases so far, and were impressed enough to want to meet him. Over the course of several meetings they planned to check him out; Kanye, on the other hand, was full of cockiness at his genius being recognised and celebration of what he was certain was a done deal. In their meeting with Ienner, according to No I.D., "Kanye danced around singing this song and saying, 'I'm gonna be the next Michael Jackson'. To us, it was like, 'This is hip-hop! What are you talking about? Are you kidding me?'" Then, in their interview with Mauldin, Kanye was asked what his niche was and couldn't answer. "He said 'I want to be better than Jermaine Dupri!'," I.D. said. "I'm like, 'Are you crazy? [Mauldin is] Jermaine's father! Why would you say that?' Just a lot of silly things happened that day."

When Kanye left the Sony offices with no deal but only the casual promise "we'll call you", he couldn't even get a cab back to the airport. But the setback didn't deter him, or derail his ambitions. He went straight back to his bedroom studio and intensified his writing; the experience merely hardened his resilience and fired his determination to make it big, one way or another.

For No I.D., however, the trip was a breaking point. "After that meeting, that was the day I said, 'You know what? I'm gonna fall back'," he said. "I said, 'You know what man? We're gonna stay friends and I'm gonna help you, but I can't do this. I'll go crazy'… because that's a hell of a personality to manage. I only have so much capacity as a creative person. That would've been a full-time job and I'm a producer. I wouldn't cheat him by sitting in some position trying to make some money off of him, when I can let capable people step in and help him get where he needed to get."

"After a few meetings, [I'd] realised that I couldn't control his personality, and didn't have the time and patience to be that role."

The capable people Kanye needed turned out to be So So Def's Free Maiden, a one-time employee at Bad Boy, and his associates. They signed a management deal with Kanye which included a 50 per cent cut of his publishing, a lucrative source of income for the artist. But they also wanted to bring in a big name to help push Kanye in the right directions in terms of selling his beats. So Maiden put in a call to Deric 'D-Dot' Angelettie, a man with some serious connections.

Having started his career in the early nineties as a rapper in Two Kings In A Cipher, D-Dot had joined Bad Boy in 1993 and become its director of management and merchandising, eventually taking on the management role of Mary J Blige. From there he'd become a major player in The Hitmen, Combs' team of producers, producing and writing major hits for Puffy himself as well as the likes of Notorious B.I.G., Blige, Jay-Z and LL Cool J. In 1997 he was basking in the glory of major smashes for Biggie ('Hypnotize') and Puffy ('Blame It On The Benjamins') and would go on to sell over 30 million records as a producer, writer or artist. He was also in the process of introducing his own rapping persona as Madd Rapper, making his debut on Biggie's *Life After Death* album. D-Dot had a coterie of producers he used on his various projects at that time including an engineer by the name of Young Guru, and Kanye shared a little background with D-Dot – they'd both produced tracks on Dupri's *Life In 1472* album. He was clearly the sort of guy Kanye needed to get in with.

"One day in '97 Free called me and at that time he said 'There's a guy in Chicago you need to meet, he wants to meet you'," D-Dot said. "Because Kanye at that time sounded exactly like my production – hi-hat, shakers, samples, big thick 808s. So we arranged a meeting and he played me his data beats and I thought he was hot. The problem was they managed him and also owned 50 per cent of his publishing. One thing I will say to Kanye, which he never thanked me for, is that I got him his publishing back. I refused at that time to take his publishing, or take anybody's publishing. I just didn't want to play that game with anyone. They owned 50 per cent of his publishing and I told them I wouldn't manage him unless they give it back to him, so in return what they said was, 'OK, but in that case we'll let you manage him but if he leaves us he's gotta leave you too'. I said, 'That's cool'."

D-Dot took Kanye in, signed him to a management deal and began organising production work for him. So with production work flowing in, tracks on Dupri's album under his belt and the major labels starting to show interest, he knew what his next step had to be.

He had to embrace his fate.

He had to become the college dropout.

★ ★ ★

Donda had been hearing the whispers around Chicago State. Kanye wasn't making his classes. He was often to be found in the student union or in the music rooms when he was supposed to be in seminars; since his mother was her boss, his English teacher told Donda she wished he wasn't in her class so that he wouldn't be her responsibility. The student affairs department notified her of his absences in the second semester of his sophomore year. Kanye was 20 years old and giving up on education.

Rather than confront him directly, Donda chose to recruit some of her colleagues and allies at the university to try to talk Kanye around to the idea of stepping up his efforts. She asked a popular tutor called Al Brown to sit him down, but Brown couldn't convince Kanye he should focus on his studies more and Al didn't want to push it too much since he saw first-hand the impetus and drive behind Kanye's musical convictions. A second volley from Robin Benny, the director of the university's composition programme, went even worse – Kanye so firmly convinced him that he was meant for music that Benny ended up canvassing Donda to let him leave.

Eventually, Donda and Kanye faced off. "He said, 'Mom, I can do this, and I don't need to go to college, because I've had a professor in the house with me my whole life'. I'm thinking, this boy is at it again. He always could twirl a word." If Donda had learnt one thing from the continual back-and-forth of raising Kanye, it was the power of understanding. As a mother she'd discovered she was learning as much from Kanye as he was from her – she'd always been open to his ideas and taught him to take control over his own life. She knew he wasn't one to conform to anyone's expectations, that he had the drive to make a success of himself and she had faith in his discretion and self-belief. "I thought I would die when he dropped out," Donda said. "But that's when I realised that Kanye doesn't respect people who don't take their destiny in their own hands."

So they struck a deal. She wouldn't hassle him to stay in college – he could stay at home for $200 a month in rent, but he had only a year to make hip-hop work out for him, and in the meantime, since he'd chosen financial independence over the security of his college fund, he'd have to get a job.

So, in 1998 at the age of 20, Kanye filed his dropout papers and launched himself into hip-hop as hard as he could.

His father bought him a car to help him get to and from jobs – sporty, new, but cheap, and he'd certainly need that day job to pay the insurance on it. Kanye's employment record would be a roller coaster. He looked into going into real estate and being a male porn star crossed his mind several times. But his first job was as a busboy at a Bob Evans restaurant, where he lasted only one day, quitting when he realised he wouldn't be able to hack it for too long. Then he launched himself into the lowly world of telemarketing. His first job on the phones didn't last long either – he wasn't allowed to doodle while he was on work calls and no matter how many times he told his supervisor how to pronounce his name she'd purposely say it wrong. It took only one too many cries of "Kanyee or Kan'yah, whatever your name is!" before he quit that job too. Donda insisted he go back and ask for the job back though, until he'd found another one. They welcomed him back, tentatively.

Within a few months, though, he'd found another firm that would let him draw while he was on the phone, and he settled in just fine. Given a little more rope, he became quite successful as a salesman, his gift of the gab earning him bonuses. He even managed to phone his mother at home and convince her he was a stranger trying to sell her his product.

Outside of the day job, Kanye worked closely as D-Dot developed his reputation as a jobbing producer and beat-maker. In 1998 he hooked him up with Foxy Brown for her *Chyna Doll* album producing the third track, 'My Life', an elastic soul bouncer, and soon, alongside Jermaine Dupri and Trackmasters, he had three tracks on Harlem World's *The Movement* record, 'Minute Man', '100 Sheisty's' and 'You Made Me' featuring Carl Thomas and Nas, which saw Kanye getting ever closer to his biggest heroes. "People that through my connects we were hooking up with," D-Dot explained. "Nothing really big because Kanye wasn't yet the producer, he was just a beat guy handing you a DAT. And then I would do the rest or if he did it for Jermaine [Dupri], Jermaine handled it."

Kanye's excitement at being involved with such big names was evident in a video shot of him at Dupri's birthday party in 1998, aged 21. In a filmed interview for ChannelzeroTV.com – possibly Kanye's first ever video interview – beaming into the camera with the exuberance of holding a microphone and looking into a spotlight, he babbled: "I wanna send this out to 87th street outfit, my man John-John back at the crib. Lennon, Aaron, Timmy. We're out here doing the tracks, get ready for this. Harlem World, it's about to drop. Harlem World, Kanye, Chi-Town represent." Drunk and on a roll, his sheer disbelief and enthusiasm spilled over. "Chi-Town made it down here boy," he grinned, "somebody from the crib made it down here, boy!"

Kanye's Chi-Town dream was on fire. Back home, his rising profile had made him something of a Chicago scene pioneer, and his local crew proudly hoisted him on their metaphorical shoulders. John 'Monopoly' Johnson had been consistently helping to push Kanye as a producer and an artist, even getting him a support slot at Jay-Z's first low-key show in Chicago. Alongside his partners in his marketing and promotions company Hustle Period – his cousin Don C (Don Crowley) and Happy Lewis – Monopoly had pieced together a conglomerate of local rapping and production talent they called Kon-Man, of which Kanye was their chief production star, getting assistance from Boogz, Arrowstar and Brian 'All Day' Miller. Kanye himself brought in some of his rapper friends to a crew that included Mikkey Halsted, Rhymefest, Miss Criss, Really Doe, Shayla G, Timmy G and GLC. "Me and my crew [Hustle Period] were always pushing his initiative," Monopoly said. "We weren't managing 'Ye at the time, but trying to help him make it in the game."

To which end, Monopoly helped Kanye set up and launch a new group, a rap trio called Go Getters, alongside Timmy G and GLC. Since his management deal with D-Dot and Free Maiden barred him from making his own solo album to showcase his rapping, here was Kanye's first chance to really expose his rhyming skills. With Arrowstar producing and some professional publicity photos printed up, Go Getters looked to Monopoly and other Chicago movers and shakers like a dream team destined for huge things.

Go Getters would record a full album's worth of material over the coming months, eventually titled *World Record Holders* and featuring a revolving cast of guests such as Miss Criss, Shayla G, Rhymefest and Mikkey Halsted alongside the three central rappers. It opened with a 30 second *World Record Holders Intro* track, introducing Kanye to the world. "Somebody said, 'Kanye the best producer out of Chicago', let's go!" the intro goes, before an urgent snippet of manipulated soul drops with Kanye rapping, "Who am I? Kanye," over the chopping beat. The album's title track then kicked in with more Kanye worship. "Standing in this corner with the platinum chain," said a boxing style hype man over crowd cheers, "trained by the platinum producer Kanye West, we've got Chi-Town's finest, the Go Getters!" The pugilism theme continued with the hook built around a *Rocky* theme horn sample and the crackling toytown beats landing like precision jabs. As the three rapped in a D-12 style about their world-beating skills, their sex appeal

("Girls get naked for us/Cause they heard we the coldest"), their rejection of hard for soft drugs and the riches inevitably coming their way, there was a consistent respect for Kanye as their leader-in-chief. "How we gonna fall if Kanye producing?" went one line, while another claimed his beats were so murderous there was talk of arrest. Go Getters clearly knew who was boss.

To drive the point home, Kanye took the lead on the next track 'Nuthin's Gonna Stop Me', his trademark soul samples – the song used here Tony Hester's 'Nothing Can Stop Me' – backing his first burst of hip-hop autobiography. "I could be in gym class," he said over the intro, "but nigga, I'm meant to be a rapper. I didn't do that much with my last three years of high school." He then broke into an assured verse stripped of the menace of his Dupri guest spot, laying into less talented producers and speed-rappers and already boasting about his superior taste in clothes while also exposing some of the attitudes that had been ingrained into him by his exposure to the Chicago scene, and some of which he'd later disown. "I hate a gold-digging bitch," he rapped, "fuck fucking, I make them kiss the tip of my dick… all that crying and shit… next time we fuck bring your friends with you." Then, later: "I hate gay niggas." He also played on the way people constantly mispronounced his name, giving his listeners an easy way to remember it with his first legendary line – "How you gonna con me when Kan half my name?"

Vocally Kanye sat out the next track 'Dem Guys', but he certainly wasn't absent. With GLC and Timmy G sharing the gangsta verses about a gangland rivalry and his own sparse, inventive Blaxploitation-style sample of skewed guitar lines, clipped tambourine and reedy bass driving the track, he got a shout out as one of "dem guys" in the first chorus, listing the Kon-Man crew right down to their "designated drive" Melvin. If that track sounded playful, Kanye's next appearance on 'Ghetto Senorita' was even more so. Led by delicate flamenco guitar and erratic woodblock beats, it sounded almost like a pastiche of the sort of Latino loverman pop that Ricky Martin would soon take global. Kanye took on the chorus hook of "Baby don't you know I need ya/I want you to be my ghetto senorita" – a hook line he'd recreate in 2007 when Missy Elliott associate Mocha would rework the song for her unreleased album *One Day At A Time* – while Miss Criss and Shayla G strutted their sassy stuff as the titular heroines, asserting their own rhyming gifts and feminine class.

Brian 'All Day' Miller took over the production helm for the next two tracks 'All I Need' and 'Foolish Game', the latter a laid-back ghetto groove rapped by Mikkey Halsted and showcasing the sped-up soul samples that Kanye had been developing alongside No I.D★. Then Kanye returned for 'No Luv', a slinky, piano-led funk piece with Kanye taking the backroom beatmaker role to GLC and Timmy G's rapping once more, a plethora of classic hustling raps about Rolexes, gun violence and the lack of love and respect between enemies on the street.

Kanye hooked up with Rhymefest and Mikkey to rap out inspirational thug life tales on 'Fight With The Best', all soulful strings and rubber rhythms reflecting the colourful Southern styles of Outkast, and went head to head with Rhymefest on the smart, shuffling 'On 10 In A Benz', painting himself as the traditional gangsta player that was far from his real life persona: "Everybody wanna be what Kanye West be in/In the bulletproof 5 what the Pres be in/With a half black, half white lesbian… my guns don't discriminate, they penetrate… before you take your last breath, any last statements?"

The most obvious hit single Go Getters recorded was called 'Uh Oh!', in some places, 'Oh Oh Oh'. Based around a catchy crib chant with a sunny West Coast hue and taking its cues from the low-riding pimp sounds of Snoop Dogg, it involved all three Go Getters rapping, Kanye upfront on a verse about mistreating a woman. "I lie to a bitch," he claimed, "that bitch thick as hell… she wanna page me all day, wanna ride the dick like yippee-kay-ey". Despite its subject matter – a later verse involved a kidnap at gunpoint – the song sounded like a radio smash.

The recordings closed with 'Mind Yo Business', a crisp eighties twist on Uh Oh!'s louche Cali groove with hustler attitude, and 'Let Em In', a seventies-inflected cut about trying to front their way into

★ Some sources have Kanye producing 'Foolish Game'.

a nightclub despite being underage. Kanye took the chorus here too, yelling, "Where my south side niggas at? Let em in! Where my west side niggas at? Let em in!" as if begging the bullish bouncer on behalf of all of Chicago.

Showcasing Kanye West as producer, rapper and singer, the Kon-Man crew were certain they had a hit on their hands. Go Getters started playing club shows all over the city to build a name for themselves while Monopoly took the chosen single 'Uh Oh!' to his contacts at radio stations. When he came up against resistance from the playlist compilers at WGCI, he even organised a picket line at the station in an attempt to get the record played. The protest didn't work, but one of the station's DJs, Mike Love, began using the track as a lead-in to advert breaks and the tune began to garner some local attention. With the help of the group's keenness to be heard, they started getting radio appearances and spot plays. "We'd be down at radio stations, at performances, floated throughout the city," said Really Doe, "and sleeping in No I.D.'s parking lot trying to hear our music heard. I mean, not really, but we would be in his parking lot, seven to eight hours, trying to present our music. Trying to get him to open his doors for us and he finally did."

As the record started to pick up some heat, Elektra Records, a subsidiary of Warner Brothers at the time, started sniffing around Go Getters. But, just as with the glimmer of hope Kanye had been given by Sony, the deal never materialised. Every time he got a glimmer of hope that his rapping ambitions might be about to launch, a door was slammed in his face. Kanye knew nothing worth having ever came easy though, and he kept badgering labels to pay attention to his music – Def Jam, Arista and Capitol were high in his sight line. He was willing to work hard for his success. But the problem he kept coming up against was his rapping – he was seen across the board as a skilled producer and beatmaker but no-one wanted him to rhyme. "He started to shop his group with GLC and all them to Columbia, they played him," D-Dot explained. "He was trying to rap to Free, they played him." Kanye's tactics to get record executives to come around to his way of thinking occasionally reached laughable extremes. "I once heard a story about him getting up on a table," said No I.D.. "Well I wasn't there. I'm not gonna act like I was there. He told me about it too. But it was just so many different things that happened. The stories are endless."

One person who did believe in Kanye's rhyming skills was D-Dot himself. In 1998 he was hosting mix-tapes called Underground Railroad for DJ Ashknuckles, and he gave Kanye a platform to rap there. While fixing him up production jobs with the likes of Atlanta's Goodie Mob and Boston's Made Men – tracks which developed his knack of straddling the country's full range of hip-hop styles – D-Dot also got Kanye production roles on three songs on the debut album of female duo Infamous Syndicate, and Kanye was allowed to rap on one, 'What You Do To Me', playing a guy cheating on his girlfriend after being messed around so many times by women out of his league that he'd become a heartless misogynist. "It seems like fine hoes is hard to find mostly," Kanye rapped, "the type of girls that give you their whereabouts supposedly/And when you check, they ain't never where they're supposed to be/I learnt my lesson, now I only fuck hoes that's close to me… I diss hoes, I'm very mean now… I bring your self-esteem down". Then, when Angelettie came to make his own album as *The Madd Rapper, Tell 'Em Why U Madd*, as well as giving Kanye a production role on six tracks he also gave him the chance to write a song for the album. Unfortunately, over the course of 1999, Free and his other managers wouldn't let Kanye rap, so D-Dot took his verse instead. "He probably would've did well if I could've let him rap," Angelettie said, "because I had a label deal and he was who he is today. He hasn't really changed much, very cocky, very arrogant but confident and a talented kid."

The *Madd Rapper* album, eventually released in 2000, would also be a pivotal preview of Kanye's work. The inventive and sinister graveyard grooves of 'You're All Alone', the cartoonish deep bass party funk of 'That's What's Happenin'', the dramatic yet sophisticated horrorcore backing a typically violent Eminem on 'Stir Crazy' and the lustrous psychedelic soul of 'Not The One', 'Too Many Ho's' and 'Ghetto', with its narcotic piano blings, formed the backbone of a boundary-challenging album. This was Kanye exploring twisted and unsettling atmospheres within the comforting realms of soul and block party sounds, the first signs of his ever-adventurous production nous. And it was work like this that, in 1999, was already catching the ear of one of the A&R scouts that Kanye had kept in touch with throughout his rise through the Chicago ranks.

Both No I.D. and D-Dot had links to Roc-A-Fella, and both claim to have had a hand in hooking Kanye up with the burgeoning label. "[Kyambo 'Hip Hop' Joshua] hit me and said, 'I want to work with him. I like him'," I.D. recalled. "Me and Hip Hop were good friends at this point, even beyond business. I was talking them up to the both of them to really make it happen." D-Dot meanwhile claimed to have been the key link for Kanye. "I actually introduced him to Roc-A-Fella so those first things were under me," he explained. "I actually got paid all the way up to the first album."

However the connection was made, Hip Hop became a long-distance friend and confidant to Kanye and began organising him production work for Roc-A-Fella artists. His try-out track was for Beanie Sigel, one of Jay-Z's most promising protégés striking out on his own with his debut album, *The Truth*. Kanye produced the title song on the album, sampling Graham Nash's 'Chicago' as a sly hometown signature for the same sort of stark, murderous beat that characterised his darker tracks at the time. On a much later track, Kanye would explain this entire breakthrough period in detail, claiming that during the Sigel session he played his demo for Hip Hop, who asked him "who that spittin'?" and, when he heard it was Kanye himself, began calling him regularly asking for beats. "I'm thinking he's trying to get into managing producers 'cause he had this other kid named Just Blaze he was messin' with," Kanye explained, but went on to say that Hip Hop then contacted No I.D. who told him, "Yo, you wanna sign him, tell him you like how he rap." So Hip Hop began talking about managing Kanye as a rapper and a producer. "I dunno if he was gassin' me or not," Kanye would say.

Hip Hop's business partner and fellow Roc-A-Fella A&R Gee Roberson would give more details on the thinking behind the deal. Around the start of 1999 he and Hip Hop began thinking about launching their own company called Hip Hop Since 1978, collecting a small coterie of producers under the banner to make it easier by having an in-house team producing for all of the label's artists. Hip Hop suggested Kanye as a producer they could take on who was currently "not getting any production credit" working for D-Dot and the post-producers at Bad Boy. So they got in touch with him. "He would give us a batch of beats on a daily basis," Gee remembered. "I thought we should sign this guy and he can be the first person we bring on board. The only stipulation was he rapped and we would need to work with him as an artist. We obliged and we planned on pushing his beats, feeding his sound and creating an opportunity for him as an artist."

★ ★ ★

Back home, Kanye's life was in flux. The year his mother had given him to make his way in hip-hop was up, and he'd made some impressive in-roads in the time he had. But his mother's patience had run out. The constant beats and endless stream of rappers through the house had gone on for too long. She told him he'd have to find his own place to work. "Mom," he said, a little hurt, "are you kicking me out?"

Donda helped find him a two-bedroom apartment above a dress shop in Chicago's Beverly area which seemed perfect – the living and dining rooms were large and there was even a small spare room he could turn into his studio. The rent was $1,000 per month, but he could just about meet it with the money coming in from his production work and selling beats to local acts for a couple of hundred dollars a time. "I be doin' like, just beats for local acts just to try to keep the lights on," he said, "and then to go out and get a Pelle Pelle off layaway, get some Jordans or something or get a TechnoMarine, that's what we wore back then." It was while he was here, listening to Dr Dre's *The Chronic 2001* album, actually released in 1999, on repeat, that he came up with a beat that would change his life. Speeding up a sample from Harold Melvin & The Blue Notes' 'I Miss You', he played it down the phone to Hip Hop who was enthused by the track – he told him to mail him the beat and even had to send Kanye the money for postage. "'Oh, yo that shit is crazy'," Kanye remembered Hip Hop telling him, "'Jay might want it for this compilation album he doin', called *The Dynasty*'." "Jay heard it and he was blown away," Hip Hop said. "He did it right then and there. That opened up the door to the whole Roc-A-Fella/Kanye thing."

Excited that he might be on the verge of the opportunity of a lifetime, Kanye strove for perfection with the track. The drums didn't sound right, so he turned to the Dre album for inspiration. Accelerating the Neptunes-style drums from Dre's 'Xxplosive' and patching them onto the Blue Notes sample, Kanye seemed to strike career gold. "Now it's kind of like my whole style," he'd say. "That was really the first beat of that kind that was on the *Dynasty* album. I could say that was the resurgence of this whole sound."

Suddenly Kanye was facing the big league right in the face. By 2000 Jay-Z was a phenomenon, having sold two million copies of his latest album, *Vol. 3… Life And Times Of S. Carter*, in its first month of release and pushing his reworking of 'It's The Hard Knock Life' from the musical *Annie* into 'Hard Knock Life (Ghetto Anthem)' deep into the national US consciousness. The label Roc-A-Fella that Jay and his partners Damon Dash and Kareem 'Biggs' Burke had started from the back of a car had grown into one of the biggest rap labels in the country. And now Kanye found himself behind the desk in a session with the big man himself, producing the track – now called 'This Can't Be Life' – for Jay-Z's label showcase album *The Dynasty: Roc La Familia*. And he found himself totally star-struck.

"You've heard the story where Kanye actually had the chance to go in the studio with Jay," D-Dot recalled, "and his first time he wanted Jay to rap a different way but he wouldn't say nothin' because he was so intimidated by that dynamic of, your idol [and you saying] 'Nigga, that ain't hot, spit that again', that's a hard pill."

On his own records, Kanye would describe the scene himself. "I got to meet Jay-Z and he said, 'Oh you a real soulful dude'," he claimed. "And he played the song 'cause he already spit his verse by the time I got to the studio, you know how he do it, one take. And he said, "Tell me what you think of this." And I heard it, and I was thinking like, 'Man, I really wanted more like of the simple type Jay-Z, I ain't want the more introspective, complicated rhyme…' in my personal opinion. So he asked me, 'What you think of it?' And I was like, 'Man that shit tight'. You know what I'm sayin', man what I'ma tell him?"

In the end the feel of the track was taken out of Kanye's hands by fate. It was intended to be a hard-hitting exploration of life's hardest knocks – Jay-Z's verse spoke about his girlfriend's miscarriage, his family's split, his risks of death and arrest and his fears of a failed career in a West Coast dominated rap scene. But it was the dark and desperate verse from another big name guest rapper, Scarface, that probed deepest. While waiting to record his verse Scarface received a phone call with the news that one of his friend's sons had died. Discarding the verse of his own troubles that he'd originally intended to put on the track, Scarface wrote a tribute to his friend's tragedy on the spot. Over Kanye's slick soul beat, it made for a devastating five and a half minutes. In the eyes of Roc-A-Fella's big boss man, he'd proved himself.

Kanye also told of his attempts to get Jay interested in his rap skills. "I said, 'Yo Jay I could rap'. And I spit this rap that said, 'I'm killin y'all niggaz on that lyrical shit. Mayonnaise colored Benz, I push miracle whips'. And I saw his eyes light up when I said that line. But you know the West, the rap was like real wack and shit, so that's all the response. He said, 'Man that was tight'. That was it. You know, I ain't get no deal then."

Having glimpsed through the crack in the door at the world he should be living and working in, Kanye went home faced with a deep dilemma. He knew he wanted to rap but his management wasn't letting him; meanwhile here was Hip Hop promising him the chance to rap as well as produce. "I just needed some fresh air, you know what I'm sayin?" he said, "'cause I been there for a while, I appreciated what they did for me, but, you know, there's a time in every man's life where he gotta make a change, try to move up to the next level."

So Kanye made the difficult decision to switch his management deal to Hip Hop at Roc-A-Fella. "That downhill slide started because [Free Maiden and his associates] wouldn't let him rhyme," D-Dot explained. "What happened was, eventually he didn't want to be stuck under me just doing beats when he had opportunities, [but] he couldn't rhyme. I couldn't get him signed to Columbia and my deal's through Columbia. They wouldn't let him rhyme, so what was he going to do under D-Dot

Angelettie besides make beats?... Eventually he didn't want to be up under me, which I applaud him for."

Kanye was so keen to follow his new opportunities that he even made Angelettie an unusual offer to keep him happy and involved in his development. "Kanye was so desperate to go do what he wanted to do – you know the type of dude he is – he actually signed management with [Roc-A-Fella] and was giving me 20 [per cent] and them 20 [per cent], just because he wanted to get on."

With his management base elsewhere, Kanye's gaze was now beginning to stretch outside the confines of Chicago. "I'm just in Chicago, I'm trying to do my thing. You know, I got groups. I got acts I'm trying to get on, and like there wasn't nothing really like poppin' off the way it should have been." He told how one of the artists he had under the umbrella of his own production company got signed by a label and rang him to say that Kanye wouldn't be involved in the deal, that he'd be going direct to the new label; his Kon-Man clique was starting to crack and Kanye had itchy feet. Chicago also seemed to be turning against him as a city – one day in 2000 he was arrested outside a mall for allegedly stealing printers from a branch of OfficeMax. The cornrows he wore then matched the description of the culprit given by onlookers and reported sightings of the perpetrator driving a cream Blazer car were ditched by investigating police and replaced with details of Kanye's white Expedition. It was a case of mistaken identity, yet his lawyers advised him to plead guilty in order to avoid any jail time, with the promise that the crime would be wiped from his permanent record in time. Suddenly Kanye felt victimised in his hometown.

The crunch came when his landlord had the same issues as Donda; the noise and stream of visitors was too much and he asked Kanye to move out. The only question was, where would he move to?

He knew he wanted out of Chicago and first considered moving to Atlanta to be near to Jermaine Dupri, who he was now selling beats to for thousands of dollars apiece. He and his mother went as far as visiting the city and finding him an apartment, even putting a deposit down. But before he could move in, New York called to him. It was where

Hip Hop hung and even No I.D. was often there now, working with the likes of Nas and Rhymefest, so there was a brotherly glow to the city.

"When I left Chicago and moved to New York, it wasn't because I didn't love Chicago," he said, "it was because I needed to go to New York."

New York was an expensive town though, so Kanye looked into other options. Donda knew a guy called Richard Johnson who was a resident of New Jersey and he advised them that the area was far more affordable. He pitched in to help and soon found them a stunning one-bed apartment across the street from Penn Station for only $850 a month.

So, 10 days before he was due to be evicted from his Chicago apartment "so I ain't have to deal with the landlord 'cause he's a jerk", and having sold beats to local drug dealers with dreams of rap stardom and his Jesus piece to No I.D. to fund the move, Kanye and Donda loaded up a U-Haul truck with all of his equipment and drove the 700 miles East. To a new apartment he hadn't even seen yet. Kanye signed up for the place from the description alone – the fact that it had a glass ceiling so you could look up and see the stars gripped him.

Little did he know he'd be beating his head against another glass ceiling, career-wise, for some years to come.

CHAPTER FOUR

Setting The Blueprint

Just from looking at him, Kanye was clearly no hustler. Jay-Z looked him up and down, noted his Gucci loafers, his oversized pink sports shirt with the collar turned up, his sports jacket and tailored trousers. He dressed more like a college geek than a rapper, let alone the drug dealing image that Roc-A-Fella Records was built on.

"It was obvious we were not from the same place or cut from the same cloth," said Damon Dash, while Jay could tell he wasn't from the projects and hadn't ever delved into the criminal life. "We all grew up street guys who had to do whatever we had to do to get by," he added. "Then there's Kanye, who to my knowledge has never hustled a day in his life. I didn't see how it could work."

"It was a strike against me that I didn't wear baggy jeans and jerseys and that I never hustled, never sold drugs," Kanye said, who at the time was prone to wearing buttoned down shirts and baseball caps with the cap turned to the front, a geeky look that had Roc-A-Fella A&R Lenny Santiago call him a real contradiction. "But for me to have the opportunity to stand in front of a bunch of executives and present myself, I had to hustle in my own way. I can't tell you how frustrating it was that they didn't get that. No joke, I'd leave meetings crying all the time."

"First of all, it was just my whole look," he said, "my whole aesthetic was very un-Roc-A-Fella. I had Italian shoes, my size medium T-shirts. I dress kind of like a producer, like all producers dress like this. Picture how it looks with me busting a hard rap with a tight T-shirt on. And I'm rapping to Jay-Z, I'm rapping to the greatest and one of the more gangster rappers out there. I was like, 'Yeah, Jay', and I've got the suction-cup T-shirt on. He's looking like, 'Yo, I don't think this is gonna work right here'... he had that look in his eyes... They were expecting [my rapping] to be outright terrible. So that was just such a shocker to them that I was actually not wack."

His beats, though, Jay loved – he quickly became one of Roc-A-Fella's hottest new producers. In New Jersey he felt inspired: once he'd taken out the carpet which was covered in cat droppings and built his own IKEA bed, the place was fabulous; he'd often call his friends back in Chicago to tell them, "You should see this place, it's like something off the TV." And once he'd got his home studio installed into the apartment and Devo Springsteen started coming by to assist him in sample selection and general home maintenance, he set about writing a new batch of beats, often working right through the night, intently focussed on his music. He'd surround himself with crates of records and go through them, picking out tunes he liked, cutting them up and mashing them into beats. The first track he came up with there would eventually be called 'Heart Of The City (Ain't No Love)', a brassy tune twisting Bobby 'Blue' Bland's strutting soul masterpiece 'Ain't No Love In The Heart Of The City' into a dusty demon of funky strings and flirting flutes, backed with Bland's inimitable chorus croon.

Jay decreed that Kanye's inventive use of soul samples would become his trademark sound – an inspired throwback. While many rappers in 2000 – Jay-Z included – were taking up cheap synthesizers in an attempt to make the genre more futuristic and cartoonish, West was harking back to a golden age of the mid-nineties when RZA, Pete Rock and Nashiem Myrick would spin soulful beats and Jay-Z's debut *Reasonable Doubt* gleamed with the gritty Super 8 sunshine of Blaxploitation. Unconsciously he was falling into line with a host of other rising producers affiliated to Roc-A-Fella, such as DJ Premier and Timbaland. He was learning a lot from the artists he was being hooked up to produce in New York too. When he worked with Dead Prez on a dense, buzzing 2000 track called 'It's Bigger Than Hip-Hop', it opened his eyes to the possibilities of writing more honest and personal, less cliché-driven hip-hop, of exploring his real thoughts and feelings without conforming to any standard rap mores. "When the smoke and camera disappear," Dead Prez's M1 rapped about rapping itself, cutting through the front and image of the scene to the power of having something true to say and calling out the misogyny inherent in the form, "it's bigger than all these fake ass records when poor folks got the millions and my woman's disrespected… if you a fighter, rider, lighter, flame ignitor, crowd exciter or just wanna get high, then say it." Later his partner stic. man declares himself ready for violent political action – "I'm down for runnin' up on them crackers in their city hall" – and claimed, unequivocally, "I'm sick of that fake thug R&B rap scenario all day on the radio… you would rather have a Lexus or justice? A dream or some substance? A Beamer, a necklace or freedom?"

"Before, when I wanted to rap, my raps sounded a bit like Cam'ron; they sounded a bit like Mase; they sounded a bit like Jay-Z or whoever," Kanye said of the influence working on the record had on him. "It wasn't until I hung out with Dead Prez and understood how to make, you know, raps with a message sound cool that I was able to just write 'All Falls Down' in 15 minutes… that's how I discovered my style. I was just hanging out with them all the time in New York. I would produce for them. You know, I was able to slip past everything with a pink polo, but I am Dead Prez."

Kanye was ripe for a little sociological awakening at this point. In 2000, shopping with his girlfriend in a Greenwich Village clothes store, he used the word "fag" derogatorily within earshot of some gay men. Common practice in his circle of friends in Chicago, but he wasn't prepared for the reaction in cosmopolitan New York City. Tutting, his girlfriend told him to "step into the new millennium". Suddenly Kanye became aware that the negative attitudes he grew up around were slowly being debunked.

Every name in hip-hop that Kanye met in New York, he'd rap at them to try to convince them of his skills. Rapper and producer 88-Keys recalls meeting Kanye around that time, at a session at Roc-A-Fella's regular studio Baseline down near the Flatiron District in Midtown Manhattan★. When Keys told Kanye who he was, Kanye was shocked, having heard of him via the work he'd done on Mos Def's albums while Keys, for his part, had heard Kanye's name around. "Within eight minutes of our conversation he told me was going to be a star," Keys recalled. "His Midwest accent was so thick I didn't know what he was saying. He spit a rap at that time, and we went back and forth rapping. His raps were really good, but I didn't really think 'star' from those raps or that moment. At that time, we both lived in Newark. We'd go to each other's apartments, going to the studio together for almost four years." Likewise, Devo's college room-mate John Stephens, who met Kanye in May of 2001, witnessed Kanye developing his material over 2001 but didn't hear anything he felt was going to turn out particularly special.

GLC remembers Kanye playing him songs over the phone back to Chicago. "He had a song called 'Dream Killers' about where you try to come up and do something with your life but they don't want you to prosper," he said. "He had another joint called 'Arguing'; he had a Martin Lawrence excerpt where he was like, 'I don't want to get rid of this girl but we constantly arguing.' He had this joint called 'Wack Niggas' - like if you got offended by that song, you must be a wack nigga." Kanye would later record 'Wack Niggas' with Talib Kweli, Common and Consequence for the *Take 'Em To The Cleaners* mix-tape.

'Heart Of The City (Ain't No Love)' was one of seven beats Kanye took along to Baseline Studios one fateful day to play to Beanie Sigel, for possible inclusion on his second album, *The Reason*. "Beans was still working on his album at that time," he explained, "so I came up there to Baseline, it was Beans' birthday, matter of fact, and I played like seven beats. And, you know I could see he's in the zone, he already had the beats that he wanted, I had nothing like that ready at that time. But then

★ Owned by Justin 'Just Blaze' Smith, Baseline would be closed down in 2010.

Jay walked in. I remember he had a Gucci bucket hat on. I remember it like it was yesterday. And Hip Hop said, 'Yo play that one beat for him'. And I played 'Heart Of The City'. And really I made 'Heart Of The City', I really wanted to give that beat to DMX [but Hip Hop said], 'No I think Jay gon' like this one right here'. And I played another beat, and I played another beat. And I remember that Gucci bucket, he took it and like put it over his face and made one of them faces like 'OOOOOOOOOH'."

Two days later, Kanye was back at Baseline when he met Jay-Z's Roc-A-Fella partner Damon Dash for the first time. "Dame didn't know who I was and I was like, 'Yo what's up I'm Kanye'. [He said] 'Yo, you that kid, Kanye? You that kid that gave all them beats to Jay? Yo, this nigga got classics'. I'm like 'Oh shit'. And all this time I'm star-struck, man. I'm still thinking 'bout, you know I'm picturing these niggaz on the show *Streets Is Watching*★, I'm lookin', these were superstars in my eyes. And they still are, you know."

Unlike Jay, Dash could see the potential in Kanye as a rapper, picturing him as a hip-hop version of clean-cut R&B star Babyface. "Dame Dash figured out a way that he thought it could work," Kanye said. "He said I would be like the hip-hop Babyface, we could do an album and it could be like *The Chronic* and we can put Cam'ron on it, Jay on it. You know, he's just a mastermind." But Jay, like so many before and after him, couldn't see Kanye making it in a hip-hop scene full of hard-nosed street gangstas.

Instead, he grabbed 'Heart Of The City' for his next album, and signed him up as one of the record's principal producers.

And, together, they set about making hip-hop history.

★ ★ ★

The Blueprint was set ridiculously quickly. In just two weeks at Baseline studios in July 2001, and with his rhymes written and recorded in just

★ The 1998 film *Streets Is Watching*, billed as 'a long form music video movie by Abdul Malik Abbott', was Damon Dash's concept to link Jay's existing videos into a cohesive story based around the more cinematic and narrative-based of Jay's raps thus far.

one 48-hour period, Jay-Z and his crack team of producers pieced together a record that would become Jay's first unified, complete piece of work, a record that sat alongside the best classic soul and Motown rather than smothering it in rhyme, technique and gangsta rhetoric. It was a blueprint not just for the dramatic, gritty soul sound of future Roc-A-Fella records but for the next decade of hip-hop. Sped-up soul samples mingled seamlessly with pop hooks, studio cuts and glitch beats gleaned from cutting edge electronica and trip-hop, and the result was an album that took hip-hop's focus back to sampling, a 'lost' practice that had made *Reasonable Doubt* so cohesive and celebrated. But *The Blueprint*'s innovation was to combine it with the modernist edge, populist nous and technological trickery.

And Kanye was very nearly not a part of it at all. Jay-Z had originally wanted Tone from Trackmasters to oversee the production of the entire album, impressed by the way he worked beats in the same way rappers worked their rhymes. Tone was an unreliable studio presence though, and missed out on the glory of being *The Blueprint*'s mastermind – "He was supposed to oversee *The Blueprint*," Jay would say, "he missed the whole opportunity. I would kill myself."

Instead, Jay took on four producers he'd been bringing through the Roc-A-Fella stable to work on the record – Bink, Timbaland, Just Blaze and Kanye West. The success of the album was built on an intense work ethic – again, Kanye would work late into the night during the sessions – and a hardcore competitive atmosphere, each producer vying to outdo their peers and get the most beats on the album. "I had two rooms in Baseline," Jay-Z remembers. "It was a big room… that I'd record in. Then it would be a small room that Just would be in doing beats. What happened was, Just would peep his head in and hear what me and Kanye was doing and would just go back mad… It was like a heavyweight slugfest. For three days they was just knocking each other out." One early breakthrough was 'U Don't Know', a pivotal song for both the album and hip-hop. Its seminal opening is now as instantly recognisable thanks to its combination of strident strings and vocal sample of Bobby Byrd's 'I'm Not To Blame', both sped up to a reedy, silvery gleam. "I remember [just] playing that joint," said Jay, "and I was like 'Oh my God'."

Kanye's work would make just as much of a splash, however. The first single to be released from the album was 'Izzo (H.O.V.A.)', Hova being a shortening of the Jayhova nickname Jay had concocted for himself, a bright pop banger that Kanye had pieced together around a looping sample from major Motown classic 'I Want You Back' by the Jackson 5. It backed one of Jay-Z's most intricate descriptions of his development from hustler to hip-hop star yet, telling how he moved from cocaine syndicate boss in Brooklyn to using the same tactics to conquer the rap world.

'Izzo…' became Kanye's first major hit song, reaching number eight on the *Billboard* Hot 100 chart. A huge confidence boost for the young hot-shot, he even got a cameo in the video, applauding Jay-Z's Presidential parade alongside Nelly, Eve, OutKast and Destiny's Child. Back west, Chicago lit up. "One day, I'm watching BET and I saw Jay Z's 'Izzo' video," Coodie recalled, "and I was like, 'Wait a minute – that's Kanye's track!' That was one of the first tracks I heard when I met him in like 1997. That's when I was like, 'Oh I got to get to New York'." Sure enough, Coodie moved to NYC and began tracking Kanye's attempts to get a record deal on camera. Often he'd walk into meetings with Coodie filming him, to be met with looks of 'Who is this guy?' from the label executives.

And 'Izzo…' was just the start of Kanye's *Blueprint* adventure.

The other Kanye track that was already well known by the time *The Blueprint* quietly hit the shelves on the fateful date of September 11, 2001 was 'Takeover', a fuzzed-up, bulbous and bluesy track built around a sample from the Doors' 'Five To One' that was already gaining a notoriety Kanye could never have intended. Premiering it at that year's Hot 97 Summer Jam showcase gig at the Nassau Coliseum, it was Jay's first all-out dive into the tradition of the diss song, and one which would instigate one of the most legendary beefs in modern rap, Jay vs Nas. It was a confrontational opening volley – it was Roc-A-Fella was "running this rap shit" on the East Coast, Jay proclaimed, while targeting Nas with the line "Ask Nas, he don't want it with Hov, no". But his primary target was Prodigy from Queens duo Mobb Deep: "I don't care if you Mobb Deep, I hold triggers to crews/You little fuck,

I got money stacks bigger than you/When I was pushing weight back in eighty-eight/You was a ballerina, I got your pictures, I seen ya". As supposed evidence for his claim, several pictures of Prodigy as a child dancer were splashed up on the arena's JumboTron screen, dressed as Michael Jackson. Laughter rang loud and long around the auditorium.

The reasons behind this slight, and the monumental beef that developed from it, are convoluted. Jay's beef with Prodigy was rooted in Prodigy taking offence at lines which he felt were aimed at himself and Nas in the lyrics of various Jay-Z tracks going as far back as 1999, and those of his Roc-A-Fella proteges. "Your lifestyle's written" went a line in Memphis Bleek's 'My Mind Right', which Prodigy convinced himself was a dig at Nas' second album, *It Was Written*. Nas and Jay had also had disagreements over the use of Nas samples in Jay-Z's songs and Nas failing to show for recording sessions Jay had arranged with him, but Prodigy and others only helped to stir up the argument.

Nas had already taken a potshot at Jay-Z on his 1999 third album, *I Am...*, when a verse from his 'We Will Survive', directed at the deceased Biggie Smalls, went, "It used to be fun, making records to see your response/But now competition is none, now that you're gone/ And these niggas is wrong using your name in vain/And they claim to be New York's king?". But Nas saw no slight worth reacting to in the bleek line and didn't want to get into a Biggie vs Tupac situation. However, Prodigy wouldn't let the beef go. He also felt that Jay-Z's shift in image from the baller lifestyle of luxury boats and villas full of models in his videos to wearing basketball jerseys in the 'Where I'm From' clip was a pointed mocking of himself and Nas, and felt that the line, "I'm from a place where you and your man's hung in every verse in ya rhyme" was an attack on the pair. Prodigy also heard disrespect to his name in the line "It's like New York's been soft/Ever since Snoop came through and crushed the buildings/I'm trying to restore the feelings" in Jay's 1998 track 'Money, Cash, Hoes', considering he'd had a beef with Snoop Dogg and Death Row.

"I was like 'Nas, what we need to do is go at these niggas'," he told Planet Ill website, "'because number one, his lil' man is trying to shit on you; talking about your life is written and all this shit... I was like these

71

niggas is going at us subliminally and I was like fuck that, we need to go at those nigga. Let's make a song about them, son. And he was like 'Nah nah that nigga ain't nobody to be doing that son...' I'm like aight cool. 'Cause in my mind, I'mma address it on my own anyway. I don't give a fuck what this nigga do. I love you Nas but I'mma handle this 'cause you buggin'."

So, on two tracks of Mobb Deep's *Infamy* album that winter, Prodigy would call Jay-Z "a female-ass nigga, the homo rapper, H to the you-know" in 'Crawlin'', adding, "Your retaliation was weak, baby pictures". Nas would be far swifter to respond, though. A week or two after the Summer Jam show, Nas guested on a radio show freestyling over the beat to Eric B And Rakim's 'Paid In Full'⋆. The freestyle would later be called 'Stillmatic, Stillmatic Freestyle' or 'H To The Omo', and in it Nas attacked Jay-Z viciously, claiming he was a hustling fraud rapping "Fake coke rhymes/And those times, they never took place, you liar/'Un' was your first court case, you had no priors [referring to Jay's arrest for allegedly stabbing producer Lance 'Un' Rivera at a music industry party in December 1999]/You master fabricated stories of streets". Next, Nas took aim at Jay's clothing line Rocawear ("your wack clothes line"), the Roc-A-Fella crew ("Rip the Freeway, shoot through Memphis... remove the fake king of New York") and mocked the lyrics of 'Izzo (H.O.V.A.)' – "For shizzle you phony, the rapping version of Sisqó/And that's for certain, you clone me".

Once Nas' freestyle broke, Jay-Z went straight back to Kanye's track 'Takeover' to exact his immediate revenge, adding a third verse that went direct for Nas' jugular. His career was over, Jay claimed, his hits had dried up and any respect, hype or talent he'd had in his early days had long since died. Jay claimed that Nas was only making one good album every 10 years and could be outrapped by his security guy. He retaliated on Nas' accusations of fakery in kind – Nas was, he rapped, "the fag model from Karl Kani/Esco ads" and "fake thug" who'd never seen a Tec-9 gun before Jay-Z had shown him one. "You know who

⋆ The use of this track itself might have been a sly comment on Jay-Z allegedly not having gained permission to use Nas samples on his records.

did you know what with you know who" he spat, hinting on some dirt he might one day let out about Nas and warning him not to end up as "the next contestant on that Summer Jam screen". Finally, addressing his use of Nas samples, he threw out one of the greatest hip-hop disses on record. "Yeah I sampled your voice, you was using it wrong/You made it a hot line, I made it a hot song".

Lenny 'S' Santiago, an A&R for Roc-A-Fella was at Jay-Z's session. "Everybody in there was obviously super-biased. Biggest Jay fans and supporters in the world. We were 100 per cent gung-ho, gassing Jay to do it." Young Guru, who was working with Kanye on producing the track, remembers Jay's calmness. "It wasn't this super-angry vibe. I've never seen Jay super-angry, or he doesn't show it, it's always the poker face." Jay himself had few words on the track. "I only could take so much," he said.

Later, Jay-Z would play down the beef as, on his part at least, a publicity stunt to put Nas and Jay on the same level as Tupac and Biggie, the most vitriolic beef in hip-hop, and ultimately they both benefited hugely. The attention helped to reassert Nas, whose profile had been slipping by 2001, as one of hip-hop's pivotal figures. And it allowed Jay-Z to further court the mainstream on the back of his biggest hit yet while maintaining his dangerous street image.

For Kanye, though, the track would ultimately be something of a headache. As a fan of both Jay-Z and Nas and with plans settling in place for him to produce further tracks for both, he felt a little caught in the middle. For the time being though, he was firmly in Team Roc-A-Fella, having a total of five tracks on *The Blueprint*, more than any of the other producers. Besides 'Izzo…', 'Takeover' and 'Heart Of The City (Ain't No Love)', he contributed the proud soul pulse of 'Never Change', created using a sample from 'Common Man' by David Ruffin and with Kanye allowed a brief cameo on the tune's memorable hook, reflecting Jay's days on the streets: "I'm still fucking with crime 'cause crime pays/Out hustling, same clothes for days/I'll never change, I'm too stuck in my ways/I'll never change".

The irony was that Jay-Z had changed dramatically. Here was a song about "still fucking with crime, 'cause crime pays" by a man purporting to have left his criminal ways far behind him. But the lyric was about something more fundamental; an exhortation to stay true to yourself and your roots, an admission that the resourceful, determined and street-honourable hustler of his youth would never truly leave him.

Again, Kanye would find his track unwittingly embroiled in controversy. The song included references to a time in his hustling days that Jay had lost his entire hoard of drugs while trying to visit Trenton High School to see a friend and was searched by the school security for trespassing – he then hit the streets for three days solid with no sleep to make up the debt he owed from the loss to his supplier. The story was too much for Def Jam's A&R chief Tyran 'Ty Ty' Smith, who argued vehemently that the line should be cut for legal reasons. Ultimately, the line stayed.

Kanye's final beat on the record was the hidden track 'Girls, Girls, Girls (Part 2)', a reworking of Blaze's earlier track 'Girls, Girls, Girls', this time over samples from the Persuaders' bubbly pop sparkler 'Trying Girls Out' and featuring uncredited vocals from Michael Jackson. Like a cheeky final wink to the album, Jay-Z leafed through his little black book to bombard us with sexual double-entendres concerning a student girl he was giving "in-house tutoring" while "moving through her student body union" and a suspicious wannabe actress wary of his busy schedule, before finally detailing what he was after in his perfect woman. Any size, height or skin tone would do so long as she had a sizable behind, was fun but faithful, an extravagant dresser, an accomplished cook and was as comfortable cooking cocaine into crack as negotiating discounts on first class airline seats. Quite a lady.

Once the album was finished, and before it hit the shelves, Kanye, Jay and the rest of the team actually watched the hysteria building. Right there, in their own studio, in front of their faces. Friends and colleagues would drop by to hear the finished album, leave dumbstruck and then turn up again a day or so later with five friends, insisting they hear it too. Eventually they could barely move in there for whooping, excited hangers-on.

"The listening sessions was getting bigger and bigger between us," Jay recalls. "People was coming back with their friends and shit, like,

'Yo, you gotta hear this shit'. And it was so much energy in the studio that I was like, 'Oh, this is special. This gon' be really serious'."

When the promo CDs hit the desks of the press, the wildfire turned to conflagration. The effortless combination of mainstream appeal and urban edge hit a critical nerve. Reviews were almost universally gushing – garnering an esteemed five mike review in *The Source*, a perfect XXL from *XXL* and a maximum five discs and Album Of The Year in *Vibe*, *The Blueprint*'s critical plaudits would eventually stretch to high placings in Albums Of The Decade lists in *Rolling Stone*, *Billboard*, *Paste*, *Rhapsody* and *Entertainment Weekly*. Kanye and Blaze were hailed as production geniuses. Retrospectives over the years would declare it Jay-Z's best work since *Reasonable Doubt* and a benchmark in modern hip-hop, spawning a generation of soul-centric sampling imitators. Despite America's shock at the 9/11 attacks, 427,000 sales in week one sent it hurtling to number one, Jay's fourth in as many years and Kanye's first taste of the top spot. By the end of the month, it'd topped one million, eventually reaching double-platinum and selling over two million copies in the US alone since 2001.

★ ★ ★

Kanye's name, in production terms, was suddenly pure gold. Virtually overnight his career was made in the rap world; he was seen as amongst the architects of the next evolution of rap. His phone rang off the hook, labels and artists keen to get a sprinkling of the same magic that had dusted *The Blueprint* onto their own albums. In 2001 he produced on three albums including *The Blueprint*, his other beats appearing on Beanie Sigel's *The Reason*, producing 'Nothing Like It' and 'Gangsta Gangsta', and on *We Paid Let Us In!* by Abstract Mindstate The M.O.D., producing 'Pain'. Over the course of 2002, he would supply beats and, where possible, verses to a total of 10 tracks.

Recognising his vastly increased profile and demand, he concocted a plan. This would be his big break, his chance to get himself noticed as a rapper as well as a producer. "At this time I didn't have a deal," he'd say. "I had songs, and I had relationships with all these A&Rs, and they wanted beats from me, so they'd call me up, I'd play them some beats.

'Gimme a beat that sound like Jay-Z'. You know, they dick riders. Whatever. So I'll play them these post-*Blueprint* beats or whatever and then I'll play my shit. I'll be like, 'Yo but I rap too'. Hey, I guess they was lookin' at me crazy 'cause you know, I ain't have a jersey on or whatever."

By the end of 2001, demoing at his home studio and working in 15-minute bursts in the professional studio from his Louis Vuitton backpack of CDs and demos, Kanye had put together an impressive demo mix-tape of his newest beats that began to do the rounds. He had 15 tracks completed to showcase his rhymes, many of which would be reworked over the coming years, the mix-tape emerging in 2013 as *2001 Demo Tape*. The tape opened with an open ode to his hometown: 'Home (Windy)' started with the sound of thunder and Kanye declaring "I wanna tell you a story, it's like a love story, kinda hurts though". As an opening statement of intent for an entire career that would upturn the clichés of hip-hop lyricism and reinvent the bedrock themes and emotions of the genre, it was a bold and revealing line, and the track continued in a similarly unconventional manner. Over a sample of Patti Labelle And The Bluebells' cover of the Rodgers & Hammerstein classic 'You'll Never Walk Alone', a soulful vocal hook★ chastised the rest of rap for getting stoned and ignoring the world's issues while soldiers were dying in the post-9/11 invasion of Afghanistan launched on October 7 2001: "Go ahead, roll it up and pass it round/Cause lately's been a whole lot of bullshit going down/A lot of soldiers aint make it through this year/So let's just celebrate that we're still here". Of course, the soldiers referenced may also have been street soldiers, or the unknowing front-line of the war on terror that died in the World Trade Center.

Over a truly gorgeous soul shuffle, Kanye then skilfully span a love story to Chicago built on the same structure as Common's 'I Used To Love H.E.R.', the similarities between the two tracks leading some commentators to believe that Windy, like the girl in Common's lyric,

---

★ On the version of 'Home' that would be dropped off *The College Dropout* following its internet leak, John Legend would sing the hook. It's uncertain who sang on the demo version.

is meant to represent rap music, but as Kanye points out at the end of his tune, "if you don't know by now I'm talking about Chi-Town". Imagining the city as a girl called Windy that he met "when I was three years old/And what I loved most she had so much soul", he rapped of how the city reared him and he adored the brightness of her downtown nightlife – complete with cheeky double entendre on 'downtown' – and then of how, one winter, the city went cold on him. "She never messed with entertainers 'cause they always leave," he rhymed, referencing the tendency for signed artists to drift away towards LA and New York, and now he'd absconded himself he felt his crew was blaming him for leaving them behind. "She said, 'You left ya kids and they just like you/They wanna rap and make soul beats just like you/But they just not you," he rapped, and though he admitted "I guess that's why I'm here and I can't come back home", he had a message of hope for his friends back in Illinois: "In the interviews I'm representing you, making you proud/Shoot for the stars so if you fall you land on the clouds". Kanye's fondness for Chicago was also evident in sessions for the demo tape at Sony Music Studios and Light At The End Of The Tunnel studio in New York. Jensen Kerp of the Hypemen even remembers Kanye having to leave the studio early one day to catch the last train back to visit his mother.

The second track on the demo, half-written with Rhymefest a full two years before it would make him a superstar, was 'Jesus Walks'. Though at this point it was only two hooks and one central verse, its impact was as forceful in 2001 as it would be when it later marched into the heads and hearts of the world. Taking a clipped choir chant of the title and a Roman oarsman bass choral backing from 1997's 'Walk With Me' by the ARC Choir (ARC stood for Addicts Rehabilitation Center), Kanye added a portentous military style beat he constructed from the drums of Curtis Mayfield's '(Don't Worry) If There's A Hell Below, We're All Going To Go', a sample given to him for the song by 88-Keys. "We had a real deep conversation on the drums that he heard on there, that he imagined using, and I told him I had that record," Keys said. "To date, he's the only person who chopped that. Everyone who has used that record has looped it."

Kanye used this menacing track to tackle some serious issues, both social and spiritual. "I need to recoup all the soldiers," he said over a drill sergeant's orders bawled out in the background, "All of God's soldiers. We at war with society, with racism, terrorism, and most of all we're at war with ourselves". His lyric attacked the idea that Western society was full of crime and violence when there were much more important enemies to fight, and that our actions were dragging us further from God. Painting himself as a dealer with "a trunk full of coke" and police harassing him, he was a hustler with a conscience and a fear of damnation for his actions – "Well Mama I know I act a fool, but I'll be gone til November, I got packs to move… God show me the way because the Devil's trying to break me down… I wanna talk to God but I'm afraid 'cause we ain't spoke in so long". The second verse would take the idea much further, but wouldn't come to fruition for some time to come.

Next up was 'Have It Your Way', a track still in its early stages of development. Some years later it would become 'Bring Me Down', but in 2001 the demo version was a rough-hewn and brooding gangsta cut, yet to feature the female hook or orchestration or its eventual lyrics. Instead Kanye rasped menacingly over the graceful piano refrain about Biggie, Tupac and his own imagined *Matrix*-level gangland gunplay, all swinging gats and flying bullets and singing a crackly, amateurish chorus hook that went "Don't want nobody to die, don't want to have to die but in this game I guess that's just the way".

'Have It Your Way' was followed by a couple of tracks that would remain unreleased. First was a tongue-in-cheek playa tune made from erratic, sparse funk grooves called 'Out Of Your Mind' in which Kanye claimed to be the kind of shameless ladies man who hides condoms around the house from his girlfriend, travels the world with a girl in every beach and ski resort and cares more about his coupé than his girl. His most comedic antic was to try to sleep with a cashier at a local grocery store because he knew his girlfriend never shopped there, but the life he claimed was just as much of a hip-hop parody. "Why don't you talk to the mouth of the horses 'bout my Porsches," rapped the guy who was seeing money flow in from his success on *The Blueprint* but was still renting a cheap flat out in New Jersey, "Condos in front of the golf courses…"

The next unreleased track was 'Wow!', a crackling, lo-fi calypso beat that would ultimately change his life. Again he was indulging in hip-hop's boastful slant but with a little more reasoning to back it up. "H To The Izzo did three thou spins in a week," he raps at some unnamed rival, "you get a thou in a month, wow… I go to Jacob [the jewellery store of choice for the high-end New York rappers] with 25 thou, you go with 25 hundred, wow, I got 11 plaques on my wall right now/You got your first gold single, damn, nigga, wow". Still, for all his proclaimed new-found riches and sardonic, deep-pitched "wow"s, Kanye was getting ahead of himself, particularly in three lines that would be used again later in Jay-Z's 'The Bounce': "Magazines call me a rock star, bitches call me a cock star, *Billboard* pop star, neighbourhood block star, Chi-Town go-getting pimps, we mob-stars, Gingerbread Man even says 'You're a monster'." This was an actual quote from the Gingerbread Man in *Shrek*, and a sentiment that would rear its head again in Kanye's work some years down the line.

The track faded out amid more aggressive gangsterisms – "see you paralysed from the top of the spine" – and gave way to the original 'Gangsta" version of 'Need To Know', a track that would later be reworked, retitled 'I Need To Know' and in 2005 included on the *Freshman Adjustment* mix-tape. Swathed in hazy seventies soul samples, whistles and honey piano plinks, in its ballsy hook Kanye laid out his message to any girls that wanted to meet him in clubs and after shows – "I need to know, you down to do whatever? Down to get it poppin'? Down to get topless?" Setting out his three "different levels" of relationships as talking at the club, having sex and then "kicking them out", he also discussed his fussiness over the sort of girl he'd get with – "never eat 'em unless that fuckin' cat looks fresh" – but then changed his tune out of sexual desperation and the "pissy-pissy" effects of cognac. "I'm lyin', I got a nine in my pants and I'm just dying for a chance, who ready to fuck?… What's scary to me, Henny make hoes look like Halle Berry to me".

Subsequent verses were exclusive to this version, talking about his radio-demolishing flow, how "they told you that I been broke but

I'm balling now" and telling his potential conquest what's expected of her – "You ain't heard the info? You don't know what you're in for?" The final verse flipped the power dynamic though, the girl now expecting expensive phones and accoutrements from Kanye, trips to the MOBO awards, high-end fashions and the most expensive drinks. Suddenly Kanye's sexual expectations made him look like the shallow and desperate loser in this scenario.

There followed a snippet of a track called 'Gotta Pose', an itchy basement wobble of Carribbean rum shack groove over which Kanye spurted more boastful wordplay about his "iceberg flows" that landed him "in the hospital dissin, flow is very sick". Mentioning his time in braces – only this time they were platinum – and his impeccable taste in shoes, the track slipped by in a blink, a glimmer of the inspired word skills Kanye was starting to work up. Taste in shoes would soon become very important to Kanye – he'd often mock rapper Really Doe during shopping trips for his cheap sneakers.

'Never Letting Go (The Stalker Song)' opened with Kanye having a wry conversation with a pitched-up sample from Pheobe Snow's 'Never Letting Go', acting as though the 1977 tune was a clingy woman he was trying to be rid of: "I thought I'd drop by, so nice to see you" Snow sang and Kanye dismissively replied, "Yeah, you can leave now". The track took up the theme, as Kanye unfolded a story of having sex with a girl called Tanisha who then started calling him in the night, boasting to her friends that she had Kanye (and his bank account) wrapped around her finger and trying to tell his actual girlfriend that something was going on. Soon she's calling him up and disguising her voice, getting her friends on the line and turning up wherever he went; at the grocery store, at shows and even in his own apartment – "pop up in my kitchen like 'oh, you wash dishes here?'/Pop up in my bathroom, 'oh, you take pisses here?'". "Restraining orders aint stopping her," Kanye complained after she'd scratched up his Cadillac Escalade with his stolen keys and smashed in the windows once he'd told her it was over and she wasn't even his main girl, "across the street now with some fucking binoculars/Screaming at the top of her lungs, 'I ain't never letting go!'". Things reached a head when she got her uncles to attack him and started telling the police he was assaulting her until he got arrested, leading Kanye to grab his gun for the ultimate retribution. Yet one of the most telling lines was the sign that, even this early, Kanye could feel his ego spiralling out of control. "I'm like a swole nigga," he rapped, likening himself to a wannabe strongman pressing above his weight, "thought that he could lift the van".

The next track was another beat that would become a defining and meaningful moment in Kanye's life and career. "I want everybody to put their hands together for me, I wanna talk about somebody real special tonight," he muttered as the cool "la-la-la"s of 'Hey Mama', lifted from Donal Leace's 'Today Won't Come Again', tripped melodically along beneath. And so began Kanye's heartfelt tribute to his mother, both thankful and apologetic. "I know I act a fool but I promise you I'm going back to school" went the gospel style hook, a classic Pentecostal choir harmonising and clapping in the background, and Kanye launched into a celebration of "a friend of mine" as much as a mother. Calling her "this little light of mine" in reference to the song 'This Little Light Of Mine' which was often sung at the sort of fifties protests that Donda attended with her father, he looked back at their time together in Chicago, from arriving in late December and being warmed by his mother's chicken soup to Donda's struggles to pay the bills and provide him with anything he needed, be it Michael Jackson costumes or training wheels for his bike, no doubt a metaphorical reference to Donda guiding him straight and preventing him from falling as a person. He told of her romantic endeavours, "You never put a man over me and I love you for that mommy, can't you see?", and of the fallout, remembering being seven years old and finding his mother in the kitchen in tears over a cheating boyfriend – "As we knelt on the kitchen floor/I said 'mommy, I'mma love you til it don't hurt no more'."

The track continued by promising Kanye would buy his "angel", a woman he called his "book of poetry", a mansion, high-class cars and meals in the world's best restaurants when he got famous and expressing his gratitude for her advice to stay in school and get a doctorate but also her support when "I did the opposite". Undoubtedly one of the soppiest but most deeply emotional rap songs written to that point, it's no wonder the Roc-A-Fella crew wouldn't feel that it fit amongst their ultraviolent raps of drugs, gangs and guns.

"Got me talking 'bout love," Kanye rapped in the opening verse of the next track 'Know The Game', as if catching himself getting emotional, "you mean me falling in love? Talking never". Over a sample of a piano rendition of 'The Godfather Love Theme' and after a hook that followed the same melody, he set about desensitising himself again, laying out a winding tale about meeting a girl outside a hospital who claimed that she no longer had a man, only for Kanye to be accosted by the guy and his friends when later leaving her house. The girl is possibly pregnant since Kanye seems shocked she's just bought cigarettes but is pleased that "her belly holdin on" during their first meeting. True story or not, it was a classic player's lament strung out over tense and tremulous strings, taut with mafia menace.

Kanye's golden ear for an affecting hook-line shone through 'Family Business', then little more than a gorgeous, heart-lifting piano refrain evocative of a New York sunrise (no sample credit is provided for this piano piece on this or the eventual version of the track which appeared on *The College Dropout*, suggesting it may have been original), one and a half verses, a rough idea of the choir segment and some sampled spoken-word wisdoms from the Dells' 'Fonky Thang': "All that glitters is not gold". The verse was a stern but touching portrayal of the West family on one of their holiday reunions, Kanye tipping his hat respectfully to "the family that can't be with us… super hard at Thanksgiving and Christmas" before going on to defend a cousin who was in prison★ and so couldn't attend family gatherings. Instead, Kanye would take him a plate of food to prison, "soul food, know how Granny do it", which the guards would search, before reminiscing about happier childhood days

---

★ It's uncertain how many of the stories on the demo tape were true, and it's unknown if Kanye did have a cousin in prison at this point. The later completed version of the song included stories from Tarrey Torae's life, and she did indeed had a godbrother called Stevie in jail, but it's not known if Torae had contributed anything to this earlier version.

and pledging his belief in his cousin's innocence. "Tell me you ain't did it then you ain't did it/And if you did, then that's family business".

Naturally the song, even at this formative stage, reflected the family's pride in Kanye's success. "Abi," he rapped to another family member, "remember when they ain't believe in me? Now she like 'that's my cousin on TV'." For now that's where the lyrics would end, the track meandering to a close around its elegant piano lilt and the warm sentiment that, compared to his family, "all the diamond rings don't mean a thing".

The last of the demo tape's recognisable tracks was 'Dreams Come True', albeit in a very rough form. This was a sunny Motown sort of song, its classic seventies strings and upbeat soul vibe typical of Kanye's predilections at the time, that would go through many changes before it would eventually become 'All Falls Down' on his debut album, the strings stripped away and the hook completely changed. Many of the lyrics would remain though, albeit re-arranged. Here, Kanye opened with his declarations of an addiction to expensive fashion brands he can barely even pronounce – "pass that Ver-say-cee" he jokes – but suggested the money with which he got "iced out, medallion heavy on the wrist" came from hustling: "Cut that coke til it's so impure".

The story of a shopaholic college girl growing tired of her course – many have pointed out the autobiographical nature of this verse – and dropping out to become a hairdresser to try to pay for her daughter Alexis' Air Jordans (the pun on the woman calling her daughter Alexis because "she couldn't afford a Lexus" has been taken by some, including Donda herself, to refer to Kanye's future fiancée Alexis Phifer. This is unlikely as Kanye and Alexis didn't start dating until 2002) was then verse two, with the final verse given over to a consideration of materialism, explaining how the higher echelons of society profit the most from it and explaining the desperation some kids feel to succumb to it out of peer pressure, even resorting to violence to get the clothes that will help them impress their friends. "Niggas got killed over Starter coats," he rhymed, "but I can feel why the shorties be mad as shit, without the Jordans he feelin' inadequate". It's an intriguing line from a man who was admitting to his own consumerist failings just moments before, and who'd soon become a poster boy for Louis Vuitton, but at least he was aware of his own materialist contradictions from the start.

The demo, as released many years later, would also include two freestyles produced with DJ Boom around this time, and were very revealing of Kanye's mindset post-*Blueprint*. The first, titled 'Jigga That Nigga', had Kanye rapping over the beat from the *Blueprint* track of the same name. His rap seethed with undisguised bitterness at not being allowed to make his own rap records, from the opening snarl of "let a nigga hear something finally" to a closing rant against closed-minded labels. "I just did beats to have some shit to rap on nigga," he argued, "why the fuck if a nigga got hot beats he can't have hot rhymes?... Why niggas just can't do a lot of shit good?... Fuckin' A&Rs, c'mon". The rhymes between were concerned with his sex appeal, his producing success and his recent riches – "I made 500 Gs in this", he claimed – but also bolstered the image he was trying to present of a gun-toting, homophobic tough guy: "I pull more steel than Sopranos... think I won't use the gat? Until paramedics gotta use the bag/'Cause in my eyes you'se the fag". His flow was impressive, but his themes at this point weren't helping him stand out.

The second freestyle, subtitled 'I Met Oprah' and recorded far closer to the release of his debut album, found Kanye weary at playing second fiddle. "This my last motherfuckin' freestyle," he said over the slick orchestral introduction, "I'm tired man, I'm sick and tired". He was tired of several things; of being hassled to provide beats for people as a favour – "Since 'Takeover'... I got the whole city on my back... this year alone I got two dozen new cousins" – of older rappers getting in the way of upcoming young talent, other inferior producers stealing his style and, again, of not being taken seriously as a rapper. His vaulting ambition was undimmed; he closed the freestyle with a spoken-word story about running into Oprah Winfrey at a stop light in town, the chat show superstar rolling down her window to ask him how to drive her G5 vehicle. Naturally he took the opportunity to try to blag his way onto her show, claiming "I'm Kanye West, a rapper."

These freestyles accurately capture the frustrations that dogged Kanye throughout 2002. Roberson and Hip Hop, alongside D-Dot, were getting him plenty of production work. He became a hand across the beef divide between Roc-A-Fella and Nas when he sampled Eddie Kendricks' 'The Newness Is Gone' for Nas' 'Poppa Was A Playa', produced tracks on Cam'ron's *Come Home With Me* and provided beats for Scarface's *The Fix*, Trina's *Diamond Princess* and State Property's self-titled debut, among others. He also cemented his connection to Jay-Z and his recent hip-hop revolution by producing three tracks on *The Blueprint 2*: 'The Gift And The Curse', including Jay's collaboration with his future wife, Beyoncé, on ''03 Bonnie And Clyde', and worked on Talib Kweli's album *Quality*, an experience that would both be a great learning experience and help him forge a relationship that he'd honour as one of the most important in his rap career, Kanye being immensely thankful that Kweli would eventually take him out on tour.

But the mixing desk started feeling like a barrier, a dead weight keeping him tied down. He'd tell his managers, "I'm not just a producer", and push for them to broaden his activities. "When I first brought him on as a producer," said Hip Hop, "I was shopping beats and they weren't getting sold. [Kanye] was like, 'I want my beats to get placed.' They started getting placed and then it was, 'I don't want to shop beats no more; I want to go to the studio and make the beats.' When we could go into the studio and work hands on with somebody, the next problem was, 'I don't want to make beats for him because he's wack and I'm better than him.' Eventually it was, 'I don't want to sell beats no more; I just want to work on my album'." On almost every production job Roberson and Hip Hop sent him on, the act he was working with would phone them up to ask "why won't he just stick to beats? Why he want to rap?" People were actually mad when he would be rapping in their session," Roberson said. "Now it's like, 'Yeah, I bet you wish you had him rapping for you now.'"

Kanye and his managers had meetings with many labels, the A&R department excited by the idea of backing him but their bosses always refusing to let them. "I played them 'Jesus Walks' and they didn't sign me," Kanye said. "You know what happened, it was some A&Rs that fucked with me though, but then like the heads, it'd be somebody at the company that'll say 'naw'." The most the labels would offer would be to buy 'Jesus Walks' from him, but he insisted on keeping it for himself. He'd even visit the offices of hip-hop magazines and rap for the editors, desperate for his big break. The brick walls reared up at every turn. "Man, people told me that I couldn't rap, that I couldn't sell a record, that I didn't have a chance," Kanye said. "And it hurt me. Nobody believed in me."

"Labels wouldn't place their bets on him," said 88-Keys. "He went through the gamut of all labels, one right after another. It was one thing to turn him down, but then [they'd] ask for the beat he just rapped on. It was a slap in the face. He'd perform 'Jesus Walks', 'All Falls Down', 'Two Words' (before Freeway and Mos was on it) and they would be like, 'The music is real good. Maybe we can use that beat for DMX… Who do we contact about that?' He was like, 'This is my album that I'm playing you. I'm a rapper. Didn't you just hear my raps?'"

Talib Kweli recalls Kanye being keen to sign with the label he was on, Rawkus Records, but the bosses not seeing the potential in the different approaches he was taking to rap. "When we'd go to offices, he'd rap and jump on the desks," Coodie said. "He had something to prove because at that time, 'producer/rapper' wasn't working."

"I was mad because I was not being taken seriously as a rapper for a long time," Kanye said. "Whether it was because I didn't have a larger-than-life persona or I was a perceived as the guy who made beats, I was disrespected as a rapper. I was making good beats before I made good raps, but I've been rapping for longer. It's hard to rap, man. You can't accidentally rap well, but you can accidentally make a good beat."

Roberson couldn't believe Kanye was being turned down so much, since he was surely a dead cert from his Roc-A-Fella connection alone – they could be signing him themselves but there they were, offering other labels the chance to get in on the action. "The lane that was wide open was being that guy in a Benz with a backpack," Roberson said. "Timing is everything, and I saw Kanye West filling that lane."

But Kanye was so sure of his eventual success that he began pulling in big names to work on the album he knew he'd one day be allowed to make. Through 88-Keys he met Consequence, whom he'd been a huge fan of for his work on A Tribe Called Quest's *Beats, Rhymes And*

Life. Consequnce had slipped off the hip-hop scene since that record and was disenchanted with rap, but Kanye was thrilled to have him over to his Newark apartment and desperate to get him on board. He told Consequence they could make a classic together, that he was going to be the next Michael Jackson and promised to let him rhyme on the beats he was putting together with big names like Jay-Z, Beanie Sigel and other Roc-A-Fella acts. "I was like, 'Man, I just met this motherfucker and he already had eighteen months of my life planned out," Consequence said. Impressed, he started writing with Kanye that very day, producing 'Getting Out The Game' early on. The two became close collaborators; Consequence would stay for entire weekends at Kanye's place, writing, partying with girls, cooking, making grape juice Kool-Aid or driving around town. They studied G-Unit, they studied the exploding Philadelphia scene, they studied Young Gunz and Grafh, looking for ways to change rap, looking for their entry point. They worked as hard as they played.

"He demoed a lot of [his debut album] in his crib," Consequence said. "It was cool because he would get up sometimes at like three in the morning and spit a verse or re-spit a verse. I remember when he first made 'School Spirit'. We was all running the house [singing], 'Can you *feeeeeel* it!'."

When GLC was in New York, he was amazed at the speed with which Kanye worked. "He would come to the studio and have all his discs," he said. "I don't know how many, but it would be a big Louis Vuitton book bag filled with discs. He would load in a disc, listen to it and be like 'nah' or he'd be like 'I might fuck with this.' He goes into a zone. He can go and cook up a beat in like 15 minutes. Sometimes he goes to a record store and buys a CD that looks cool and old and he's somewhat familiar with, then he'll chop that shit up. It's amazing."

Other rappers noted Kanye's inexperience in the studio in those early days in New York, perhaps due to his introverted way of working. Olskool Ice-Gre recalls hiring Kanye to produce a track called 'Pain' on the debut album of his Chicago-based band that Go Getters used to open up for at club shows, Abstract Mindstate, and then went on to work with him on tracks for Kanye's own material. "He didn't know his way around the studio," Ice-Gre said, "he didn't know how to communicate to people what was in his head. He didn't know how to verbalise what he wanted them to do. I stepped in and gave the technical terms because I lived in the studio growing up. The song he recorded that night that happened was 'Two Words'. He was working with the Hezekiah Walker Choir that night, but he ended up using the Boys Choir of Harlem. I got him through that session. He was like, 'I like how you move in the studio. I'll pay you to stay with me and help me out while I do all this stuff… I know you're a star yourself but I'm about to be the biggest star in hip-hop and I need your help.' The ego MC in me was like, 'Are you serious? You want me to be your personal assistant? And I'm a bigger artist than you in my city?' This was in my head. But then I thought about it, and… I said I would be his personal assistant but only if I ran his production company, Konman Productions. 'Deal.' We shook on it."

The closest Kanye came to a deal was through an A&R called Joe '3H' Weinberger up at Capitol. 3H first met Kanye at Right Track Studios in Manhattan when 3H, a young A&R for Interscope, was buying one of his beats for one of his acts. Having been kicked out of the studio while DJ Clue was working in there, Kanye played 3H 'Hey Mama' and 'I Want To Know' in the waiting room and 3H "lost my shit". "Kanye was never down on himself," 3H said. "He'd be ready to rap on the spot, ready to tell his story on the spot, ready to make a record on the spot. He was probably the hungriest dude I ever saw. Whatever it takes. He wasn't all caked up yet, but he still had his Kanye swagger. It was definite star quality the day I saw him. He played me three songs and I was like, 'What!?' His flow was different, his beats were great, he was performing the whole time. The energy was there, it was some real star-quality stuff."

"I saw in him what he saw, but not many others did, so we became fast friends. I said, 'I want to bring you to Capitol, if you don't mind?' He was like, 'Let's do it.' We had a similar goal."

Joe called relentlessly, really enthusiastic about working with Kanye, claiming "we gonna change the game, buddy". Kanye began to make his own demands, telling Capitol that he wouldn't be anything less than a priority for them, he refused to be put behind any other act. Roc-A-Fella was pleased that this time it looked good. "Dame was like, 'Yo you got a deal with Capitol, OK man, just make sure it's not wack," Kanye said. To show them what 3H was so excited by, Kanye played Dash the demo of 'Wow!' "I wanted to play some songs, 'cause [Cam'ron] was in the room, Young Guru, and Dame was in the room. So I played... 'Wow'. 'I go to Jacob with 25 thou, you go with 25 hundred, wow, I got eleven plaques on my walls right now. You got your first gold single, damn, nigga, wow'. I play that song for him, and he's like, 'Oh shit, I ain't gonna front, it's kinda hot'. And I'm sure Dame figured, 'Like man. If he do a whole album, if his raps is wack at least we can throw Cam on every song and save the album, you know. So Dame took me into the office, and he's like 'Yo man, we, we on a brick, we on a brick. You gotta be under an umbrella, you'll get rained on'."

Dash was impressed by Kanye's self-belief and work ethic too. Just Blaze would refuse to flip a beat for him, but when he asked Kanye to work up Queen's 'We Are The Champions' for a track called 'Champions', he was quick and professional about it. He could tell Kanye had something to prove, and something special. "It was like his fear made him fearless," he said. "I realised that he was going to make it happen and he didn't mind being an asshole. If you don't mind being an asshole, you're not going to lose. He wasn't scared, he had gall. I needed Kanye to knock on the door because of the way he was dressed. When they opened the door, Roc-A-Fella would be hiding behind him and we'd all run in the house. He was someone that could articulate authentic culture in a way that was safe to white people."

Though Kanye was happy to be courted by Dash, he was a man of his word and the Capitol deal was all but signed. But like so many times before, the Capitol dream dissolved right within Kanye's grasp. The deal was on the table, the papers were all but signed and then, at the last minute, someone in the company told the president of the company making the final decision that Kanye was really just a producer and that the records wouldn't sell. "The day I'm talking about," Kanye would say later, "I planned out everything I was gonna do man, I had picked out clothes, I already started booking studio sessions, I started arranging my album, thinking of marketing schemes man, I was ready to go. And they had Mel call me, they said, 'Yo... Capitol pulled on the deal'."

"I didn't have much authority," 3H explained. "I finally got a meeting with the head of the company. Andrew Slater was running Capitol. This was maybe six months after I met Kanye for the first time. I was like, 'Look, there's two acts that I really think are special. I'd love to sign them both. One is this guy named 50 Cent, who just got dropped from Columbia and this other guy is called Kanye West'. He was like, 'Cool. Set up the meetings.' I told [Kanye], 'Let's fly you out when Jay-Z is doing the 'H To The Izzo' video. I brought my boss down to the video shoot. I figured the more hype I'd create around Kanye the more it'd help me because he was such a different type of artist at the time. We flew him to LA and then flew 50 Cent to LA. The boss said, '50 Cent is too scary. I don't want bodyguards at my house. I'll sign this Kanye guy. Even though I don't get it, even though it doesn't seem interesting to me at all.' I said, 'Thank you. It means a lot.'

"We were ready to go. 'Jesus Walks' was done, 'Slow Jamz' was done, 'Breathe In, Breathe Out' was done, 'All Falls Down' was done but on a different beat, but... I saw this album. Two months later, he fired a lawyer for me and hired a new one just to be really easy to deal with. [But] a new person came in to head the Urban department and this person just cut the deal. I don't know why but it was not only a 'no', it was a 'don't bring it up again.' So I had to call him and say, 'You're going to hate me but there's no place for you over here but I hope we can remain friends.' He was mad, but wasn't mad at me."

Downcast, Kanye told Capitol that Roc-A-Fella had expressed an interest in signing him. "I don't know if they thought that was just something I was saying to gas them up to try to push the price up or whatever," he said, but it made no difference. Capitol had pulled out of the deal and Kanye turned back to his last available option. "The Roc-A-Fella deal was more like a default," Hip Hop said, "we couldn't get no other deals and that's where I was at and that's where, of course, they're going to at least let me do that."

There was a little subterfuge in Kanye's shift onto the Roc-A-Fella roster. He'd told Dash that he'd make a compilation album for all of the acts on Roc, but in reality he planned to use the studio time to start work on his own record. "We all knew he's been recording the album," said GLC. "That was his dream. But Dame didn't know. He fooled Dame and told him that he was doing a compilation album. That's how he got his deal. He was going to produce the beats for all the Roc-A-Fella artists but [instead] he said, 'Fuck that, I'm going to make my own album'." "We all thought he was making a compilation album for Roc-A-Fella," producer Patrick 'Plain Pat' Reynolds agreed, "but when I met with him, he's like, 'Nah, I'm rapping!' It was shocking because nobody (at Def Jam or Roc-A-Fella) knew he was going to rap the whole album."

"He had no history [at the time] and no one listens if you don't have any history," Dash said. "The only reason I was listening, regardless of whatever, was because I was going to put out a record where he was the producer. I could sell 500,000 records for the compilation with everyone on it who was on Roc-A-Fella. That's what I was thinking. When he came in and had beats that had him rapping on it, 'I was like, OK then'… I thought his album was going to be a compilation, but all of a sudden he'd be playing his songs. But, I wasn't really looking for a producer that was rapping so heavy. I was looking for someone who was working hard. We were looking at him as a producer that could rap, 'cause that's what he was doing with us. He was the best producer that can rap, while Jay-Z was, still is, the best rapper of all time.

"It was his consistency that did it for me. It was what made him rap on a table and rap for people. I remember I took him to London 'cause he was doing it like that. I remember when I had him perform at the movie I funded for Lee Daniels [*Shadowboxer*]. I had Kanye come to Sundance. When he was performing, people weren't paying attention and he demanded their attention. This was before anyone knew who Kanye was. I respected that he demanded the attention and respect before he had a record out. That came from a place of no fear. I then knew what he was going to do. I was also trying to evolve away from the gangsta rap. Biggs really recognised, put it on my radar, and said, 'Listen, he's working'."

"By the time Dame heard the compilation album was really his album, he revealed he had offers at record labels like Capitol," said Ice-

Gre. "Dame wanted his first dibs on his beats, so he got him the record deal so he could have first dibs." "It seemed to me, what [Roc-A-Fella] were selling, Kanye didn't fit: street," added Devo. "He wasn't signed 'cause of his raps. He could rap but [Damon Dash] wasn't buying him as an artist. He had Roc-A-Fella and the street thing was prevalent. Dame Dash wasn't trying to hear Kanye. He just wanted the beats."

Nonetheless, Dash signed Kanye West to Roc-A-Fella gladly. "I was definitely feeling a little bit of anxiety 'cause my man Jay-Z is retiring★. People were on me like, 'What you gonna do after this?' I personally signed Kanye, and I wanna take credit for that because I feel good that I believed in him and I saw his vision. What I didn't see was how big his vision was and how he was going to attack it himself. He's like me and Jay put into one. He's a businessman, he's an artist, he's a producer. On a bigger level, he's positive."

Roc gave Kanye a $150,000 advance. He used $100,000 of it to buy his way out of his previous management contract using the lawyer that had negotiated Prince out of his record deal with Warners. The rest went on status symbols to suit his preppy 90210 look of polo shirts, shades and green khaki Louis Vuitton backpacks. He sprung for a Mercedes SUV, a watch from Jacob and a Rolex for his mother's Christmas present. Both he and Dame's joy at working together would be evident on 'Champions', recorded for a compilation album of Roc-A-Fella talent that Dash was putting together. "God damn Kanye! I bet niggas didn't know you could rap, huh?" Dash said on the track, a showcase for label talent including Cam'ron, Sigel, Young Chris and Twista. "That's my motherfucking producer, this the producer on Roc, he rap better than most rappers!" "Had the Chi' on lock when they finally heard I signed with Roc," Kanye responded.

"It finally gave me a platform to put the message that my parents put inside of me," Kanye would say of the deal and his Roc-A-Fella association, "and that Dead Prez helped to get out of me and Mos Def

---

★ Jay-Z would 'retire' for several years following 2003's *The Black Album* in order to take up a position as head of Def Jam. His retirement would prove short-lived; he returned with *Kingdom Come* in 2006.

and [Talib] Kweli, they helped to get out of me: I was able to put it, sloppily rap it, on top of the platform that Jay-Z had created for me."

So began Kanye's life on Roc-A-Fella.

A life that, within only a matter of months, would very nearly be cut tragically short.

CHAPTER FIVE

Through The Wire

The streetlights growing hazy. The warm hum of the engine, the melting shuttered shopfronts, soothing voices on the radio. A slipping away.

A swerve. A monumental crash. The world revolved.

The Lexus came to a stop, flipped onto its roof in a wreck of shattered glass and crushed metal. Kanye, shocked awake, struggled to comprehend where he was. A second ago he'd been driving home, eyes drooping at the wheel, at 4am from a lengthy late night studio session in LA with 3H, Ludacris and DJ Whoo Kid.★ Now he was suddenly suspended upside down by the seatbelt that had just saved his life.★★

His jaw was a hot ball of pain. He checked his reflection in the rear view mirror; his face had begun swelling on the right hand side, the

---

★ 3H believed they might have been working on 'Breathe In Breathe Out' that night, but others claim Ludacris' part for that track was delivered by Fed Ex. While in LA, he'd also been producing for Beanie Sigel, Peedi Crakk, Young Gunz and The Black Eyed Peas.

★★This wasn't the first time Kanye had flipped a car. On a previous occasion he'd walked away virtually unscathed, to the degree that his mother told him "you must have angels with you". He'd commemorate those words by getting a gold angel pendant on a chain.

side where his head had hit the steering wheel when the airbag failed to deploy. His jaw had cracked in three places and his front teeth were grotesquely askew.

Around 4am on October 23, 2002, Kanye's girlfriend, Sumeke, got a call from Kanye from the wreck of his car in Hollywood. "I remember calling my girl, and the first thing I said to her was, 'I'm sorry for hurting myself' 'cause I knew how it would affect [her]," Kanye said. "So she called my mother, and my mother called back and said, 'Ah, baby, are you OK?' I just remember saying, 'It huuurts!' like a little kid. It hurt bad as hell."

As Kanye hung there watching his face swell to twice its usual size, it took just 10 minutes for the emergency services to arrive at the scene. They quickly ascertained the situation. Kanye had fallen asleep at the wheel of the Lexus that Roc-A-Fella had rented for him and drifted into the path of an oncoming car – the driver of the other vehicle sustained broken legs. In fact, Kanye hadn't liked the Lexus and had asked instead for a bigger car in LA, but Def Jam had a policy to only splash out on high-end cars and first class flights for its platinum-selling acts. (He even had similar issues when Def Jam was finding him an apartment while recording in LA – every listing he'd be sent by a guy called Plain Pat in the administration department, he'd complain the place was too small. He'd tell them his Newark apartment had floor-to-ceiling windows and he expected certain standards.)

As was standard procedure, they tested Kanye's blood alcohol levels three times despite his distress and difficulties breathing and his repeated requests to be taken to hospital.

"I was sitting in the car after the accident and they kept asking me questions," he recalled. "I was just telling them 'I want to go to the hospital, I'm in so much pain right now, I'm gagging on blood right now'. I was just trying to breathe. Then they finally put one of them hard-ass neck braces on me and it hurt. Then they put me on the stretcher and it was like on *There's Something About Mary* because they dropped me, and I hit my head and jaw."

Kanye would be convinced that his colour earned him worse treatment, from the constant questioning at the scene of the accident to the emergency crew's failure to tell his mother which hospital they were taking him to, being dropped from the gurney when they finally got him to Cedars-Sanai and the hours he spent waiting for treatment. He'd sustained nasal fractures too, so his nose bled profusely every time he tried to talk. Donda got herself and Sumeke on the first flight to LA and when they reached his hospital room they were shocked at the way his head had swollen so much. They both masked their horror well – "Baby, you're going to be just fine," Donda said, while Sumeke hugged him and told him, "It's not so bad". Kanye kept his humour through the ordeal: "I look like the Klumps," he joked.

His thoughts instantly flew to music too. Roberson remembers getting the call about his accident and flying straight to LA. "I get to the hospital," he said, "the guy's face is the size of a building. I can't even recognise him. He's talking all crazy because his jaw is dislocated. My thoughts are going everywhere. I'm trying to make sure he's going to be able to stay alive. I say, 'You all right? Hang in there.' Do you know the first thing this guy told me? Is this exactly who Kanye West is? He goes, 'Yo Gee, we out of here.' I'm like, 'We out of here? What you talking about?' I'm thinking, is he on some drugs? Painkillers? What's going on? He's like, 'Wait till I tell the world the story about my accident and what happened. I almost died. We out of here – you understand what I'm about to create?' I'm looking at him like, 'Wow. OK, I got one of the ones, no doubt about it.'"

The coming days would be the most painful Kanye had ever experienced. While his entire family waited outside the theatre eating Thai food and praying for him and nurses sucked blood from his mouth constantly, surgeons wired shut his jaw but set the wire incorrectly, so the first wire was removed, the jaw rebroken and set for a second time. He also had four hours under the knife for reconstructive plastic surgery in order to repair the damage to his face and make him look like he was before the accident. The very idea of surgery terrified Kanye; he'd heard stories of patients dying on the operating table and was worried that the operation might affect his breathing for life, let alone his ability to rap. Little did he know the surgery would be the making of him.

Over the two weeks he spent in hospital, Kanye had plenty of time to reassess his life. "He came up with a healthy respect for God," Donda said, "but the accident had a profound impact on him. He particularly knows that by the grace of God he was spared, and spared for a particular purpose. I've never witnessed him as a card-carrying Christian, he's just too hip-hop for that. But I think he has an appreciation for the fact that he could have been dead, and he feels there are angels watching him and protecting him."

In hospital, Kanye underwent an awakening. Realising how limited his time on Earth might be, how it could be cut short at any moment, he came to see that he'd been giving his time to other people's projects, as if brainwashed into working on records he wasn't interested in rather than focussing firmly on his own work. "So simply, the accident gave me the opportunity to do what I really wanted to do," he said. "I was a music producer, and everyone was telling me that I had no business becoming a rapper, so it gave me the opportunity to tell everyone, 'Hey, I need some time to recover'. But during that recovery period, I just spent all my time honing my craft and making *The College Dropout*. Without that period, there would have been so many phone calls and so many people putting pressure on me from every direction – so many people I somehow owed something to – and I would have never had the time to do what I wanted to… I think that people don't make the most of their lives."

"That was the first time in my career when I could tell people, 'I can't go to the studio with you', and people weren't trippin'," he'd add. "Because at that time I was an established producer everybody wanted me to go to the studio to work on they music and they didn't even take it seriously when I said I was going to work on mine. But when I had the accident, my manager had to tell them I couldn't go. They were like, 'OK, he almost died'."

No I.D. remembers the first conversation he had with Kanye after the accident as a turning point in his career. "He was kind of a gangsta rapper," I.D. said. "Most of those early years he was really rapping gangsta raps... His goal was to be tough as possible. Some of it was overcompensation for the fact that he wasn't a street guy at all and he felt like people wouldn't respect him it if it was not tough. The Go-Getters were street, so he tried to keep up with them. I remember when I first talked to him after the accident, and his mouth was all messed up. He was like, 'I figured it out.' I was like, 'What did you figure out?'

He said, 'I'm going to rap about this accident. I'm going to use a song and change the direction. I'm going conscious with my music.' In my mind, actually not even in my mind, I may have said, 'But you're not conscious how are you going to do that?' He's like, 'Nah trust me, this is going to be my direction. I know how I'm going to do it. I got it now. I figured it out'."

Gee Roberson remembers a similar conversation. "I knew I was dealing with a different human being after the accident. I went to visit him at the hospital and the first thing this man tells me is, 'Man, we're out of here. You don't understand. I almost died. Do you know the song I'm about to write?' I was like, 'God, you did it. You blessed me with a whole other human being.' The last thing I'd be thinking about is work. I'd be thinking about my health. Talk about focus and vision. I was in it all the way. From that day forth, it was game on."

Kanye claimed that the accident merely gave him greater access to a deeper part of his art that was already there, though. "I think it opened up that side of me. I already had 'All Falls Down' and 'Jesus Walks' though, all completed with the same lyrics. But I wrote 'Never Let Me Down' after the accident, 'Spaceship', 'School's Spirit'. So I already had that vibe. It's not like I had the accident and became a conscious rapper afterwards. I'm not really a conscious rapper. I'm just a regular person. And regular people have a conscience."

From his hospital bed, Kanye started writing some new lyrics about his accident. "How do you console my mom or give her light support," he wrote, "telling her, 'Your son's on life support'? And just imagine how my girl feel on the plane scared as hell that her guy look like Emmett Till★… I use two lifelines in the same hospital where Biggie Smalls died/The doctor said I had blood clots but I ain't Jamaican man… looked in the mirror, half my jaw was in the back of my mouth, man… thank God I ain't too cool for the safe belt… I must gotta angel 'cause

★ Till was a 14-year-old boy who was murdered in 1955 by having his eye gouged out and being shot in the head. His mother insisted on giving him an open-casket funeral in order to expose the brutality.

look how death missed his ass… look back on my life like the ghost of Christmas Past".

The words gave him a new strength, a fresh determination, and a dizzying perspective on life and the breaks he was getting. "The only thing this accident's saying is, 'I am about to hand you the world, just know at any given time I can take it away from you'," he explained. "To nearly lose your life, to nearly lose your mouth, your voice, your whole face, as a rapper... and I had to be on TV!" But he also saw the benefits in his misfortune. "Death is the best thing that can ever happen to a rapper," he'd say later. "Almost dying isn't bad either."

He rang Consequence three days after his accident and rapped the lines down the phone to him. "I'm thinking to myself, 'What the fuck is wrong with you? Why the fuck are you rapping right now?'" Consequence said. Soon Kanye was asking Dash to get him a drum machine so he could work from his bed; a bemused Dash agreed.

When he was finally released from hospital after two weeks, he begged Roc-A-Fella to let him straight back into the studio – he told them he wanted to work with other artists but really he wanted the studio time to record this new track. But his injuries meant that he couldn't get on a flight to New York, so instead Kanye moved into a two-bedroom suite at the W Hotel, very close to where his accident had occurred. His mother took one of the bedrooms and acted as his nurse, giving him his medicine every four hours, 24 hours a day, and feeding him soups, broths and juices she prepared in a bought-in microwave through his wired jaw, using a straw. Here, desperate to tell his story as soon as possible, he set up a studio, worked up a pitched-up backing from a sample of Chaka Khan's 1985 single 'Through The Fire' and, with the aid of painkillers, recorded his rap while his jaw was still wired shut. As it happened, sampling 'Through The Wire' would become a huge headache for Kanye. As the release of *The College Dropout* approached, it proved difficult to clear the sample for use on the record. Eventually, A&R guy JB Marshall ran into Chaka's son Damien by chance – he was a wannabe rapper too – brought him to one of Coodie's weekly Sunday barbecues and played him the track and its video surrounded by Kanye and everyone that had worked on the record. Angling for a spot rapping on the record, Damien convinced his mother to clear the sample, although Kanye would end up getting no writing credit on the track.

His vocals muffled and restricted by the wires – he would spend several months learning not to slur his words following the accident – Kanye's pain and determination shone through the track, the infectious hook lifting his story to an inspirational level, his good humour and resilience sounding almost heroic. No wonder, when he played it to Roc-A-Fella, it was the track that finally green-lit his work on a solo album.

And 'Through The Wire' wouldn't be the only honourable thing Kanye would do following the crash. Since the driver of the other car had broken his legs and Kanye falling asleep would make him immediately responsible and therefore open to extensive damages in a negligence claim for the months the driver would spend off work, Kanye's insurance broker advised him not to admit he'd fallen asleep at the wheel and instead say he was swerving to avoid another car. For several months he went along with the ruse, then Kanye rang Donda to tell her he'd be telling the truth about the accident, even if it meant he'd be paying every cent of his earnings. "I'm not lying any more," he told her. "I don't care if I have to pay millions and I'm down to my last dime. I'm telling the truth. I'll just make more money. I'll just pay it. That man was lying in the hospital because of me."

With all systems go on his album the W Hotel, where Tupac had once done much of his recording, became a hive of activity. He'd been hoarding his best beats for this moment all his life and had the album largely written already, but with a fresh batch of ideas he'd written in hospital, Kanye now began to master his vision as the fulcrum of a huge cast of producers, rappers, engineers, arrangers and videographers★ assembled between the W – where everyone from the label convened, many with a studio setup in their rooms until Roc-A-Fella controlled

★ Coodie recalled Kanye phoning him up in NYC and rapping down the phone to him while his jaw was wired shut, insisting he come to LA to film him undergoing a life-changing experience.

an entire floor to themselves – and Record Plant Studios. "The only thing he had to do was get up out of bed, go into his living room, and create songs," Roberson recalls. "That's when the whole album went to overdrive. From that point, it was just recording every day."

From 9.30am to 3am every day, Kanye ran a tight ship – time was money and if you were in the studio with him, you were there to work; time-wasters and loiterers were soon made to feel unwelcome. Those working on the album would describe the beat-making process as one of constantly being on high alert. Whenever anyone would come up with a great beat, it was "code red" and everyone would rush to work on it. "I feel like the album was my medicine," Kanye said. "It would take my mind away from the pain – away from the dental appointments, from my teeth killing me, from my mouth being wired shut, from the fact that I looked like I just fought Mike Tyson. The record wouldn't have been as big without the accident." "All I kept thinking about was D.O.C.," he added, referencing the NWA co-writer whose voice was permanently altered when his larynx was crushed in a near-death car accident in 1989, "how he was in a car wreck. I was at the concert in Chicago that he was supposed to go to the night of his car accident… At the point before the accident, my whole goal in life was to eventually be able to do nothing. Now that I see the type of impact I'm gonna make on music and the community, my responsibility is now to do everything for the fans, for the community." Indeed, several of his friends felt Kanye's accident had changed his voice too, but for the better. "The accident wound up being a blessing for him," said Consequence. "Whatever diction issues he had, he came back with a super clear voice."

Kanye moved his entire hometown crew out to LA, including his hairdresser Ibn, and for the coming year, the W Hotel acted as Kanye's HQ. "We had a big suite at the W Hotel that Dame got us," Coodie said. "We were living up in there maybe a year working on the album. I remember it was my birthday on January 18 and we were in the rooms riding on moped scooters. The hotel smelled like gas for a week. We had a ball man." With further sessions taking place in New York, what he emerged with was the culmination of his entire adult life's work; beats that had begun in Chicago or New York full of self-belief and vaulting ambition, fed through a machine of intense creativity and then reworked and remixed with a fanaticism and perfectionism unprecedented in rap music.

It was a record called *The College Dropout*. And it would change the game.

★ ★ ★

"Kanye, can I talk to you for a minute," mumbled someone sounding suspiciously like famed Chicagoan comic Bernie Mac, playing a jive-friendly school teacher. "Me and the other faculty members was wonderin', could you do a lil' something beautiful, somethin' that the kids is gon' love when they hear it? Tha's gon' make them start jumpin' up and down and sharin' candy and stuff?"

It sure sounded like Bernie Mac, guesting on 'Intro', the first track on *The College Dropout*, but it wasn't. Back in Chicago, Coodie was doing stand-up on the side, between his video work, and Bernie was his mentor during his comedy career. Kanye asked him if he could get Bernie to appear on his album, the perfect introductory voice to link Kanye to the biggest names of his hometown. Sadly Bernie was unavailable, but the pair found the next best thing. One of the rising comedy stars Coodie knew out of Chicago was one DeRay Davis, who'd moved to LA by the time Kanye started recording there. When they needed a lift home from one of Kanye's many dental appointments, his jaw still wired shut, DeRay stepped in and, for his trouble, Kanye played him 'Through The Wire'. His quick wit while he was listening to it – footage of DeRay joking "without an arm I spit!" that day would make it into the video for 'Through The Wire' – got him the job; he'd introduce Kanye's debut.

In the vocal booth, Kanye gave him his concept – a graduation scene, with Davis playing a teacher – and threw ideas at him, but Davis improvised a variety of accents before landing on his best Bernie Mac impersonation. He'd never been to college, or improvised a skit before, so simply babbled whatever he could think of that was vaguely school-related. "It was really informal," Davis recalled. "Kanye was just listening, watching, and laughing. I didn't expect that much of it to be on the album. I never knew how big it was going to be. People on Twitter still be like, 'Bernie Mac was great on Kanye's album.' And then someone will at me and say, 'That's actually DeRay Davis.' People will be like, 'Oh, I never knew that!'"

"Oh yeah," Kanye said in reply to DeRay's request, "I've got the perfect song for the kids to sing." And so began *The College Dropout*, already warming to its theme. And its style, class and game-changing panache would blast forth from its first track proper. 'We Don't Care' was a breezy soul saunter full of reverb saxophone, heavenly gospel choirs and jubilant beats, which sampled Jimmy Castor Bunch's cover of Gino Vannelli's 'I Just Wanna Stop', and its lesson to the nation's youth was one of survival by any means. Originally eight verses long and called 'Drug Dealer', according to Roberson it prompted a serious discussion about whether to go with the original or a more mainstream title. It was Kanye's submission to the hustler rap world he was surrounded by at Roc-A-Fella, a track about "drug dealin' just to get by" and the lifestyle of crime and addiction that, according to a report in the eighties, put the life expectancy of black males in the projects at 25: "We wasn't supposed to make it past 25," sang an innocent school choir, defying their own short futures, "joke's on you, we still alive."

Telling of how "as a shorty I looked up to the dopeman", as this was the only adult he saw around him with any money, Kanye explained that selling drugs was many people's only chance of a future – "this dope money here is lil' Trey's scholarship, 'cause ain't no to tuition for having no ambition". He also acknowledged people selling drugs despite having full-time minimum wage jobs as well as music bootleggers, tax fraudsters and those many hopeless millions "scratchin' lottery tickets, eyes on a new house". He even told of Really Doe taking to crime since he couldn't find work. But rather than just lay society's problems on a plate and shrug, Kanye looked into the causes behind such issues. "You know the kids' gon' act a fool when you stop the programs for after-school, and they DCFS, some of 'em dyslexic," he explained, and criticised the high rate of referral for black kids to Special Education across the country: "We ain't retards, the way teachers thought, hold up, hold fast, we make more cash, now tell my momma I belong in that slow class."

Roberson remembers the track as one of the tunes that was immediately leapt on as one not to sell★ but to keep for the record, while Consequence remembers it taking some time for Kanye to come around to writing the lyric about drug dealing, gathering stories and information from the people around him as he himself had never been out on the streets in the same way. "He had to extract it," he said, "he got me to stop hustling. I was moving things in Queens and I got arrested. He kind of had that Puffy/Biggie talk with me like, 'Yo man, you gotta put that shit down.' He rapped from an outside-looking-in standpoint." (In a separate interview, Consequence claimed Kanye had arranged for a mentor to have this conversation with him.) "He was mixing Roc-A-Fella with what he was, but still speaking to Roc-A-Fella fans," added Hip Hop. "He was trying to find his way to blend the two worlds, to appeal to street people without doing it blatantly – these are conversations we had."

GLC agreed. "He was thinking to hit muthafuckers from a different angle. People look at him as a backpack, positive rapper. He got the 'hood involved. Nobody ever would have thought Kanye West's first song on his album would be 'Drug dealing just to get by'. For a lot of us, this is our only way out that we know. He was thinking how he could put that into writing, into music and still be Kanye. If you listen to the song, it's still conscious, though. It was a celebration of the ghetto."

The track was also a good example of the way that Kanye would seek out opinions and advice from the people he trusted, rather than

---

★ Over the course of writing *The College Dropout*, Kanye also provided beats to a host of other acts including Cam'Ron, Lil' Kim, DMX and Memphis Bleek. He'd also rack up a major hit with Alica Keys' number three smash 'You Don't Know My Name' and use these sessions to garner advice from other rappers. The first time he found himself in the studio with Ludacris, for example, Kanye was so sure of his future stardom that he asked Luda if he had any tactics for going out in public without being hassled by fans. Ludacris told him to get used to staying in more, as it was simply unavoidable.

believing that he always knew best. "The version you hear of 'We Don't Care'," said Consequence, "he had a bunch of different rhymes to that shit because he wasn't content initially of how it was sounding. For the most part, he critiques himself pretty well, but he'll ask, 'What you think about this?' I think every good rapper has an idea of what they like and don't like, but they will ask if they're a man."

"'We Don't Care' definitely set the tone to what the album is," said Consequence, "and of where a majority of his friends were. All of us were kind of fucking around with some shit, and here we were with this opportunity to be a part of something great and extract greatness from ourselves."

Then came the teacher's rebuttal. In the 'Graduation Day' skit, over a pitched-up take on 'Land Of Hope And Glory', DeRay returned as Bernie Mac furious at Kanye having used children's choirs to put across his hustling morality tale, and throwing him out of school on the spot, refusing him the chance to "walk across that stage" at the graduation ceremony and highlighting a raw point of 21st Century racism – "you's a nigga, and I don't mean that in no nice way". Kanye's response was sung by Devo's old room-mate John Stephens, who would earn the stage name John Legend from Kanye and poet J. Ivy during the *College Dropout* sessions. Kanye repeatedly played Ivy a track Stephens was singing on and Ivy was blown away by how refreshingly soulful his voice was. When Stephens arrived at the studio an hour later, Ivy accosted him – "I heard your music," he enthused, "it's so amazing, it sounds so old school. Man, you sound like one of the legends. You're a legend. Matter of fact, that's what I'm going to call you from now on: The Legend". When Stephens walked into another session several days later, Ivy shouted at him "John Legend!" and Kanye backed him up, saying "you're John Legend from now on, that's your name". And it was.

Through the medium of Auto-Tune, sometime before T-Pain made the technology a central part of his style and popularised it in the urban community, Legend laid out Kanye's quietly confident ethos behind the record he was making. "I'm about to break the rules but don't tell anybody/I got something better than school but don't tell anybody," he sang in his luscious soul falsetto, "my momma would kill me but don't tell anybody." Even when he was about to revolutionise rap music, he was still concerned that his mother would disapprove of his life choices.

There followed the reworking of the fashion-addict rap 'Dreams Come True' from his demo tape as 'All Falls Down', but drastically altered from its original form. The lyric and theme remained largely the same, with the original lyrics merged into the first two verses and a new third verse added which delved further into the mentality of the outward consumerist showiness of downtrodden black Americans. Claiming that splashing out money was a form of retaliation against oppression and racism – "We shine because they hate us, floss 'cause they degrade us" – he went on to explain that, "We'll buy a lot of clothes when we don't really need 'em, things we buy to cover up what's inside, 'cause they make us hate ourself and love they wealth". He makes pertinent points about the white hegemony profiting from every step of the consumerist chain, be it the drug dealer buying Nike sneakers or the junkie buying crack, but ultimately owns up to how he himself is just as much of a victim of the process. He bought his first $25,000 piece of jewellery, he told us, before he'd bought a house, putting a show of his status and standing ahead of more essential concerns. And his declaration was a telling one for his future intentions in rap music, not just in relation to the honesty he was willing to explore his own psyche with, but that he was alone in being able to expose his failings so blatantly – "I got a problem with spending before I get it/We all self-conscious, I'm just the first to admit it".

The final line of the track, "now Syleena, you just like a self belt, you saved my life", told a different story though. Like the seatbelt that kept him from flying through the Lexus windscreen, Illinois R&B singer Syleena Johnson had indeed saved Kanye's bacon while recording the track. Far from the soulful strings that adorned the demo, the finished version had gone through a previous incarnation with a different beat called 'Self Conscious'⋆, and was now a miasma of bouncing beats, flamenco acoustic guitars and a hook that Kanye had sampled from Lauryn Hill's 'The Mystery Of Inquity': 'When it all falls down,

---

⋆ The 'Self Conscious' version was performed on Def Poetry Beat.

I'm telling you all, it all falls down". The track had evolved from 'Self Conscious' during a session at Baseline studios in NYC, where incense filled the rooms for a permanent state of chill and two CDs held permanent pride of place above the mixing desk, an Anita Baker album and Lauryn Hill's *MTV Unplugged No 2.0*. As his team – 88-Keys, JB Marshall and Consequence among them – were working up 'Self Conscious' for the album one afternoon, a time of day Kanye would call "the time before the madness" of the busy evening sessions when the likes of Jay-Z and State Property would show up, suggestions started arising that they should incorporate the Hill track since 88-Keys had been trying to forge connections with her to work on her scheduled follow-up to 1998's *The Miseducation Of Lauryn Hill* album. Hill wasn't simply accepting tracks from producers to work with, she was insisting on hearing what they'd sound like if they worked with her, so requested potential producers to go to her *Unplugged* CD and work on tracks from there. 88-Keys suggested Kanye, as a close collaborator, should work up a track too and that afternoon in the studio Marshall pointed him towards 'The Mystery Of Iniquity'. Back at his Newark apartment, working on his cheap 18-track Roland VS 1680 digital recorder – this home-made version was the one that would appear on the record – Kanye was struck by the bolt of inspiration. "He's like, 'I can die right now'," Marshall recalled. "I'm playing pool, and he comes around and he starts singing: 'When it all falls down'."

By the time 88-Keys got around to asking him if he was going to submit his track for Hill's album, Kanye had decided to keep it for himself. And there his troubles began. Everyone working on the record knew that the track had the potential to be a breakthrough hit, but Hill was notoriously difficult to get hold of, and clearing the sample became a living nightmare. Hill was unresponsive largely, it's believed, because she wasn't happy with her own version of the track, let alone anyone else working with it. Hill hadn't actually written the track herself, so the team were easily able to clear the lyrics and the backing track, but the vocal performance was the sticking point. Kanye and Monopoly even flew to Miami, where Hill lived, and drove the streets in the vain hope of running into her on the street or tracking her down through contacts. "That's the kind of stuff that we were doing, we were so 'by any means necessary'," Monopoly said. "'Oh, she lives in Miami? We'll just go find her'." They did manage to hunt down an email address for her via her husband, Rohan Marley, but that proved of little use. "We flew down to Miami and talked to the Marley brothers," Monopoly said. "I was even in communication with Mrs. Hill. I thought we came to terms, but because of what some other people that were in the mix did, it didn't happen." A cheque was sent out to her to entice her, and eventually Hill did respond, granting clearance for the sample. Then, at the eleventh hour, close to the due date for the album to be delivered, she pulled the clearance from under Kanye's feet.

"Biggs called me [to tell me about her decision]," Kanye remembered. "He sounded like he had a frog in his throat. He said, 'Man, you got a Plan B?'" Kanye had one, John Legend, but his take on the hook didn't fit right. Luckily, the stars aligned. On the last day of cutting the record at Record Plant, Johnson was recording her *Chapter 3: The Flesh* album in the studio across the hall, working on a track Kanye was producing called Bull's-Eye, featuring Common.

"It was six o'clock in the morning and [Kanye] needed clearance for the Lauryn Hill sample and she wouldn't give it to him," Johnson said. "And so, I came in to sing that hook for him and I ended up saving his deadline because he was going to have to push [back] his album if he hadn't gotten it done."

Johnson came into Kanye's studio and sang over Hill's original note-for-note, but Kanye wanted something different. "Do what you do," he told Johnson, and so she added her own flavour to the hook. "The song actually came out sounding better than the original," Kanye said. "I wasn't satisfied with how the original had came out. That's why I was thinking about using a different single. Syleena really had that soul in her voice, she had the perfect voice for it." The next day, having finished cutting the song at 7am, Kanye's crew told Johnson that the track would be a single, and they'd be filming the video the following week. "People love that song," Johnson said. "Probably because that's the song that launched him into superstar status. So, forever I will be that girl that sang on the song. That was a big song, not just for him, but for a lot of people. It changed the tide for hip-hop in a way."

After such a confessional track, Kanye sought redemption. 'I'll Fly Away', written in 1929 by Albert E Brumley, is accepted as the most recorded gospel song ever, and Kanye used an upbeat, jazzy take on it, the piano played by Ervin Pope and with DeRay and Tony Williams providing vocals, to give his record a spiritual grounding before beaming up to 'Spaceship'. Built from an intricate chopping and rearranging of Marvin Gaye's 'Distant Lover', originally this tale of a wage slave dreaming of a spaceship to whisk him out of the daily nine-to-five grind began life as a track intended for GLC's radio breakthrough in Chicago. GLC had just quit his job in a clothes store and was hustling on the side, and Kanye wanted to do whatever he could to keep his friend out of prison. So he told him to come to New York and throw himself fully into the rap world. In Newark, the pair went through Kanye's extensive record collection listening to potential samples for a track that would thrust GLC into the attention of his hometown DJs until they came across the Gaye record. Kanye put the beat together on the spot.

When GLC put his downbeat verse on the track, in December 2003, he was suffering; partly from a heated phone call he'd just had with his ex-girlfriend, griping at him for not being signed when he was claiming to have label interest, and partly due to the fact that it was the anniversary month of the death of his mother in a car accident. (GLC's mother had died when he was 12, and he nearly died himself two years later, slipping into a coma from undiagnosed diabetes and being pronounced legally dead before being resuscitated.) "Lost my momma, lost my mind," he rapped over the brooding soul backing, "my life, my love, that's not mine/'why you aint signed?'" He lamented his tedious job and described how he asked Kanye to help him escape his dead-end life, rap music his own personal spaceship. It was a touching, self-knowing verse that would change GLC's life★. When Kanye would play it to

---

★ GLC would receive numerous label offers and a tour slot with Talib Kweli off the back of his verse, eventually signing to Kanye's own G.O.O.D. label in 2005. Everyone from Jay-Z to Andre 3000 congratulated him on the song.

people like Plain Pat with only GLC's verse on it, intending it for one of the Akademics mix-tapes he was working on around that time, they'd unanimously tell him it should be on his own record. When he told GLC, his friend was sanguine about the news. "Cool," he said, "you signed to Def Jam; I'm signed to nobody. Let's go."

Before long producer Miri Ben-Ari had infused the track with a cinematic doomsday vibe and it had a verse from Consequence on it, which Consequence had rapped for GLC and Kanye over dinner before a promo show, detailing his own struggles after his success with A Tribe Called Quest had faded: working a humiliating day job while the music industry turned its back on him. "A lot of people have told me it was one of their favourite verses on the album," Consequence said. "People loved the whole scenario of me explaining being in Busta's video because it was actual factual. It was an emotional, 'this is where my life is,' introspective verse. 'Spaceship' was like the people's record... It's the blue-collar anthem of the album." Once Consequence's verse was down, again recorded in Kanye's apartment, Kanye added his own verse about his days in summer employment as a greeter at the Gap. He painted a picture of widespread hypocrisy, both in his anger at being questioned about missing khaki trousers while admitting to stealing himself, and on the part of his managers, who'd treat him like a criminal behind the scenes yet rolling him out front of house as a shining example of the multi-racial employment policies. Then he went on to describe his lengthy period of writing beats to sell to local Chicago rappers – "doing five beats a day for three summers" – as proof that he'd earned his dues and deserved the millions of sales he expected for *The College Dropout*, and the fancy cars that followed, once his own rap spaceship had blasted him out of obscurity.

The final piece of the 'Spaceship' puzzle, like Syleena Johnson's part on 'All Falls Down', would arrive at the very end of the recording process. Tony Williams would regularly see Kanye when he picked him and Donda up from the airport in Oklahoma City every Christmas on their annual family trip home. On the drives, they'd always play each other the music they were working on – Kanye was particularly impressed by Tony's Christian band Souljah and suggested that he should produce them. Kanye invited Tony out to the W Hotel in LA and re-produced some of the Souljah tracks early on in the *College Dropout* sessions. While he was there, witnessing first-hand the incredible creative churn of work across the entire floor of the W Hotel, week in week out, he asked Kanye if he could sing a line on the album. Kanye told him John Legend would be doing the singing.

The following year, on the Christmas drive from the airport, it was Kanye's turn to impress his cousin. He played him 'Spaceship' and Tony started riffing over the end of the track: "I want to fly," he sang, "I want to fly, I said I want my chariot to pick me up and take me, brother for a ride". Kanye stopped him, rewound the CD and asked him to do it again. "'That's what I need," he enthused. "That's the feel that I've been wanting for the album that I haven't been able to get." In a week Tony was back in LA, two weeks before the album came out, adding his final flourish to 'Spaceship'. "It was a very p-funk-inspired," Tony explained, "loose, unrefined and raw feeling. He wanted free soul -- an unrestricted kind of vibe." Kanye was so impressed with him that he asked him to try parts on another song, then another. By the end of recording, Tony was singing on five of the songs.

Next came 'Jesus Walks', re-recorded with John Legend singing a melody line through Auto-Tune, Miri Ben-Ari adding more spiritual marching touches★ and with Kanye expanding his lyric to include a second verse it took him 12 months to piece together, and only then with a lot of help from Rhymefest. Yet it seemed a deeply personal and brave assertion of his faith and how Christian rappers could act as a positive influence on the scene. "Now hear 'Ye, hear 'Ye," he rapped, referencing his own name in Biblical language as he attacked radio for refusing to play religious rap music, "they say you can rap about anything except for Jesus/That means guns, sex, lies, videotape/ But if I talk about God my record won't get played, huh?" Yet still he dreamed of the day his faith would inspire people via his music, "and bring the day I'm dreaming about, next time I'm in the club everybody screaming out 'Jesus Walks!'"

★ Ben-Ari would find it ironic that she'd win a Grammy for 'Jesus Walks', since she's Jewish.

"One verse of that song now, he's rapping through another nigga's eyes," said GLC. "He tried to do the whole song like that and it wasn't really happening. Some people was like, 'You need to put Scarface or somebody else on there.' He knew he could make it happen, so he did it. But he wanted to switch it up where it can get across to everybody. He put so much into that shit, like, 'I have to get it perfect'."

Once finished, the inspirational track had a huge impact on the team. It was the moment that Hip Hop could tell that Kanye was a truly special artist, and the likes of Common and Coodie were amazed when they heard it, this Christian rap tune in an unexplored beat. When Kanye went down to Atlanta to work on T.I.'s Trap Muzik album, he played T.I. 'Jesus Walks' and the rapper warned him it sounded risky, but Kanye was convinced it would blow up. Roberson and Kanye had many discussions about how to go about releasing the song – there were arguments that it should be the album's first single, but Roberon considered it so strong yet challenging to mainstream radio that they should hold it back until Kanye was established, for fear of it being lost. Ultimately, they decided to sit on the track until the world was ready for it.

The world was definitely ready for a Jay-Z guest spot, though. Continuing the spiritual theme, 'Never Let Me Down' bounced along on a gospel choir hook sung by Legend and singer Tarrey Torae, a tune sampled and extrapolated from 'Maybe It's The Power Of Love' by Michael Bolton's early band Blackjack. Tarrey, who had been working on vocals for the record in Kanye's apartment in NYC, was asked to fly to LA to sing on the track, only to arrive with her voice shot to pieces by the airplane's air conditioning and unable to sing. So Kanye hired a choir to come in to sing the part, only for them to realise there was cursing on the song and leave, despite Kanye's protests that the message was a good one. So, a few days later, her voice recovered, Tarrey sang every part of the choir.

Over the continuing hook and dynamic shuffling beat, Jay-Z spat a verse from his *Blueprint 2* era 'Hovi Baby (Remix)' – a verse that arrived at the very last minute, added just two days before mastering – following his rise from owning the streets to owning the charts, winning over the public, outlasting lesser rappers and keeping others off the number one spot until he was back in the studio again, the charts cast as his home that "y'all niggas visiting". It was typical Jay-Z self-aggrandisement, and Kanye's verse was equally autobiographical. Paying tribute to his grandfather and his mother for their bravery in getting arrested at the sit-in at the Oklahoma lunch counter "where white folks ain't want us to eat" when Donda was six, thereby making Kanye "born to be different", he then brought the civil rights story up to date, pointing out that racism was still bubbling under in society, inherent in the likes of club entry policies, while African-Americans had become obsessed with flashy consumer goods rather than voting – "now niggas can't make it to the ballots to choose leadership/But we can make it to Jacob's and to the dealership". The verse ended on personal notes, however, referencing his heaven-sent luck at escaping death in the car crash and paying tribute to his girlfriend of seven years, Sumeke Rainey, whom he'd promised her father on his death-bed that he'd marry. It was a promise he'd ultimately break: over the course of writing and recording *The College Dropout*, Kanye split with Sumeke and started dating aspiring fashion designer Alexis Phifer.

The verse was also born of a certain amount of adversity. On November 25, 2003, Jay-Z held his retirement party at Madison Square Garden, a night of many stars that features guest spots from Missy Elliott, Memphis Bleek, Beyoncé, R Kelly and Pharrell Williams, among other acts that Jay had worked with over the course of his career. Jay was set to leave rap in favour of running Def Jam, and this was his final blow-out. Having rapped on 'The Bounce' on *The Blueprint 2*, Kanye felt he had a place on the stage alongside those huge names and, on Hip Hop's advice, asked Jay if he could make an appearance too. Jay said "No, he ain't ready for that yet" and instead offered him two tickets to the show, at face value. He wasn't even offered a backstage pass. Hip Hop offered him his own tickets, but Kanye refused, instead deciding to spend the night at Sony Studios working on 'Never Let Me Down'. "Fuck that show!" he told his mother. "Next year I'll have my own show at Madison Square Garden!"★

★ Kanye would indeed play Madison Square Garden the following year, playing a 45 minute set supporting Usher.

Being unable to perform his verses live was a frustration Kanye had already faced that same year. When Jay-Z and 50 Cent's Roc The Mic tour hit Chicago in July 2003, 'Champions' was on the set list, alongside several tracks for which Kayne had written the beats. Kanye even got so far as to be waiting in the wings for the part where his verse should be. But the music shifted, another track dropped before his moment came; his mother remembered him being almost in tears from the disappointment, his rap ambitions still thwarted at every turn.

The third verse of 'Never Let Me Down' was, according to its author, a gift from God. J Ivy, Tarrey Torae's boyfriend and an acquaintance of Kanye's from Chicago, recalls getting a call from Coodie to say that Kanye and Jay-Z had a song they wanted to get a poet on, and Coodie had suggested Ivy. "You need to get to LA," Coodie told him; Ivy, who was yet to be involved with the *College Dropout* sessions, assumed he was joking, Coodie being a comedian. "Dog, that ain't funny!" Ivy said, knowing Jay-Z was retiring, "A joint with Jay-Z?" But Coodie was insistent: "Dog, you need to get to LA right now. You ain't got much time. You get out here tomorrow if you can." Coodie went into Kanye's studio at Hollywood's Record Plant and played Ivy the music down the phone to prove he was for real. Though he was broke and alone in the projects of Bedford-Stuyvesent, New York, barely even being able to afford a train fare into Manhattan, Ivy promised to find some way out there, but first he needed a poem. Grabbing a piece of paper, he wrote down the title of the song and scribbled a first line, then nothing came. He started banging on the page, saying "God, I need a piece right now, give me a piece!" then put his hand back on the paper. His hand started moving, almost of its own accord, scribbling out a full page of poetry. He read it back four or five times, surprised at how eloquent it was, then got Coodie back on the phone. "I spit it to him over the phone," Ivy said. "He goes in the other room and I hear a bunch of people talking. The music goes down and the people get quiet. He put me on speakerphone, and I spit the piece as if I had done it a million times. When I finished the room exploded... I hear Kanye say, 'Man J, spit it again.' I did the joint for a half hour, and the piece was only a minute long. So I did it over, over, over and over again.

114

Coodie finally got back on the phone and said, 'Guess what? Kanye is flying you out here tomorrow.' I found my way."

Within days, Ivy was in LA having practised his verse 1,000 times on the plane trip. He performed the piece at the Improv theatre, then was whisked by limo to Kanye's studio to pull off his poem in just two takes, the first shrieked at the top of his voice and the second toned down perfectly. Ivy's lines fit Kanye's religious tone neatly, his poem concerning his feelings that he was merely a conduit for God's words – "I get my hymns from Him… I'm a Heaven-sent instrument" – with the intention of decrying racism and becoming a freedom fighter akin to Kunta Kinte from the TV series *Roots* or Joseph Cinqué, who led the slave uprising against the Amistad in the 19th Century. It was a sentiment that put Jay-Z's final verse of rap braggadocio to shame – reminding us of his slew of number one albums and plugging his next record as *Eighth Wonder* – the working title of *The Black Album* – Jay used religious imagery rather more flippantly, to describe himself as "the Pope John Paul of y'all niggas". Jay's verse seemed to detract from the sincerity and spirituality of Ivy's poem, but it was a star turn nonetheless.

Damon Dash would claim the track was a success due to the inherent competition Kanye felt with Jay-Z. "I don't think it's a negative thing," he said, arguing that there was an essential friction since Jay had to fight his way up from the streets while Kanye was rather more blessed, having been handed the credibility of Roc-A-Fella from which to launch his career. "It's just a human thing… But as long as they both work hard, they're both legends, they're both going to go down in history."

Kanye's weed anthem 'Get Em High' was a late addition to the record, and a track that several artists were scrambling over. Kanye first produced the louche beat for Talib Kweli's album *The Beautiful Struggle*. Kweli would tell of the shift in dynamic between he and Kanye by now – Kanye had had some big successes so rather than come and play him a selection of beats to choose from for his record, he was now too busy to put together a selection, so simply agreed to come and make some in Kweli's studio, putting 'Get Em High' together from scratch in 15 minutes. Kweli loved the beat but wasn't keen on the weed lyrics that Kanye came up with, or the hook line "throw your motherfucking hands in the air – get 'em high", which was a line Kweli had already used in his career. So Kweli passed in favour of using 'I Try' and Kanye decided to keep 'Get Em High' for his own album, despite the track at one point being bound for Busta Rhymes and John Monopoly wanting to get it for a Jive signing called Dirtbag.

Kanye had been talking to Common for some time, trying to get him on the album considering his Chicago connection, and 'Get Em High' seemed the right place for him. Common was under fire from critics claiming that he'd lost the edge of early tracks like 'I Used To Love H.E.R.', so he used his verse to revisit his volatile, bullish rhymes about those he saw denigrating hip-hop. "Real rappers is hard to find, like a remote, control rap is out of," he spat, going on to pinpoint Lil Wayne as the sort of "illiterate nigga" he was gunning for in his attempt to resurrect rap by putting down weak acts that too readily believed their record label's high opinions of them and were too keen to fill their singles with featured guest stars. Kanye added his own verses, the first biting back at the college tutors who said he'd be a loser for dropping out or thought that he was withdrawn – "You thought I was bashful, but this bastard's flow will bash your skull" – with great swipes of belief in his future success. And for the second he recruited Sumeke to play the part of a girl he's trying to seduce by telling her he knows Talib, even going so far as to call Kweli to get him to rap down the phone as proof, and this meant that, at the last minute, Kanye had to get Talib onto the album.

Kanye, like Jay-Z, would never write down his rhymes – often he'd make sure Coodie was filming him when he tried something out, and then watch the tape back to remember the lines. Often he'd build his rhymes in the booth itself, using noises as placeholders until he found the right word. Coodie remembers this happening on Kanye's 'Get Em High' verse.

Knowing Kweli had already turned the track down once, Kanye turned on the charm. "I cannot do this album without you being a part of it," he told him on the phone, "but you gotta do it right now." Kweli was on tour in Europe, so managed to find a studio to record a verse in response to Kanye's – sure, he'd help him have sex with the girl in return for some new beats – and send it over via email. However it arrived, it was laid over a different section of the beat than Talib had originally rapped over, a full bar late, so when he heard the record on its release he was furious that Kanye had made such a glaring mistake. "Yo, this is crazy," he yelled at him down the phone. "How could you do this to me? You gotta fix it for the second print of the album." "I'm sorry, I didn't mean to do that," Kanye replied, "but that shit sounds hot." "It doesn't sound hot and I don't rap like that," Talib replied, "I'm way doper than how you have me sounding." But Kanye was right, Kweli began receiving numerous messages saying how great he was on the track. Gradually, he came to love what he'd call a beautiful mistake.

'Workout Plan', a skit featuring three girls discussing the miracle of Kanye's workout video, bled into 'The New Workout Plan', an excitable groove of hyperspeed beats and high-pitched harmonies which Kanye used as the bedrock for a satire on perceived ideas of gender politics. Women in good physical shape, his theory went, are more likely to bag rich men or rappers, although from lines such as "excuse me miss [a reference to Jay-Z's song 'Excuse Me Miss'] I forgot your name/Thank you, God bless you, goodnight, I came", they shouldn't expect any respect or consideration to follow. Here was a track that showcased Kanye's voracious sexual appetite, declaring that there "ain't nothing to talk about" with a girl "unless she's talking about freaking out", as he went on to try to seduce a gym girl in his second verse, finally admitting that he'd sleep with her even if she wasn't fit. Yet he spat his disrespect with pride, even adding fake testimonials to the results of his workout at the end, a series of girls claiming to have bagged rich men after following it.

As it went through numerous versions before arriving at the final take, taking a full 70 hours to produce, the track split Kanye's camp. Roberson found the concept hilarious, a great example of Kanye's comedic side. John Legend loved writing and singing the final hook – "eat your salad, no dessert, get that man you deserve". But producer Patrick 'Plain Pat' Reynolds hated the song, calling it goofy and saying it drove him crazy, and Kanye would play it so loud that JB Marshall would claim he lost his hearing for a day after one blast. Marketing guy Ferris Bueller also wasn't a fan, as Plain Pat pointed out to Kanye during one session. "You don't like 'Workout Plan'?" he asked Ferris, who replied, "Put it like this: you don't hear 'Workout' on a classic album. When I listen to *Midnight Marauders*, I don't skip any songs. I let it ride through. When your album comes out, I'm going to skip 'Workout Plan'." It's a sign of Kanye's steadfast self-belief that Bueller's name was nowhere to be found on the album. Indeed, when he'd come to play it live, 'The New Workout Plan' would be a huge fan favourite.

As would the following track, the result of some of Gee Roberson's most inventive industry manoeuvring. Taking the lead from a skit on a Consequence mix-tape called *The Baby Pops*, Kanye had been drawn to work up a beat called 'Slow Jamz' from sampling Luther Vandross' cover of Burt Bacharach's 'A House Is Not A Home' – a beat Kanye originally intended for GLC – and Roberson saw a great opportunity for it. He and Hip Hop had been made Senior Vice Presidents at the A&R department of Atlantic Records, and given a list of acts to work on. Amongst them was Twista, who'd been around for a few years but hadn't had the sort of success the label had expected and also had no obvious first single from his forthcoming album. Meanwhile, they were also out to find more money to fund Kanye's album and the forthcoming videos and promotional work that would have to be done on it. Also, Kanye knew already that he wanted Twista on his album somewhere, since he'd been working on his album *Kamikaze*. The new beat offered them all a solution – if they gave the beat to Twista as the lead single from his album then Atlantic would pay for a video that would give Kanye some great exposure, after which Kanye could release the song himself from his own album.

"Kanye was like, 'I want to hear you on this song right here'," Twista said. "He explained the concept and I remember pacing in the studio, thinking to myself, 'I'm going to name a bunch of different classic singers in this song right here'."

The concept was a look back at some of the greatest groove balladeers of the R&B world, and all of the sex they helped along. From the Whispers to the Isley Brothers to Teddy Pendergrass and Vandross himself, Twista name-dropped legions of the most famous and effective romancers in his super-speed verse, punning on their names as he smooth-talked a girl into bed. Kanye's verse took a similar tone, telling of playing a girl tracks by Gladys Knight and Luther Vandross as he prepared for a night of Cool Whip-based bedroom antics, but also marked the moment that he recognised his own limitless potential, when he came up with the killer line, "she got a light-skinned friend, look like Michael Jackson, got a dark-skinned friend, look like Michael Jackson". "I held on to the last moments of [anonymity]," he said. "I knew when I wrote the line 'light-skinned friend look like Michael Jackson', I was going to be a big star. At the time, they used to have the Virgin music [stores], and I would go there and just go up the escalator and say to myself, "I'm soaking in these last moments of anonymity." I knew I was going to make it… I knew that this was going to happen."

Kanye needed a female voice on this inventive R&B slow groove, playing the girl Kanye was trying to get with, demanding he "do it faster", the implication being that the girl wanted faster sex which Kanye comically interpreted as to mean faster rapping, and Twista was amongst the fastest around, as he proved in his subsequent verse. By chance J Ivy shared an attorney with TV actress Aisha Tyler and he brought her over to Record Plant studios in LA to hear the track. With her contribution in place, there was only one slot left to fill, the hook. And for that, they went all the way to Hollywood royalty.

Jamie Foxx vividly recalls the day Kanye West burst into his life. "I threw all of these parties," he said, "and I threw a party one day for Puffy and Jay-Z and MIA, Missy… way back in the day when Puff was really going hard. There was a guy who walks into my house, his jaw was a little busted and he had a backpack on. I said, 'Who's that kid?' They said 'That's Kanye West'. I said, 'What does he do?' They said, 'He raps'. Well if you come to my house, you have to perform, so I walk up to him and say, 'Man, they tell me you rap?' He says, 'Yeah'. He rapped and it was absolutely amazing. I said, 'Dude, why don't you have a record out?' And he says, 'Well I produce for Jay-Z, but I have a song for you'. I said, 'Well I got a studio in the crib' and we went back in the crib and he said, 'This is the song, (sings) 'she wants some Marvin Gaye, some Luther Vandross'. I said 'I got it, (sings more soulfully) 'she say she wants some Marvin Gaye…'. He said, 'What are you doing?' and I said, 'Well, I gotta put the R&B sauce on it, that's the sauce'. He says, 'Don't put that on because you're gonna screw the song up. Music has changed, sing it simple.' So I sung it but I sung it begrudgingly, thinking, 'This is wack, he's never gonna make it, he's terrible, this is a terrible song'."

Coodie remembers the session in Foxx's home studio with a picture of Ray Charles above the mixing desk, claiming Jamie hit the booth with a lacklustre vibe until Coodie came in with his film camera to shoot his part, at which point Foxx came alive, playing to the camera and injecting his hook with depth and life. The result made the track magical. "Kanye came by the Bel-Air like, 'I just did a record with Jamie Foxx'." Dash said. "I was like, 'Why? I hate when actors sing.' But that shit just worked." Jay-Z was just as enthusiastic. "When Kanye played it back for me [with Jamie Foxx on it] I was like, 'That's phenomenal'," Twista said. "But what took it to the next level was when Jay-Z was like, 'What's up with that song that you and Kanye got? That 'Slow Jamz' song?… I think that's a good look. That should come out as a first single for both of y'all.' So Jay-Z was actually the one that put 'Slow Jamz' being a single into effect."

If Jamie Foxx wasn't star power enough for *The College Dropout*, Kanye swapped three of his most sought-after beats for an appearance on *Breathe In, Breathe Out* from Ludacris. Over another manipulated trumpet-speckled soul groove, put together from a sample of Jackie Moore's 'Precious Precious', Ludacris' hook urged rappers that talked about having lots of jewellery and impressive cars to prove it, but ironically money was becoming an issue for Kanye by the time the track was recorded. At first the budget for the album from Roc-A-Fella was set at around $250,000 but with the constant recording, hotel bills and travel across the country for Kanye and numerous guest acts, the record would inch towards costing $1million to make. This was beyond Roc-A-Fella's means, and as bills kept arriving for guest slots and so forth, the cost looked to be getting out of control. Eventually

Roc-A-Fella capped the budget for its entire roster besides Jay-Z, and Kanye was recording on borrowed time – Plain Pat wasn't supposed to be allowing him to record at all, but let him keep going, holding back the bills from Record Plant. "Some days I would pay for something myself, like a studio," Pat said, "because we just wanted to get it done so bad that it didn't matter. We just loved the music so much, it was important to us."

The one hope was Lyor Cohen, the head of Island Def Jam and the man with the power to approve Kanye's increased budgets. He and Damon Dash conferred over where best to spend Def Jam's money – Lyor was keen to invest more in Young Gunz rather than Kanye, since their song 'Can't Stop, Won't Stop' was getting airplay and Kanye hadn't begun to work his album yet. Lyor didn't want to put any money behind Kanye at all despite Dash and Biggs arguing his case – "We need to chase both if we're going to chase anything," they'd argue but Lyor said, "Nah, we don't have the budget for it." "I was getting ready to put him out through Def Jam," Dash explained, "but we had a certain amount of money to spend and, at the time, the Young Gunz's 'Can't Stop, Won't Stop' single was doing well. It was the time I wasn't putting out the money myself, and I went to tell Lyor and he said 'I think we should put the money behind Young Gunz.' I said, 'You guys are dumb'."

Then one day Kanye was hanging out in the New York Def Jam offices with the marketing director Shante Bacon and Plain Pat – Pat had held back $40,000 to $50,000 of bills from Kanye's album and was terrified he'd be fired for his budget transgressions. Cohen wandered by the office and Kanye was on him, talking his way into Lyor's office and playing him all of his best tracks. It was 'Breathe In Breathe Out' that sealed the deal. "This is my favourite one!" Lyor exclaimed, and when they next tried to play him 'Jesus Walks', he said, "Don't fuck it up Kanye, I only like this one." The next day the budget was opened up for Kanye's album, much to Pat's eternal relief.

Perhaps it was Kanye's money-aware theme that grabbed Lyor's attention; Kanye's first verse flipped the entire concept of the baller rapper, the cliché of having risen from the streets only to flagrantly show off your attained wealth: "Golly, more of that bullshit ice rap," he began, before apologising openly to the likes of Mos Def and Talib, conscious rappers who took an anti-materialistic stance and tackled more important political and social themes than this, a standpoint Kanye himself aspired to. "Always said if I rapped I'd say something significant," he acknowledged, "but now I'm rapping about money, hoes and rims again."

Kanye's lyrics did contain a certain amount of deeper analysis of the baller image though, as he questioned whether it was OK to rap about wearing lots of gold if it came from Ghana or Mali, where you'd be seen to be supporting weaker economies, and claimed to be the first rapper to cross the boundaries between the backpack-wearing intelligent hip-hop acts and the Benz-driving types obsessed with status symbols. Yet he inevitably fell on the side of the ballers, almost disgusting himself as he listed his extravagant purchases – "I'm so broke I look back like 'damn, was I on crack?', I mean, 12 platinum chains?" Subsequent verses backed up the traditional image, as he hit the club to meet girls he'd convince to give him head to annoy their rich boyfriends, or impressed them with his car or his watch.

Despite being over the moon to have got a hook through from Ludacris for his album – JB Marshall recalled the CD arriving by Fed-Ex at 1.30am, he and Kanye rushing into the studio and playing the hook all night, they were so pleased to have landed it – Kanye wasn't sure the track should go on the album. Its theme was a little too mainstream and it didn't have a strong concept behind it, plus there were other tracks that people like Consequence thought fit better, such as a John Legend song called 'Gettin Out The Game' or his own 'Magic Man' track. 'Breathe In Breathe Out' would appear on a mix-tape before the album came out and got a few radio plays off the back of that. While Kanye was on the fence about including it, and would question the decision after the release, Roberson was a champion of the song, arguing that it could be single-worthy. Consequence believed he kept it on out of sentimental value as it was one of the first he made for the album, and having Ludacris on the record was important to him. But it was a decision he'd eventually come to regret. "The beat is not so awesome, and the song doesn't have a melody or message," Devo would say. "It's just a song."

At which point DeRay returned, in his own voice, in a satirical skit called 'School Spirit (Skit 1)' on the benefits of finishing college, in comparison to grabbing the chance to make the music we'd been hearing from Kanye. He painted a portrait of virginal, nerdy students leaving school having picked up a crack habit during their partying years, landing a $25,000 bottom-of-the-ladder job at a high street chain where they'd be lucky to work their way up to reporting to the company boss' niece. This and the later 'School Spirit (Skit 2)', which parodied people who stayed in further education gaining qualifications that would never benefit them in the real world, came from an hour that DeRay spent freestyling in the booth, later cut into the sections Kanye wanted to use. They sandwiched 'School Spirit', Kanye's treatise on how further education was superfluous and unnecessary, built around a pitched-up sample from Aretha Franklin's 'Spirit In The Dark' which Kanye had found in a crate of records given to him by Sumeke's father.

Roberson claims to have lost years of his life trying to clear the Aretha Franklin sample. Initially Franklin refused clearance, but Kanye wouldn't take no for an answer, so insisted Roberson get clearance one way or another. The team had three fallback versions of the song without Aretha's voice on them, but the only one Kanye liked was the one with the sample, the track would have been very weak without it. Taking on Kanye's 'no ifs, no buts' attitude, Roberson went crazy trying to achieve what he thought was a "mission impossible", and eventually, with the mediation of the head of Atlantic, Craig Kallman, Franklin cleared the sample on the assurance that the song wouldn't include any profanity. Hence all official versions of 'School Spirit' have the swear words obscured, even on the album's uncensored version, although uncensored versions of 'School Spirit' would be available to hear online. "I was learning this from the living example himself, Kanye West, that you never take no," Roberson said. "There's no choice for me but to have the same mentality because I'm speaking 24/7 to the guy who's living his life and being the example of all examples of that.

In the midst of the no's, I had to figure out a way. And I figured out a way."

To Franklin's catchy gospel melody, Kanye listed fraternity houses – Alpha, Omega, Kappa and Sigma – on the hook, almost as a warning rather than a recommendation. The lyric expanded on Kanye's success since dropping out of college after being told he'd always have to wait to follow his rap dreams; starting his own Kon-Man Productions business and making good on his promises to his mother that he'd end up on TV. Noting that the valedictorian from his high school had ended up as a waiter in a branch of Cheesecake, Kanye lauded his relative high-rolling, from his ability to get with sorority girls without having to join, to his impressive Roc-A-Fella chain and Jesus piece.

The sloping, funky track was a favourite, even if the plethora of skits was a sticking point. 'School Spirit (Skit 2)' was immediately followed by another skit called 'Lil' Johnny', a conversation with the son of one of the serial degree-studiers from the previous skit, who'd been left homeless and penniless because his father had spent his whole life studying rather than earning money to support him. Roberson thought the skits were genius, a great way to give the album an overall character and tone, rooted in the theme of education and the worthlessness of too much of it. Others battled the proliferation of skits, telling him it was too much to put two skits back to back, but he kept adding them during the mastering process – the more his team told him "no more skits" the more he wanted on the record.

'Lil' Johnny' gave way to 'Two Words', the song Kanye started working on with Ice-Gre some years before. It had come a long way since then; now it was a dark and dramatic cut full of harsh guitar and sinister piano, built from a sample of 'Peace & Love' (Amani Na Mapenzi) – 'Movement III (Time)' as performed by Bed-Stuy seven-piece Mandrill, a favourite act for use on movie soundtracks. The track also sampled drums from the 5th Dimension's 'Rainmaker'. The style of classical strings and ominous doom-mongering was something he'd recruited Miri Ben-Ari to add to the record, Kanye having wanted to work with Miri after seeing her perform with Jay-Z. 'Two Words' was the first of *The College Dropout*'s tracks that Ben-Ari would work on, and

Kanye gave her little direction in adding her own touches to the track, simply watching her work in her inimitable way, writing and producing on the spot and giving the engineer strict instructions on how the track should sound. She was excited by how theatrical and expansive the beat sounded. "*The College Dropout* is when Kanye developed his own unique sound," Miri explained. "He did that by having people [whose] talent he trusted. He let them do them and he learned from them because he's very open-minded. He loves to learn… The whole classical strings, orchestra was very new to Kanye. He wanted that sound, my writing… it was a fresh new sound, no one had done it at the time. Kanye liked to just sit and listen. I introduced him to that whole sound of classical strings and orchestration and he fell in love with it… he was thirsty, he wanted to learn."

Kanye loved the orchestration so much that he considered putting out the album with only the strings on the song, but his team talked him out of it – this was an era when, if a hip-hop act put out an instrumental they liked, 50 Cent would rap over it and virtually own the track, since every radio station would play 50's version. And anyway, they had some great opportunities to get good names on the tune. Roc-A-Fella's self-styled freshman Freeway had heard some of Kanye's tracks and knew he was a good rapper even if others disrespected him, and as a rapper who liked working on beats that challenged him and his flow, he readily accepted Kanye's offer to rap a verse. The structure of the concept appealed to him; every line, wherever possible, should be made up of two words or syllables, giving the track a clipped momentum. In the event, Freeway was so enthused with the track that he continued to play it at his shows for many years to come.

"Kanye was great at making those kind of records where you could spit your heart out," Freeway said, even though he bent the rules during his verse of classic gangsta posturing – "Freeway slightly retarded" went his excuse. But the track's other guest rapper Mos Def, a conscious rapper from the far end of the spectrum from Freeway's hustler persona, stuck far more rigidly to the brief. He created an entire world, capturing the frustrations, violence and degredations of Bed-Stuy and the wider American political situation in rapid-fire two-word bursts: "United

States, no love, no breaks/Low brow, high stakes/Crack smoke, black folks/Big Macs, fat folks, Ecstasy capsules, Presidential scandals".

Mos Def ended up on the track after a fraught trip to Europe. Dash was keen for Kanye to connect with London as it was such a major musical hub, but the trip got off to a stressful start when one Chicago rapper that Kanye had made a record with started threatening him if he didn't show up to an event that clashed with his trip. Dash eventually had to "apply a bit of gangsta" to get the rapper to leave Kanye alone so he could make the flight. Once in London★ he did get the chance to battle Mos Def at Dash's London apartment. "The one thing about Kanye is, he's brave," Dash said. "Even though you know him, how do you get in front of Mos Def and go rap for rap with him? That's when I was like, 'He's fearless.' Because most people wouldn't have done that shit. He wasn't scared to be himself."

For Kanye's part of 'Two Words', he introduced the song by recreating lines from his appearance on State Property's 'Got Nowhere': "It's only two places you end up, either dead or in jail/Still nowhere to go". And his verse once again celebrated his rise, from name-checking Chi-Town and the Go-Getters (who, he says, "should've been signed twice") to pointing out his five-mike ratings for *The Blueprint*, the plethora of platinum discs on his walls and giving an accurate prediction that he'd soon become the "most imitated" producer in rap. Adding in nods to his religion – "On Judgement Day, who's gon' blame me? Look, God, it's the same me" – and the ongoing racial struggle in America – "We get racially profiled, cuffed up and hosed down" – the verse built up a sense of import that needed a certain amount of drama to it. So he and Consequence set about hunting out a choir.

So leaving the session at Quad Studios in NYC, four hours out of town by car, in a compound deep in the woods of upstage New York, Kanye and Consquence tracked down the 16-strong Harlem Boys Choir to the only place they could find to record them, and for $10,000 he got them to sing a purposely off-kilter backing track. "I was like, 'They don't sound in the pocket'," said JB Marshall. "And he's like, 'That's

★ Kanye also went on to France during the same trip.

the magic. They're not supposed to'. It bothered me, but I have grown to understand through the years that it's about capturing the emotion that you want the listener to get."

'Through The Wire' followed, and then a reworked version of 'Family Business' from his demo CD. Extended to three verses, polished so that the sweet soul piano gleamed afresh and with choirs, John Legend vocals★ and cute lines from young children added to enhance the family feeling. The extra lines on Kanye's lyrics were tough for him to come by – he wanted the song to reflect everybody's family life rather than just his own, so needed to draw on other people's experiences to add colour. As the eldest of 48 grandkids just on her mother's side, Tarrey Torae was a very helpful source of material about being part of a large extended family, telling him about her aunt who was so bad at cooking they'd warn people not to eat her food and about the times she had to take baths or share beds with her cousins – some of them at the top of the bed and some at the bottom. The line saying "let's get Stevie out of jail", spoken by a young child at the very end of the track, was about Torae's godbrother Stevie who was in prison at that time.

"I was breaking down some of the funnier parts of how we grew up," Torae said. "That song was definitely my family to the core. There was no switching it, he wrote it exactly as I described it, and he went from there. And he's a great MC so he did an excellent job."

For his third verse, Kanye brought the track back to the personal, talking about how he woke up from his accident with "a new state of mind" that didn't involve thug raps any more, but more heartfelt and honest rhymes, and morals for life. "Keep your nose out the sky, keep your heart to God, and keep your face to the rising sun", he advised, advocating a humble but self-assured life, then touchingly paid tribute to his Chicago rap family, hoping that they'll learn to love and respect each other rather than in-fight all the time.

★ Dash would be a little wary of the fact that John Legend was all over the album, since he felt he was being pushed at Roc-A-Fella's expense without being signed to the label. When Legend eventually signed a deal with another label, Dash was even more frustrated.

The album closed with the most heartfelt and extensive autobiographical track of the entire album. 'Last Call' had several meanings – just as a bar calls last orders for drinks, a last call for anybody wanting beats from him, as he would be doing much more rapping from now on, and it was also the last song on the album so a chance for everyone involved to get together and celebrate it. And everyone joined in. A drunk-sounding Jay-Z opened proceedings with a hearty "fuck you Kanye first and foremost for making me do this shit", before Kanye raised a toast to himself and his Roc-A-Fella family over a stoned soul sample from Bette Midler's 'Mr Rockefeller' and set about lauding his achievements once more. 'Last Call' also samples the Whatnauts' 1970 track 'She's Gone To Another'. Kanye had originally shopped the beat around, offering it to Jay-Z for *The Black Album* and to Memphis Bleek before deciding to use it himself after it was turned down.

Pointing out that he'd overcome major barriers to his career by reaching this point, where once he was the label's backroom guy and stylistic outsider – "the Rudolph The Red Nosed Reindeer of the Roc" – he rapped about being given his Roc-A-Fella chain onstage with Jay-Z at a show in Chicago and how he lived up to the expectation that came with it by changing the game with his debut album. At a Jay-Z show, Kanye was introduced after 'Heart Of The City', Jay telling him, "You've gotta make an announcement". Kanye told the crowd, "I'm the newest member of the Roc-A-Fella team" while Damon Dash placed the chain over his head. Since Jay hadn't wanted to part with his own chain on the occasion, the chain Kanye was awarded actually belonged to Dash, who still hasn't had it back. In fact, one night Dash had to rescue Kanye from a late-night diner when a group of thugs were threatening to steal his chain. "Nobody expected Kanye to end up on top, they expected that college dropout to drop and then flop", he rhymed as a prediction of the album's success, "was Kanye the most overlooked? Yes sir/Now is Kanye the most overbooked? Yes sir".

His second verse delved further into his story, putting his success down to recreating the Tribe Called Quest feel while putting incongruous rappers together – Mos Def and Freeway or Kweli and Jay-Z – and bridging the gap between disparate strands of rap. He also justified his supposed arrogance at length, claiming it was the only thing that kept him going when every label was turning him down and telling him he couldn't rap while he was shopping around his demo: "I could let these dream killers kill my self-esteem/Or use my arrogance as the steam to power my dreams… I don't listen to the suits behind the desk no more". It was his self-assurance, he argued, that helped him guide his own fate, change the cards that life had dealt him and turned him into the self-declared "Louis Vuitton don" and a combination of those famous hip-hop moguls Damon Dash, Russell Simmons and Puff Daddy. To bring his whole story full circle, he ended the album with the first line he'd written for it – "mayonnaise coloured Benz, I push Miracle Whips", a line he'd first rapped for Jay-Z aged 21, before *The Blueprint*. "The last line you hear on *College Dropout* is the oldest line," he said, "so I call that the beginning."

Finally, for a full eight minutes, Kanye reeled out the story of his career so far, his rambling recollections of his roller-coaster rise from Chicago to Roc-A-Fella adorned with guest lines from the key players – Jay-Z, Hip Hop, 3H and even Donda spoke their words on the piece. "No one did the story stuff on their first album," Roberson said. "No one took use of the journey on leading up to it like, 'I'm finally here, I'm delivering the world my first album, let me give you a snapshot of what it took for me to get to this point.' The outro is genius because he's giving you the premise of the inspiration of these songs."

The outro did, however, spark Kanye's first beef. "I was messin with D-Dot also," he said at one point in his story, "people were like this, started talking about the ghost production, but that's how I got in the game. If it wasn't for that, I wouldn't be here." D-Dot would feel slighted by the idea that Kanye had been his ghost producer. "The beef came in when he started using this term called 'ghost producer' which I hate, which I felt was disrespectful," D-Dot said. "'Ghost' means you're not seen or heard. Not only did he get credit, he got money, he got signed to Roc-A-Fella as a result of it. How were you 'ghost producing'? It'd be co-produced by me and him. 'Ghost' means you get the beat and you do not get a credit, you don't get a cheque, you don't get a piece of publishing. That's 'ghost producing'. I got him back his publishing!

I threatened to fuck him up afterwards. Now you're forcing me to go another direction which I'm pretty known at, I'm known on that side of town. I'm not a thug, I'm not a gangsta, but I roll with those guys. One phone call… now you're gonna play me and say 'ghost producer', I got you back your publishing and introduced you to the people who made you a star."

The beef lasted until Kanye spotted D-Dot while in the Bahamas and ran up to apologise to him. "I didn't know what he was apologising for," D-Dot said. "He said to me 'Yo, they cut you out, I didn't mean to cut you out but they cut you out'. I said 'What you talking about?' They did a *Behind The Music* on Kanye West and he went from No I.D. to Roc-A-Fella. Three years are missing from that story, and that's the D-Dot story and it's not there. I said 'Don't apologise motherfucker, the reason I'm not there is because you've been hating on me since, like I did something to hurt you. From that point on we're straight, we have no beef, but I'm not gonna be the guy running around helping promote the fact that I put you on because you're not showing the reciprocation'… He started eventually showing me some love. I know he's a talented kid, I know he's eccentric too, but he deserves every accolade he gets because he worked hard for it. He was a savage when he was under me."

'Last Call' was one of only two tracks on *The College Dropout* on which Kanye shared production credit. The Bette Midler beat had originally been the work of Evidence from Dilated Peoples, who'd been brought the record by a crate-digging friend called Porse. Evidence passed it to Kanye, who'd produced for Dilated Peoples, in the hope that he'd play it for Jay-Z for possible inclusion on *The Black Album*. "He was puzzled by it," Evidence said, "like telling a kid that he can't have this candy. He said, 'No, I'm the new Mr. Roc-A-Fella.' But he wasn't even out yet. In my mind, I'm like, 'You're pretentious'." The Jay-Z film *Fade To Black* includes footage of Kanye playing the 'Last Call' beat to Jay, but Jay passed, so Kanye convinced Evidence to let him use the beat to prove a point to Jay.

The next thing Evidence heard about the track was when an A&R friend at Capitol Records called him to tell him he was at Larrabee

Studios in Hollywood and could hear Kanye mixing it. Evidence drove over to ask what was going on, claim ownership of the beat and demand an advance; when he arrived he found that the sample hadn't cleared and Kanye had had the whole thing recreated by other musicians, with musicologists on hand to say when it was just different enough to bypass the copyright rules, all of which meant that Kanye's team kept the publishing for the track, a substantial sum. The track was now vastly different from the beat Evidence had originally put together, and stunningly impressive. Kanye pulled Evidence into the recording booth for privacy and started to discuss their approach to press interviews, since he was convinced *The College Dropout* was going to be the biggest rap album of all time – he told him to say that he had made the music and Kanye had put the drums together.

Evidence couldn't help but laugh at this guy claiming to be the saviour of hip-hop, but he agreed, little knowing that he'd be supporting Kanye on tour within months and would one day hang a platinum disc on his wall for 'Last Call', and be handed a Grammy.

And that, too, for an album that *The College Dropout* was never supposed to have been.

CHAPTER SIX

Jesus Walks

When news of the leak broke, Kanye was devastated. He'd put so much of himself into *The College Dropout*: his faith, his life's story and a whole year of intensive work, reworking and remixing the tracks in obsessive detail and arguing over every mix with a team of 30 advisers, producers and rappers. "When it got leaked, everybody was like, 'Who the fuck is responsible for this?'" said GLC, "but all the greats get leaked. If Jay-Z gets leaked, what makes you think you gonna be exempt?"

It was particularly crushing news because, until that point, Kanye's star had been gradually ascending exactly as he'd planned. In 2003 he'd teased the hip-hop world and raised his profile with two mix-tapes, *Get Well Soon…* and *I'm Good*. The first, titled in reference to his recovery from the car crash, featured tracks and freestyles on beats he'd produced or guested on from 50 Cent, Jay-Z, Mos Def, Scarface, Beanie Sigel and more, alongside snippets and teases from *The College Dropout* including 'Jesus Walks' and 'Two Words' and a live track from an Irving Plaza show alongside Talib Kweli and Mos Def, spitting lines from 'Last Call' and 'Breathe In Breathe Out'. The second, *I'm Good*, featured some of the same tracks as well as more of Kanye's productions and guest spots and a few unreleased tracks such as the impressively savvy soul slink of 'Half Price' and several tracks he'd made with John Legend and

Consequence. But, crucially, it ended with 'Through The Wire', the first public appearance of the song.

Unsurprisingly, the track blew up. DJs started picking up on it and spinning it on radio shows and in clubs, excited by the way it managed to bridge the chasm between the underground hip-hop scene and the mainstream. DeRay Davis remembers walking up to a club one night hearing 'Through The Wire' being played inside, yet still being held back by the doormen. "We're standing behind the rope. We're like, 'Yo, for real we standing outside?' I'm like, 'This motherfucker's song is on right now.' They're like, 'That's Kanye? Oh shit!' This is before he was getting carried in the club."

This upsurge in interest in the track wasn't down to any label push; Kanye was still a long way from being any kind of priority artist for Def Jam or Roc-A-Fella, with some of his crew going as far as to say that his label bosses didn't care about him at all until his radio profile took off. Instead, it was groundwork from his inner circle that forged the success of 'Through The Wire'. "From when he got the deal to when his album came out, there was a lot of grinding from us," said Devo. "It wasn't Roc-A-Fella pushing Kanye. We needed a hot record for Roc-A-Fella to put money behind [*College Dropout*]. There needed to be some buzz and momentum. In order for there to be marketing, there needed to be a demand for it. We'd push music to DJs, went to clubs and pushed. 'We' being Kanye, me, Don C, John Monopoly, Gee, Hip Hop doing all this. Kevin Liles, who was Def Jam at the time, took me to the side and said, 'You should know this was all you guys. You did all this. Not Roc-A-Fella, not Def Jam, it was you guys.'"

'Through The Wire' was getting the sort of attention that Kanye always knew it would, cementing his belief that the song should be the first single from the album. But first it needed a video, and at that point Lyor Cohen had yet to free up his budget to promote the album. So Kanye was going to have to pay for the promo clip himself, and they needed a concept, and cheap. "No one at Def Jam or Roc-A-Fella believed in that record," West said. "So I shot a video for it using $35,000 of my own money, and they didn't even bother to clear the sample until after MTV2 added it to rotation."

It was from spotting an Adidas advert in *BlackBook* magazine that Kanye got the idea for framing his life story in Polaroids. "I don't like gettin' ideas from direct shit," he'd say. "I like to pull ideas from all the way over here. Sometimes my vision can't be explained in words, 'cause I couldn't have even told you in words how I envisioned that video ending up."

After Kanye was signed by Roc-A-Fella, one Yasmine Richard from MTV got in touch with Coodie wanting to put together a piece called *You Heard It First* using the footage he'd been shooting of Kanye through the years. At MTV, Coodie was introduced to a motion graphics guy called Chike. "What's so good when I met Chike is that he had a passion to do videos, but he wanted to change the whole video game," Coodie explained. "That got me to be like, 'Oh hell yeah'." So, when Kanye and Coodie came up with the idea of putting his first video on Polaroid, using Coodie's footage, it was Chike who they called to make it happen – they cut together the footage they wanted and then they'd sneak into the MTV building every night saying they were visiting Chike in order to get the video made on MTV equipment. "History was made at MTV, right beneath their nose, and they didn't even realise it," Chike said. "I told my boss at the time like, 'He's not gonna be able to walk in here like this, y'all don't realise really what y'all have sitting in here right now.' He would come up and walk in regular, nobody would say nothing to him, he'd be sitting next to me on the computer the whole day. I was showing him all different types of sites that had cutting edge typography and other visual stuff that I thought he'd be interested in, that's how we bonded." Chike also introduced Kanye to such sites and processes as MK12, fashion site Show Studio, QBN.com and K1OK, all of which Kanye would soak in and use in future projects.

The video included grainy footage of Kanye's time in hospital – surgical procedures and paying his medical bills – as well as shots of his swollen face after the accident and clips of him rapping the song with his jaw wired shut, all framed within Polaroids scrawled with slogans: 'History In The Making, Nov 02' or 'DeRay Stupid As Hell, Nov 02' below a clip of DeRay in a car joking about Kanye rapping despite his vocal restrictions, yelling "without a arm, I spit!" This would become something of a cult, other rappers using it for hooks and mix-tapes, and people still stop Kayne today reciting the catchphrase. As it went on, the footage included shots of Kanye at talent shows as a child, onstage at Power 92 and in the studio with Jay-Z or the kitchen with Donda. His entire life was laid out in the promo, right up to sleeve shots of *Get Well Soon…* and his 'Chaining Day With The Roc', and it ended with Kanye gazing at all of these polaroids of his journey on a pinboard, amazed at how far he'd come and handing a kiss to a poster of Chaka Khan as a thanks for clearing the sample.

It was a moving and revealing video, humanising hip-hop and laying Kanye's journey out for the public to see exactly what he'd been through to get here, opening up an underground world to a mainstream TV audience. Already taking his inspiration from Steve Jobs, he knew that if people knew your story, they were more likely to buy into you, and the unconventional format fitted with his ambitions to shake things up in rap. At first Lyor Cohen wasn't convinced, frustrated that Kanye wasn't rapping in the video, but he got on the phone with Cohen and argued his case. Ultimately, the video was a huge boost to Kanye amongst his team; the premiere party at Jay-Z's 40/40 sports club in New York blew the Def Jam contingent away and they began to take him far more seriously than they had previously. "If we would have wrote a treatment [for that video] they would have shot that down," Coodie said. "They had to see it to understand. Otherwise they'd have said, 'No, Kanye should be rapping at a party, with lots of girls poolside'."

The TV video stations were just as impressed. 'Through The Wire' shot up the play lists, this strange, haunting new slant of hip-hop at its most vulnerable and wounded. It hit number one on the MTV charts on its way to being awarded the Video Of The Year award at the *Source* Hip Hop Awards in 2004, but some around him immediately saw Kanye's success go straight to his head. Watching him interviewed on Rap City when his video was sitting atop the chart, Coodie was surprised when Kanye was asked by Big Tigger where the idea for the video came from and took all of the credit himself, without mentioning Coodie or Chike. 'OK,' Coodie thought, 'something's going south'.

To help boost the profile of 'Through The Wire', Kanye hit the road with Talib Kweli, funding the trip himself, the concept part of his ambition to break down the segregated barriers between different types of hip-hop artists. The authorities couldn't see anything different about him from other crime-flaunting rappers though. On reaching the Canadian border on one leg of the tour, Kanye was pulled aside and asked if he'd ever been arrested for stealing printers from OfficeMax. The charge he'd accepted clearly still hadn't been wiped from his record. Feeling the wrath of his grandfather bearing down from above as he stood humiliated and angry in the customs detention room, he swore to himself he would never, from that point on, accept less than he deserved in life. Whatever he was offered, if he thought he was worth more, he'd demand it.

At the same time, he felt quite the opposite urge. With decent money coming in, he'd splashed out on a lot of accoutrements he wanted – a huge flat screen, a pool table, a Merc, designer clothes by the armful. But even as he was considering buying his first apartment in Manhattan, he was asking his mother how best he could give something back. At first he had the idea of giving 10 per cent of his net income to a random person he felt needed it, but Donda suggested a more rational plan. He should set up a foundation, tax deductible, to help those 50 per cent of black and Latino kids who dropped out of school before graduation each year. Ironically, this advocate of ditching school to follow your dreams decided he wanted to encourage these teenagers to graduate, so he came up with a programme to put studios into school so that musically leaning kids might stay on until graduation to learn to produce music. "In school I could never make music I heard on the radio," he explained. "If kids have opportunities to do that maybe they'll stay in school."

Inspired by the Hoop Dreams project which encouraged schoolkids who hoped to become basketball players, Kanye's programme was called Loop Dreams, the first project from the new Kanye West Foundation that he created alongside Miki Woodard from Creative Artists Agency and his aunt Beverley Williams, who retired from her teaching job to help run the scheme. The Kanye West Foundation website carried a message from Kanye explaining his thinking behind the project. "For as long as I can remember, I have dreamed of making a substantial impact on the music world," it read. "Hard work and other values such as commitment, respect, discipline, integrity and responsibility conspired to drive me towards my dream. Over the past few years, I have had the opportunity to meet hundreds of young people across this land, and contrary to popular belief, they also have goals and dreams. Consequently, I have concluded that prospering in the world of music is only a piece of what I really want to accomplish. So I was encouraged – in fact, driven – to found and develop Loop Dreams, the first initiative of the Kanye West Foundation. This rap-writing and music-production program is designed to involve students in learning through a hands-on curriculum we believe will motivate and compel them to stay in school and graduate. Loop Dreams is an unprecedented approach to engaging students in not only the study of hip-hop and the way it can be used to better our world, but in the development of habits of mind that are critical to student success no matter what path they ultimately choose to follow. I fervently believe that, as someone has said before, 'when you change the way you look at things, the things you look at change'. I want to help change the way young people look at school and, hence, the way they look at their futures."

In the fall of 2003, Loop Dreams launched at Accelerated School in South Central LA as a one-semester pilot project. Seventy-five eighth grade students signed up and took Loop Dreams classes daily, where they were taught about the history, personalities and culture of rap, both positive and negative lyrics, how to create loops and beats and forge their own careers in the music industry. The classes were a roaring success, helping students' literacy and self-worth as well as their production skills, and Loop Dreams would continue and expand, with Kanye putting half a million dollars into the scheme up to 2007.★

★ This wouldn't be Kanye's only charitable contribution. He donated heavily to the Katrina fund in the wake of the disaster in New Orleans and to Tiffany Persons' Shine On Sierra Leone fund to aid the children affected by the Sierra Leone diamond mines, after Tiffany asked him personally for a contribution. He would also play shows in aid of colon cancer.

"I like simple ideas," he'd later say of the project. "I thought, 'Why did I go to school?' I didn't go for math class, I went for gym, for lunch, for art. Back then people used to love to play basketball, everybody had hoop dreams. Nowadays the average student wants to be a rapper or video director or producer or something like that more than playing basketball. So why not start a curriculum that teaches music production? Come on, get with the times. People are so behind. There's poetry classes, but why aren't there rap curriculums? It takes people like myself to stand up and say this is part of our culture, why not use it to educate."

When Kanye would later perform special shows at schools and colleges to promote the scheme, he'd take the opportunity to encourage the students not to follow his example and drop out. "It is true you can be successful without [college]," he'd say, "but this is a hard world, a real world, and you want every advantage you can have. I would suggest to people to do all that you can. When I dropped out of school I had worked in the music industry and had cheques cut in my name from record labels and had a record deal on the table, and when I wasn't successful and Columbia said, 'We'll call you,' I had to go back and work a telemarketing job, go back to the real world, and that's how life is. Life is hard. Take advantage of your opportunities."

Donda was proud that one of his first thoughts as his star ascended was of helping others from his success, particularly because as a youth and only child he never had to share anything and failed to bond very well with others.

But Kanye was about to bond with an entire hip-hop nation.

★ ★ ★

'Through The Wire' hit the streets on September 30, 2003. The following night, Kanye played a launch show at SOB's in New York. "The night Kanye played SOB's," said Common, "I knew that hip-hop was about to change. He was the first artist to bring together the backpack crowd along with the Roc-A-Fella ballers. I remember seeing people throwing up the Roc, but it was all underground hip-hop backpackers doing it. That album, he bridged the gap."

"I was like, 'Man, hip-hop is back again'," Common continued. "It felt so good that it was coming through this brother. I'm honoured to be on his album and geeked what the brother is bringing to hip-hop. I don't think nobody is coming with beats and rhymes, putting that package together like this right now." And from that show onwards, as Coodie would put it, "He was bona fide, he was popping. It was full-on Kanye season."

The critics frothed. "As riveting and moving as everyone says it is," wrote PopMatters, "[it] may be the album's most startling personal horror story (though it's also a song of hope and gratitude)." "A daring way to introduce himself to the masses *as an MC,*" said Allmusic's Andy Kellman, "[he] couldn't have forged his dual status as underdog and champion any better… [despite his] inevitable slur, his words ring loud and clear." "A wounded hero beating the odds," said *The New York Times*, "['Through The Wire'] gave him a chance to prove that he was the exception to the rule that producers can't rap", while *Vibe* magazine claimed "West's sideways approach to music making stands out… [the] raw, teeth-clenching narrative falls in line with his gut-wrenching soul beats."

The public were just as enthused. 'Through The Wire' debuted at Number 94 on the *Billboard* Hot 100, a modest arrival but not the end of the track's lifespan. Over the next six months, as Kanye's profile, celebrity and hip-hop standing rose and the album campaign kicked in in earnest, it would rise with him, eventually hitting number 15 and staying there for a full five weeks. In the Hot Hip-Hop/R&B Singles chart it made number eight, number four on the Hot Rap Tracks chart and number one on MTV2. In the UK, it made number nine.

But that would all be down to the monumental success of Kanye's next single.

A matter of weeks after 'Through The Wire' started making its modest waves, Twista released his version of 'Slow Jamz', and the world lit up. No-one really expected it to take off the way it did – Twista wasn't particularly hot at the time and Kanye had produced a lot of records that hadn't automatically become big because his name was attached. Kanye had been coming up with plenty of excuses as to why it shouldn't be the first song to emerge from his album; it was too slow, he'd argue, or it didn't have a major hook. But 'Slow Jamz' struck a national nerve. "That song was definitely the biggest thing that happened in my career," Twista admitted. "It didn't hit me until we got to a couple of radio stations and they was telling me how 'Slow Jamz' was getting thousands of spins and people were calling about it."

Released on October 21 with Twista's version of the song upfront and Kanye's as the B-side, 'Slow Jamz' swept like a tsunami through the airwaves, and the video hit heavy rotation hard too. A crib party with Jamie Foxx as the loverman DJ, it saw Aisha Tyler guesting as a friend of Kanye's who takes all of these serious players for a ride at poker. "I was very specific that I'm not a video vixen," she explained. "Girls in hip-hop videos are accessories and I didn't want to be an accessory, I didn't want to come in and drop anything down or back anything up… He was like, 'Well why don't we play cards and we'll let you win.' I was actually on the celebrity poker tour at that time, so it fit me."

By the time Kanye flew back to Oklahoma for Christmas 2003, he had much to shout about. His second single was causing a storm on radio and he had an entire album to play to his family. He was particularly interested in playing 'Jesus Walks' to his aunt Shirlie, who'd directed several church choirs. As his cousins waited in the car for Kanye to go to the mall, Shirlie listened intently to the track, and declared herself deeply moved. He'd made a record that could touch every generation.

So when the album leaked, months ahead of its scheduled date, Kanye felt violated, frustrated and abused. His meticulous working techniques and perfectionism had seen the release date pushed back twice already, from August 2003 to October and then to January 2004. And now, he vowed, he was going to have to revisit it, rework it, make it a different beast entirely to the one that the pirates had given out already – otherwise, why would anyone buy a record they already had for nothing?

"Kanye was like, 'OK, I'm just going to make the album better'," GLC said. "'I'mma put strings on some shit, have choirs come in. I'mma switch up verses. I'mma make the drums sound stronger.' He went in and refined his whole album. At that point a person usually panics.

Kanye just redid shit." "He remixed and remastered the album several times," added Monopoly. "He's so meticulous. His ears work like he's on some daredevil super shit. He remixed his album like two or three times. He's really into his craft. He would [pay] out of his pocket for certain things, like orchestras."

The original 2003 version of *The College Dropout* was a significantly different entity to the one which eventually came out. It included no 'We Don't Care', no 'Spaceship', no 'School Spirit', no 'Get Em High' or 'Last Call'. These songs, and the skits, were put in to replace the tracks Kanye decided to drop after the leak. He ditched 'The Good, The Bad, The Ugly', giving this ghetto speed-soul groover to its guest rapper Consequence – and fair play too, since Consequence exhibited some masterful wordplay on his verses, riffing on what was good, bad and ugly about American life. He cut 'Keep The Receipt', an intriguing and innovatively spooky Eastern-themed ego track about Kanye's hit-making skills, featuring ODB under the name Dirt McGirt, which he took when he signed to Roc-A-Fella, and a hook built from an Auto-Tuned vocal wail manipulated to sound like a snake-charmer's flute.

Out went 'Heavy Hitters', a sweetly delicate music box piano piece with classical overtones and an itchy click beat over which Kanye gloated once more about his chart success, his vastly improved income and fooling the world into thinking he was making a compilation when "I was really making myself they competition". 'My Way' hit the cutting room floor too, a gospel-style sway constructed from Irene Reid's cover of Paul Anka's much-recorded standard around which Kanye wove his own tribute to his talent, his ways with a more sentimental branch of rap – "When you walk straight, niggas tend to look at you sideways," he rapped – and belief in himself – "I took the road less travelled, the unbeaten path/I've been beatin' but never broken through the darkest past" – but also to the ghetto kids surviving by getting into the crack game. 'My Way' also includes a comic twist where Kanye accuses his hometown hip-hop critics of being "a little arrogant with all your comparisons" while, in the very next line, boasting that he's got more gold and platinum discs than any rapper ever to come from Chicago. A different take on 'Jesus Walks' was swapped in and, finally, he sliced off the final track, 'Home', his tribute to Chicago that had first appeared on his demo and would stick by him, unreleased, for some years yet.

"It's so much that goes into one of these records," Kanye explained to MTV of his motivations to rework the album. "It's not contrived and it's not a copy of anything. It's also so from the heart, and I feel so connected with it. When it comes out, I feel people are going to be connected with it. I looked at it as a kid wanting to open up their Christmas presents too early."

It was in Kanye's nature to make the best art he possibly could, to refuse to be beaten by the bootleggers and turn a negative positive, a disaster into a triumph. The album he finally delivered was a far better one than he'd originally put together, a work that somehow married sensitivity, rampant ego, invention, familial love, faith, sex, brotherhood and aspiration in a way no school class could ever teach. A gleaming example of the benefits of taking the path that's right for you rather than the one expected, it was an education in itself.

Kanye was rightfully proud of the record he'd made. In Sony Studios in New York, he called together a host of journalists, tastemakers, rappers and radio execs, stood on a table and made an impassioned speech. "I'm asking you all, I'm begging you all," he said, "if y'all feel this is a zero, give it a zero. If you feel like it is a five, give it a five. If y'all believe that this is the future, which is what I believe... If y'all feel like this is what the game needs right now, if y'all feel that this anticipation... I delivered what y'all been waiting for, then let it... what's the word? Reciprocate? I dropped out of college, can I have a thesaurus?... I'm asking you all not to let the future pass you by and be a part of history, 'cause this is history in the making, man." He then played the assembled media congregation tracks from the record, dancing and singing along, punching his chest and screaming out his raps, even stopped the track if he saw someone in the room that he thought wasn't feeling it, and restarting it to be sure they were concentrating fully. His determination to prove himself the next evolution in rap was infectious, and the quotes he gave to the press were full of Pentecostal fire. "I'm a pretty smart dude," he said, "I knew that if I could rap even anywhere near the calibre of my beats, I would kill the game. Murder the game... I try to see how I can express things in my life that other people will relate to and feel like, 'Man, I'm glad that somebody said that.' There are so many people that vent through other stuff other than shootin'."

His display would immediately have interviewers asking him about his arrogance. "Would it be arrogance or confidence?" he replied. "Because I'm outspoken? Or because I feel confident? I feel like I have the right to tell you. My thing is, I just like to debate. I really like my raps ... But it's not from arrogance, it's from me just debating and wanting to get my point across. Like, 'You all need to understand.' Any situation I'm in, I just wanna stand out... I think I've got a lot of growing to do. I've got a lot of energy. I'm growing and growing every day, and I'm finding out ways to wear my success with more dignity. The younger you are, the newer your money is, the more ignorant you're gonna act. I need to learn and have the opportunity to be around people like Quincy Jones and Oprah Winfrey... He consults me about handling fame, about shutting down malls and dealing with so many people pulling at you. Different moves, what records to go to next. Some of the stuff I wouldn't even put it on the air. It's stuff for me to personally have in my mind. 'Cause if I give away the secrets, people can go around it."

"I don't see what's wrong with going in and saying, 'I'm going to sell three million records'," he said. "Not even saying 'I want to' but 'I'm going to'! What if someone was like, 'I'm going to finish school'? 'You're kind of arrogant for that!' What if it was just as hard for that person to finish school as for me to sell three million records? But in order to give themselves that confidence, they say, 'I am going to do it!' And people turn around and say they're arrogant. Now they even doubting them. They're saying, first of all, you can't do it. And secondly, your method to build your esteem up so that you have something to believe in and to set your goals, your methods are wrong also. So they bashing you on both ends. It's basically like saying, 'Fuck you! You have to be a fucking loser!' You can't believe that there is something greater for you out there. You can never believe that you'll be performing for 20,000 people every night. Why?! Why you?! Who the FUCK are you to think you can have anything in life? And if you say, I am going to do it. I will sell three mill. I will be the biggest artist. You ain't NEVER seen the likes of me. NEVER seen nobody like me in front of you. NOBODY's going to do what I'm a do. Oh, he's so arrogant! He has dreams. Why the fuck should he dream? And if he does dream, don't let him say it loud!"

His friends and work associates would back up his declarations of brilliance. Alicia Keys' 'You Don't Know My Name', produced by Kanye, was then enjoying a 15-week run in the *Billboard* Top 10 and sat at number one on the Hot R&B/Hip-Hop Songs. "We've heard him from a production standpoint for a minute, and he's always come through in a major way, but he really has crazy rhyme skills," Keys said of Kanye. "The way he puts his thoughts together, the way he puts everything in this mixture, it's something everybody can feel… [When] we worked together on 'You Don't Know My Name' we'd be in the middle of doing something and he'd break out and start rhyming. This is how passionate he is about what he does. He'd be like, 'Feel me on this,' and start putting together this idea he's working on. That's what I love about him. You really feel the genuine love from him."

Writers such as MTV's Shaheem Reid would argue that Kanye's significance was that he rapped about the frustrations of everyday life and working low-paid retail jobs in an age when everyone else was trying to copy G-Unit's murderous thug attitude, and *Vibe* would argue that he was becoming influential in shifting the image of rappers, as well as Afro-American men in general, from that of the gangster with "limited life options as well as limited life" to something more sensitive, conflicted and mysterious. "I'm glad to be able to give people that option," Kanye said. "But I'd like people to have this alternative, even if it isn't me."

It was an approach that was certainly paying dividends. When Alicia Keys' stay at number one on the R&B/Hip-Hop chart finally ended, it was 'Slow Jamz' that replaced it, on its way to reaching number one on the *Billboard* Hot 100 chart proper.

Suddenly Kanye was the phenomenon he'd always expected.

"It's all a matter of a turning tide," he said, somewhat modestly, of his grasp on the hip-hop zeitgeist. "Compared to movies, there's a time of mad gangsta movies, then it's comedies, then it's family films, then it's back to gangsta flicks, [because] we missed the gangsta flicks. I'm doing this little wave [of music], it's going to make people fiend for good gangsta music again after my wave is waving goodbye. I realise that time will happen. I enjoy it and I realise that it's all entertainment."

The slam-dunk smash hit of 'Slow Jamz' was a development that left Roberson both overjoyed and a little terrified. He'd taken a song from the first act he'd ever managed and given it to an artist who was essentially his day job, and it was a smash, a US number one, a number three in the UK and Top 10 in Belgium and New Zealand. It was also helping 'Through The Wire' pick up in sales. But because of the deal, Twista's album was due out first, two weeks before Kanye's, and would now get the biggest lift from the song's success. Twista's *Kamikaze* album sold a mammoth 312,000 copies in its first week, which put Roberson in a tough spot. It would have been devastating for Kanye's album to come out two weeks later and sell half as many on the back of Kanye's song. "I'm shitting bricks," he admitted, "I'm saying an unlimited amount of prayers… You can imagine my life as I was going through it. Those things mess you up mentally."

Much to Roberson's relief, *The College Dropout* crushed Twista's album. The press rose as one to praise it. "2004's first great hip-hop album," wrote Kelefa Sanneh of *The New York Times*. "One of those wonderful crossover albums that appeal to a huge audience without sacrificing a shred of integrity," said Nathan Rabin of The A.V. Club, hailing its "substance, social commentary, righteous anger, ornery humanism [and] dark humour". *Stylus* magazine claimed that Kanye "subverts cliches from both sides of the hip-hop divide" by "trying to reflect the entire spectrum of hip-hop and black experience, looking for solace and salvation in the traditional safehouses of church and family".

Several critics focused on Kanye's move away from the gangsta cliché. "Not only does [West] create a unique role model, that role model is dangerous," wrote Robert Christgau of *The Village Voice*, "his arguments against education are as market-targeted as other rappers' arguments for thug life", while *Entertainment Weekly*'s Michael Endelman wrote, "West delivers the goods with a disarming mix of confessional honesty and sarcastic humour, earnest idealism and big-pimping materialism. In a scene still dominated by authenticity battles and gangsta posturing, he's a middle-class, politically conscious, post-thug, bourgeois rapper – and that's nothing to be ashamed of."

Even though Pitchfork's review called the record "flawed, overlong, hypocritical, egotistical", it concluded that it was "[an] altogether terrific album" and awarded it a notable 8.2 out of 10. But more troubling to Kanye was *Vibe*'s review. "Dog, *Vibe* only gave my album a four," he said to the magazine's music editor during an argument over whether Kanye should give the magazine an interview for a non-cover feature. "I know my shit is better than a four. A horrible album with just 'Jesus Walks' on it is a four! C'mon dog, the demo version was a five! You need to rate it again, but you'll have to create a new rating system… It's like this, by not giving my album a classic rating, you diminish your magazine's credibility. And that's real. Right now, I feel like I deserve a cover and that doing another feature will just hurt my chances at a cover later. I don't want you to be talkin' about giving me a cover in three months, and then have you ask me if I stole a printer from OfficeMax. You feel me?"

Some years later, noting the contradictions in the album – the way Kanye used the record to express fundamental disgust with his own materialism, seeing it as a sign of insecurity and powerlessness, for example – *Slate* magazine would look back at the record as an instant game-changer, Kanye emerging racked with the juxtaposed forces of arrogance and self-doubt at a time when mainstream rappers simply weren't meant to appear vulnerable, paving the way for the likes of Kid Cudi and Drake. Meanwhile, *Vibe*'s music editor John Kennedy would sum up the record's import. "[Its] real message was a middle finger at societal norms. Be you. Do it your way… For every posturing moment there's a self-aware or self-deprecating one to balance it out. It taught many of us that it's OK to be yourself. Whether you're a God-fearing man who enjoys threesomes or a Louis Vuitton mannequin with a knack for wholesome spoken word poetry."

The public certainly declared *The College Dropout* a five star record. With its cuddly cover of Kanye dressed as a college mascot called the Dropout Bear, the sleeve was put together by Roc-A-Fella's in-house artwork designer Eric Duvauchelle, chosen from pictures Kanye had already taken of himself dressed as the Dropout Bear. Drawn to the bleachers photo due to the way it captured the loneliness that encapsulated many people's experience of school, Duvauchelle bordered the picture with gold ornaments from a book of 16th century illustrations to add elegance, the inner booklet featuring pictures of the album's guests in a college yearbook style. Record-buyers from across the spectrum snapped up 441,000 copies of the album in the first week after its February 10 release, shooting it to number two on the *Billboard* chart and number one on the R&B/Hip-Hop chart. Kanye had estimated that 450,000 people would buy his record, a figure he reached by adding together 150,000 backpackers, 150,000 college kids, 100,000 women and 50,000 Roc-A-Fella fans. His mother, who'd never heard the whole thing in full before, actually bought 10 copies at a local Best Buy store and listened to it loud on her car speakers in the parking lot, glowing with pride at his religious declarations on 'Jesus Walks', wanting to shout out of the window at passers-by that her son had made this record. All her concerns about his future and his quitting school instantly evaporated, and a few days later she went back and bought more.

The College Dropout would go on to sell almost 3.5 million copies worldwide and garner numerous press plaudits – Album Of The Year in *Rolling Stone* and *Spin*, one of the top 100 albums of all time according to *Time*, the fourth best album of the past 25 years and the best album of the decade according to *Entertainment Weekly*. "It was one of the most hip-hop albums in a while," said Kanye, explaining the record's across-the-range appeal, "but one of the most pop albums at the same time. So it kind of broke the barrier of people saying that hip-hop wasn't pop, because pop has a negative connotation. But pop just means 'popular' – Michael Jackson was pop… The album has so many messages, broke so many walls. The stigma of the rapper-producer. The Chicago hip-hop artist. The hip-hop artist. What hip-hop artists talk about. How hip-hop artists dress. The death of the compilation producer album. The rebirth of… the real."

With the huge sales of *The College Dropout*, Kanye's career was on autopilot. "That gave confidence to Def Jam and Roc-A-Fella to push

Kanye all the way," said No I.D., "that was the moment we knew the machine was behind him and there was no question it was gonna work."

The album would have a huge impact on the careers of virtually everyone who worked on it. Tony Williams would eventually release a solo album, far later in life than he could have expected to. GLC was exposed to a huge national audience and got five offers of record deals from his one verse on 'Spaceship', with fans across the world accosting him in tears, telling him that they'd lost a parent too, or just wanting to show their appreciation. "I always was a popular guy, I always had girls competing for my affection," he said. "But after that 'Spaceship' verse, my lady rate went through the roof! And I embraced it!"

John Legend was inundated with label offers too, while Plain Pat was promoted to A&R at Def Jam after Kanye demanded he get the job. Even DeRay Davis felt the benefits when, a few years later, Kanye wandered up and handed him what he'd describe as "a big-ass bulk of money" for his work on the skits, enough to buy a decent car. J Ivy would tell of college professors who'd told him they were teaching his work in classes, and of people who'd showed him his verse tattoo'd on their arms. Consequence saw a swift turnaround from the people who were previously mocking him for getting involved with Kanye. "At first people were like, 'Consequence, why you fucking with him? He sucks'," he said. "I was like, 'Nah he don't suck. I promise you he don't suck.' The album dropped and the same motherfuckers is now on his dick. Like, 'I remember you straight fronted on that nigga'… The landscape of music got hit with an uppercut… In this game, nothing sparks more interest than a major release that's successful." The record even changed Donda's life; after 31 years she dropped out of Chicago State herself to work for Kanye full-time.

And Kanye's life would certainly never be the same again. "I'll never be able to relive making the first album. I'll never be able to relive being able to walk through the airport and nobody knows who I am."

He was, after all, changing both music and lives. "The album got people through school, through depression, through death in the family, through relationships, through bad jobs, through career decisions," said J Ivy. "People said that they were considering taking their lives but they heard my verse and they reconsidered committing suicide. It called forth a huge ripple effect. So many artists came after it were inspired. So many people were inspired to write poetry, so many rappers were inspired to rap, so many producers were inspired to produce and those who were doing it already were inspired to do it better. Every song did something to your spirit, and the world came around it collectively… It was the perfect medium of street and conscious. It was backpack but it was hood."

"It came from frustration because no one was paying him attention," GLC said. "That's why it was so good. He came from an angle that wasn't really in. It wasn't really cool to be an emotional male in hip-hop. It was a time of 50 Cent. Gangsta rap was doing what it was doing. He had to separate himself from the status quo. I believe he succeeded by going to that extreme, being 'I am the supreme, emotional male who don't take no shit.' He was the rapper who had a Mercedes-Benz and a backpack. He showed he was about the culture, but also liked real expensive shit too."

"There's pre and post-*College Dropout*," Devo Springsteen agreed. "There are a few kind of tribes within [the rap] demographic. You're a gangster, a baller, a backpacker or you're a seller. If you're going to rap, which of the lanes are you coming from? I think with Kanye, his approach brought in different types of influences away from these categories. I can be from the suburbs, Midwest, I can wear Polo shirts and I am still hip-hop. As long as you're honest about yourself, you're hip-hop. I think most rappers that come now since then are post-Kanye."

When Kanye's colleagues talk about *The College Dropout* they describe it as a "tipping point of rap", "ground-breaking" and a record driven by Kanye's determination to prove himself against all the odds and obstacles. But the one word that comes up again and again is 'classic'. And few records so deserve the accolade.

★ ★ ★

Meanwhile, the album campaign continued apace. On March 16 Kanye hit the road on the School Spirit Tour to support the album, opening at Virginia Tech University and crossing the country over the next two months. Playing 34 dates, the tour swept through the likes of Washington DC's 9:30 Club,

Rhode Island College, the Rave club in Milwaukee and Seattle's Showbox on its way to three nights at LA's House Of Blues. From there Kanye headed back East, through Vegas, Phoenix, Denver and Indianapolis towards New York, Philadelphia and three homecoming shows at Chicago's House Of Blues alongside Dilated Peoples, climaxing on May 5. Fans spoke of sensational sets, with onstage guests including Jay-Z and previews of coming classics such as 'Hey Mama'. Playing his songs to rapturous crowds, he saw first-hand the effect his record was having on people, and the wide-reaching range of stars who wanted to get involved with it. At a gig at Webster Hall, Coodie and J Ivy convinced actor and comedian Dave Chappelle to wear the Dropout Bear costume and wander amongst the crowd.

His fantasy of being unable to walk through airports unrecognised wasn't quite coming true yet though. In one airport in Milwaukee a woman noticing Kanye surrounded by reporters and cameras, asked him if he was local. He told her he was heading off to a radio show and she asked him if he was a musician. "You don't have a TV?" he asked, grinning at the media reps. "I just figured if you had a TV you'd know who I was. 'Through The Wire' is my song. It was the number one video on MTV2 last year. You might have seen it." She hadn't but she did let on that she was related to Oprah Winfrey, and suddenly the self-promoting Kanye leapt back to the fore – he filled the woman in in detail about his number one productions and 'Slow Jamz' and urged her to lean on Oprah to get him on the programme.

Just two weeks after *The College Dropout* hit stores, Kanye's second official single was released – 'All Falls Down', accompanied by a video directed by Chris Milk and featuring Damon's cousin Stacy Dash as well as guest vocalist Syleena Johnson. The video, from Kanye's eye view, followed Kanye and a gold-digging girlfriend played by Dash riding up to Ontario International Airport in a limo, and their journey through the airport, from having their tickets checked by Johnson, playing a member of the airline staff★, to Kanye getting his pink polo shirt sprayed

★ Johnson was also supposed to appear at the end of the video alongside Common but since no-one said anything to her about it on the day, she simply got changed and left.

with mustard by a passing child. Hitting difficulties at security when his high-end chain and watch keep setting off the metal detectors, Kanye decided to save time by lying on the conveyor belt and feeding himself through the x-ray machine, rapping as a skeleton as he travelled through. Passing Common, GLC and Consequence as they raced for the gate, the video ended with Dash in tears as she flew away.

The video made a point of showing off Kanye's preppy fashions. "I had a style that was over-the-top, overly expressive, and it forced me to just lay back and be a little cooler," he said. "One of the problems with being a bubbling source of creativity – it's like I'm bubbling in a laboratory, and if you don't put a cap on it, at one point it will, like, break the glass. If I can hone that... then I have, like, nuclear power, like a superhero, like Cyclops when he puts his glasses on."

Damon Dash would claim that Kanye's "fly" style was something he'd learnt from being around him and others. "[The Pink polo] wasn't nothing to me because Cam was already wearing pink and we was already wearing Polos. That's the kind of pressure I used to put on him, be like, 'Yo, football jerseys and Polo is basic… You got to go ahead and show me something different if you want to impress me on a fashion level.' Him and Just Blaze, they didn't come fly. They became fly after they were around things that educated them and they had enough wherewithal based on what they were doing to buy shit. But they had to be educated. He always wanted to be doing things outside of the urban, that's kind of like how I am."

The video would earn four nominations at the VMA awards, including Breakthrough Video and Best New Artist In A Video, and with its help 'All Falls Down' would peak at number seven in the *Billboard* chart and number 10 in the UK. And it continued Kanye's growing obsession with the visual side of his work. His next single, 'Jesus Walks', would go through three videos in all. The first was directed by Michael Haussman, although Kanye had originally wanted Hype Williams but Haussman got the job after it emerged that Jay-Z was planning to use Williams for his '99 Problems' video. With a budget of $650,000, it featured Kanye as a preacher in a church, a gospel choir swaying along in the balcony as his stirring sermon summons angels to help drunks, prostitutes and shot-down gang members. Intercut with footage of riots and natural disasters, the rescued are drawn to Kanye's pulpit, ready to be properly saved.

Despite its hefty budget, Kanye didn't feel that the video properly captured the essence of what he was trying to get across with the song, so he convinced Damon Dash to fund a second clip to the tune of another $500,000. Directed by Chris Milk, the second version was rather more complex and metaphorical. Opening on a white-clad Deep South chain gang marching to their guard's barked orders, it focused on Kanye performing in a flame-filled corridor beneath a flickering neon halo, interspersed with monochrome footage of a prisoner being singled out for punishment by the prison guards, hoiked into Christ poses before being beaten to the ground. The symbolism of the downtrodden and subjugated black American male was writ large, juxtaposed against the innocence of skipping girls singing the hook line; salvation, went the message, came not just from religion but from within yourself.

Further imagery poured from the screen: classical religious paintings, doves of peace flocking out of a boot full of cocaine, a Klan member dragging a burning cross up a hill. As Milk would explain, his concept was to highlight the duality of man by merging hateful characters with Biblical imagery to make the point that Jesus is even with the worst of us. Of the Klan member who lights his cross on top of the mountain, watches it tumble to the bottom and rushes to carry it back up again, still alight, Milk explained: "His hate is so all-consuming that he tries to carry the burning cross back up the mountain. That's the physical manifestation of his hate, and he wants it to get to the top of the mountain for the world to see. He's so blinded by his hate that he doesn't [consider that his robe will burn]. But God forgives him and causes it to rain, therefore extinguishing [the fire], and that's a sort of baptism; washing away his sins. I doubt anyone's got all that, but it's nice to at least make an attempt to build in some layers. I know a lot of it is going to be lost in the translation of just being a music video, but the song is so deep and powerful it necessitates going the extra step with the visual metaphors."

The video certainly had the layers of meaning that Kanye was looking for. But he felt the song still needed something a little more literal. With

$40,000 from his own pocket he funded a third video from Coodie and Channel Zero's Chike Ozah, co-directed by himself, this time a montage of grainy black-and-white footage recorded around Chicago in which Kanye grabs some money from his dresser and walks the streets literally accompanied by Jesus. (Kanye originally wanted Dave Chappelle to play Jesus in the third video but it didn't come to pass.) Together they perform miracles, Jesus filling an empty fridge and curing a man on crutches so that he can dance along. Ultimately, Kanye and Jesus find themselves in a Pentecostal church, where Kanye takes to the pulpit for a passionate rap sermon while a – now black – Jesus is seen dancing with children.

Disowning none of the videos, Kanye premiered all three at the Tribeca Cinemas on June 21, telling the assembled media "That song evokes so much emotion, and four minutes of imagery limits the ideas that you're supposed to give for the songs, so I had to do three." Of the three, it would be the third version that premiered on MTV.com on June 23 but the second that would be the most garlanded. It received nominations for Video Of The Year at the 2005 VMA Awards and BET Awards, picking up the BET award and the VMA for Best Male Video.

The single itself came heavily hyped too. Critics were amazed that such a religious song was getting radio play. "On 'Jesus Walks' Kanye proclaims his devotion to Jesus as seriously as the most devotional hymn singer would," wrote PopMatters, "while illustrating the way he falls in and out of what he perceives as the good path to follow. 'I wanna talk to God but I'm afraid 'cause we ain't spoke in so long,' he confesses, but then he goes ahead and asks us all to join him in that conversation, to push the song onto radio and push the divine into the heart of public dialogue. Extra dimensions are added to the song by the intense, cinematic presence it has, with all of the drama of a gangster film's climactic scenes, and by a Curtis Mayfield drop that makes the song ripe for a study of intertextuality."

"Kanye makes his spiritual toil sound like triumph thanks to martial drums and a little gospel choir fervour, sounding a clarion call of salvation to all would-be doubters and haters," said Josh Love at *Stylus*. "He swears that he's not trying to 'convert atheists into believers', but

153

listening to *The College Dropout* might just convince you that Kanye West is the Sound City's Second Coming."

Some of Kanye's colleagues were just as surprised at the radio's acceptance of the track. Common remembers hearing 'Jesus Walks' on Hot 97. "It's not like… he got played at a gospel station," he said. "The song was on Hot 97. That's ground-breaking in itself because in hip-hop we definitely talk spirituality, but most of the time it comes from an Islamic perspective because you had the Five-Percent Nation. It wasn't even like people talking about Christianity was the coolest aspect of hip-hop. I really appreciated that he made that cool. That's a testament to his talent, how he can make anything [accessible] for the average person. But it's a testament to hip-hop too, like if you put it in the right form, people can appreciate almost anything you talk about."

In interviews, Kanye would link the theme of the song back to his childhood. "My father had me going to church three times a week," he said. "Had me going to church so much that I didn't want to go no more. I was born into it. And all I did, when it came time to do my album, was just not deny it. The thing is that 'Jesus Walks' is not so new in hip-hop. It's not that new. It's just that the beat it's on this time is a club banger. Usually people don't make them God songs over beats like that." And when asked about religion, which he was regularly as a result of the track, he would also reference his car crash. "I think that God spared my life to make music and to help people, to always put out positive energy," he said. "One of the reasons why I don't have beef with any rapper or with anybody is because of the positive energy I put out. So even if I hold myself up, I'm not putting anybody else down."

His management, on the other hand, could see the issues behind the scenes. After the countless discussions they'd had about waiting for the right time to release the track, once Kanye was big and established enough to get a song about Jesus onto regular rotation, they could clearly see radio's reluctance to play it as much as Kanye's previous songs. Yet John Monopoly saw the influence the track was having within the industry. Then working at Jive Records, 50 Cent's representative came into his office to insist he was going to get 50 on the remix.

Hip Hop was also pointedly aware that Kanye knew he could do better. When the Game's *The Documentary* album came out around the same time it sold twice what Kanye sold with *The College Dropout*. Despite being more culturally significant, Kanye knew he could do more, knew he was under-performing compared to other major rappers who were selling four million copies of their albums. And he wouldn't rest until he was the biggest player in the game.

'Jesus Walks' certainly pushed him further in the right direction. Released on May 25, it would enter the *Billboard* chart at 68 and climb to number 11 by mid-July, selling half a million copies and, come the end of the year, declared amongst the best tracks of 2004 by *The Village Voice*, *Rolling Stone* and *Blender*. The gospel Stellar Awards even considered short-listing *The College Dropout* thanks to 'Jesus Walks' and many religious commentators would credit it with bridging the gap between rap and the church; ministries began using hip-hop in services and Mase, the rapper turned pastor, even came out of retirement to add a guest verse to the official remix. Suddenly, Kanye was hip-hop's most prominent missionary.

What the church would have made of the follow-up single, 'The New Workout Plan', however, is unrecorded. This sex-obsessed gym bunny track needed a suitably comedy video, so Kanye flew to Miami with director Little X with a treatment that Plain Pat would call "goofy" and "stupid-ass" but which had Roberson on the floor in stitches. "That video goes back to the comedy of Kanye West," he said, "having that lightheartedness. He made sure to always have that throughout the project… We were having conversations about who would make sense to be in the video, but someone outside the box that would be entertaining. It was Kanye's idea to have Anna Nicole Smith. Kanye was convinced about it being her and whenever Kanye is convinced then there ain't no plan B. He was like, 'Yo man, you got to find her.' And I did and she was genuinely on board for it."

She wasn't alone. The video would also feature cameos from GLC, John Legend, author and musician Fonzworth Bentley, glamour model Vida Guerra and actress Tracee Ellis Ross, daughter of Diana Ross. Together they formed the cartoonish exercise instructors in this spoof advert for Kanye's workout tape, leading a crowd of girls around a foam rubber maze on the promise of bagging themselves a baller, or helping them with their training regimes as slogans popped and rolled across the screen – 'results vary, don't get your hopes up' – and the guests gave impassioned testimonials to the wonders of the workout. Essentially throwaway, it certainly wouldn't have the impact of the 'Jesus Walks' videos – 'The New Workout Plan', on its August 31 release, would fail to bother the *Billboard* chart, failing to get anywhere other than the R&B chart, and then only hitting number 59.

But by August, Kanye's life was such a whirlwind he wouldn't have much time to concern himself too much with chart positions.

★ ★ ★

"I'm sorry to bother you right now," the nurses would say, "but would you sign this T-shirt?"

Ludacris was right. Even sitting in the waiting room outside his grandmother's hospital room surrounded by his extended family, Kanye couldn't turn off his new-found celebrity. He'd developed a plan to avoid being bothered while out shopping; he'd cover his head and feign a headache if stopped. But here there was no hiding. Still, he signed the nurses' shirts despite his confusion that they'd bother him at such a difficult time. His grandmother Lucinda Williams, having survived bladder cancer back in 1986, was now, they feared, approaching the end. And, just as they had on the day Kanye had his reconstructive surgery after his crash, the roses had gathered to support her. As they waited for news of the results of critical surgery, they hung onto each other, and Kanye made himself a promise; he'd honour his grandmother, and the love of his family, in music.

Ultimately, Lucinda pulled through, but the trauma wasn't the only upheaval in Kanye's life during 2004. Jay-Z had declared his retirement with *The Black Album* and Roc-A-Fella was in flux. Jay had taken up the role of President at Def Jam Records and, despite Dash vigorously promoting Roc signings such as Kanye, Cam'ron, the Diplomats and State Property since, he looked to be taking on more control of the label in Jay's absence. But Def Jam had purchased Roc-A-Fella alongside

Jay's move, and after fraught negotiations Jay, Dash and Burke sold their 50 per cent stake in the company to Def Jam. "I was like, let me get *Reasonable Doubt* and I'll give up [the rest of] my masters. I'll give up Roc-A-Fella Records, I'll give up president and CEO of Def Jam Recordings, everything," Jay-Z said of the negotiations. "Just give me my baby to hold on to so 10 years down the line, I can look back and I got something, I'm not empty-handed. And I was the one being offered everything. I thought it was more than fair... And when that was turned down, I had to make a choice. I'll leave that for the people to say what choice they would've made. That's about it. I don't really wanna talk about Dame or Biggs. I don't have nothing negative to say about them." As Jay was President, he retained control of Roc-A-Fella, but his erstwhile partners were out.

Which left Kanye with a dilemma. Dash and Burke launched a new label, first called Roc4life, then Dame Dash Music Group, and Kanye was given a choice – to follow the man that had shown the most belief in his talent to his new label or to stay where he was with Jay-Z, with whom he'd now built up a strong relationship. Feeling like a child caught between warring parents in a divorce, Kanye decided to stick with Jay and Roc-A-Fella; Jay was now his gold standard of hip-hop quality and a good friend, the man he would always try to beat whenever he wrote his rhymes. Being associated with Roc-A-Fella also helped Kanye avoid tangling too much with the gangsta element of rap. "I'll only speak about [gang culture] as lightly as possible," he told Jamie Foxx in a Business Network interview, "but the gangstas are a strong element in hip-hop that controls a lot of it. I definitely feel like I avoid a lot of problems because I am with Roc-A-Fella Records. But what's so crazy about the gangstas is they got star power at the same time."

When questioned, Kanye would own up to accusations of disloyalty to Dash. "You gotta make that decision," he said. "I felt like with the relationship that me and Jay built after I was on Roc-A-Fella, we had built a different type of relationship, it was a working musical relationship because of the production, and I built more like a business relationship with Dame because of all the ventures he wanted to involve me with. And not to be cliché, but it's like I was between a rock and a hard place. Me and Jay are really close. You know, Jay is one of those people where... you can't never [truly stop being star-struck around] Jay-Z. I idolise him for certain aspects and he would be my greatest competition, so if I'm writing a rap, I'm writing a rap to beat Jay."

As Roc-A-Fella split, however, Kanye made moves to unite his own coterie of stars. Alongside a plethora of new business, music and design projects that he was being offered – a clothing line called Mascott, a range of jewellery he set out to design for Jacob's the jeweller and plenty more production and guest rap work★ – virtually every major label had offered him the chance of starting his own label, and Sony/BMG were the ones that got him. Through them, in the fall of 2004 he formed G.O.O.D. Music, with John Legend and Common the inaugural signings. "I think that the three of us complement each other really well," Legend said, "with me as the singer and musician, Kanye as the sing-songy rapper/producer with the overtly pop sensibility, and Common as, like, the old wise man."

They were soon to be followed by Mos Def, Consequence, GLC, Fonzworth Bentley, I Crisis and Sa-Ra, amongst others. The concept of the label, initially based around those who'd worked on *The College Dropout*, was of a collective of classy, well-dressed and skilful rappers making uplifting music, an alternative to the gangsta guerrilla attitude being touted by the likes of 50 Cent, and the name was inspired by Kanye's belief in thinking big. "Regular life has so many fun things that happen, live interesting things," he said. "Regular people's lives are so much more interesting than performer's lives. What's a performer's life? I went and bought a Benz today. There are things that regular people go through – which I still am even though I have this good-ass job – that are real problems. Love. Pain. Work. Dreams. Following your dreams. That's why the name of my label is Getting Out Our Dreams."

★ Besides producing tracks on albums by associates including Twista, Consquence, Dilated Peoples, Talib Kweli, Mos Def, Cam'ron and John Legend, Kanye had production or rapping credits in 2004 on albums by Judakiss, Janet Jackson, Brandy, Shawnna and Jin, amongst others.

"I knew a lot of talented people and I figured I could use my name to build a label that would allow them to get out their dreams," Kanye would say. "I can't sign every talented person in the world and every talented person in the world isn't gonna get their shot, but the ones I do run into, I provide them the opportunity." Indeed, that year he ran into a kid introducing himself as Scott while shopping for CDs at a Virgin Music Store. Scott complimented Kanye on his 'Jesus' piece and talked about how he couldn't afford CDs himself but he was trying to get his break as a rapper. He asked whether Kanye might want to sign him, and Kanye told him not to give up on his ambitions; four years later, now named Kid Cudi, Scott would end up as one of Kanye's greatest protégés.

Kanye's belief in his G.O.O.D. label artists was quickly proved right. The label's first release was John Legend's debut album, *Get Lifted*, and was a huge success. The record would sell 2.1 million copies in the US alone and earn Legend three Grammys out of six nominations in 2006. For now, the label was flying, as was Kanye's profile. Interviews came thick and fast, and with them, revelations. In *Details* magazine he claimed to be able to see sounds as colours, a condition known as synaesthesia. "What I see, you get to hear," he'd say. "I describe it with the music. I see how round the kick drum is, I see how dark the bassline is, I see the volume if something is really loud, say an instrument is red. I don't mean red in real life, I'm talking about the colours the sound makes that I see in my head."

In the *Telegraph* he revealed that he was just as inspired by Ben Stiller and Adam Sandler movies as he was by rap records, and that he had the plans laid out for his next four albums, keeping with the theme of school and its aftermath – there'd be forthcoming albums called *Late Registration*, then *Graduation* and finally *Good-Ass Job*. And on a trip to Dublin for two sold-out club shows, in the *Irish Times* he continued his barrage of self-belief in the press. "I'm providing a service to people who need real music with real meaning," he said, "so it was important that the lyrics had as much heart as the beats. They're songs for someone who thinks 'I'm going through this today and he's singing about what I'm feeling'. They needed that from a rapper. Alternative music had

that, but hip-hop had no-one doing that. But right now, they do...
[*The College Dropout*] had a positive feel to it because all the songs are
really inspirational. They show how you can get over a situation, they're
about taking the worst possible thing and turning it into a good thing,
like the accident. At the end of the day, you're overcoming something."

He painted the album as a record for rap connoisseurs. "[This is a
record] for those who appreciate that the 10 seconds of strings which
appear in the middle of 'Jesus Walks' contain 100 tracks of strings.
Those who appreciate that I drove to the Harlem Boys Choir's summer
camp to record them in a barn for 'Two Words'. Those who appreciate
the layers of piano, the layers of vocal and the poetry on 'Never Let
Me Down'. If I was to die on the plane going home, people would
go back to *The College Dropout* album and hail it as one of hip-hop's
greatest works," he continued. "As long as I am here, though, they
can't give me that credit, they won't give me that. The only thing you
can do with this album is praise it. I'm really annoyed that some people
have the audacity to knock it. All these songs like 'Spaceship' and 'Jesus
Walks' were made to help people out. For people to knock these songs
would be like someone knocking a philanthropist who is helping out
his community for not giving enough to the kids. When something is
helping someone, how can you knock that? People can knock me for
saying I'm arrogant or if I mess up or if I sleep with some girls before
I get married or whatever. But *College Dropout*? You can't touch that."

He was also asked about his past, and the injustices he'd been
harbouring from as far back as his youth talent shows poured out. "I
would help the others because I just knew I was going to win," he'd say
of the competitions. "Then the teachers said, 'You know we're going
to change this to a talent showcase, this ain't meant to be the Kanye
West show'. But now they can't stop me. It's all in the fans' hands now.
They tried to stop me at art school. I got scholarships. They put the suck
work up on the board to give the students esteem, instead of putting
my work up. But now they can't stop me. At school, I used to be fresh
to death. I worked at the fucking Gap. Instead they gave some kid who
wore [inferior brands] best dressed. They didn't even nominate me. But
now they can't stop me. I'm on the red carpet. I am the best dressed."

Kanye West attends the 9th Annual Soul Train Awards at the Pasadena Civic Auditorium in Pasadena, California, August 23, 2003.
FREDERICK M. BROWN/GETTY IMAGES

Kanye during his days as a thwarted Stevie Wonder impersonator.

Roca-Wear and Roc-A-Fella Records CEO Damon Dash and Kanye arrive for a party promoting Dash's clothing line, New York, August 15, 2002. GETTY IMAGES

Rosario Dawson and Kanye in happier times. JOHNNY NUNEZ/WIREIMAGE

Stalked by the Dropout Bear at the Grand in San Francisco, April 3, 2004. TIM MOSENFELDER/GETTY IMAGES

Kanye West and Alicia Keys.
LARRY BUSACCA/WIREIMAGE FOR EMI MUSIC PUBLISHING

Pretty in pink; Miri Ben Ari and Kanye. JASON SQUIRES/WIREIMAGE

Jay-Z and Kanye throw Roc-A-Fella diamonds during G.O.O.D Music and Groovevolt.com Presents XXL Appreciation Celebration Hosted by Kanye and Common at Seventeen in New York City. JOHNNY NUNEZ/WIREIMAGE

Kanye poses backstage with his awards for "Best Rap Album", "Best Rap Song", and "Best R & B Song" during the 47th Annual Grammy Awards at the Staples Center in Los Angeles, February 13, 2005. CARLO ALLEGRI/GETTY IMAGES

Donda West - Kanye West's Mother. BARRY BRECHEISEN/WIREIMAGE

Kanye communes with his fans.
JASON SQUIRES/WIREIMAGE FOR PMK/HBH

Kanye and girlfriend Brooke Crittendon arrive at the 48th Annual Grammy Awards at the Staples Center in Los Angeles, February 8, 2006. STEPHEN SHUGERMAN/GETTY IMAGES

Kanye holds court with his mother Donda and guest at the Brit Awards Universal after party at Nobu in London in 2006.
DAVE BENETT/GETTY IMAGES

Kanye and his date Alexis attends Conde Nast Media Group's Third Annual Fashion Rocks Concert at Radio City Music Hall in New York City, September 7, 2006.
PETER KRAMER/GETTY IMAGES

Kanye and Rihanna. KMAZUR/WIREIMAGE

The unusual suspects: (L-R) Rappers Timbaland, Kanye, Singers Robin Thicke, Rihanna and Chris Brown pose for a photo during a special Video Music Awards nominee taping of MTV's Total Request Live in New York City, August 7, 2007.
SCOTT GRIES/GETTY IMAGES

Kanye and his "angel" Donda at a book signing for her book *Raising Kanye: Life Lessons From The Mother Of A Hip-Hop Superstar* at Borders in Los Angeles, May 9, 2007. VINCE BUCCI/GETTY IMAGES

Again and again he was asked about his perceived arrogance. "People either love it or hate it," he said, "but people loved and hated Muhammad Ali. My grandfather loved Muhammad Ali and my grandmother hated him. But I bet more people love and remember Muhammad Ali than less. He used to talk shit like 'float like a butterfly sting like a bee' and I think I say the same kind of things partly to provoke people. But don't worry, I know you can't please everybody… My flow isn't like Jay-Z or my voice still can't be compared to Nas but I've figured out things. On the next album, I will have developed as a rapper and my flow will have improved because I now know how to use less words to get my point across."

At times he felt the press focus on his personality traits was overshadowing his music, forcing him to try to sell himself to every interviewer even harder. "There are a lot of people that have new and fresh ideas that just always suck," he'd say, "but the ultimate thing is the quality of the songs. The fact that I'm actually talking about something new, that's somewhat on the positive side, is just an added bonus."

Reading back his most big-headed quotes, and descriptions of his actions which sometimes made him look a little foolish – arguing with magazine editors over being on their covers or freestyling in hotel lobbies mid-interview, insisting his tour manager write down his lines for later use – Kanye developed an early discomfort with press interviews, having his words taken from him and woven into an article he had no control over. Kanye wanted his words to have many meanings at once and to inspire his fans and he felt that, in order to achieve that, he needed as much control over his words and image as he had over his music. So he began asking people attending his pre-release parties not to tell anyone anything he'd said there, so he couldn't be misrepresented or his outbursts taken out of context.

Instead, he let his performances and actions do the talking. On September 18 he was asked to play at David Chappelle's legendary Block Party in Brooklyn and used the opportunity to try out an unusual staging of 'Jesus Walks', taking the song off of the outdoor stage and into the street where he was joined by a full marching band. He landed a support slot on Usher's huge The Truth tour, stretching from August to October 2004 and closing with Kanye playing a 45-minute set at

Madison Square Garden, just as he'd promised himself when he'd been denied the chance of rapping there with Jay-Z. Throughout the tour Kanye was a huge hit, although he managed to miss one show. When the tour route veered close to Oklahoma he decided to stay and see his father, and also perform at a youth revival service – following his performance of 'Jesus Walks' as 300 children pledged themselves to Christ. He planned to make the next day's show by plane, but the plane was grounded by weather – which showed scant appreciation for his effort on Christ's part – so Kanye was forced to race 200 miles by taxi to reach the show. By the time he arrived, he'd missed his slot, but Usher allowed him onstage during his set to rap a couple of numbers, much to the delight of the fans who'd been disappointed by his no-show.

Come the award ceremony season, however, Kanye did little to dampen public opinion that his was an ego ballooning. On November 14 Kanye attended the 32nd annual American Music Awards where he was nominated for three awards, New Artist Of The Year, Rap/Hip-Hop male Artist and Rap Hip-Hop Album. Despite playing live at the ceremony, he came away empty-handed, and fuming. When the last of his nominations, for New Artist, was presented to C&W singer Gretchen Wilson – a former bartender from Pocahontas, Illinois, whose number one single 'Red Neck Woman' had shot her to fame as a trailer park party girl who'd had a child at 16 by an absentee father – Kanye stormed out of the ceremony frustrated, just as he was when he wasn't allowed onto his school basketball team, that he'd been denied the credit he was due.

Taken to the press run after the awards, Kanye couldn't hold back his disappointment. "I feel I was definitely robbed," he told the reporter from Associated Press, "and I refuse to give any politically correct bullshit-ass comment. I was the best new artist this year. I don't know if I'll be back at this award show next year." He'd go on to say that he was happy that 'Jesus Walks' was getting such good airplay and that he was more sad than angry at the award result, blaming a huge conspiracy against him and calling the award's voting process into question.

His mother would back up his comments, agreeing that Gretchen hadn't had anywhere near the cultural impact Kanye had had during

2004, but almost immediately Kanye felt ashamed of his outburst. "I came up to Gretchen [before the Grammy press conference] and apologised," he repented in *Entertainment Weekly* some months after the event. "And I want to apologise to my black role models, like Jay-Z and Oprah Winfrey, for being overemotional. I was doing a disservice to everything my forefathers have done to allow black people to get to this place."

At the AMAs, Kanye may have still been bruised from the MTV Music Awards in Miami on August 29. "From the depths of his soul, he will elevate the hip-hop game before your very eyes!" declared Marc Anthony as Kanye emerged out on the main floor to the opening chant of 'Jesus Walks', rapping out amongst a congregated crowd all bearing candles, at the head of a marching platoon of gospel singers. Reaching the stage, he was joined by Legend and Syleena Johnson for 'All Falls Down', before Chaka Khan herself appeared on a flame-strewn second stage to croon out the hook for 'Through The Wire' along with a full orchestra. "This right here history in the making!" Kanye rapped as the show-stopping set bounced to a close, yet he went home without any of the four awards that 'All Falls Down' had been nominated for.

"Just to have Syleena Johnson up there [was great]," he'd say about his performance. "'Cause it was a whole thing where they said, 'Yo, Lauryn Hill might be able to perform 'All Falls Down' with you'. And that's one of those things that you say, 'Damn, I could perform with Lauryn on the VMAs'. That would be incredible, but I had already got Syleena Johnson her ticket to come out. And I could've gone to Syleena and been like, 'Yo, Lauryn is gonna perform'. But on the song I said, 'Just like a safety belt, you saved my life'. Do you think that I'd turn around and tell Syleena she not gonna perform?"

Four days later, the MTV Europe Music Awards in Rome had a far better fallout for Kanye. On the flight over to Italy, he found himself sitting in first class next to Adam Levine from Maroon 5, on his way to perform at the ceremony. The pair got chatting over a remix of Levine's song 'This Love' that Kanye had worked on that year, and Kanye enthusiastically hunted through his iPod to play him one of the songs he'd been working on since the release of *The College Dropout*. "I just always like to play people new music," Kanye said, "and 'Heard 'Em Say' was the first song I had recorded for the new album. So I had it in my iPod, and on the plane over we were sittin' up in first class, where artists sit. And I played it for him and he said, 'Yo, this reminds me of a song that I wrote but I don't know if my band will want to do it. It sounds kind of R&B. But I want to do the song'. I said, 'Yo, we should work together'. And that's all it was."

"He was rhyming over it, and I had just written a hook that was so perfect for it," Kanye recalled. "It was one of those natural collaborations where you're so excited because it's all very pure and very easy." Once they'd arrived in Rome and Kanye saw Maroon 5 perform, he was sure he wanted Levine to guest on the track, little knowing the huge audience crossover he was setting in motion. "They were so big that I thought they'd be less ill," Kanye said, "but I heard them rehearsing backstage at the Grammys and he was hitting all them mockingbird notes and I said, I have to get him in the studio'." And the ceremony itself? "I didn't win, I got robbed again," Kanye joked. "I was really more upset that you couldn't actually see my outfit on the show. I had this dope-ass, pink-and-brown outfit."

The College Dropout would get an extended lease of life via the release over the coming years of three compilation mix-tapes called *Freshman Adjustment* 1, 2 and 3, featuring a plethora of unreleased material, remixes, live tracks, demos and alternative versions of album tracks from the dozens of mixes Kanye had made. Though it's uncertain whether these were official releases, they are of interest to the Kanye completist as they trace the development of lyrics such as the first verse from 'All Falls Down', and include demos and lines which would emerge on future albums. If these releases were officially endorsed, they prove that Kanye couldn't leave his debut alone until he'd allowed the public to sample every worthwhile element that went into its making. The pinnacle of the current campaign, however, came with the 47th Grammy Awards on February 13, 2005 at the LA Staples Center where Kanye arrived bearing the most number of nominations of anybody – 10 in all – and the eyes of the world upon him. The media had worked itself into a frenzy over the possibility of another Kanye blow-up if he weren't to win, and he made reference to the controversy during his performance of 'Jesus Walks'. On a church set complete with preacher, congregation, a wall of stained glass and Donda herself getting a close-up at the line "my mama used to say only Jesus can save us"★, Kanye gave an energetic performance before disappearing behind a white cloth screen and, in shadow, being knocked down by a car, a metaphor for the car crash that had made his career and also the one so many millions were tuning in to see, were he was denied a prize. Then, with the Blind Boys Of Alabama singing 'I'll Fly Away' over his coffin as the mourners shuffled by to lay their flowers, Kanye rose again, the doors of the church flying open to find him in a crisp white Yves Saint Laurent suit muttering, "Y'all look like you've seen a ghost or something", spitting the final verse and then flying over the worshipping congregation wearing huge angel wings.

Having played up his heavenly qualities, it was a relief that Kanye did win, taking home three of his 10 award nominations, for Best Rap Song for 'Jesus Walks', best R&B Song for Alicia Keys' 'You Don't Know My Name' and Best Rap Album for *The College Dropout*. His speech was just as legendary as his AMA outburst. "Y'all might as well get the music ready because this is going to take a while," he said, taking his time to savour the applause of his peers. "When I had my accident, I found out at that moment, nothing in life is promised except death. If you have the opportunity to play this game called life, you have to appreciate every moment. A lot of people don't appreciate their moment until it's passed. And then you got to tell those Al Bundy stories: 'You remember when I…'. Right now it's my time and my moment." His voice bulged with excitement. "And I plan to celebrate and scream and pop champagne every chance I get, 'cause I'm at the Grammys baby! I know everybody asked me the question, they wanted to know 'What, Kan', I know he's going to wild out. I know he's going to do something crazy. Everybody wanted to know what I would do, if I didn't win."

He hoisted the Grammy above his head. "I guess we'll never know!"

★ Donda threw herself into rehearsals for her part, so into the choreography of the show that Kanye would comment "My mama can bust some Usher moves!"

As he headed off to the Miracle Mile district for his own after-show, a party so dangerously packed it would be shut down by fire marshals at 1am, Kanye felt defiantly on top of the world.

Not least because, with his second album already 75 per cent finished, he knew what he'd soon be unleashing on it.

CHAPTER SEVEN

Late Registration

"White people!" Kanye would say, peering out at packed audiences ranging across the racial spectrum, "this is your only chance to say the word 'nigga' and get away with it. Take advantage of it."

The track he was introducing, onstage during his *College Dropout* shows, was called 'Gold Digger', a crackling pop groove woven around an extrapolation of Ray Charles' 'I Got A Woman' sung, once more, by Jamie Foxx. Many would assume that Kanye was inspired to work on the Charles track after watching Foxx play Charles in the biopic *Ray*; in fact the track was older than the film. While the idea of getting Foxx to sing the hook to replace the original sample did indeed come from watching the film, alongside singer John Mayer, the vocal take took several attempts, with Foxx re-recording to remove expletives, and was only used on the opening hook, with Charles' vocals sampled for the rest of the track. Kanye had produced the beat for Shawnna's 2004 album *Worth Tha Weight* at Ludacris' house, with the verses written from a woman's perspective: "I'm not sayin' I'm a gold digger," went the chorus, "but I aint messin' with no broke niggas".

Bizarrely, Shawnna turned the track down, so Kanye rewrote the song for his second album, one of many tracks he'd been working on ever since coming off of the Usher tour in October 2004 and the first he'd made with film score composer Jon Brion. Kanye would claim that the *Late Registration* project began "with Common turning down beats" during sessions for his album *Be*, which Kanye would then think up rhymes for and jump on in the studio. Although Ray Charles hadn't inspired 'Gold Digger', cinema did have a major impact on the follow-up to *The College Dropout*; having been exposed to Brion's work on the soundtrack to Michel Gondry's *Eternal Sunshine Of The Spotless Mind*★ Kanye made the link that this was the same guy who had produced Fiona Apple's *When The Pawn Hits ...* (not the full title – it's very, very long) album. Tiring of his high-pitched sample style which was now being copied across the hip-hop spectrum, he'd been very taken with Apple's album and was interested in merging similar orchestral crescendos of horn and drum roll with Quincy Jones' Chicago sound on his next record, as well as emulating her sense of emotional exposure; he saw himself developing into the rap Fiona Apple, laying bare his pain in song. The world might be gaining an impression of Kanye as a hot-headed young rap auteur, but he was keen, out of sheer respect and reverence, to see if he could work with other producers from entirely different areas that he thought highly of and from whom he might learn new techniques.

"I always loved that [Fiona Apple] so much," he said "It hit me in a way and I wanted to know, who got the drum sounding like that? Who went into these dark chords, these string arrangements? Who brought Fiona's pain to life? I needed someone that could bring my plight to life. And the Fiona Apple album kind of sounded similar to Portishead, too. I just felt no one was doing that in hip-hop, no rapper has ever captured that sound and rapped on it. It's like, how many more sped-up soul samples do you want? We gotta push the envelope a little bit. And I always wanted to feel like I was rapping at the top of a mountain or something."

So Rick Rubin, the man Kanye called 'Hollywood Yellow Pages', introduced the two at Kanye's request, and they clicked immediately. During their first afternoon in the studio together they'd completed

---

★ Brion had also composed music for *I Heart Huckabees* and *Punch Drunk Love* as well as producing Aimee Mann.

the basic tracks for 'Gold Digger'. "Jon Brion definitely changed my life," Kanye said. "He didn't call any labels or anything like that, he just started working on the project right there. We were thinking, 'We'll let the lawyers clean up the mess, but we have to be creative, this energy, this thing needs to happen right now'… He wants you to feel the music, and that's like me, I want you to feel the music." "It was completely apparent that he was open to investigating new ideas," said Brion. "I was playing something on a track and he was completely psyched, and then he left after a few hours and said, 'I'll see you tomorrow'."

Kanye already had the majority of a second album complete by the time he and Brion began working together in March of 2005, but was unhappy with it. He wanted lush orchestras, grand experiments, a new form of rap inspired by the deep, narcotic tones of trip-hop pioneers Portishead, sounds that he wasn't hearing in his recordings so far. "Seeing the album cover [of Portishead's *Roseland NYC Live*] did so much for me," he'd say. "This picture inspired me. I saw it years back, but on my first album I couldn't afford real strings. So after I won those Grammys, the first thing I did was run to Jon Brion, and then I ran and got a string section. Hip-hop never had strings that lush with drums that hard. But Portishead had that. And they sounded hip-hop, and people vibed to that. I said, 'OK, what if we do that and I drop my poetry shit on top of it?' Drink it in San Diego, it goes down smooth."

Brion's influence altered the project dramatically, steering it towards the opulent feel that Kanye was after, and in turn Brion was impressed by Kanye's adventurous and open-minded approach to his music, as well as his authoritative studio presence. "On your sophomore record, that's the ultimate time to not fuck with the formula, right?" he said. "And he gets *me*, a guy who has never made a hip-hop record in his life, and gives me half the reins? That is not an egomaniac… [People might say] 'Oh, [Kanye's] gone off his rocker, he's going to make an art record with some crazy, left-field music guy'. That's not the case whatsoever. It's very much a Kanye West record… When he hears something he likes, he knows it. He has vision, and when the guy makes quick, intuitive decisions, he just *has* it. I'd watch him take a rough track that I had worked on and completely stand it on its head in 10 minutes, and it's just *better*. It was mind-boggling… There are colours and ideas that make [the album] different from average hip-hop, but Kanye is already different from the average hip-hop guy. He's got this sense of pop record-making which is really solid, and he likes tracks with a lot of things going on in them, which is not necessarily common for hip-hop. He was already barking up that tree. This is definitely not just a hip-hop album. But it is also by no means overtly arty, or non-hip-hop. I don't think it's a weird record by any means."

For Kanye, Jon's studio was a playground. Keen to explore and experiment, he'd pick up and record the strange and unfamiliar instruments scattered around to add to the basic song structure he would bring in. The pair spent a full year recording the album at a cost of almost $2million, largely at Sony Studios in NYC, though other sessions for *Late Registration* took place in LA, at the Record Plant and Grandmaster Recording Studios and Chalice Recording Studios in Hollywood, with Brion as co-executive producer on many of the tracks and helping Kanye's imagination fly. A fly-on-the-wall MTV2 camera crew joined them in the studio for a portion of the recording process, capturing the high spirits of the sessions. "We're mad fun to be around," Kanye said, "I'd want to be around us." The cameras caught Jon joking that "There's something really delightful about seeing a piece of written music that says Crack Music on it. Where is your Beethoven now?", Kanye explaining why they nicknamed engineer Anthony Kilhoffer 'Tyrone' ("Because we don't know any white people called Tyrone – it was funny to us") and Brion and West laughing over news that Jon had "doubled the flugelhorn". "I remember I doubled the flugel back in high school," Kanye double-entendred.

They also shot footage of the various guests arriving for their takes, with Kanye explaining the energy added by each one. Tony Williams, he explained, was "a great writer, he's got a cutting-edge voice", Really Doe was "still connected to the streets and the struggle and having to pay his rent" and Jamie Foxx, there to recreate his Ray Charles part for 'Gold Digger', was a gift from God. "The whole energy with him coming off the Oscars and me coming off the Grammys and having that song out for the summer, all I'mma saying is God times things."

"If you see someone that's really hot and talented, you take their energy, you use them," he explained. "I love saying that because the word 'use' has such a negative connotation, but really it's misused, because it's a give and take… It's like I'm on this hunt to find the best musicians we can find."

In the documentary that emerged from the filming, Kanye unravelled his creative process. "When I start working on a beat," he said, "sometimes I'll just take a couple of days to listen to samples. It'll be Puffy or somebody, I'll be working on this project and he comes in and I'm sitting up here watching TV and listening to music for a couple of days. Like what are you doing fam?' 'I'm working'. When I turn around and make the beat, I'll make the beat in 15 minutes, I'll just chop it all up. In hip-hop we're always talking about 'you're biting my style', but hip-hop itself is based off a bite, it's based off taking segments of people's music and taking something that people said on the street and taking this pattern here… one of the fundamentals of hip-hop is biting."

He also explained his ambitions for his second album. "I'm thinking about the history of music," he grinned, "I'm thinking about where's my place in history. I want it to mean something to somebody. I want people to say 'just like Kanye' 20 years from now. Because when people say 'Stevie' it means something. They say 'it's not like you're Stevie' and you can say that because his name is so synonymous with something outstanding… I almost died, I'm not scared of death, but I will be remembered and what I say while I'm here will help people forever."

And, whether it achieved it or not, *Late Registration* sure set out to fly high, leap huge genre canyons and change the world.

★ ★ ★

"I knew I was gon' see you again!" exclaimed DeRay's Bernie Mac-alike college tutor, back for the sequel. "Where your goddamn book bag at?"

As the piano refrain from Natalie Cole's 'Someone That I Used To Love' struck up in the background, Kanye swiftly fell asleep in DeRay's class, until a yell of "Wake up Mr West!"

The wake-up call wasn't just meant literally, but to jolt Kanye out of his social stupor and wake up to the ills of the world around him. Thus, the piano melody bled into *Late Registration*'s first track, the song that Kanye had dug out of his iPod to play to Adam Levine of Maroon 5 on the plane to Rome, 'Heard 'Em Say', something of a gift from God Kanye believed.

"He came to the studio right after the Grammys and he sang the song and the melody fit perfect with it," Kanye recalled. "He added something to it, it was just like the magic, the frosting on top. And that's one of those times that God is working in the studio with you. Those are those days that he's really on his job. One of the reasons I defended the first album so much was I was scared that I couldn't make an album comparable to the first one. Again, 'cause I know I didn't make it by myself – I know that God had heavy involvement in it. And I didn't know if he might have been tryin' to focus on someone else's career, to get 'em to the point where I'm at. Not that he can't do two things at once. But there's times with 'Jesus Walks', with the blood diamonds, with 'Crack Music', where I know that God is speaking through me. I know that's something he wants me to say. I know he's connecting people. He put me on that plane with Adam to bring out that song."

Brion remembers the session being short on time since Levine only had a few hours free: "Adam had something, Kanye loved it and the three of us went at it like banshees, and there it was."

'Heard 'Em Say' was a track that would lay out Kanye's intentions for the record. Inventive in style, it combined subtle hip-hop beats with Cole's piano melody and the kind of restrained experimental electronic squelches and glitches that post-rock laptop acts had been developing since the late nineties. And over this sparse but compulsive backing, the lyric took a cutting view of American life from the perspective of a downtrodden citizen struggling with the ills of society, government and religion. "Nothing's ever promised tomorrow today" was the song's repeated refrain, rapped by Kanye or crooned in a luscious falsetto by Levine, and the idea of struggle against the odds of society rang loud through the rhymes. Kanye tackled the injustice of the minimum wage, the idea that AIDS was a man-made disease invented by the government to control populations, the hypocrisy of rich religious leaders and his belief that the police want to see all black men in prison. His second verse turned to the elements of society that keep the public tamed – religion, acceptable drugs like cigarettes and the false hope of lotteries – while the track also highlighted the plight of the poor ghetto kids watching rappers on TV flaunting their material goods and feeling that riches and fame are far closer than they really are, when the real rock stars in their neighbourhoods are the drug dealers.

Kanye certainly wasn't blameless in presenting an image that the rap kids would dream of and aspire to. "Equal to the music is the style," he said. "You take the average crew, there might be one person who can dress good. But me, Don and Ibn were the three best-dressed people in Chicago. Now we're together all the time, we go to Japan, we go to London, we go to a store and say 'What do you think?' Of course I'm gonna be talking to you with the Gucci shirt and Yves St Laurent with the sleeves rolled up. Why wouldn't I?"

Likewise, the next song 'Touch The Sky' painted a classic portrait of hip-hop success, again tracing Kanye's journey from Chi-Town to Roc-A-Fella over a rousing, instantly recognisable slowed-down sample from Curtis Mayfield's 'Move On Up'.★ "Come up in the spot looking extra fly," he spat on the hook, "'fore the day I die I'm gonna touch the sky", and then delved back into the past to talk about the days "when they thought pink Polos would hurt the Roc" and he couldn't get signed: "The doors was closed," he rapped, going on to reference the poor job Puffy's team did on trying to break a group called the LOX, "I felt like Bad Boy's street team, I couldn't work the LOX". He recalled driving the U-Haul truck to New York, standing in line at clubs and hitting Jacob the jeweller an hour after he was signed, and wondered at the point he'd now reached, with Jay-Z considering him amongst his contemporaries. "I think I died in that accident," he gasped, "'cause this must be heaven".

★ 'Touch The Sky' was the only track on the album that wasn't produced, even in part, by Kanye. Just Blaze produced the song.

The second verse was virtually an open letter to his girlfriend, Alexis Phifer, with whom he'd split in 2005 – he was now dating actress Brooke Crittendon. Crittendon would later star in BET's *Harlem Nights* show, but at the time she was a rising starlet who claimed their short time together was like a trip to Disneyland. It had been a bumpy ride for Kanye though, as he explained in the verse. Looking back to his pre-fame life when nobody wanted his beats, he'd stretch himself to afford Gucci loafers and "me and my girl split the KFC buffet", he then fast-forwarded to apologise to Phifer for his errant ways. "Couldn't keep it at home," he admitted, "thought I needed a Nia Long [a character in *The Best Man* who tempted the lead character to cheat on his girlfriend], I'm trying to right my wrongs". Success, it seemed, was bringing Kanye all manner of unexpected personal problems.

In keeping with the G.O.O.D. ethos, Kanye turned the third verse of 'Touch The Sky' over to an upcoming Chicago rapper by the name of Lupe Fiasco. Lupe – aka Wasalu Muhammad Jaco – had caught Kanye's ear with a remix of a later track on the album, 'Diamonds Of Sierra Leone' (Lupe's remix was called 'Conflict Diamonds') and he let him loose on an introductory, show-stopping verse full of tongue-twisting references to anime, Abbott & Costello and expensive foreign cars, all spun with elaborate and poetic wordplay to prove Lupe's evident rhyme skills stealing the song from under Kanye's nose, like a baseball player on third. Here was another of Kanye's inspired discoveries, a talent he was using, while himself being used.

And talking of being used, next came 'Gold Digger', the Ray Charles-looping story of a rich man being bled dry by a woman only after his bank account. Since it was originally written from a female perspective for Shawnna, the rewritten 'Gold Digger' appealed to both sexes equally – its male fans felt it made fun of the fine art of hunting out and manipulating rich men, while its female fans thought it belittled the superficial concerns of men and empowered the women out to get what they want from a relationship. Either way, like the two tracks that preceded it, it was a massive hit-in-waiting, as Jamie Foxx crooned "she take my money when I'm in need" – though in Charles' original song, the roles here were reversed; it was the woman giving Ray her money

– and Kanye kicked in with the assertion that "I aint sayin' she's a gold digger, but she aint messin' with no broke niggas". The woman Kanye was rapping about didn't fit the precise definition of a gold digger since she wasn't targeting wealthy men, just ignoring the poor ones but, according to the song, he'd soon be trapped into a life of penury by her. Meeting in a beauty salon he's impressed by her small Vuitton bag and sizeable behind – "I'm looking for the one, have you seen her? My psychic told me she'd have a ass like Serena, Trina, Jennifer Lopez" – and she's drawn to his Roc chain and expensive watch; the next thing he knows he's driving her, her four children and all their friends to dinner in his Benz, and footing the bill himself. He soon discovers she's been having relationships and children with other rappers – Busta Rhymes, Usher – but despite the amount of money he has to spend to be with her, he's smitten.

Come the second verse, originally performed in July 2004 on Russell Simmons' TV show *Def Jam Poetry*, when it was just a spoken-word piece called '18 Years', Kanye delivered a warning to potential gold diggees, that once a partner has had their child they're responsible financially for the 18 years it takes to raise them, and if the story of one NFL player he knew was anything to go by, the mother might well be spending the child support payments on fancy cars, big apartments and plastic surgery. His advice is to ensure you get a prenuptial agreement, "'cause when she leave your ass, she gonna leave with half". And the irony for the NFL player in question, is that when his child hit 18 they discovered it wasn't even his child. The original verse ended with the line "He killed that bitch, they gave him 25 years".

The final verse flipped the song's sympathies and viewpoint to advise women on the dangers of gold-digging; that it's often best to find an ambitious, hard-working man and wait for him to become successful, since the rich man they have their eye on may well just be after a trophy wife and is prone to "leave your ass for a white girl". Hence 'Gold Digger' cleverly straddled the gender divide on the issue, both mocking and sympathising with each player in one of life's fundamental power struggle games. The album's first skit, named simply 'Skit #1', put Kanye's crew firmly in the poor but ambitious category, as DeRay led the house chant of a new sorority for broke guys as an introduction to 'Drive Slow', an enigmatic casual slink of a groove sampled from Hank Cranford's sax cover of Skylark's 1973 hit 'Wildflower'. The original plan was to have MIA guest on the track, but her schedule was too full to fit in the session, so instead GLC and Houston's Paul Wall, whom Kanye had met during a photo shoot for a piece in *King* magazine entitled *Coming Kings*, accompanied Kanye on his extended car metaphor for a variety of lifestyles. Based around hooks that found the threesome cruising around town in a luxury car fitted with TV screens galore, hunting for women, they each span car-themed verses, Kanye's the most elaborate. Here, he told the story of a schoolfriend called Marley who'd inherited money from his father and spent it on becoming the school's biggest baller, buying Chevy Caprice cars with high-end rims and a detachable stereo front. Marley became so popular and desirable he even had a baby at 16, and Kanye – then "a virgin, a baby" – would admire him as a young aspiring rapper, envious of his notoriety. Yet Marley would tell him not to put pressure on himself, to grow up at his own pace: "He told me don't rush to get grown, drive slow homie".

Paul Wall's verse took a more traditional bragging stance, singing the praises of his Mercedes with its elaborate rims and immaculate paint job, drawing women like "dime pieces and sexy ladies", a 'dime piece' being a woman considered a perfect 10. Not that Wall needs it, he boasts – "I could still catch boppers if I drove a cab". GLC's verse took a more reasoned approach, pointing out how ridiculous it was to focus so much on your car, but complaining it was in his nature because "I got the baller genetics" and going on to show off about his tyres, interior and near-silent engine.

The track's final hook, using the opposite technique that Kanye had become known for, was actually pitched down, reflecting the mental effects of the cough syrup-based lean drink that GLC rapped about in his verse, and it was a new twist that Kanye continued into the album's next song, 'My Way Home'. For this brief track, he pitched down Gil Scott-Heron's 'Home Is Where The Hatred Is' to create a soupy, narcotic haze of a track, otherwise leaving the original largely un-meddled with, giving Common a sinister base on which to build a stylish and thoughtful verse of social discontent. The addict and dealer trapped in ghettos – "grassless jungles" – filled with hate and hopelessness, fighting against the bonds of racism and poverty but so often succumbing to the dual prisons of drugs and crime. "Show money becomes bail, relationships become jail," he rapped portentiously, mirroring Scott-Heron's proto-rap style, "children are unheld". And his solution? Just get out: "I bail, and it…" he rhymed as Gil's sample completed the sentiment, "might not be such a bad idea if I never, never went home again."★

Because home, as the next song would remind us, was the front line of a drug war America was rapidly losing. The syncopated martial beats, gospel choir, chopped up brass sample taken from 'Since You Came In My Life' by the New York Community Choir, although the choir itself isn't sampled and instead the voices on the track are those of Tony Williams, Keyshia Cole and Charlie Wilson, while the drumbeat is taken from 'It's Your Thing' by Cold Grits. The woozy, warped backing represents the crack high, creating a juxtaposition of lushness and tension that perfectly reflected the sort of issues the lyric tackled. Kanye's efforts to fight against the clichéd traditional tropes of hip-hop, and particularly its drug-related numbers, by replacing the word "nigga" with "homie" throughout failed – "that's the crack music, homie", he decided, just didn't have the same impact as the more stereotypical "that's the crack music, nigga". But he rammed home his point anyway. "How we stop the Black Panthers?" he asked, "Ronald Reagan cooked up an answer", and went on to condemn the CIA and the Reagan administration's role in the alleged invention and export of crack cocaine in the early eighties by the Contra rebels and its flooding of American projects with the intention of enslaving and suppressing the restless black populations. Kanye referenced the rocketing murder rates it caused in Maryland and Washington DC, and the fact that the black communities were

★ Common was such an inspiration for *Late Registration* that Kanye kept a copy of his album *Be*, which he was producing in tandem with recording his own album, in the studio with its track listing side-by-side with his own to make sure his album would turn out to be just as good.

complicit in their own destruction, with many turning to selling the drug as an economic escape route: "We invested in that, it's like we got Merill lynched/And we been hanging from the same tree ever since". He saw hip-hop as the only antidote to this collective affliction, cooked up, packaged and distributed much like the drug, tested and criticised by reviewers but still feeling pure on his tongue.

The second verse widened the issues to take in US political corruption, from the harsh actions of Illinois attorney general Lisa Madigan towards Chicago's gang crime, locking up abandoned children in under-18s prisons, to the conspiracy theory about George Bush Sr. selling anthrax to Saddam Hussein for use in his chemical weapons programme. Bush's actual involvement in or knowledge of such deals is unknown, although according to a *Washington Post* report Donald Rumsfeld, then a pharmaceutical company executive, helped Hussein buy viruses including anthrax and bubonic plague from American companies. But inevitably Kanye returned to the problem of drug abuse and hustling in the ghettos, America's own chemical assault on its people, still in operation decades later, the gangland perpetrators and facilitators, taking Jay-Z as their hero and role model. Kanye here name-checks two Chicago gangs, the Folk Nation, or Folks, and the Black P. Stones, or Moes.

For the song's more empowered closing address, Kanye made way for spoken-word poet Malik Yusef, whose final lines praised the crack-like addictive nature of rap music and the way it was helping the black community take back the wealth and self-respect that was stolen from it by white America. "We ooze it through they nooks and crannies," he rhymed, "so our mommas ain't got to be they cooks and nannies... now the former slaves trade hooks for Grammys/This dark diction has become America's addiction". 'Crack Music' was Kanye the socio-political force really stretching his wings.

And as he developed the social side of his conscious persona, he also expanded his emotional palate. Though 'Roses', forged around a sample from Bill Withers' 'Rosie', was fast-paced, it was a minimalist and mournful piece recounting the time the Williams family gathered outside Lucinda Williams' hospital room in fear for the life of the grandmother he'd nicknamed Chick. Touching details emerged: that the doctors were afraid to operate in case the anaesthesia killed her, that Kanye tried to comfort her with memories of his childhood and that Kanye begged the doctors to fly in the best doctors they could find, since rich people seemed to get better treatment – "If Magic Johnson got a cure for AIDS, and all the broke motherfuckers passed away," he rapped, "you telling me if my grandma's in the NBA, right now she'd be OK?/But since she was just a secretary working for the church for 35 years, things s'posed to stop right here?". But amongst the snapshots of the event – his hardy grandfather finding the strength to keep himself together, the nurses asking him to sign T-shirts, his clutch of aunties gathering together – the most moving and unifying lines were those explaining that the family saw themselves as the flowers that other families might have sent in absentia, and the "all-time high" they felt when news arrived that the operation was a success.

Brion had been very proud of his keyboard and beat work on 'Roses', until Kanye stripped it all away so that the vocal would provide the rhythm, leaving Brion's instrumentation for the chorus. Brion would compare the decision to Prince's famous removal of the bass track from 'When Doves Cry'. "His attitude was, 'See if you can make me like this'," Brion said. "All the authority [and] groove is from his voice, and when the chorus comes in, it's just this extravaganza of stuff going on." Ultimately, Kanye would seriously consider dropping the track from the album, but it was Brion who convinced him to let it stay.

The next track, 'Bring Me Down', was another backwards glance. It had originally begun life as 'Have It Your Way' on Kanye's 2001 demo CD, but now its dark gangster groove was adorned with Brion's bombastic orchestral flourishes, the most dramatic track on the record, and multi-tracked honeycomb harmonies from Brandy on the hook. As she was a nineties pop starlet who'd taken a hiatus from music to become a mother and returned to a lukewarm reception, Kanye found her an interesting figure to sing the lines "always knew that one day they'd try to bring me down/Way down", and she certainly brought a heartfelt sweetness to the hook. Kanye's lyrics had softened since the original too, a verse he'd first freestyled on BET's *Rapcity: The Basement*.

This was a classic case of hitting back at the haters, the rappers desperate for one of his beats despite never helping him when he was a struggling producer or trying to drag down his dreams. Declaring he'd have to die for his creative drive to ever be quenched, he laid into these two-faced industry types with a vigour: "Dawg, if I was you I wouldn't feel myself/Dawg, if I was you I'd kill myself... I'mma look in the mirror if I need some help".

Not that Kanye wouldn't admit to his own failings. 'Addiction', an Afrobeat concoction of Etta James' version of 'My Funny Valentine', shuffling, morphing, metallic beats, bongos and sunny guitar licks, was one of the tracks turned down by Common for *Be*, but Kanye turned it into an itchy slice of self-reproach. "Why everything that's supposed to be bad make me feel so good?" he spat, frustrated at his own addictions to sex, money and dope, "I tried to stop man, I tried the best I could... I've been afflicted by not one, not two but all three". Yet he's messing with a girl whose addictions are arguably worse – "She's got a lover, so the lies, and the lust, is a rush... I guess that means I'm her drugs". Kanye does everything he can to encourage her addiction though, getting her drunk and high so that she can fully indulge her habit. Eventually Kanye gets hooked on their sexual activities too – "I keep co-coming over 'cause it's never over," he rapped with an addict's stutter – and as the final female-voiced hook, sung by Cash Money Records' Strings, proved, the feeling was mutual.

The track ended with a nervous request for a threesome with the girl's friend, but if that seemed unlikely then Kanye's next attempt to make a wild but desirable connection happen seemed near impossible. After a second skit continuing the marching chant of the Broke Phi Broke fraternity – a spoof on the Divine Nine fraternities which used the phi symbol and created chants and steps in this style – the next two tracks acted as an attempt to heal rap's biggest rift and reconcile Jay-Z with Nas. First up, Jay-Z guested on 'Diamonds Of Sierra Leone (Remix)', one of 14 remixes that Kanye produced of a later track on the album and an attack on the blood diamond trade and the tragedies of the children forced to mine them and fight in the civil wars that were waged over the trade. The natural sample for the song was Shirley

Bassey's legendary Bond theme 'Diamonds Are Forever', a tune that would resonate with the public in the same way as Jay-Z's use of 'It's The Hard Knock Life' from *Annie* had, and also fulfil Kanye's ambition to rap over huge crashing drum rolls and glowering billows of brass. On 'Diamonds', he said, "When the harpsichord and the music crescendos with the horns in the back and the drum rolls and everything... that moment in that song right there is what hip-hop is about."

But Kanye's populist sample was set to an even harder-hitting message. Over the urgent and energised almost electro-rock track that Kanye created from Bassey's original, including a comedy extrapolation of the "forever? Forever-ever?" line from OutKast's hit 'Ms Jackson', and drums that were bizarrely played by celebrated film director Michel Gondry who was visiting the studio on the day the track was recorded, there were two strands to the verses based on the two types of diamond the song addressed. Kanye's verse explained the horrors of the "conflict diamonds", the rocks that rappers strived for in the US unaware that "people lose hands, legs, arms" over these diamonds back in Sierra Leone – "My chain, these ain't conflict diamonds, is they Jacob?"★ he asked, "I thought my Jesus-piece was so harmless/Until I seen a picture of a shorty armless". Here was Kanye's most pin-point political and social commentary yet: "Over here it's a drug trade, we die from the drugs/Over there they die from what we buy from drugs".

On MTV, Kanye explained how his interest in blood diamonds came about. "Mark Romanek, the director that did Jay's '99 Problems', and Q-Tip both brought up blood diamonds. They said, 'That's what I think about when I hear diamonds. I think about kids getting killed, getting amputated in West Africa'. And Q-Tip's like, 'Sierra Leone' and I'm like, 'Where?' And I remember him spelling it out for me and me looking on the internet and finding out more."

★ We can only assume Jacob the jeweller's diamonds weren't conflict diamonds, since Kanye would unite with the firm to design his first line of Jesus-pieces; a diamond-encrusted rendering of Jesus' face, available in both black and white, with white diamond crown of thorns.

He learnt about the children being killed and maimed in West African countries, where the Sierra Leone Revolutionary United Front would attack diamond mines and amputate the limbs of workers and children as a terror tactic, mutilating 20,000 people including women and children in their 10-year war. He dug deeper, reading about the corruption of mine owners mistreating their miners, the widespread use of slave labour and the people murdering each other over these glistening stones. Kanye felt the bling-obsessed hip-hop scene needed to know the truth behind their jewellery. "I think that was just one of those situations where I just set out to entertain, but every now and then God taps me on the shoulder and says, 'Yo, I want you to do this right here', so he'll place angels in my path and one angel will lead to another angel and it's like a treasure hunt or something. And I finally found the gold mine... With the remix verse, the diamond industry's thinking I'm doing something to try to hurt them. But how is it hurting y'all for me to just tell people that there was a 10-year war in Sierra Leone where black people were killing each other over diamonds and that it was a monopoly and that there are still situations that are next to slave labour, with people working for two cups of rice a day?"

When asked if the fact that he still wore diamonds was a little hypocritical, he was unrepentant. "'How are you a human being?', would be more of the question, like, 'How are you still human when you know what's going on? How do you still wear what it took your whole life to get?' [But] a whole part about being a human is to be a hypocrite. They say that if you're an artist you have to stand for this, and they try to discredit you. Like they'll try to discredit Dr. King or Bill Cosby or Jesse Jackson 'cause they say that they saw them with a woman or something. So what does that have to do with what Cosby's TV show meant for us, what it meant for the black image and meant for our esteem, like 'Damn, we could do that, we don't have to be like 'Good Times' all in the projects'? What does that take away from Martin Luther King, from what he did?"

'Diamonds From Sierra Leone (Remix)' was a lyric Kanye was very proud of, in widening the perspective of hip-hop. "'I'mma kill you, nigga, I'mma kill you, nigga, I'mma *kill* you, nigga'," he said, mocking a standard gangsta lyric, "but saying, 'I'm going to dinner with a white woman' or 'diamonds come from Sierra Leone' is way more disruptive, but I had to get it off my chest."

Kanye's verse also hinted at the other diamond reference; the Roc-A-Fella sign, a diamond made with both hands. If the ice around his neck was tainted, the Roc-A-Fella family and Kanye's devotion to it was truly eternal. "The Roc is still alive every time I rhyme," he rapped, keen to assert that despite its internal splits, Roc-A-Fella was still alive and well. As Kanye began to delve further into this topic, rhyming "Where Dame at? This track the Indian dance that bring our reign back" – a play on the term 'rain dance' – Jay-Z interrupted him to make a more formal statement about the state of the label. "The chain remains, the gang is intact," he asserted, admitting "The name is mine, I'll take blame for that" before boasting "I had to get off the boat so I could walk on water". The rest of his verse followed a familiar line for Jigga fans, retelling the story of his rise from crack dealer to music mogul by way of one of his most memorable lines, "I'm not a businessman, I'm a business, man" and claiming that, despite their detractors hoping to watch them fail, this Roc-A-Fella comeback song was proof that his Roc dynasty will endure forever: "People lined up to see the Titanic sinkin', instead we rose up from the ash like a phoenix/If you're waiting for the end of the Dynasty sign, it would seem like forever is a mighty long time".

Having got Jay-Z onto *Late Registration*, Kanye now set about getting him in close proximity with his adversary. Unbeknown to Jay, Kanye invited Nas to guest on the next track, 'We Major'. He knew he was being disloyal to Jay and the Roc, but his intentions were good – he wanted his Roc mentor and a rap hero to whom he'd become close to settle their very public differences. "We made this Jay's favourite song on the album," Kanye said. "So the thing is, when something is so good, you can't deny it. When you hear the horns on 'We Major' and you hear the chorus come in and you hear Nas, that could warm somebody's heart. Good music can break through anything and maybe start to break down the wall between two of the greatest MCs that we have."

The tactic worked – Jay-Z not only loved the track, but would indeed make up with Nas to the point of rapping alongside him at his comeback I Declare War show at the annual Power 105.1 Power House show at the Continental Airlines Arena that October, which Kanye also played, and eventually signing Nas to Def Jam. And it's not hard to see why. Sampling Orange Krush's early eighties classic 'Action', We Major' was a sprawling and ambitious seven-and-a-half minute epic of tinkling electric piano, ecstatic horns and gritty disco beats and scratches so ostentatious and expansive that it truly stretched the barriers of how big a rap tune could get. One of few tracks produced by Kanye and Brion with an additional producer, in this case Warryn Campbell, over the glistening piano and strident trumpets, Really Doe delivered a hook of narcotic and alcoholic bliss – all high-end dope and chasing Hpnotiq with Hennessy to get as high as possible, a metaphor for how successful, or major Kanye and his crew had become. Its homonym also referred to the album's collegiate theme, the chorus line "We major? C'mon homey, we major" suggesting that Kanye and his guests have hip-hop as their central focus of study.

Kanye's opening verse painted another portrait of how tough it could be growing up in the projects, where teenage boys joined gangs, carried guns, accidentally had children young and risked being killed for showing off any material wealth. And the girls barely had it better – "Asked the reverend was the strip clubs cool/If my tips helped send a pretty girl through school". Nas' verse, meanwhile, was rather more meta, opening in a state of uncertainty as he decided whether he should rap about traditional gangsta concerns or more conscious issues: "First line, should it be about the hoes or the ice?/Fo-fos or black Christ? Both flows'd be nice/Rap about big paper or the black man plight". Within seconds he'd summarised and discarded much of rap music's main themes, and here he turned to Really Doe at the studio console and asked his advice on what he should rap. Doe told him "write another *Illmatic*", and what emerged was a memorable verse about his longevity in hip-hop and how he now wanted to "build my very own Motown" since he believed the existing record labels were killing the genre by treating their artists so badly, a theme Nas would continue on his album *Hip Hop Is Dead*.

That hip-hop was actually alive and thriving was evident in 'We Major' itself, a track so enjoyable Kanye didn't want it to end. As Tony Williams' soul outro faded to a close, he sparked up again to shout out to his guests and producers, apologise for being late – ironically, the release of *Late Registration* would be delayed by 49 days – and explain the title: "They ask me, 'Why you call it *Late Registration*, 'Ye?'/'Cause we takin' these muh'fuckers back to school".

A third skit took us back to the Broke Phi Broke fraternity, as its leader explained the origins of the brotherhood, "founded by broke slaves years ago", and its line about a family so poor the mother has to pretend to be the Christmas tree gave way to 'Hey Mama', written back in 2000 and revived from his 2001 demo tape, a song that had become so important to Kanye that he had it tattooed on his arm. The track had developed Auto-Tune backing vocals but retained the heartfelt devotional sentiment that would soon lead to Kanye being called a 'mama's boy' in the press for the first time, in a newspaper in Chicago. "My mama's my best friend," he told the reporter for an article titled 'Kanye: A Mama's Boy After All', "I talk to her every day." Donda was worried about the connotation at first but her fears that the tag might damage Kanye's rap credibility were quickly allayed when Kanye told her how proud he was of the label.

There followed one of Brion's proudest moments on *Late Registration*, 'Celebration', which included a sample of the KayGees' 'Heavenly Dream', and another track that he had to fight to keep on the album. Conducting a 20-piece orchestra whose members were constantly in fits of giggles at the lyrics – "You know what this is?" went the intro hook, "it's a celebration, bitches! [a line intended as comic, quoting Dave Chappelle's sketch Reconciliation Of Rick James And Charlie Murphy]/Grab a drink, grab a glass, after that I grab yo ass" – Brion constructed a twisted, askew take on lush orchestrated soul onto which Kanye dropped laid-back verses about trying to lure a girl into bed with promises of fine champagne, the best dope on the planet and the promise of a well-hung baby – "I vow that my child will be well endowed, like his daddy," he promises her. The drink seems to go to his head by the end of the track, as he imagines a conversation with his unborn child, explaining that he was "my favourite accident" after "we was practising til one day your ass bust through the packaging". "[Rap music] is so formulaic," he'd say of the track, "16 bars, chorus, 16 bars, chorus. I had just one verse. It was a mad long verse, but that's all I had to say."

The fourth and final skit of the album saw Kanye being thrown out of the Broke Phi Broke fraternity during a secret meeting for lying about being poor – making beats behind his brothers' backs and using his ill-gotten gains to buy new shoes and "eating every day". And with Kanye's fraternity journey complete, so ended the album, with a farewell track called 'Gone' attempting to outdo the orchestral vibe of the entire album so far. "It's just a drumbeat, an Otis Redding sample [from his cover of Chuck Willis' 'It's Too Late'] and Kanye going to town over it," Brion said. "There's a whole string section, and it turns into crazy soundtrack music. It's a big piece of work."

'Gone' was certainly the most elaborate arrangement on the album. Leading off with a stark piano line and sprightly beat, it gradually grew into staccato bursts of chamber pop violin and viola, the strings and beats interweaved masterfully to create a theatrical swell of 10 violins, four violas and four cellos. To this graceful backing, Kanye, Consequence and Cam'Ron rhymed some of the best verses of their respective careers. Referencing Big L, LL Cool J and Eddie Murphy movie *The Golden Child*, Kanye's opening verse bragged of his Vuitton luggage, Gucci and Roc-A-Fella style, screen-festooned car and pickiness with groupies, sleeping with them even if he takes them to chain restaurants. This was an artful take on the sort of materialism that he'd been questioning just a few tracks before on 'Diamonds From Sierra Leone (Remix)', and he continued in a boastful tone, going on to warn any rappers thinking of starting any beef with him to try to get on his albums instead so they might learn how he makes such impressive beats – "'Damn 'Ye, it'd be stupid to diss you'," he rapped from his opponent's point of view, "'even your superficial raps is super-official'." Meanwhile, incongruously, he told the sorry story of his friend Aaron, who liked unprotected sex despite already having three children, but paid for it when he picked up an STD on the Usher tour. The relevance of the story is questionable; perhaps Kanye wanted to highlight the sexual profligacy his crew enjoyed.

Cam'Ron's verse worked on wordplay rather than developing a coherent theme, his lines of general rap self-aggrandisement smartly skipping around homonyms such as "You ever dealt with a dealer? Well here's the deal, ma, we're going to the dealers". But Consequence's verse was even more intricate, getting the song's title into virtually every line. He recounted a story of a dealer who, having lost a friend who may have been informing for the FBI, finds one of his street pushers has run off with his money. Tracking him down to a bar, he goes in shooting, only to land himself with a 20-year jail term. Con's hero is 'gone' for the rest of his youth.

Kanye's final verse on 'Gone' is often considered the best of his career. Musing about the fact that he's so far ahead of the game that "the powers that be won't let me get my ideas out", he considered taking his money, giving up rap music and moving out to Oklahoma, retreating from the spotlight into the life of obscurity he had before he managed to get a beat on a Jay-Z album: "before model chicks was bending over or dealerships asked me 'Benz or Rover'". This idea may be a tribute to Dave Chappelle, who left comedy and retreated to the countryside after his plans to inject more social commentary into his comedy were stalled by his producers. "I'm the rap version of Dave Chappelle," Kanye said. "I'm not sayin' I'm nearly as talented as Chappelle when it comes to political and social commentary, but like him, I'm laughing to keep from crying." But then he recalls how lucky he's been to rise from minimum wage jobs in Chicago to spending euros across Europe and being able to set up G.O.O.D. Music and remembers his importance to rap. He closed the album with a warning to the world not to let his talent go to waste, for the good of the next generation of rappers who take their cues from him: "Shorties at the door 'cause they need more inspiration for they life, they souls and they songs/They said 'Sorry, Mr West is gone'."

It was something of a downbeat note on which to end an otherwise ground-breaking and boundary-stretching record, but of course it wasn't actually the end. *Late Registration* had a bonus track in the shape of the original version of 'Diamonds From Sierra Leone'. Recorded before the theme of the song changed to focus on conflict diamonds, and before

Jay-Z got involved with the track, this version was concerned with pettier issues. Kanye bitterly sniped at the four star review that *Vibe* magazine had given *The College Dropout* – "Does he write his own rhymes? Well sort of, I think 'em/That mean I forgot better shit than you ever thought of" – at people still mispronouncing his name, including even George W Bush who called him Kanway before correcting his error, or spelling it wrong on his gold discs, about the A&R men who didn't sign him when they had the chance and his snubbing at the AMA Awards – "only playa that got robbed but kept all his jewellery". He hinted that Alicia Keys had tried to talk some sense into him after his tantrum and admitted that the world now saw him as "the international asshole", but defended his actions by pointing out his achievements in rap within such a short period: "When he came in the game, he made his own lane". And he asserted his role as a natural leader once more, right from childhood. Telling of the time his father took him to get baptised, he claimed "The preacher said we need leaders/Right then my body got still like a paraplegic/You know who you call, you got a message, then leave it".

On the UK version, there was a further bonus track entitled 'We Can Make It Better', featuring Talib Kweli, Q-Tip, Common and Rhymefest rapping over a sped-up sample of the Three Degrees' cover of 'Make It Easy On Yourself'. It had Kanye revisiting the fraternity theme in his verse, taking a girl on a tour of campus on her first day and promising to cure her of her fear of dating black men after leaving an abusive relationship. Meanwhile Talib, Common and Q-Tip drew sketches of the dangers of the city, with its drug addicts, parasitic hustlers and trigger-happy cops, and Rhymefest wrapped the track up by pointing the finger at the government and their cynical tactics to suppress the Afro-American population with "terrorism on blacks".

And *Late Registration* still wasn't done. As it approached the 70-minute mark, a hidden track emerged by the name of 'Late', as though the track itself had been delayed in getting to the album – "Just throw this at the end if I'm too late for the intro," he joked. It saw Kanye returning to the pitched-up soul samples of his earlier work, sampling 'I'll Erase Your Pain' by the Whatnauts, as well as dropping in some laughter from Notorious B.I.G.'s 'What's Beef', and to the running theme of the album itself. He was racing to school with his mother's warnings of a life of poverty if he couldn't get on the best courses ringing in his ears, only to find he was too late to register – "You mean I missed my major by a couple of seconds? Now I'm in the shop class or the basket weaving". But as the second verse would explain, being on time was over-rated; having missed out on school, Kanye was now successful and famous enough not to have to be on time for anything, be it the world's most exclusive parties or an encounter with "two dykes that look Christina Milian-like". The *Late Registration* of the title was, in the end, the making of him.

And the press would agree. "This is killing everything out there!" Kanye exclaimed at a media listening session at Sony Studios before the album was finished. "I wanted to take this opportunity to play [the album] and show off... [Imagine] when you had dreams of being writers and writing about the Rolling Stones or Prince ... yes, only Kanye would put his name in that group. Seriously, how many perfect albums is that under my belt? I'm sorry. Actually, no, I don't apologise." He played the attendant journalists Hype Williams' video for the first single, the original version of 'Diamonds From Sierra Leone'★, which opened with cinematic black-and-white portrayals of the cutthroat life of a diamond miner as a voice-over declared, "When I was a boy, I worked in the diamond mines deep in the dark mountains of Sierra Leone. Children worked there day and night under the watchful eyes of soldiers. Every day we feared for our lives. Our only hope came from when we would sing". These troubling images were intercut with shots of Kanye wandering the medieval streets of Prague, heartless diamond traders and blood pouring from the jewels that suitors present to their fiancées in mockery of De Beers diamond adverts. The video ended like a charity appeal film, with the legend 'please buy conflict-free diamonds', and struck quite a chord with the writers in the room, even if it wouldn't match up to Kanye's hopes or expectations, despite his concerns that he'd be criticised for making a video with Hype Williams,

★ At the same time as the press listening, the video premiered on television.

who'd been known for style-over-substance videos. On its May 31 release, the single would hit the *Billboard* chart at only 43, charting in another 11 countries and reaching number eight in the UK.

Then Kanye played tracks from the album, stopping some before a guest would appear that he didn't want to reveal yet. It was enough. Critics heaped praise on the record in the months and weeks leading up to its August 30 launch. "On *Late Registration*, the Louis Vuitton Don doesn't just set out to create pop music, he wants to *be* pop music," wrote *Rolling Stone*. "So he steps up his lyrical game, shows off his epic production skills, reaches higher, pushes harder and claims the whole world of music as hip-hop turf." "*Late Registration* is more cumbersome and burdened than its predecessor," said *Entertainment Weekly*, "a little less cohesive, a lot less fun, but it rarely fails to engross at nearly every step… [A] fascinating sprawl of an album, West throws our messy, stressed-out, multiculti world in our faces and dares us to make sense of it, and of him." "A follow-up as ornate and bloated as West's ego," claimed *Spin*. "There's hardly an ounce of humility here - every track aims for the anthemic."

Looking back on it some years later, however, Kanye himself would claim he'd overthought the record. "The second album, I was trying to prove something and over-rapped songs, or used too many instruments," he said. "It was like a good movie, but a long movie." "I think it had a lot of great songs on it, but I think the songs were indulgent and that the album itself was poorly put together. I put too much shit on it. Songs are too long, there are skits that I would have left off. It could have been a tighter package. When you listen to it, you have to fast-forward some shit."

The hype around *Late Registration* reached melting point a few weeks before release when the second single, 'Gold Digger', blew up. Following the disappointing chart performance of 'Diamonds…', the Jamie Foxx effect kicked in once again; 'Gold Digger' sold 80,000 downloads in its first week of release, becoming the fastest selling digital download of all time to date and going on to sell over one million downloads. The track came with a second Hype Williams video, this time featuring Kanye and Jamie performing the song between shots of girls acting out classic scantily clad magazine covers. Kanye would recall Def Jam head LA Reid "talking me out of doing the 'Gold Digger' video and making it all slaves ... Sometimes as a creative person, you go off the deep end a little. The downside is, you don't always know when to stop." Initially hitting the *Billboard* charts at number 19, it would shoot to number one the following week and stay put for 10 weeks. In the UK, the single would be just as big a hit, selling almost 300,000 copies and spending 48 weeks in the Top 100. "It uses profanity, and it's shocking and controversial and fucked up and funny," Kanye said of the song's popularity. "It's so perfect and out of the park."

And *Late Registration* itself, helped by a TV ad showing the Dropout Bear wandering the London streets, matched the single's success. Selling 860,000 copies in its first week, almost double what *The College Dropout* had achieved and the best first-week sales in Def Jam's history, it went straight into the *Billboard* chart at number one and held the spot for two weeks, by which time it had sold 1.14 million copies. It would eventually sell over three million in the US and top charts around the world – it made the Top 10 in Canada, the UK, Ireland, Switzerland and Norway.

Kanye's star had gone supernova. And he was just about to use his position to fire up a whole new storm.

CHAPTER EIGHT

Who Will Survive In America

In rehearsal, Kanye stuck to the script. Word for word, just like the autocue said. But the words he recited didn't come close to expressing his true feelings – his anger, frustration and horror at the events he was seeing unfold on TV.

When the category three Hurricane Katrina struck New Orleans, killing 2,000 people, causing $100 billion of damage and displacing hundreds of thousands of families, many of whom lost their homes and were stranded on rooftops, it came down hard on some of the poorest people in America. Almost 30 per cent of the New Orleans black population lived below the poverty line, and now many had lost everything they owned. What's more, the desperate were treated like criminals. While normal citizens commandeered boats to help save their neighbours, the authorities responded badly – officials locked thousands of people urgently in need of food and shelter out of the Superdome where supplies were limited, and those trying to walk out of New Orleans over the Crescent City Connector bridge into Gretna were turned back by policemen bearing shotguns.

And all the while George W Bush flickered over Kanye's TV screen, his rescue campaign non-existent, the President of the United States utterly ignoring the horrific plight of his poorest people.

No autocue was going to say what Kanye had to say.

September 2, 2005 and at an NBC Concert For Hurricane Relief telethon broadcast live on America's East Coast, Kanye, hosting a segment alongside actor Mike Myers, looked firmly down the lens and strode defiantly off-script.

"I hate the way they portray us in the media," he said. "You see a black family, it says, 'They're looting.' You see a white family, it says, 'They're looking for food.' And, you know, it's been five days [waiting for federal help] because most of the people are black. And even for me to complain about it, I would be a hypocrite because I've tried to turn away from the TV because it's too hard to watch. I've even been shopping before even giving a donation, so now I'm calling my business manager right now to see what is the biggest amount I can give, and just to imagine if I was down there, and those are my people down there. So anybody out there that wants to do anything that we can help – with the way America is set up to help the poor, the black people, the less well-off, as slow as possible. I mean, the Red Cross is doing everything they can. We already realise a lot of people that could help are at war right now, fighting another way – and they've given them permission to go down and shoot us!"

Bewildered, his co-host attempted to bring the broadcast back onto its allotted track. "And subtle, but in many ways even more profoundly devastating, is the lasting damage to survivors' will to rebuild and remain in the area," he said. "The destruction of the spirit of the people of southern Louisiana and Mississippi may end up being the most tragic loss of all."

More words rolled up in Kanye's eye line, pre-written statements about the issues facing the victims of the disaster; it was his cue. He tightened his jaw, stared direct down the camera, spoke from his heart.

"George Bush doesn't care about black people," he said.

The phones lit up. Some viewers were so appalled by Kanye's outburst that they demanded donations they'd already made to be refunded; others rang in support. His speech was edited out of the West Coast broadcast, which was on a delay and NBC swiftly issued a statement. "Tonight's telecast was a live television event wrought with emotion," it read. "Kanye West departed from the scripted comments that were prepared for him, and his opinions in no way represent the views of the networks. It would be most unfortunate if the efforts of the artists who participated tonight and the generosity of millions of Americans who are helping those in need are overshadowed by one person's opinion."

Watching the news channels cover the story from her room in New York's Dream Hotel, Donda was worried Kanye had thrown away his career, that he'd be blacklisted by the establishment for his comments. She was reminded of Eartha Kitt being blacklisted for coming out against the Vietnam War at a luncheon with Lyndon Johnson in 1968, or the Dixie Chicks' fanbase collapsing after they criticised the Iraq War onstage in 2003, some ex-fans even gathering to crush their CDs with bulldozers. But when Kanye called her to talk over the event, she told him she was proud of him and he said he wasn't sorry for what he'd said, that he'd been overcome by the emotion of the moment and had to speak his mind. "I've never met George Bush," he'd tell her, "maybe one-on-one he's a cool dude."

Over the coming hours and days, reaction to Kanye's outburst was strong, and largely positive. Mike Myers issued a statement in support of what he'd done. "I went to the Katrina telethon because I was very moved by the plight of the people of New Orleans, and I wanted to make a difference," it read, "I think that the frustration that Kanye expressed was valid."* And the public at large seemed to agree. This was a country, remember, where one third of black men in their twenties were in prison, 70 per cent of black babies were born out of wedlock or in orphanages, 30 per cent of African-Americans lived below the poverty line and unemployment amongst blacks was double that of whites. In such a society, Kanye's words rang ominously true; he looked to many like a mouthpiece for their plight, and his popularity surged.

And the people stood by him. Some printed up the words "George Bush doesn't care about black people" on T-shirts and watched them sell out. Al Gore pledged his support. When Kanye appeared on the Ellen Degeneres show a week after the incident and said, "I might lose

---

* Myers would later give Kanye a role in his movie *The Love Guru*.

my endorsements for what I said but… people have lost their lives, lost their families. It's the least I could do to go up there and say something from my heart", rumour went round that Pepsi was considering pulling its endorsement of Kanye in the wake of the scandal. A boycott of the soft drink was begun and the company soon quashed what it claimed was a false rumour, upping Kanye's exposure on MTV and BET.

During interviews over the weeks that followed, Kanye discussed his words at length, always probing but never repentant. "I knew I wasn't going to read the whole script, because we'd practised that earlier," he told *Rolling Stone*. "I didn't think about Bush until the telethon. I saw him [on the TV]. I'm like 'Wait a second, dude, that guy over there, he doesn't care'. But America was always headed that way. I think it was a common opinion." "I said what I said emotionally," he told the *Australian Sunday Mail*, "I dealt with the praise and I dealt with the backlash. It is what it is. My main goal is to let people know I'm a musician, not a politician. I don't know anything about politics. I care about people."

Kanye also felt the outburst had helped get his persona across to the nation too. "I think it changed my life for the better," he told *Nightline*. "I think people understood me a little bit more. And instead of this guy like, has little baby Tourette's maybe not diagnosed – but the truth just comes out, like accidentally, like what's on the top of his mind. I'm working off the cuff here, I'm working off the top of my mind, I'm not reading the teleprompter, I'm speaking from the heart and that was that. I mean, I have a hard time believing that George Bush cares about anyone so, sidebar, black people also. I guess it's a very pop moment of a lifetime or generation. I mean, my dad's generation is a generation of messaging, you know? But that's just a piece of me being the opinionated individual that I am. It was pretty bugged out. When you think about it, I was wearing like, a Juicy Couture men's polo shirt. We weren't there, like, ready for war."

Donda also spoke out in defence of her son. "In my view there is to be some consideration for what is politically correct," she said, "but there is to be more consideration for telling the truth and making the most positive impact on society that we can. Kanye is really, I think, a very good spokesperson. He's very critical and thinks analytically, as he was taught to does... if you think that what is happening is very unjust, and you have the platform like Kanye to call attention to it, I think it's very responsible of him to do that, and it's the responsibility of the person listening to decide if they agree."

To put his money where his mouth was, Kanye and a team of eight, including his father, Ray, but with no camera crews allowed, went to visit the victims of Katrina themselves. He wanted to go to New Orleans itself to see the devastation first-hand but was told that the water there was contaminated so he should go to Houston to visit the survivors being housed at the Astrodome there. The people he spoke to thanked him profusely for what he'd said and had horrific tales to tell; of being stranded on their rooftops and thrown body bags from helicopters with instructions to put their loved ones inside if they'd died. "What do people need most?" he asked them. "I can't do as much as I would like to, but I can do something. I want to talk to the victims myself and ask them what they need. I'm doing this as a regular citizen, not a celebrity."

On his first trip he took essentials such as toiletries as well as make-up and perfumes for the adults and masks and sweets for the children. On his second visit he took more substantial aid and was told he'd be able to address the 2,000 people at the Astrodome via the in-house PA, but was ultimately stopped from speaking by the Red Cross. While he was in the South, Kanye also visited several churches, where victims laid out their most basic needs, for jobs and shelter. With the help of the Urban League, the Kanye West Foundation found and furnished homes for 15 families in need, his own contribution to rebuilding this shattered city.

Suddenly, Kanye found people looking to him for answers. "When I made my statement about Katrina, it was a social statement, an emotional statement, not a political one," he said. "After that statement, people were coming to me for these magical statements to sum up the emotions of the entire country. They don't always come to me."

Years later, George Bush would say the event was a low point in his time in office. "I didn't appreciate it then and I don't appreciate it now," Bush told the *Today Show* "It's one thing to say 'I don't appreciate the way he's handled his business, it's another thing to say 'This man's a racist'. I resent it, it's not true and it was one of the most disgusting moments of my Presidency." Kanye, by now more reflective about the incident, responded on the same show. "As far as it being the worst moment of his Presidency, I can't really speak to that, but his take, his explanation, I completely agree with and I empathise with, and I felt like that the entire time I was being hailed as a hero and everyone's saying 'I'm so happy you said that, I didn't like you before but now I like you 'cause you said this'. You sit there and know in your heart as a person that in a moment of emotion to peg someone as a racist is just not right… I don't want to speak on the word 'regret', I think a lot of things that happen in America, period, are because of race, just the way this country was built and the struggles we've had to have to get into positions through media, social positions, though gentrification, it's a way bigger conversation than that… I wanted to say something to him right after the fact… I would tell George Bush, in my moment of frustration, that I didn't have the grounds to call him a racist… I'm here to man up to different mistakes that I made and speak to the moment when I pegged George Bush as a racist… I made mistakes and I've grown as a person and it's not as easy as boxing someone into a villain role or a race role. I did not have enough information in that situation to call him a racist. That might have been the emotion I felt but me being a rational, well thought-out, empathetic human being and thinking about it after the fact, I would have chosen different words. Even in these times when I was considered to have done something so wrong, my motivation was from a good place. Maybe mistimed, maybe not the right wording, maybe not realising the power of my words and the way they would stop the internet, but nonetheless it's very pure and from a good place."

The campaign around *Late Registration* would often reflect the tone Kanye took on the record itself. He was finally speaking his mind on social and political issues as well as his own life and achievements, and he took every opportunity to raise awareness of wrongdoing wherever he saw it. Of course he'd regularly compare himself to Muhammad Ali, Prince, Bill Gates and Michael Jordan in interviews or make statements such as, "I really believe in myself, and I want to apologise to everybody out there who says I'm arrogant. I apologise to everyone for believing in myself," and "I feel like a spoiled kid, someone who's got a little scooter hooked up to a generator that powers a city… this is me trying to become more comfortable with the position I'm in. The last album was ground-breaking. Now the process is to strive for greatness." But he tempered them with stark social commentary. "My songs are mad pro-black political songs," he claimed, and at his appearance at the Philadelphia stop of the Live 8 AIDS Awareness concert tour, he took the opportunity to reiterate his belief that "[AIDS is] a man-made disease. [It was] placed in Africa just like crack was placed in the black community to break up the Black Panthers."

Def Jam's Tracey Waples would remember an event from Live 8 that illustrated Kanye's crossover appeal: "I was sitting in Sting's dressing room at Live 8," she said. "And Sting, Bono, John Mayer and Kanye were making up a song. In that moment I understood why he was able to be there. 50 or T.I. would never be able to be in that room." This is unlikely to have happened during the global Live 8 event, however, as the stars played in separate cities – Kanye in Philadelphia and Sting and Bono in London.

Later that month, when presented with the 2005 Million Man March Image Award for his achievements, he spoke further about his viewpoint. "I brought up in a song about [how] the government administers AIDS. I think the figure I learned when I was at Live 8 was that there was over 6,000 people in Africa dying every day from AIDS. But, I said the government administers the AIDS. This is the whole thing. If you've got something that you want to get to, and there's a people that are strong people, a people that are warriors, in order to get to their resources you've got to weaken them. What else has the strongest people you know in more of a fetal position than the AIDS epidemic?... I say in another song, you know the best medicine goes to people that's paid. If Magic Johnson got a cure for AIDS and all the broke mothers passed away. So that means a cure for AIDS. So who has a cure? Maybe the same people that administer it that want to get to the diamonds… That's one of the reasons why I think God let me live.

But, there must have been a deal made when He spared my life in an accident. He said, 'At any given moment I'm gonna just use you. I'm gonna speak through you at any given moment and you gotta just run with it'."

Another message that Kanye felt God must have been using him to get across concerned something much closer to home: the issues that created rap music. "A lot of hip-hop comes from the hate that hate made," he told *Time Out* in the UK. "People are making music to try to come out of those situations, but they still speak about what they do to get out of there. Frustrated heavy rock came out of abused white kids and drug addicts, right? On *Late Registration* I have a track called 'Crack Music', which is about the music made by the crack generation. This is music that came out of the 'hood, out of the worst situations. You don't know why it's rude, well, look where it came from."

And, bolder still, he tackled the thorny problem of rap homophobia head-on. In an MTV interview *All Eyes On Kanye West*, Kanye introduced a gay cousin who'd been out for 15 years and who'd brought his partner to many of Kanye's Christmases in Oklahoma. "I would use the word 'fag' and always look down upon gays," he told the cameras. "But then my cousin told me that another one of my cousins was gay, and I loved him, he's one of my favourite cousins. And at that point it was kind of like a turning point when I was like, 'Yo, this my cousin, I love him and I been discriminating against gays'. But everybody in hip-hop discriminates against gay people. Matter of fact, the exact opposite word of 'hip-hop', I think, is 'gay'. Like you play a record and if it's wack, 'That's gay, dog!' It's not just hip-hop, but America discriminates against gay people. And I wanna just come on TV and just tell my rappers, just tell my friends, 'Yo, stop it fam'."

Amongst his peer group, this statement went down far worse than his criticism of Bush – some friends stopped wearing *College Dropout* T-shirts as a result. "I got more backlash for that than for the Bush comment. It's wrong, and so many of my friends do that. We gay-bash. We feel like it's OK to call a gay person a fag. We fought so hard to make it so white people couldn't say the word 'nigger' to our face. But it's not far-fetched to picture a black person calling a gay person a fag to their face. So that shows you the climate, where we're at right now. It's not about racism, it's about discrimination."

When asked if he'd take a similar stance towards the denigration of women in rap music, Kanye wasn't quite so forthright, believing homophobia to be more widespread and honestly felt within the genre. "I think in the daily life of a black male, we gay-bash way more than we disrespect women," he said. "We would call a gay guy a fag to his face. But if we walked up to a woman and said 'ai'ight bitch!' we would know that was disrespectful… my level of consciousness has since been raised. And I actually think that standing up for gays was even more courageous than bad-mouthing the President. In the black community someone could label you gay and bring your career down. But that was me showing what black people are really about today, or at least what we need to be about."

Kanye was magnanimous in his response to his friends shunning him for his comments. He decided he'd say what he felt and leave it to his friends' consciences to agree with him or not. He'd rather be criticised for speaking out in favour of civil rights than stay quiet when he saw things he felt were wrong. "I do think that Kanye is a voice that can definitely be used and should be used not only in hip-hop but across the arts, period," Donda said. "I think he is broader than a genre. I think he has a calling to reach a number of people. Kanye keeps it real. He touches the people. You never know how words can save a person's life, physically or otherwise. People like Martin Luther King or Mahatma Ghandi or, in my view, Barack Obama, or Jesus Christ – people whose job it is to tell the truth – I see that in Kanye. Now, people like you are going to go, 'Oh, Kanye's mom said he was like Jesus!' But when you have a gift, you don't get it by yourself. Your truth is your truth."

As he travelled the world telling journalists and DJs about *Late Registration* Kanye took it upon himself to point out unfairness in every corner of society and the media. He became the conscience of MTV, feeding the channel regularly with exclusives and specials but also criticising it for exploiting people with personal or legal problems. At times Kanye's temper got the better of him. During one radio appearance in Canada he tried to discuss the fact that the station in question was editing out the phrase 'white girl' from 'Gold Digger': "I am never coming on this station again unless you unbleep 'white girl'," he said, "I can't say the word 'white'?... There's nothing racial about that line, it's an observation about social issues. If anything it's more offensive to black people. This is the real world, as long as there are racists there'll be racism." But when the DJ interrupted him mid-sentence while he was explaining himself, Kanye blew up – "I'm talking man!" he yelled, and walked out of the studio.

Not that Kanye was ultra-confident about everything he was doing at this point, even while he was being named amongst *Time* magazine's 100 Most Influential People In The World and pictured on the cover of *Rolling Stone* wearing a crown of thorns. "How could you be in this situation with this amount of pressure and this many people looking at you, waiting for you to show them a magic Houdini trick or a David Blaine, waiting for you to not make it out of your chains when the casket goes into the water, and *not* be self-conscious?" he asked MTV. "How could you not be scared when you step out on that stage? How can I not be scared on the second album? How could I not be scared when I dropped 'Diamonds'… and there's people who say, 'I don't like "Diamonds"…'?"

Nonetheless, his comments had gained him a level of notoriety that would stick with him for years to come. Whether you saw him as a self-centred, un-American egotist causing offence to the national sensibility in a time of emergency or an outspoken hero tackling injustices wherever he can, everyone now knew Kanye West's name and had an opinion on the man himself.

And his actions over the coming year wouldn't help change either party's minds.

★ ★ ★

"If I don't win Album of the Year, I'm gonna really have a problem with that," Kanye ranted to the MTV cameras, backstage at a special show at Santa Monica High School, head spinning with rumours that *Late Registration* would be nominated for the Best Album Grammy but wouldn't win due to his criticism of George W Bush. "I can never talk myself out of [winning], you know why? Because I put in the work. I don't care if I jumped up and down right now on the couch like Tom Cruise. I don't care what I do, I don't care how much I stunt - you can never take away from the amount of work I put into it. So I don't wanna hear all of that politically correct stuff. You put the camera in front of me, I'm gonna tell you like this. I worked hard to get here. I put my love, I put my heart, I put my money [into *Late Registration*]. I'm $600,000 in the hole right now on that album and you tell me about being politically incorrect? People love these songs. You talk to somebody whose grandmother just died and listens to 'Roses', and you tell me about being politically incorrect. I'm talking about history. I never got five mics [top rating] in *The Source,* I never got five stars from *Vibe*. They said it's not a classic. So 'Jesus Walks' is not a classic? 'Roses' is not a classic? 'Gold Digger' wasn't song of the year? 'Oh, but Kanye, you can't say that'. Why? Who are you? I don't know you… I said I was the face of the Grammys last year. I'm 10 times that [this year]. Get your cameras ready. Two things: do not let me get up on that stage and do not let me get up on that stage. Either way, we going crazy!"

It was understandable that Kanye would be getting even more full of himself than usual as 2005 drew to a close. In August he'd stolen the show at the VMAs once more, emerging on a revolving stage back-to-back with Jamie Foxx to sing 'Gold Digger' in designer lounge suits, as jet cannons pumped flumes of fake dollar bills into the air. That night he also picked up one of the three awards he was nominated for at the 2005 VMAs, Best Male Video.

Then, looking to emulate the sumptuous tones of Portishead's *Roseland NYC Live* album, in September he'd flown to London's legendary Abbey Road Studios to record a live performance album backed by a 22-piece all-female orchestra in eye-slash make-up and watched by 300 invited guests in the home of the Beatles. Swathed in spotlights and clad in a flashy blazer, crisp white shirt and trousers and red rose at his lapel, his set merged *Late Registration* tracks with the likes of 'Jesus Walks', 'Through The Wire' and 'The New Workout Plan' from *The College Dropout*, with Lupe Fiasco, GLC, John Legend and Consequence making guest appearances. From the tense, urgent cinematic crescendos of 'Diamonds From Sierra Leone' to the passionate spinning-on-the-spot performance of 'Drive Slow' and an emotional piano-led 'Heard 'Em Say', the 13-track album was a gorgeous coda to *Late Registration* that allowed the political messages, lustrous emotion and inventive twisting of word sounds to fit incongruous rhymes on the likes of 'All Fall Down' and 'Bring Me Down' to cut through loud and clear – on the latter Kanye leapt onto a piano stool to conduct his inner pain out of the orchestra. The album and its accompanying live film swept fans further into Kanye's ambitious world and even left the man himself dumbstruck at times. "This is gonna fuck people up," he muttered when he first heard scratching over a grand piano during rehearsals, and the show itself was peppered with proud pronouncements. "This is a dream come true," he said of playing the legendary studio, going on to remind the crowd how lucky they were to have bagged one of these incredibly hot tickets and how they should show their appreciation by dancing more wildly. "The lights, the strings, I just wanna soak it in, but what I want you all to know is I'm about making music that you feel, and for us to feel it I gotta feel y'all… I would suggest to take advantage of this opportunity and have a good time."

Late Orchestration would be released on April 24, 2006 and reach number 59 in the UK.

The following month the album's third single, 'Heard 'Em Say', was released to widespread critical acclaim – "probably the best hip-hop lullaby to come along since Slick Rick's 'Children's Story'," said PopMatters, while Robert Christgau lauded the track's inventive use of Chinese bells and berimbau. As with 'Jesus Walks' the song came with multiple videos: since the track was originally planned to be released for Christmas, Michel Gondry directed a live-action promo set in Macy's department store in New York over the festive season. It featured Kanye as the father of a homeless family allowed into the store by Adam Levine's errant security guard, where they turn the store into a magical playground where you can turn beds into cars that drive around, Christmas dinners cook themselves and Jon Brion plays the delicate piano line on a parade of marching toy pianos. When the release date was pulled forward to November 8, however, Kanye dropped the Christmas themed video and a new clip of pencil-drawn animation by Bill Plympton was premiered on Channel 4 in the UK instead. Plympton's whimsical work in such late-eighties shorts as 'How To Kiss' and '25 Ways To Quit Smoking' had had a major impact on the young Kanye. "He told me he's always loved my work, and that my images were important to him as a kid," said Plympton. "And he was always curious. He would call me from all over the place: 'Oh Bill, I'm watching 'I Married A Strange Person' right now. How did you do this and that?'"

In Plympton's video, Kanye was portrayed as a poorly paid taxi driver in an oversized cab picking up a mother and child. "The child is meant to represent Kanye as a young boy and the film is about his experiences," Plympton said. "Conversely, he wanted the mother to be very sexy, so we did that, too." With Kanye morphing into Jesus and the devil as they're mentioned in the lyrics, they eventually stop at a petrol station where the child spots his mother's cigarettes lying on the cab seat, tries one and throws the lit match out of the window into a puddle of gasoline. The cab rockets into the air, where both Kanye and the child grow angel wings – the child remains in the heavens while Kanye's angel returns to earth to continue his taxi job, a kind of living purgatory. "He wanted a scene at the end of the video where his character went to the pearly gates and was rejected," Bill explained. "I had to tell him, 'We only have one day to go, and getting the pearly gates right would be almost impossible.' Thankfully, he understood."

As the song entered the *Billboard* chart at 100 and began a slow climb to peak at 26 – a crucial crossover hit for both Kanye and Levine – Kanye's Touch The Sky Tour kicked off in Miami at the university's Convocation Centre. His second ever tour – redesigned alongside his new production advisor Es Devlin just a fortnight before the first date after he was overheard yelling at his original designer "I'm not excited about going on tour. All y'all have is moving lights!" – would wend its way across the country playing large theatres and arenas; Kanye was stepping straight into the live big leagues. Stretching right up to December 11, Kanye played such venues as the Thompson-Bowling Arena in Knoxville, the Mizzou Arena in Columbia, the AJ Palumbo

Center in Pittsburgh and two nights at the theatre at Madison Square Garden in New York with Fantasia and Keyshia Cole as opening acts. Kanye spelt out his vision for the show: "I want people [seeing the Touch the Sky show] to feel inspired," he said. "I want them to go to work the next day and feel like they can take whatever they're doing to another level. It's not just about sitting there being in awe. Making the world better – that's one of our missions with music and with visuals. So my pain is everybody else's pleasure – how I stress, how I was up all last night, how I'm about to kill myself because it's not perfect. Well, maybe people can feel that when they're in the audience, like, 'Yoooooo! This really took a lot of time. He really put a lot of work in this.' Anyone that's ever been backstage or seen a lot of shows is gonna give this show credit for being so different… Visually, there was nothing [in the shows I saw growing up] that captured me. I have a really high bar and low tolerance. How small my gauge is for what's good is what makes me the artist I am today. Basically, I think ninety-nine percent of the shit is wack. I don't want to be in that ninety-nine percent."

"Performing live is the reason why we make this music, spend so much time and thought and craft on it," he said in a statement to launch the tour. "It's never been about the critics or the album sales. It's about the fans, and I love having the opportunity to bring this music – that I've poured my heart and soul into – to them. I think about how audiences are going to respond to hooks and intros and certain lines when I'm in the studio recording. Bringing these songs to the stage is the ultimate fulfillment of the creative process."

The show strived to live up to the lavish nature of the album. Accompanied by a glamorous string section sawing out Shirley Bassey's 'Diamonds Are Forever' and the orchestral version of the Rolling Stones' 'The Last Time'*, Kanye leapt around the stage in designer blazers, giving the likes of 'Touch The Sky' and 'Hey Mama' the feel of a soul spectacular. By the time this first leg of the *Late Registration*

---

* This was a brave move – when the Verve used the same string segment for their huge hit 'Bitter Sweet Symphony', Allen Klein, who controlled the Stones' music publishing, insisted they give up all of their profits from the song.

touring schedule reached an end, Kanye was at home on the big stages, and comfortable taking on support slots on U2's mammoth *Vertigo* tour over four dates at the end of 2005. The shows were an eye-opener; every night he'd watch Bono take to the circular stage to ecstatic receptions, commanding eye-blitzing extravaganzas on transparent hanging curtain screens and holding vast arenas in the palm of his hand. This, Kanye thought, was a lesson in how he should be upping his own game.

So, Christmas arrived on another fantastically successful year, *Late Registration* topping many magazines' end of year polls and his mother celebrating by having a pair of Louis Vuitton millionaire sunglasses flown in from Paris as his festive gift, to which Kanye would reciprocate by buying his mother a house with an ocean view for her birthday. Kanye certainly felt cocky enough to be demanding Grammys. In the event he was nominated for eight, Album Of The Year and Best Rap Album for *Late Registration*, Record Of The Year and Best Rap/Solo Performance for 'Gold Digger', Best Rap Song for 'Diamonds From Sierra Leone', Best R&B Song for his part in writing Alicia Keys' 'Unbreakable', a second nomination in Album Of The Year for his work on Mariah Carey's *The Emancipation Of Mimi* album and Best Rap/Sung Collaboration for 'They Say' from Common's album – although this last nomination bugged him since 'Heard 'Em Say' and 'Gold Digger' had been overlooked.

Come the ceremony itself on February 8, Kanye picked up three awards, for Best Rap Solo Performance, Best Rap Album and Best Rap Song bringing his Grammy tally to an impressive six for his first two albums. His performance on the night was characteristically colourful, bringing rap further into the sphere of the mainstream pop revue. Dressed as the leader of a full white-clad cartoonish marching band and mocking his own arrogance with his introductory speech – "I been here two years in a row, if I don't win there's gonna be a problem, we don't want no problem do we?" – he took on Jamie Foxx's rival band in a frenzy of chocolate box hip-hop, the two marching bands standing off against each other throughout the hi-octane performance of 'Gold Digger' on a block party set full of jiving band-members. The show switched to a second stand-off, this time between a troupe of gold diggers and the Broke Phi Broke fraternity adopting the "broke stance" before Kanye reappeared in a glittering mauve and white suit for a celebratory verse of 'Touch The Sky'. His speech was similarly comic and ostentatious. "I had no idea," he said, accepting the award for Best Rap Album while pulling some pre-made signs from his pocket, reading his thank yous from the back of a sheet marked 'THANK YOU LIST' and rounding up with a cry of "Feels good to be home!" In photos later, he was pictured holding up another sign: 'I TOLD YOU SO!' it read. Even the night's big winners U2 paid tribute to West – "Kanye, you're next," said Bono as he accepted the Best Album award. The 48th Grammys was a good night for the G.O.O.D. Music label all round, with John Legend also picking up three awards.

At the Brit Awards the following month, Kanye put on another big show, his rendition of 'Diamonds From Sierra Leone' adorned with fireworks, orchestra and gymnasts and a huge parade of writhing, gold-painted dancers in bikinis emerging for 'Gold Digger'. He ended his performance hoisted on a crane at the end of 'Touch The Sky', a proud statement borne out by taking home the award for Best International Solo Artist.

Meanwhile, the promotional tour for *Late Registration* rolled on well into 2006. During his Brits visit to the UK he played a swathe of major shows including the Birmingham NEC Arena and Manchester MEN Arena, and touched base with his UK fans. "I think I'm gonna move to London. Get a fake-ass British accent like Madonna," he told one radio station while claiming that UK audiences would get his new record, which he likened to Marvin Gaye's seminal *What's Going On* album, more than US listeners since they'd understand the emotion and passion of it rather than merely concentrate on the radio-friendly pop side.

As his 20-song set travelled the globe, grossing over $8 million over 46 dates, backed by DJ A-Trak and his string section and occasionally including appearances from Common or De La Soul and a cover of the Beatles' 'Eleanor Rigby' or Twista's 'Overnight Celebrity', Kanye revealed more about his plans for the year. His elite fashion line was now due to launch in April 2006 and renamed Pastelle, the theme being pastel shades of high quality clothes, including some Polos in his trademark pink. Explaining that he was a shopaholic, always in stores with Ibn, Really Doe, John-John and Don C when he wasn't up against album deadlines, and very passionate about fashion, he claimed that smartly dressed people might listen to Franz Ferdinand, Culture Club or George Micheal in the pop sphere, but only himself and Jay-Z in hip-hop. Hence, he saw an avenue where his vision would improve the current ranges. "I went to art school, so I'm getting heavily into design – you know, shoes and clothes," he said. "I'd go to Polo, Louis Vuitton, Marc Jacobs or whatever and say to myself, 'Man, if they dial the colour like this, I would like it better'. I'm just looking for opportunities to really apply my art to stuff I love."

But Kanye wasn't just going to stamp his name on someone else's design. He envisioned his branching out into fashion as an expansion of his brand – he'd often liken himself to Disney, Coca-Cola or McDonald's in terms of the global brand reach he was aiming for, and looked for guidance to Jay-Z's Rocawear clothing line that was in the process of making Hova $200 million, 50 Cent's water brand or Puffy's sprawling empire of commercialism. So if he was going to get involved in the fashion world then he was going to have as much control over the product as he was used to in music. The clothes would have to encapsulate everything the name Kanye West was coming to mean – quality, opulence, open-mindedness, self-assurance, the setting of trends. And often the labels he approached wouldn't give him that much control. "A lot of celebrities walk in, and there will be designers who have worked on stuff their entire lives, and the [designer] says, 'Hey, you take this, this is what I picture for you'," he said. "[But] people couldn't do exactly what I wanted to do. Just like with producing and making my own videos and stuff like that, I had to learn how to do it so I could present the world something new and different. I want something that's really respected. I wanted to be a designer before I wanted to be a rapper. Rapping has given me a plateau to meet with some really dope designers. It's taken years but I'm learning a lot."

Hence, the launch of the line would eventually be postponed, as Kanye would have to learn about fabrics and industry standards so that he could properly communicate his ideas to the designers. And his move into funding a water company didn't go to plan either. Using his own money, Kanye backed a store dedicated to selling water that his father Ray wanted to open in Maryland, keen to support his father's entrepreneurial spirit. To mark the opening, Kanye hit Maryland to lead a walk for World Water Day and make a speech about the importance of the idea of clean water for Maryland. Unfortunately only 50 people turned out for the walk, and the store itself wouldn't stay open for more than a few years.

So, for the time being, music remained Kanye's main business focus. As the *Late Registration* tour reached Australia in March, Kanye readied his next single, 'Touch The Sky'. "'Touch The Sky' is what my life is about, it's what this year's been about," he told MTV. "To anyone that feels like something is so far away, [the song is] just the concept of actually being able to leap above the environment that you're in. All the naysayers and the haters and people say, 'You'll never make it that far, you'll never make it out of this town, we'll call you,' and all those things, and finally you get the opportunity to touch the sky. That's what this year's about, so no matter what they give to me or try to take from me, there's nothing you can take from me. We've already touched the sky. With or without any accolades, whatever it is, the fact that people listen to this music and it's connected with people, the fact that you see fans crying in the audience - you can't tell me anything after that because there's so many places and establishments where people are out of touch. When someone hears your song and cries, then you're in touch and that's what matters. At that point, you feel like you've touched the sky."

Such a rousing tune – the track that closed many of Kanye's live shows on the tour, including his memorable appearance at the Coachella Festival on April 29, where he drew one of the biggest and most mixed crowds of the weekend – would need a pretty sensational video to go with it. So Kanye turned to director Chris Milk and together they came up with the Evel Kanyevel concept, the star-studded million-dollar tribute to Evel Knievel's failed leap across Snake River Canyon in 1974.* It turned out to be a fantastic video, a fitting end to a string of classic promos that Kanye intended to release as a compilation in cinemas. And a video that would get him into a whole heap of trouble.

Late in 2006, long after the track had charted across the world – it made 42 in the US and six in the UK – and the video had received a huge amount of airplay, Knievel struck back. "That video that Kanye West put out is the most worthless piece of crap I've ever seen in my life, and he uses my image to catapult himself on the public," he said, issuing a lawsuit against the use of his name and image in the clip in December. Now very ill with hepatitis and having undergone a liver transplant, Evel – aka Robert Craig – perhaps felt his legacy was worth protecting at this late stage in his life, and took offence to what he saw as the vulgarity of Pamela Anderson's role in the video as well as the damaging impact to his reputation of the whole clip. His suit demanded that the video stop airing, and damages be paid, but Kanye's lawyers argued that the image was part of the public domain. With both sides agreeing to mediation, the case was put on hold, for now.

Unlike Kanye's self-worth issues. After being wholeheartedly embraced at festival appearances across the summer of 2006, including shows at Lollapalooza, the Heineken Open'er festival in Poland and Belgium's Rock Werchter, and having had his romantic life bolstered when he split with Brooke Crittendon in April and returned to Alexis Phifer, to whom he proposed over a lobster and pasta meal on the island of Capri on August 11, he still felt under-appreciated when it came to the autumn award ceremonies.

Kanye would remain intensely private when it came to his relationship. "Even though I will tell you mad shit about porn, I don't go into depth about me and my fiancée's relationship," he told *Rolling Stone*. "'Fuck you, this is my life'. I dedicate a lot of my time to make music and

---

* For the original leap, Knievel had planned to jump over the Grand Canyon but was foiled by the Californian authorities. Instead he bought a section of Snake River Canyon in Idaho and launched himself from one side in a rocket. He failed to clear the canyon but parachuted to safety and collected a $6 million fee for the attempt.

provide something for the fans that they'll enjoy, but my relationship isn't for the fans to like and enjoy. It's for me to like and enjoy… I think real rock stars get married and have little rock-star kids. At some point, you have to add some sort of stability to your life. You have to have something real that you can hold on to. There can be a point where your records don't sell as much, or you're not as popular as you used to be. The best thing that any of the Backstreet Boys could have had was a really good woman in their life. I'm sure they had a lot of good pussy, but good pussy is fleeting. What's another word for 'good pussy' that's less vulgar?"

November 2, 2006: Kanye's award show stage invasions began. When the envelope for Best Video at the MTV Europe Music Awards ceremony at the Bella Centre in Copenhagen was opened and the presenter read out the words "Justice Vs Simian" where they should have been saying "Kanye West's 'Touch The Sky'", something snapped. The age-old issues of fighting for what he deserved rose up; before he knew it Kanye was out of his seat and on the stage, grabbing the microphone from the winners, arguing for his rightful recognition with the boos of the crowd ringing in his ears. "This video cost a million dollars, fam! I had Pam Anderson, I'm jumping across canyons and shit! Oh! Hey, if I don't win the award show loses credibility."

Later admitting to having had a "sippy-sippy", Kanye's televised rant continued backstage. "It's complete bullshit," he railed to members of the press. "I paid a million… it took a month to film; I stood on a mountain; I flew a helicopter over Vegas. … I did it to be the king of all videos."

MTV would revel in the media storm that Kanye's outburst provoked. "His finest tirade," it said, "an outburst so succinctly jingoistic and, well, downright *American* that it's no wonder the EMA audience booed." But unlike his George Bush statement, this looked to the watching world like egotism run wild. The idea that the cost of a video justifies awards rang hollow with music fans and Kanye's rant looked like the childish strop of a self-important show-off. Even Donda disapproved of what he'd done, even though she could understand it and always supported him in what he said. She always encouraged his passion in life and the way he'd always express his own opinion and view of the truth – it was what she believed would help him make a difference in the world – and she knew that he'd been robbed of prizes enough times to be able to see the shallowness of such ceremonies, to see the machinations of ratings at work behind the façade. But here was a time he'd stepped over the line, been too sharp and disrespectful, stolen someone else's moment. This time he was adding to the unfairness he'd set out to challenge.

"When I saw it on MSN the next day, it looks like I went into an orphanage and bit a baby's head off," he said, admitting that he would constantly keep an eye on his public persona via blogs and websites. "I felt like the Earth was on top of me."

So, realising his error, Kanye dutifully apologised on the biggest platform he could find. Having played his first stadium show as support for the Rolling Stones at Giants Stadium in New Jersey on September 27, he flew to Australia to play a string of stadiums with U2, the last dates of the year and the *Late Registration* tour. Here, onstage, he made his apology to 83,000 fans, and would also spoof himself on *Saturday Night Live* in a sketch he wrote himself alongside SNL's Seth Meyers, where he interrupted a variety of award presentations such as the Nobel Prize for physics and the Kids' Choice Awards, and snatched the winner's ribbon from an eight-year-old girl at a pumpkin contest. "Hell no!" he yelled, "I got the best pumpkin. This pumpkin cost a million dollars... It got Champagne in it. ... You got a lot of years, you can win this. I've been doing this too long."

The apology and spoof were received well by his critics, moments of humility that hinted at a real self-awareness of his foolishness. He'd later claim he'd been messing around at the ceremony and hadn't expected his rant to be taken so seriously, and that he'd do his best to rein himself in in future.

Self-control at award shows, however, would soon become one of Kanye's weakest traits.

CHAPTER NINE

Graduation

"**Y**ou're from MTV?"

The camera crew nodded and a snarl crept across Kanye's face. Not only was it rude for the crew to appear out of nowhere at a party to film him being interviewed by a major US publication, but a rift was widening between Kanye and MTV. He put his hand over the camera lens and held it there throughout the interview, explaining that he had no beef with the crew members themselves, but with their company.

The spat originated at the 2007 MTV Video Music Awards in Las Vegas on September 9, 2007. The ceremony took a different approach that year, with few performances taking place in the theatre where the awards were given out and several acts instead performing longer sets in suites at the Palms Hotel for the cameras. Kanye took one of the suite spots, playing seven songs, five of which were from his new album, in the Hugh Hefner Sky Villa on the condition that no other act of a similar style and level of success as him performed in the few theatre slots. As Kanye was passed over for all five of the awards he was nominated for he reportedly seemed upset, and when he saw Justin Timberlake, who'd also filmed a suite set, performing during a closing medley on the main stage alongside Timbaland and Nelly Furtado, he blew up, claiming he'd never return to MTV. Inevitably, his outburst was captured on tape and hit the internet.

"Kanye was watching the closing performance on a closed-circuit monitor, and he started getting upset," an onlooker claimed. "He started asking anyone who'd listen why he wasn't allowed to perform on the main stage. 'Why did I perform in just a suite?' he was saying. 'Justin's my boy, but even *he* gets to perform in both a suite and on the main stage? Something's wrong here'."

"I wasn't mad that I just didn't win any awards," he told a radio show a few days later. "For me, [MTV] made it seem like performing on the main stage was a bad thing, and the suites were just so great." His issue wasn't with Timberlake either, whom he had great respect for – he'd claim Timberlake should have won Grammys instead of him. "My biggest inspiration and biggest competition is Justin Timberlake. He's the only other person that gets an across-the-board response and respect level on black radio, white radio. If Justin hadn't come out and killed the game, I can't say that my album, singles and videos would be on the same level that they're on. We push each other. I look at me and Justin like Prince and Michael Jackson in their day."

But his frustration with MTV lingered. "Let me do the politically correct disclaimer and say that MTV has done a lot for me through the years," he said before listing every time they'd passed him over. In an interview with *Spin* he continued his diatribe. "The people at MTV know where I'm trying to go. And I feel like, 'Why do you not want me to reach my full potential?' If I've got a record like 'Stronger', which is blowing up all across the world, call an audible! It's like, 'Yo, let's let him take over the fuckin' world the way we helped Justin take over the world'. Because at the end of the day, if Justin can charge, like, two million for a private event, I think partially it's because MTV helped make him the number one artist. OK, now I work my fuckin' ass off – first to fight back from all the award show backlashes, then to have the number one song in the world. And a song like that as a black man? That is next to impossible. Yet you're gonna open the show with Britney and close with Justin? To me you're saying, 'We don't want another Michael Jackson, we want Elvis'."

He'd also criticise the network over its decision to broadcast Britney Spears' notoriously stilted and under-dressed opening performance, her hotly anticipated return to the stage during which pole-dancers writhed on the artists' tables and Britney mimed her way through a confused performance. In the run-up to the ceremony Kanye played a show at the Joint in the Hard Rock Hotel in Vegas where, before a crowd including Chris Brown, Eve, Pamela Anderson, Ashlee Simpson, Nelly, Ne-Yo, Ashanti and Spears herself, he changed a lyric to "I can't believe she would perform/She hasn't had a hit record in years", and in the aftermath of the ceremony, he turned his sights on the channel. "They exploited Britney in helping to end her career," he said. "Near the end, I felt so bad for her. I said, 'Man, it's a dirty game. This game will chew you up and spit you out'."

Appearing on the *Ellen DeGeneres Show* a week later, he expanded on his comments, claiming that the performance had been so bad in rehearsal that MTV shouldn't have let it go on. "I just felt like she wasn't ready and I felt like they had to get their ratings. At the end of the day, they did what they had to do. It shows you it's not a black-and-white thing; it's a money thing. Someone had to be at that practice and be like, 'Wow, this is not good', like all the lip-syncing and everything. I mean, that performance, if it had been pulled off perfectly, still wouldn't have been up to par to start off the MTV Awards. 'Cause I'm a fan of these award shows. I told these guys at MTV, I said 'Look, there are only a couple of things important in music this year, 'Umbrella', Amy Winehouse – it's just not me. Britney Spears is not important to music right now. She's important to the tabloids and stuff like that. I felt bad for her, bad for everyone involved."

Yet, in the same interview, Kanye chastised himself for his latest outburst. "I'm trying hard, man," he said. "I got the number one record, man. I was wrong for spazzing out and people would ask me about it [in] the days afterwards and I would just keep on talking about things they did wrong, which is just a justification. But as a man I need to own up to what I do and I can't justify."

The number one record he was talking about was his third album, *Graduation*. It was so named to mark Kanye's graduation to the highest levels of hip-hop success in a year when he'd have his birthday party hosted by Louis Vuitton and his new loft apartment in Manhattan redesigned by Armani's Claudio Silvestrin as a "hyper-masculine minimalist installation" in polished limestone and stark angular shapes. The party at New York's Vuitton store would be attended by Mariah Carey, Jay-Z, Pharrell and dozens of other superstars admiring the dancers in Vuitton bathing suits but, in interview, Kanye would play down his 30th birthday celebrations. "We had a little get-together with less than 20 people, my close, close friends," he said. "We had some mad-good barbecue chicken, and my mom gave me a painting of some angels, which was really thoughtful… Fuck the thirties! I hate my thirties. It's going to take me a while to get used to it. I envy people who like getting older, because I don't."

"It makes me proud as someone who's watched his growth from the beginning, when he came in as a hungry producer, to now he's a rock star," said Jay-Z. "I'm happy for him on that level. And I'm excited for creativity as well, because I think that's a win for that as well. You know, people mimic success. And in order to mimic that success, you have to put in a lot of work. You have to really care about the music."

Kanye had begun writing *Graduation* as soon as *Late Registration* had been released, with the intention of making a stadium hip-hop record inspired by his shows with U2 and the Rolling Stones. The shows had convinced him that complex lyrical gymnastics didn't capture huge crowds in the same way that simple, easily digestible musical messages could. "[Those crowds were looking at me like, 'I don't know what you're talking about'… If you come in the room and say one thing, it better be the most powerful thing." So he planned on making a 12-track record on more personal topics rather than the social statements he'd made on *The College Dropout* and *Late Registration*, wanting his songs to cut direct to the heart of the masses and become theme songs to people's lives. Listening to folk and country music by Bob Dylan – Kanye was turned on to Dylan by the friends who told him that his lyrical storytelling and approach to the press were redolent of the folk legend – and Johnny Cash to try to find new ways of writing hip-hop. "Somebody played me a Johnny Cash song, and the story was so dope," he said. "It came together better than any story I had – a father had named his son [Sue]. I haven't reached the level of what Johnny Cash did. The closest thing in hip-hop is 'Girls, Girls, Girls' by Jay-Z."

He also studied the likes of *The Eraser* by Thom Yorke, *Sam's Town* by the Killers, *We Were Dead Before The Ship Even Sank* by Modest Mouse and Keane's *Under The Iron Sea* to pick-up stadium rock tips and noticed, "When I hear the records of my favorite bands – the Killers or Coldplay – you only hear one voice from start to finish." So he vowed to use less guest performers this time, and he'd reach beyond his traditional soul samples to bolster his music with samples from hard rock, eighties electronica, house, euro-disco, reggae, dub and prog. In his vocal style he would try to emulate Bono's bawl.

Recording was, once more, a painstaking process. Whenever Kanye felt a track might be ready for public consumption, he'd take it out and play it to people, from his iPod, in clubs or in his office. Whatever reaction he got, he'd note it down and go back and change the track according to the comments. This meant that some tracks had a huge number of mixes, a dizzying array of options from which Kanye could pick the perfect version. "I've been working on this album for maybe a year and a half now," he said. "I'll work on songs for a year. I go back to them, I listen to them more. That way I already know if they're classics and if they'll stick with you. The youngest a song is by the time it comes out might be four or five months and the oldest song might be two years old before it hits the album. So it's had a chance to stand the test of time in my car before I give it to the world."

Kanye's control freakery and his inability – bordering on obsessive compulsive disorder – to let a song go until he'd tried every single option available to attain perfection was exhausting to the army of mixers and producers who worked with him in Chung King Studios and Sony Music Studios in New York, or Chalice and the Record Plant in LA. "It's pretty much how much he cares about it; it's not done for any other reason but to be the best music out at that specific time," Jay-Z said. "At times you could hear [other] people's music and you hear, 'OK, that's your girl single, that's the thug single, that's the…' No, it's none of that. Every single song he makes, he makes because he thinks it's the best record at that specific time. He may not think it next week, but that week he thought that was the best record that he could make. We have 75 mixes of 'Stronger' [to get the bass guitar right]. Who does that? When I was sitting in mastering to make sure the album got done, he was somewhere in Sweden sending through mixes of 'Good Life' – 16 different mixes of the song. Who does that?"

Graduation would be tighter, leaner, more seeped with synth and bereft of skits. "There's just serious songs, hooks, chords and ideas," Kanye said, "no special effects or antics, and no fake Bernie Mac!" In place of the skits, Kanye had originally composed two instrumental pieces to break up the album, constructed around African rhythms, but neither made the final track listing. Indeed, the album itself would still be in an amorphous stage, with Kanye still aimlessly writing songs with no fixed concept beyond the *Graduation* theme right up until the release of the album's first single, 'Can't Tell Me Nothing', on May 15, 2007.

"I'm graduating from a school called Universe City," he said of the *Graduation* theme. "I think the sound is bigger this time. It's bigger and simpler, where the notes really connect with you and I say lines … I know the power of my words, so when I rap, I know it's gonna impact the world. I know I'm gonna be performing anywhere from the Summer Jam stage [at New Jersey's Giants Stadium] to [New York nightclub] Speed to the House of Blues in L.A., to London to Brazil to Ireland. … I'm making music for somebody sitting in a car on their way to work trying to get through traffic and my music is helping them zone out, to a 60,000-seater where I'm opening up for the Rolling Stones or U2… Like I say, 'Why would I do a song with you two when I just got offstage with U2? I'm not even talking to you two'. That's how I feel. I'm ready to take over the world once again. I have a lot to say. I got a lot more music to make… I make music people can relate to every day. My music just isn't about my story. … There's not one artist in the world that has as much responsibility as me. When I deliver a piece of music, it has to connect with the most genres of music. I don't care who you name. If you name rap artists, their only responsibility is to rap crowds. If you name a pop artist, their only responsibility is to a pop crowd. If you name some French dance music, their responsibility is to the cool crowd. But I have to deliver songs. All these people are looking at me from super-middle America to the hipsters like, 'What's he gonna do next?'"

What he was going to do next, according to 'Can't Tell Me Nothing', was doomy arena anthems. With sonorous horns, cinematic strings and atmospheric synths creating an evocative, lugubrious backing inspired by the Rolling Stones and Led Zeppelin and vocals from Connie Mitchell from Australian dance act Sneaky Sound System, Kanye spooled out a moody, slow-paced glower of a tune written in imitation of rock song structures. Mitchell had come into Kanye's sphere when he met her bandmates Daimon Downey and Angus McDonald in a Sydney diner while touring Australia with U2. Kanye asked McDonald if he had any musical ideas that might help him develop his sound and he recommended he work with Mitchell. West was recording on the road and had a studio space called Studios 301 in use; Mitchell came along to sing on a track and soon found herself with an invitation to fly out to the Record Plant in LA to sing on several of the album's tracks. "Connie didn't know who Kanye West was," said McDonald, "I had to say, 'Trust me, you'll probably want to sing on his record'."

"I hear records that are super hot for two months," he said of his thinking behind the new style, "but the records won't last in people's minds. I set out not to just make records that could hop off the radio instantly, but stuff that will speak to people. People still bring up 'Spaceships' to me. And people compare 'Can't Tell Me Nothing' to 'Spaceships' saying that's a song that inspires them when they going to work. But the chords itself, is like a Led Zeppelin rock melody. Yeah, you thinking it's made for the car and you thinking it's made for the club, and it works in the arena because DJ Toomp did the drums and all that, but the actual melody is made to rock 50,000 people."

The song's opening verse was, ironically, about losing control. As if writing a self-help lesson in getting his money right, Kanye harangued himself once more for his shopaholic, materialistic tendencies and spending ridiculous sums on jewellery. "I had a dream I could buy my way to heaven/When I awoke, I spent that on a necklace," he rapped, starting a verse with strong religious overtones, in which Kanye saw himself having his faith tested like Job by being granted fame and riches, taking leave of God while he indulged himself in reckless acts. "To whom much is given, much is tested," he opined, "I feel the pressure under more scrutiny/And what I do? Act more stupidly/Bought more jewellery, more Louis V/My momma couldn't get through to me". For his stupidity, he admitted, he was being sued by Knievel for realising his vision and lambasted by the right wing for speaking his mind to the TV cameras as though talking to a friend. As he looked at himself from the public's skewed point of view – "I guess the money should've changed him/I guess I should've forgotten where I came from" – and entered the hook with a defiant statement that nobody could tell him what to do or how to be, 'Can't Tell Me Nothing' marked the start of what would be called his "freak baller period", a line in the sand that marked the end of his predominantly socially conscious era and the birth of Kanye's more self-analytical raps.

For the rest of the track Kanye, like anyone admitting to faults in their personality or ideology, wrestled with his own hypocrisies. He believed in God but couldn't believe God would allow wars; he stood up for himself and his actions yet at the same time chastised himself for speaking too hastily – "Don't ever fix your lips like collagen/And say something when you gon' end up apologising". He ended up finding a sense of balance for himself and his battling conscience, admitting that if "the devil wear Prada, Adam Eve wear nada, I'm in between but way more fresher".

The video, directed again by Hype Williams, didn't find Kanye racked with such insecurity and uncertainty. Striding around a desert throwing gestures of unrestrained confidence or snarling down the camera in a room full of smoke and neon, he returned looking as defiant and self-assured as ever. And once again, the single came with two videos; while the first premiered on Kanye's website on May 25, an online-only alternative appeared in July, directed by Michael Blieden and featuring comedian Zach Galifianakis and musician Will Oldham singing the track while carrying out farming activities, throwing hip-hop shapes on a tractor or walking down country lanes in pimp pyjamas and fake chains. Kanye's personal trainer had introduced him to Galifianakis' comedy and Kanye had invited him to appear in the video after seeing him perform in LA. Ironically, the comedy video went down better than the original; *Rolling Stone* declared it the third best video of 2007. The single, however, only reached number 41 on the *Billboard* chart and didn't even make the top 100 in the UK, a dip in Kanye's inexorable rise.

Hype Williams returned for the next video too, a shoot which turned into the *Apocalypse Now* of rap promos. In April 2007, Kanye had approached LA Reid, Def Jam's chairman, with a track called 'Stronger', created from a sample of 'Harder, Better, Faster, Stronger' by France's retromodern vocoder synth-pop robots Daft Punk. DJ A-Trak had played Kanye the song on tour the previous year, and Kanye had been gripped by it. "What's great is that I really look up to Daft Punk," he said. "I see shit they're doing and bow to them. I feel they've created music and visuals that surpass what I'd heard up to that point. One day I can be on the level of sophistication that Daft Punk are. But that's the way the French are, you know? Their art, fashion and style are at the highest point on the globe. I completely believe in stereotypes! Like, the best rap music is from America, mostly from the East Coast, as that's where hip-hop was born and that's the best there is. The absolute best animators now are, to me, from Asia. The best clothing and heart of fashion is obviously Paris. And it trickles down from there, so you're not too far off when you get to London. And you're not too, too far off once you get to New York. And you're not too, too, *too* far off when you hit Chicago… and by the time you get to LA, it's gone."

The track was a real evolution for Kanye's music, catapulting him into the futuristic realm of disco electronica, and when he played it to Williams before it even had drums on the track, Hype urged him to go down the futuristic route with it. Inspiration struck – the aimless songwriting process for his third album suddenly had a focus. He went back to the studio to rework already recorded tracks in this theme, watching sci-fi films such as *Total Recall* to help the mood. *Graduation* would be a futuristic album, its beats crisp and electronic and its artwork designed by Takashi Murakami in a Japanese neon advert style. And he needed a video for 'Stronger' to match.

So, with no storyboard planned, only a vague idea of what he wanted and the song's second verse not even written yet, Kanye asked Reid to front him $1.2 million for four videos to be shot over nine days around Tokyo. The idea was that Williams would film Kanye guerilla-style as he wandered the streets, shooting without permits or advance warning, explaining as best they could to the locals what was going on and pulling favours from friends to get shots in locations such as the BBC store or in BAPE.

"When we went to Def Jam for the money, it was like, 'LA Reid, we need $1.2 million to shoot four videos. And the treatment for the first one ['Stronger'] is right here'," said Don C, "The treatment was just 'Kanye and Hype in Japan,' that was it. … Thank you very much. Let's go shoot. We just went and did it. Kanye and Hype had the vision in their brains, but they didn't have anything on paper. It wasn't no storyboard. They just went out there and was like, 'We're going to get a bunch of footage'… Kanye has always been inspired by Japanese animation and follows a lot of Japanese directors. He was inspired by wanting to shoot in Japan, the whole setting of *Graduation* being in the future. He wanted to have a futuristic look with the neon lights and bikers in Japan."

In the lead-up to the shoot, the storyline developed. Kanye would play a member of a Japanese motorcycle gang getting into a fight with a rival group (the gang in the original video was a real Japanese motorcycle gang) and ending up in hospital, under the scrutiny of a hi-tech CGI scanner, his body being rebuilt like the *Six Million Dollar Man*. The clip would include homage scenes to the 1988 anime movie *Akira* and feature guest appearances by the actors who played Daft Punk in the film *Daft Punk's Electroma*, in full robot costume. The film even included footage of a real-life riot that broke out outside the pair's hotel. "It was some type of political figure that was in town," Don explained, "and the people didn't like him and they started rioting outside the hotel [where] Hype was staying. Kanye was like, 'Let's go shoot it right now.' We ran out, shot the riot scene."

Once they got the footage home and constructed the video from it, however, Kanye wasn't happy with the results, and his intense perfectionism kicked in once more. Over 10 weeks in editing suites, the video going way over even this huge a budget and Hype Williams threatening to quit the project three times, he threw out the plot altogether and made a video based purely on the coolest shots they had. The colours of the film were too close to those used in recent videos by 50 Cent and Maroon 5, so Kanye demanded five days of reshoots, not least so that his performance sections could feature him wearing a pair of white Alain Mikli shutter shades that had taken him three months to track down to Paris and would soon become his trademark. The shutter shades were also worn by a cartoon of the Dropout Bear on the single's sleeve. "I wanted something you can't get in stores," he explained.

"The video went through so many different stages," Don said. "It was a story going on, but it didn't fit. Kanye almost had a brain aneurysm, editing this video for three months. Literally, 10 weeks of editing going back in. Then he still was not satisfied, so he shot more footage in New York... Kanye put everything else on halt. He was in the editing suite till four or five in the morning. He went way over budget editing, sitting in them expensive editing suites. He kept going – and not only kept going, but he wanted to shoot more footage. We were so far over budget, Hype couldn't shoot no more. So Kanye hired a local crew and he shot at [New York's Jacob K. Javits Convention Center]. The footage with him against the wall with the white glasses, now known as the 'Stronger' glasses, that was shot in New York. But the [director of photography] at this time wasn't Hype's DP, so the shots didn't come out looking as ill as Hype's shots. That's why Kanye distorted the film so it would look like something on TV, like an old tube television with the lines and stuff. He knew it wasn't going to match the Hype Williams footage. Then the special effects came in with robotic arms and glowing starbursts. The editors put all the magic that everybody shot together."

Further filming in LA even allowed Kanye to get the real Daft Punk into the clip, since they happened to be in town and came down to the shoot. They would also take time out from the Lollapalooza tour to visit Kanye's studio in Chicago to hear *Graduation*, which they loved so much there was talk of a collaboration. "This is one of the first times we got to make a video like how we make music," Kanye explained as he premiered a rough cut in June to select journalists and industry insiders at five hours' notice, at the Tribeca Cinemas, "we got to go back to it."

The video would be worth all of the effort Kanye put into it, going on to win Best Hip-Hop Video at the BET Awards and Best Video at the MOBOs, and prompting Michael Jackson to call him up to ask him where he got the coat he wore in the clip. And he'd put even more work into the song than the video, producing 75 mixes with 11 different engineers in three studios in Tokyo, New York and LA. Once a final mix was chosen, recorded with engineer Manny Marroquin over 26 hours in LA and New York and featuring 100 layers on Pro Tools, after its release Kanye would still be feeling unhappy enough with it after he heard it in a club back-to-back with Timbaland's 'The Way I Are' to turn to Timbaland for help with the drum programming, convinced his song was inferior to Daft Punk's original. Hearing the song on a San Francisco flight, Daft Punk themselves would disagree. "Our song had a good sound," Guy-Manuel de Homem-Christo said, "but when [the radio DJ] put Kanye's record on, the sound was really fat. It sounds really big." "The challenge when you're taking a sample is to make it fit your own universe," added Thomas Bangalter, "the interesting thing here is how he took our music and really made it his own in terms of his personality…. He distorts the initial meaning of the song, and that's what's interesting."

Basing his hook around Friedrich Nietzsche's famous dictum "that which does not kill us makes us stronger", West twisted this philosophical truth onto a more physical plane. It was his lust for a girl that he'd been longing after "since Prince was on Apollonia, since OJ had Isotoners" that was almost killing him, and his patience making him stronger. Kanye was particularly proud of the Apollonia rhyme. "That shit's crazy, right?" he said. "It's just retarded. Certain lines are so pure. There's a lot of rappers that get into freestyle battles, and they use prefabricated metaphors and similes. Like referencing guns to sports: 'I got a nine on me like…' some quarterback who wears number nine. You see those rhymes coming a mile away, and they're unimpressive, after the fact. The lines that are genius are the Apollonia/ Isotoners, just out-of-the-blue shit." Inviting her to be his "black Kate Moss" – Moss would reciprocate by posing for photos covered in black paint in *The Independent* – and his "secretary" in reference to Maggie Gyllenhaal's submissive sexual employee in the film *Secretary*, Kanye's seduction technique was one of sheer ego display – "Bow in the presence of greatness," he rapped. "How the hell could you front on me?/There's a thousand yous, there's only one of me". As the lyric went on and Kanye got drunker, he let slip a predilection: "I'd do anything for a blonde dyke". Some commentators would take this as a reference to his growing fondness for actress and model Amber Rose – who sported a blonde suedehead haircut – even while engaged to Alex Phifer.

"The way that ['Stronger'] was put together, especially at the end – I've never accomplished that level of musicality," Kanye said of the track. "I think I've fallen short every time I've attempted to do something like it. But falling short of that is still way better than everything else in hip-hop."

A snippet of 'Stronger' first crept into the public domain in May, on the *Can't Tell Me Nothing* mix-tape that Kanye compiled with Plain Pat, alongside the debut track from *Child Rebel Soldier*, Kanye's supergroup with Lupe and Pharrell, and cuts from other G.O.O.D. label acts including Common, Consequence and Really Doe. With all of the long hours he was putting into his album and videos, by mid-2007 Kanye had found that he couldn't give G.O.O.D. the amount of attention it needed to thrive, and sales were dipping despite every act on the label getting a guest spot on *Late Registration*: Common's *Be* album had managed a respectable 800,000 copies in 2005 and his 2007 follow-up, *Finding Forever*, would notch up half a million sales with the help of Kanye's production credit. By now Kanye's production side-projects had become largely limited to acts on the G.O.O.D. label or close associates; over 2006-2007 he produced tracks on albums by the likes of Rhymefest, Talib Kweli, John Legend, Lupe Fiasco, Jay-Z, Nas and Consequence while only rarely branching out to work with Chris Brown, Lil' Wayne, Diddy or Janet Jackson. However, Consequence's 2007 album, *Don't Quit Your Day Job*, sold only 140,000 on its March release, so to rejuvenate the label, Kanye signed a rising Big Sean in May and hired No I.D. to take over the everyday running of the label as President.

"Sometimes those titles are glorified," I.D. said. "I can't even say that things were set up so that it could really be constructive in that sense. I think it was more-so Kanye needed a break, and I was a competent guy that everybody could talk to and respect. I said, 'OK, cool. Take a break. Let me see what I can do'. I tried to bring a business structure. The first thing I did was figure out who's actually signed. I said, 'Who's signed? OK, Big Sean is signed. Who's what?' It led to me putting a lot of effort into Sean and Common, which as a producer, is something I would have done anyway. Working there gave me the authority to exercise those relationships without feeling like I'm stepping on toes."

The *Can't Tell Me Nothing* mix-tape was rapturously received by critics, some calling it a potential album of the year even before its parent album *Graduation* was released, with *Vibe* magazine declaring it Mix-tape Of The Year, and 'Stronger' was one of its stand-out moments. The track was snapped up by Brendon Joshua's podcast and Radio One and given a huge boost by Kanye performing it at his comeback show at the Concert For Diana at Wembley Stadium on July 1 to a televised audience of 500 million. The concert marked the tenth anniversary of the death of Diana, Princess Of Wales, and Kanye's set also included 'Jesus Walks', 'Gold Digger', 'Diamonds From Sierra Leone' and 'Touch The Sky'. On its July 31 release it was the highest new entry on the *Billboard* chart at 47 and over the coming weeks it climbed to number one, a position it would hold in the UK, Canada, Turkey and New Zealand as well. That it would reach number one on the US Pop Chart, a rare feat for a rap song, was testament to Kanye's crossover appeal and it would go on to sell five million downloads, and break Daft Punk to a US audience, not least when they'd be pictured on the cover of *Spin* magazine alongside Kanye as it declared 'Stronger' its record of the year. It's arguable that 'Stronger' was one of the key elements in starting America's obsession with electronic dance music, which rolled through the country like a tsunami over the coming years and dominates the club scene today. 'Stronger' would also land Kanye in a little legal hot water as a musician named Vincent Peters would claim in 2010 that the song was a rip-off of a track he handed to John Monopoly in 2006 and which, he claimed, found its way to Kanye. The tracks were both called

'Stronger', both mentioned Kate Moss and reworked the Nietzsche line. Peters' claim was dismissed by a federal judge and the Court Of Appeals.

There were some naysayers, though, irritated by the crossover of electro and hip-hop. "I faced some backlash when the single first came out," Kanye said. "I think the electronic community was saying, 'How dare you sample this holy grail?' and the hip-hop people were saying, 'You have to always do what we're used to you doing'. But I think hip-hop is about always being new and cutting-edge and coming up with a combination you haven't heard." "What you want," added Daft Punk's Thomas Bangalter, "is for the next generation to destroy what you've done and start from scratch."

The album *Graduation* was set to swiftly follow the release of 'Stronger', its street date proclaimed at the opening of the *Can't Tell Me Nothing* mix-tape as arriving in August. But as the album was shifted around the schedules by Def Jam, it eventually fell on September 11, the same release date as 50 Cent's new album, *Curtis*. Suddenly the spectre of a sales race between two of the biggest rap stars in the country reared up, and 50 Cent was a formidable opponent for Kanye to take on. He was the ultimate thug rap icon, the Ivan Drago to Kanye's plucky Rocky IV, and his previous album, *The Massacre*, had shifted 1.14 million copies in its first week in 2005, substantially more than *Late Registration* had achieved. "When I heard that thing about the debate," Kanye originally said, "I thought that was the stupidest thing. When my album drops and 50's album drops, everybody wins because you're gonna get a lot of good music at the same time."

But as Jay-Z explained the power of a great rap rivalry to him, taking from his own experience of the publicity his spat with Nas generated, Kanye's head was turned. He saw the huge sales potential in the rivalry, and even managed to talk his way around setting up the face-off on September 11, a day of mourning for America. "I was a little worried about that day," he admitted, "because I didn't want to be offensive to anyone, to act like I was neglecting that. But people also want to celebrate and have a good time and have something to uplift their spirits. And I believe that my music is inspirational, so it's the perfect album to come out on a day like that. The songs dial into the energy that people need at that time: 'Did you realise that you were a champion?'; 'Throw your hands up in the sky'; 'That which don't kill me can only make me stronger'; 'I did it for the glory.' Barack couldn't have given a better answer than that."

His chart contest with 50 Cent would be far more friendly than Jay Vs Nas. Throughout the run-up to the battle Kanye praised Fiddy ceaselessly, showing him the utmost respect even as he was claiming it was only a matter of when he outsold his rival, in the long term. The challenge went a little to 50 Cent's head, however; he put his whole career on the line. "Let's raise the stakes," he said, "if Kanye West sells more records than 50 Cent on September 11, I'll no longer write music. I'll write music and work with other artists, but I won't put out any more solo albums."

Kanye was rather more sanguine about the challenge. "I'd rather come out on a day like that, up against 50 – where people are excited about going to the stores and it's an event and people talk about it – and be number two on that day rather than come out and be number one on a day nobody cares about," Kanye said. "It's about things going down in history. It's not that much exciting stuff in hip-hop right now. I think people are going to make it more than what I'm making it myself. At the end of the day, I'm making music and I'm trying to sell."

50 would retract his words in a later MTV interview due to his contractual agreements with Interscope and Aftermath, but would point out that he saw no personal advantage to the battle. "It's great marketing – for Kanye West," he said. "But I sell way more records than Kanye West, and I generate way more interest than Kanye West. They think they can match us up, but they'll find out when that week goes by and the sales come back. This is no rivalry." Kanye agreed. "Oh man," he said, "he sold me so many records by saying that."

The media lapped up the story, turning the rivalry into the sort of classic head-to-head that had made the Beatles Vs the Stones or Blur Vs Oasis so iconic. The show *Top 10 Live* on BET pitched the two acts head to head in the weeks running up to the date, with both performing on the show. Having won a coin toss, 50 Cent performed first, playing his major single 'Ayo Technology', and then sat down for an interview in which he claimed Kanye had no chance at all of beating him and that, although there was no beef between them, he thought Kanye had made a mistake in taking him on. When Kanye emerged for his comeback slot, however, he looked for all the world a champion, hammering through the rock riff slathered 'Big Brother', stealing the show. During an interview alongside 50 Cent, West fought his corner, claiming *Graduation* was the best hip-hop record of all time. 50 Cent even relented a little, saying that if Kanye did beat him, it would be because Fiddy had been the champ for so long that the public wanted to see him fall, tired of watching him constantly win.

The *Graduation* campaign was further boosted by a series of huge live appearances worldwide. A week after the Concert For Diana, Kanye was in another stadium, performing at the Giants Stadium leg of Al Gore's series of benefit concerts Live Earth, aimed at combatting climate change. Carbon neutral and the longest show ever recorded, Live Earth featured the likes of Genesis, Metallica and Snow Patrol performing at Wembley Stadium while the New York leg included Kanye high up on a bill that also featured Roger Waters, Smashing Pumpkins and the Police. Kanye slipped 'Stronger' into his seven-song set, broadcast to a huge global audience, and also into his sets at global festivals such as Canada's Cisco Systems Bluesfest, Sweden's Way Out West and the UK's V2007. And then there was the publicity and notoriety he garnered around his spat with MTV following the September 9 MTV Video Music Awards in Vegas.

Before the registers started ringing on September 11, both Fiddy and West had already won. "The amount of press we got was real," Kanye said. "Everything was real. You're dealing with real people in that environment. The press wanted to make it a beef because that's what they want. They want the black guys to be up against each other, about to shoot each other. And that's not what they got. What they got is two black guys selling a lot of records. I knew it was going to take off as soon as we were going to come out on the same date. Think about it – you got the two biggest shit-talkers in rap history. There's no-one known in rap history for talking more shit than me and 50… it was a complete publicity stunt."

A huge number of records, in fact. In the first week, *Graduation* sold 957,000 copies, outstripping *Late Registration* and putting *Curtis'* tally of 691,000 in the shade. While 50 took the number one spot in Switzerland and Ireland, Kanye clinched the top spot in the UK, Canada and, crucially, the USA, as well as making the Top 10 in nine other countries. The underdog had bitten back★.

And once they heard the winning record, most fans would feel they'd made the right choice.

★ ★ ★

Pow! Eyes to the sky and chain flying, the Dropout Bear cannoned out of the gaping mouth of a monster resembling an entire university campus come to life, with joyous animal graduates waving him off. After two album covers reflecting a dark and dour attitude towards college life, it was a bright cartoon introduction to *Graduation*, a sign of Kanye taking off into a hyper-coloured future.

The sleeve was designed by Takashi Murakami, known as Japan's own Andy Warhol for his post-modern superflat images of cute cartoonish animals with wicked undertones. Kanye had met Murakami during a trip to his Kaikai Kiki studio in Tokyo while on tour for *Late Registration* and loved his twist on his beloved anime style. During the design process Kanye would come up with a storyline for the Dropout Bear's cartoon adventures and email them to Murakami to bring them to life: the bear waking up late for his graduation from the University Of Universe City, finding his DeLorean hover car failing on him and taxis and buses leaving him stranded, having to race down rainy streets watched by many-eyed mushrooms and chased by a cloud with monster teeth and finally reaching his graduation ceremony, only to be shot into the stratosphere by his animal classmates.

"[Murakami's] work has been stunning to me because pop art is really expressive, representative and emotional, and it looks like something you can do yourself," Kanye said. "[But] you cannot do no Murakami shit yourself. You cannot do this at home. He has this studio out in

★ 50 Cent, despite his declaration, continued to make solo albums.

Japan that has 30 artists working at one time. I love Japanese culture and I was always into art, and Murakami is really a god in the art world… I've heard people come up to him and say, 'You're becoming more godlike every day'. Every single that's coming out for my album, he did the artwork for the covers. … And all the merchandising for the new album is Murakami."

"The cover is based on Kanye's theme of student life," Murakami explained. "School. It's a place of dreams, of righteousness, a place to have fun. It's also occasionally a place where you experience the rigid dogma of the human race. Kanye's music scrapes sentimentality and aggressiveness together like sandpaper, and he uses his grooves to unleash this tornado that spins with the zeitgeist of the times. I too wanted to be swept up and spun around in that tornado."

Just as the bear was simultaneously stressed and triumphant, so the album seemed to catalogue Kanye's own existential dualities. Here was an album that ricocheted between arrogance and doubt, aggrandisement and self-criticism, a talent deeply analysing itself to the tune of its latest giant leap.

Although it was never released as a single, Murakami animated his Dropout Bear cartoons for a video to accompany the album's first track, 'Good Morning', a heady, slow-paced song that wafted by like a daydream, weaving samples from Jay-Z's 'The Ruler's Back' and Elton John's 'Someone Saved My Life Tonight' around a laid-back, insistent groove of cowbell, synth drone and enigmatic piano. The lyric sounded like Kanye's graduation speech, harking back to the opening to *Late Registration* with its opening line of "wake up, Mr West", he declared the album his "dissertation" in hip-hop, having flunked so many real-life school classes because he was "looking at every ass, cheated on every test". "On this day we become legendary, everything we dreamed of," he boasted, imagining himself a smarter, more fashion conscious Malcolm X by punning that he would "buy any jeans necessary" and marking the album as the moment that he finally escaped the shackles of the streets: "You graduate when you make it up outta the streets/From the moment of pain, look how far we done came".

His final lines, each verse shortened to help get his points across more directly, took aim once again at the serial student, "the valedictorian, scared of the future while I hop in the DeLorean [referencing the *Back To The Future* films, where the DeLorean car was used to boldly hop into the future] … some people graduate but be still stupid". Education, the song argued, robbed you of street credibility; a questionable idea, you might argue, to be putting to people who might be encouraged to drop out of school and then fail to become huge rap stars.

Having celebrated his hip-hop graduation, he started thanking the people who made it possible. His mother had already been lauded in song, so now he turned to thank his father, Ray, in 'Champion', a song based around a sample of Steely Dan's 'Kid Charlemagne' which had blown him away when Brian 'All Day' Miller had found it for him – Kanye personally contacted songwriter Donald Fagen to beg for its clearance. "Kanye actually sent us a sample of his tunes," said Fagen, unimpressed, "and frankly, Walter [Becker, co-writer] and I listened to it, and although we'd love some of the income, neither of us particularly liked what he had done with it. We said no at first, and then he wrote us a hand-written letter that was kind of touching, about how the song was about his father, and he said, 'I love your stuff, and I really want to use it because it's a very personal thing for me'. My mind doesn't work like that – I would never use someone else's stuff if I was writing something personal, but I guess that's how he was thinking about it. It was such a good letter that we said, all right, go ahead… and we made a deal with him."

"Me and my father's relationship is a little strained," Kanye said, "so when I started writing… something came out of me to speak on that but to say, in the end, that my father was a champion in my eyes, even with our ups and downs."

A modern electro R&B piece with jazz-rock hints, 808 handclaps and heavy fuzz synths, it addressed his father with no little respect. "Did you realise that you were a champion in their eyes?" went the sampled hook, relating to both his feelings towards Ray and how Kanye's fans, in turn, idolised him. After an opening bout of braggadocio – "You don't see just how fly my style is/I don't see why I need a stylist/When

I shop so much I can speak Italian" – he paid tribute to his father's entrepreneurial nous, claiming that "every summer he'll get some brand new harebrained scheme to get rich from" and yet he'd still somehow manage to buy Kanye new clothes for each school year.

The second verse saw Kanye take on his father's inspirational aura, both as a living example of how it pays not to give up when "living's harder than dying", and as a motivational speaker, admitting that the one and only Dropout was visiting schools to talk students into staying on. "They used to feel invisible," he rapped of the way he'd changed the students' lives, "now they feel invincible." The song itself definitely had an impact; despite not being released as a single it would leap into the *Billboard* Top 100 on download sales alone, prompting Kanye to make a video for it to be released on his website the following year, directed by NEON and filmed at Adolfo Camarillo High School in California. The video featured a puppet Kanye competing in the 100m sprint at the fictional Unified Games, following the puppet's intense training for the race, the live TV vote that allowed a puppet to compete against real-life athletes and its inevitable victory.

'Stronger' wound up a powerful and inspired opening trio, at which point things got emotional. Taking its inspiration from U2's stadium anthems that Kanye had watched awestruck the previous year, and particularly their track 'City Of Blinding Lights', 'I Wonder' was a nagging piano hookline, sampled from Labi Siffre's 'My Song', swarmed with crunching beats, arena pop synths and Kanye intonating his lines slowly and clearly enough for any stadium crowd to comprehend. "I've been waiting on this my whole life," he stated, enunciating each syllable as if ramming home his pride in his own success, "These dreams be waking me up at night."

He then became philosophical, considering the nature of dreams and how we so often stop ourselves fulfilling them. He turned to address a woman who'd had an argument with her abusive boyfriend yet, after some time away, still goes back to him, unable to realise what she might become outside of such a crushing relationship. Likewise, in his third verse, he considered all of the women in his audience who would give up their independence for a family, something he seemed to look on as a weakness at this point in his life. In keeping with the album's title, the theme of 'I Wonder' was intended to mirror the concerns university graduates have when leaving school. "It talks about… what do you do in your life, like where are you headed, how do you make these decisions?" Kanye explained. "I offer a little – a little – advice, but more just posing that question and letting them zone out to the music and figure it out themselves."

Keen to explore every avenue of his own potential, for the next track, 'Good Life', West further dabbled with the world of Auto-Tune, by inviting T-Pain onto the track's choruses. The track originated from a sample of Michael Jackson's 'PYT' which Kanye was playing with in the studio.★ "All of a sudden he was like, 'Yo, I always wanted to do something with this… I want to hear it in a different key'," said his production partner on the track, DJ Toomp, though Mike Dean also helped produce the track. "Because we were in the same room, he just transferred the sounds over to my keyboard and… we just started playing with the sample and once we got it in the right key we wanted, that's when he started singing the melody and I started adding more to the beat. We then had a few players to come in with the synthesizers and the shit was crazy."

"Michael Jackson is my favourite artist of all time," Kanye enthused. "Every time I hit a stage, every time I write a song, every time I rap, every performance I do, every time I pick an outfit, I think about Michael Jackson. Michael Jackson is synonymous with the greatest that you could possibly do in music."

Kanye worked the pitched-up and slowed-down 'PYT' sample around anthemic synthetic brass and squelchy soul electronics while he celebrated his baller lifestyle. Ferraris, well-proportioned women, copious liquor, champagne and oral sex on private planes, lenient drug cops and haters that merely help to increase your bank balance; these were all part of Kanye's jubilant "living spree" – the opposite of a killing spree – as he envisioned *Graduation* catapulting him into ever greater

★ The album was recorded between Chung King and Sony Music Studios in New York and the Record Plant in LA.

stratospheres of success thanks to his decision to "switch the style up" to appeal to larger crowds. The condemnation of his own shopaholic nature had diminished by now, presumably in correlation with the increased size of his shopping budget, making it less of a problem – "I always had a passion for flashin'," he rapped, "but when I get my card back activated, I'm back to Vegas."

'Good Life' would be the third single released from *Graduation*, hitting the charts on download sales on September 22 before the record was even officially released and eventually reaching number three, accompanied by a video directed by Jonas & Francois of Kanye and T-Pain surrounded by animations of the lyrics, fine cars, girls, roller coasters and cop cars. The video was at the centre of Kanye's continued spat with MTV however. "I had a meeting with them and we were supposed to squash [the beef]," he explained, "but they never played 'Good Life'. I had 'Good Life' as Video Of The Week and halfway into the week they took it off and put up 50 Cent and Robin Thicke. How credible is that? I apologised to them for my spazzes but I think it's fucked up that I had a meeting with them and they still didn't play my video."

'Can't Tell Me Nothing' followed, darkening the mood for 'Barry Bonds' which included a sample of 'Long Red' by Mountain; a sinister gothic zombie-hop piece featuring another major rising star of rap, Lil Wayne. Named after the baseball player who broke the MLB all-time record for home runs★, West and Wayne hailed themselves as hit-makers in the same league. "They want something new so let's get reacquainted," Kanye spat in reference to his constant chameleonic shifting of styles, as he bragged about becoming the "hood favourite" despite not being from the hood himself, and living the "life of a Don", hitting clubs in the finest clothes with a woman on his arm. And to drive home the reliability with which he writes hit records, he snatched the catchphrase of baseball commentator Duane Kuiper, used whenever someone hit a home run: "We outta here, baby!"

★ Shortly after the release of the song, Bonds was uncovered as a steroid-taker, so the braggadocio of the track is somewhat tainted today.

For Kanye's verse, he continued bragging about his constant international travel, being declared one of the top five hottest rappers by MTV, how he doesn't need any writers to help him make his tunes and his immaculate fashion sense, all tempered with some of his most egotistical statements yet: "I'm doing pretty good as far as geniuses go". "I want to drop songs where other rappers are like, 'I wish I had that'," he said when questioned about calling himself a genius. "If I heard *Graduation* and it was made by somebody else, I would go to the bathroom and take a shit, because I would be scared. This record speaks to me so much... If you have a series of genius moments, then you can be considered a genius. Genius moments can be created when a new idea is met with an overwhelming response. Like Timbaland right now – he at that point. He keeps dropping shit like, 'Oh, my God! That was genius! How did you think of that?' He's in a genius zone. But if someone didn't have the intention of creating a genius moment, then it's just dumb luck, and you're not a fucking genius. That's like the George Bush comment – because I didn't know shit about politics. Everyone was like, 'That was genius', but it wasn't. Not really. It wasn't premeditated."

Wayne, in his verse, praised his own diamond-covered teeth and bank balance in an attempt to prove his claims that he was the "best rapper alive". If this was a face-off of hip-hop greats in the same vein as Kanye's chart conflict with 50 Cent, many felt that Kanye won this rap battle too.

Jon Brion returned to help Kanye compose the next track, the charmingly titled 'Drunk And Hot Girls', a title Kanye had misheard while listening to Can's 'Sing Swan Song' – the original lyric was actually "drunky hot bowls" – the track he sampled for the song. Already a bold step into uncharted territory – Can were a revolutionary German motorik act from the seventies krautrock scene, a long way away from the rap, soul and pop samples Kanye started out working with – he messed with it even more, drenching its inebriated waltz in Brion's warped, wicked strings and distorted circus synths to form an inter-galactic Balkan drinking song with Mos Def as its reflective ringmaster. It was a song that encapsulated Kanye's entire life to that point in its sorry, regretful tale of cruising the clubs to find pretty drunk girls and then getting them home before they manage to sober up, or start talking about their burgeoning singing career.

"That's my life-defining song," he said, even though the track ended with a cautionary tale – the girl gets pregnant and he has to stay with her forever. "Jay-Z said that that's the anthem, a stadium-killer. I'm going to tell you, on some real shit, out of all the songs I've done – 'Touch The Sky', 'Jesus Walks' – that song represents me the most… At the end of the day, everything relates back to trying to do something for a girl. We go through too much bullshit just to mess with these drunk and hot girls. It's my entire life, from being a five-year-old trying to reach for that porno magazine all the way to the 30-year-old getting into an argument with his girlfriend. It sums up my whole fuckin' life. Guys will go through a lot to chase women. A guy will get on a plane and go to the other side of the world to hit it for the first time, and won't cross the street to hit it the second time. But as a man, your whole life is to provide for that girl in that white dress, that missing picture in your wedding photo. That was poetically put, if I do say so myself."

The girls occasionally stuck in his head too, as evinced by the next song on *Graduation*. 'Flashing Lights', co-produced with Eric Hudson, was all about being in thrall to a girl and also the unpredictable tastes of the public he was constantly trying to satisfy, as well as the press intrusion. To elegant swells of strings and suave eighties synths that painted a picture of Studio 54 at the cusp of soul turning to thumping disco, Kanye told of two different girls, a lover and a partner. The lover is a materialistic type bereft of romance – "She don't believe in shooting stars/But she believe in shoes and cars" – with whom he's having an affair, taking her to exotic beach-side restaurants and watching her dance sexily in his hotel room while fending off calls from his actual girlfriend. His frustration comes when his plan is foiled by paparazzi snapping him with his mistress: "I hate these niggas more than a Nazi", he spits. Following a slick chorus from Dwele (a hook originally meant to be sung by Charlie Wilson), the story jumps forward a year, with Kanye having split from his girlfriend, heartbroken and missing her dreadfully. "Feeling like Katrina with no F.E.M.A.," he rapped of losing his soulmate, "like Martin with no Gina [a reference to Martin Lawrence of the nineties sitcom *Martin*, and his estrangement from his onscreen girlfriend Gina, played by Tisha Campbell, over behind-the-scenes harassment issues]… In my past, you on the other side of the glass of my memory's museum." The track was a telling flip between the old, womanising Kanye and the new sensitive rapper facing the prospect of marriage and all of the emotional consequences of lifelong partnership. Kanye was starting to see the error of his youthful, sex-obsessed ways, and before long 'Flashing Lights' would ring very true to him indeed.

The song would become *Graduation*'s fourth single, released in November after he'd had another hit with a guest verse on Kid Sister's 'Pro Nails' single, adding his verse to the track for his *Can't Tell Me Nothing* mix-tape and Kid Sister, A-Trak's girlfriend, released her version of it, hitting number 21 in the Hot Singles Sales chart. Initially, at an album listening party in New York in August, Kanye had premiered the song over a snippet from a Hong Kong movie called *2046*, but by the end of its lifespan it would accumulate a total of three videos, as was Kanye's visual wont. They'd be released to the public in reverse order. The last to be made was co-directed by Kanye and Spike Jonze and first shown to a select audience of 200 guests at an *Entertainment Weekly* Grammy Awards after party on February 10, 2008, a week after the single had peaked at number 29 on the *Billboard* chart. It saw a Ford Mustang Bullitt pull up deep in the Nevada desert in slow motion and *Playboy* model Rita G step out, strip down to sexy underwear and burn her clothes. Then, she trod slowly back towards the car, barely clad, opened the trunk and revealed Kanye tied up in the back. She tenderly stroked his face, kissed him and then, pulling a shovel from beside him, stabbed it into his chest, out of sight of the camera. The physical violence gave a new twist to the song's line "she don't believe in shooting stars" – she evidently believed in stabbing them instead. This, West would later claim, was his favourite ever music video experience.

The other two videos were rejected clips which somehow leaked online without Kanye's knowledge or permission. In one, told in a series of snapshots, model Charlotte Carter-Allen woke up, dressed for a night on the town and then hit the clubs, only to be robbed – and possibly worse – on her way home. The other, filmed in Berlin, took on the tone of a horror movie whodunit, as Kanye joined a grotesque dinner party in a spooky gothic mansion house, where gold chalices overflowed with blood, pale waitresses hovered around vampiric diners and the guests became sheet-draped corpses one by one. Pursuing a woman in black through the shadows of the house, Kanye ultimately flings himself at her, only for her form to dissipate and send him hurtling through the window behind her. Though an expensive cast-off, the video made number two on the Viral Video Chart.

The final guest appearance on *Graduation* came from one of Jay-Z's early producers DJ Premier, scratching a Public Enemy sample, the line "here we go again" from 'Bring The Noise', a sample he brought to the track after Kanye played him an early version – for the hook on 'Everything I Am'. It seemed amazing that Common would have passed on such a gorgeous track, the album's stripped-down ballad masterpiece; a Rhodes piano twinkled with honeyed melody, a sample of Prince Phillip Mitchell's 'If We Can't Be Lovers' oozed soulful panache and Kanye gave a subtle and restrained performance that resonated with a philosophical depth. "Everything I'm not made me everything I am," went the track's central tenet, an idea Kanye felt was as deep as any he'd ever had. "In my humble opinion, that's a prophetic statement," he'd say. "Gandhi would have said something like that. Picture somebody going up to him saying, 'This is bad about me, blah, blah, blah'. And Gandhi would come back and say, 'Everything you're not made you everything you are. Leave, my son'."

Over the course of the first introspective verse, Kanye used this basic theory to lay out how he came to be the man he was. "I'll never be picture perfect Beyoncé," he ruminated, admitting to his flaws and failures in order to envisage how they'd come to shape his character, "be light as Al B or black as Chauncey… I never be as laid-back as this beat was". Yet he'd made it to the highest echelons of hip-hop just the way he was, he pointed out, without following fashions or taking on the fake gangster persona so many expected of him – "I never could see why people reach a fake-ass façade that they couldn't keep up" – or keeping in check his tendency to flare up at award ceremonies – "so say goodbye to the NAACP Award/Goodbye to the India Arie Award… I'll just take the I Got A Lotta Cheese Award".

The final verse, in an unprecedented move for a Roc-A-Fella act, attacked the prevalent gangster rap scene for promoting violence, stating that "just last year Chicago had 600 caskets", so this wasn't a lifestyle he wanted to promote or propagate: "Do you know what it feels like when people is passing?" he asked. Predicting a backlash to such a viewpoint, he closed the track by imagining himself being shut down by a disinterested public, "My 15 seconds up but I got more to say/'That's enough Mr West, please, no more today'." 'Everything I Am' was a bold and brave statement, as pertinent and controversial within the rap world as his comments on George Bush had been on national television, but Kanye was standing proud for what he believed once more. With tracks like these, he'd slowly turn the tides of hip-hop.

As a sop to his earliest fans, Kanye threw 'The Glory' into the album towards the end. A classic West pitched-up chipmunk sample broke out over a meaty soul beat and symphonic gospel strings, while Kanye pledged his faith to fame once more. Taken from Laura Nyro's very religious 'Save The Country', the beat was originally produced for Common's *Finding Forever* album, produced by Kanye, but was rejected, so once again Kanye picked it up. The hook line "gonna take you to the glory, oh I can't study war" related to both religion and success, but the track leant far more heavily towards the worship of self than deity. "Can I talk my shit again?" Kanye rapped, repeating his line from 'We Major', as he launched into an opening verse bigging up his top-end clothes, hit-making abilities – "Class back in session, so I upped it a grade… while y'all was in limbo I raised the bar up" – and rapid rise – "two years Dwayne Wayne became Dwayne Wade"*. He boasted of how his tour with Common featured "after each and every show a couple dykes in the van" and so many photographers taking his picture that he had to cover his eyes in the style of Yayo's trademark dance move.

---

* Dwayne Wayne was a geek character from nineties sitcom *A Different World*, whereas Dwayne Wade was one of the highest-paid players in the NBA.

Yet, since he was admittedly doing it all "for the glory" of attention, there were still frustrations. The second verse complained about other rappers trying to copy his slick dress sense – "How I'm suppose to stand out when everybody get dressed up?" – while maintaining that he rose above them all – "At the Grammys I went ultra Travolta/Yeah that tuxedo might have been a little guido/But with my ego I can stand there in a Speedo/And be looked at like a fucking hero". The result, he claimed, of his inexorable rise to his current position as a very rich artist threatening Biggie Smalls' legend as the best rapper ever from his lowly beginnings driving his mother's Volvo and necking bottles of NoDoz to stay up and make rhymes. "Back when I was breaking into the game, I spent every waking hour focusing," he explained. "I'd take a couple of NoDoz – all the time. But aside from the fact that my girl won't let me take NoDoz, they don't even work any more. I'm completely numb to NoDoz at this point. I've taken so much that my body is immune to it."

After several tracks of ego inflation, Kanye was in need of being pulled back down to earth. To Chicago, to be precise; 'Homecoming' finally saw the track 'Home' from his demo tape make it onto an album, the tribute to Windy – the romantic female metaphor for his hometown – now stripped of its soul feel and John Legend hook and based around a strident arena piano loop with Coldplay's Chris Martin providing a new, elastic pop chorus. It was Kanye's idea to collaborate with Martin, one eye on the immense crossover potential of working with a huge mainstream rock band, having first met him during a jam session at Abbey Road Studios in 2006. But having heard the track Jay-Z decided to also ask Martin to guest on one of his raps – 'Beach Chair' from his comeback record *Kingdom Come*. Jay was quick about it; his track appeared in 2006, while Kanye's wasn't out until 2007. Kanye was initially angry about his plan being snatched by his label superior, and refused to play him *Graduation* for a while.

'Homecoming' would also be the final track released as a single from *Graduation*, on February 18, 2008. Promoted with a monochrome Hype Williams video of Kanye enigmatically wandering Chicago landmarks, it made a modest impact on the *Billboard* chart, at number 69, and broke the UK Top 10.

"What's so funny is, he is really mad cool with Chris Martin, they hang out," Kanye later repented. "Are they not allowed to go into the studio because he did a song with me? So that was pretty bitchy on my part. He had the right to do it, but it was like me wanting to be the first one to wear Jordans. It was just me being competitive... I was complaining that I didn't want to play the album for Jay, because of the Coldplay thing. Then Jay hit me back, like, 'What the fuck do you mean, you can't play the album for me? You forget who I am? I'm your big brother'."

The phrase stuck in Kanye's head. Before long he had an entirely new track out of it, a tribute to his label boss and mentor and the closing track on the album, 'Big Brother'. The only track on the album which Kanye didn't have any production input on – the distorted, muted take on glossy eighties hair rock was done by DJ Toomp – it would also be hailed as one of its most legendary moments, largely due to the impassioned lyrics paying honour to Jay – "A idol in my eyes, god of the game" – while also daring to criticise him for things he'd done to Kanye along the way. Both hero worship and diss track in one, the track opened with some background on Jay – "My big brother was B.I.G.'s brother/Used to be Dame and Biggs' brother" – before going on to trace the highs and lows of his relationship with Jay, from right back when Kanye was a fan attending the Hard Knock Life tour in 1999. When he meets him, he's too shy – or, possibly too Chi – to play him his beats even though Jay could change his life if he liked them, and sure enough he eventually does: "He got me out of my momma crib/Then he helped me get my momma a crib".

Verse two moved the story on to New York, Kanye's arrival at Baseline studios and how he impressed Jay with his beats enough to create the foundations for *The Blueprint*. Yet the resentment of being overlooked to rap at the Madison Square Garden show lingered. "I guess big brother was thinking a little different," he pondered, "and kept little brother at bay, at a distance... only thing I wanna know is why I get looked over/I guess I'll understand when I get more older". By verse three he was making huge hit records and suddenly Jay was his competitor on an even playing field: "To be number one I'mma beat my brother". Admitting that Jay's verse on the 'Diamonds Of Sierra Leone (Remix)' had "kicked my ass", Kanye went on to honour Jay as "my big brother who I always tried to be" but also chide him for getting Chris Martin on a song after Kanye had done the same thing, for guesting on verses for his own personal ends and for pushing Beanie Sigel more than him. Though it ends with a heartfelt respect for Jay, 'Big Brother' was a two-handed tribute.

"I played him a piece of it," Kanye said of the first time Jay heard the track. "I had that first verse done, that line where I said, 'You got me outta my momma's crib/And then you helped me get my momma a crib'. Which are two major turning points in any man's life... All I will say was that it was a very serious moment. The song was like an apology for me. Jay had so many good ideas for the record, and I was acting like a bitch and not wanting to play it for him." Jay would later say the song was Kanye's best since 'Jesus Walks'.

The song also gave a nod to No I.D., calling him "my mentor". "My reaction when I first heard the big brother thing, an engineer that was working with him called me, like 'Man, we need to put you in this song'," I.D. said, modestly. "I was like 'OK', I was on the first album when he did the 'Last Call' doing a little part and he was talking about it too, so to me it really wasn't nothing."

Various versions of the album in different formats and territories came with bonus tracks attached, including remixes of 'Stronger' and 'Can't Tell Me Nothing' as well as two original songs. 'Good Night', available on the iTunes, UK and Japanese versions, provided a satisfying rounding-off of an album that had opened with 'Good Morning'. With Mos Def on the toytown reggae intro and hook, it found Kanye revisiting dreams of his childhood, when his grandparents would take him to museums and he'd be itching to touch everything on display. It was a bittersweet verse, rapped over a modernist ragga shuffle, as Kanye wished he could pull his grandparents out of his dream into real life – "It's sorta fly you get a chance to say hi to people you never got a chance to say bye to". With Al Be Back providing a short verse encouraging the listener to "dream beautiful", it was a sweet closer, followed on the Japanese album by one last song, 'Bittersweet Poetry'. With the help of John Mayer on the hook, a love poem penned to a girl called Bittersweet with whom he has a love/hate relationship, Kanye furthered his reputation as an emotional rapper by delving into the minutiae of the affair, claiming it's his first experience of true love: "Never did this before, that's what the virgin said". Set to a rough, loping beat of harpsichord and melodic pop synthesizer, verse one lays bare the foundations of an argument, Kanye's girl riling him by telling him she was only after his money and a mixture of anger, alcohol and "a little bad advice" causing him to boil over, starting the sort of cruel and violent row that had seen them break up and get back together numerous times. Their arguments begin driving Kanye to drink, a problem exacerbated by the couple's bedroom problems – every time he'd try to have sex with her she'd yell at him for having slept with other women during their breaks. Ultimately, Kanye admitted he was in the wrong – "I fucked up and I know it G" – a rare sign of weakness and fallibility in a genre that, until now, had thrived on self-assurance and strength. Like so much of Kanye's work, it was yet another game changer.

★ ★ ★

Once more, the critics frothed. *Entertainment Weekly* and *USA Today* named *Graduation* the album of the year. "Those who have admired Kanye as a sharp producer while detesting him as an inept MC might find the gleaming synth sprites ... to be one of the most glaring deal-breakers in hip-hop history," wrote Andy Kellman at AllMusic, while Stylus Magazine's Jayson Greene argued "musically, at least, it's the most accomplished thing he's ever done". *Rolling Stone*'s Nathan Brackett said "given the lousy year hip-hop has had, the music needs his spazzed-out, neurotic creativity more than ever", and *Time*'s Josh Tyrangiel wrote, "Thin as *Graduation* is on material, it delivers knockout hooks at a Louis Vuitton price point... West plunders the best and meticulously layers every track with enough surprises that there are thrills and discoveries a dozen listens in".

"*Graduation*'s intricate musical environments take a while to comprehend," wrote Ann Powers of the *Los Angeles Times*, "and at times they seem at odds with West's confrontational lyrics. But this contradictory music makes sense when heard as an attempt to express an internal struggle – between the Kanye West hip-hop made and the West who can't be contained by it or any other genre. It's hard to stop running with the crowd, even for a trendsetter. But West is on the verge, and moving forward … a joker who couldn't be more serious, displaced and mobile because of race instead of class and an innovator in a genre that he must at least partially destroy to renew." *Slant* magazine's Eric Henderson was rather more direct: "[It grabs] your ear on the first listen (notably bypassing your brain), your balls on the second, and your soul from there on out".

Kanye wouldn't return the affection of the press. Over the course of the media campaign for *Graduation* he'd repeatedly explain why these would be the last print interviews he'd conduct, deciding to grant only broadcast interviews in future besides a very few select press pieces with magazines he could trust. "People who write stuff paraphrase," he said. "They take what I'm saying – and I speak in colours – and flip it to black and white. Sometimes I might say something that has four or five meanings. If I'm being sarcastic, they'll take out the setup or the punchline and I sound like a jerk. It's the edit."

So it was with intrigue and fascination that his fans devoured these last printed glimpses into Kanye's life and psyche. He spoke of his belief in *Graduation* as his emergence into rap maturity, the beginning of the rest of his hip-hop life. "This new album is simple, sweet and perfected," he said. "I think it's one of the best albums in history. In life, people are living their own movie. I wanted to make the soundtrack to that… A lot of hip-hop artists don't have the ability to make classic songs because they spend most of their time rapping about themselves rather than what people care about. My songs are songs. They are songs to help in life, to inspire. Let me speak in the third person for a second – a Kanye West album is like a brand, like Louis Vuitton or Nike or the latest Jordans. You buy a pair of Jordans, take them to school and everybody goes 'wow'. Second pair, 'incredible'. Third pair, you don't even have to say it. It's like me. People just know. It's a Kanye West."

"This CD is for everyone," he told *ABC Newsline*. "I don't please everybody with who I am as a person. I'm just trying to please myself with who I am as a person. But I make a product. And I am the Coca-Cola, the Walt Disney... who else can we say just has free reign?"

"Before, the music was more self-conscious," he told *Spin*, "and now it's more about everyone... I'm talking lyrics and chorus-wise, giving them something to sing along with. Even a song like 'Can't Tell Me Nothing', that's a rock chorus over straight ghetto drums... [I've made] a conscious effort to take it to the next level in every form of success. More black people bought this album than any I've made... Because I made the album blacker... Way blacker. 'Can't Tell Me Nothing', how hood is that record? 'Good Life' is straight Steve Harvey all day long. 'Flashing Lights'? I never had a record that was that black. But it's white at the same time. Certain things are so good it doesn't have to be white or black. That's what *Graduation* is. Take 'Harder, Better, Faster, Stronger'. It's a white sample but everything I do to it is to make it as black as possible... I'm a pop enigma... I rock a bespoke suit and I go to Harold's for fried chicken... as a tastemaker I find the best of everything."

His ambition to straddle the race divide was key. "There's certain things that white people are the best at and certain things that black people are the best at... On Christmas, I don't want my food to taste white, and when I go to purchase a house, I don't want my credit to look black."

Elsewhere, he was espousing very forward-thinking ideas for rap music, claiming that he wanted to shift the genre towards a more positive vibe after years of gangsta rap domination which, he said, was a form of acting. "I think America just needs to get real when it comes to the way our kids speak and communicate," he said. "They need to understand what happens in rap. Tupac and Biggie might talk about violence, but in action movies there are stuntmen who have actually died on set. The amount of people who talk about guns versus who actually uses them is not even close in this millennium. People need to understand that hip-hop that has gun talk is just for entertainment, similar to if you were watching a movie. Film schools don't have anything against movies with violence. If you can approach hip-hop from a standpoint of 'how did you put this together?' and get past the fact that they use profanity, realise that you are a reflection of your parents, more so than the music. Let's get more into the music itself. How does Dr Dre, a musical genius, layer all these sounds? What about engineering and Pro Tools and the poetry aspect? We can teach each other about hip-hop history, we can teach about legends, hip-hop theory. It's been around so long that text books can be written about it. This is a perfect time to capitalise on and get kids excited about [musical] education."

"I feel like my lyrics are – if not the – then equal to the realest lyrics out," he added. "I connected with so many people without talking about guns and drugs – it's harder to go to work 365 days than shoot a person in one day. There's nothing about wearing a pink Polo that would make anyone believe that I would hold a gun."

He'd argue that his lyrics took rap to a new plateau of originality, poetry and philosophical discussion, and this made him an anomaly in modern hip-hop. "I think I might have some problems with being accepted and just fitting in because… there is a lot of things that are different about me," he said. "I just don't fit into the cookie cutter, you know… who you're supposed to be as a rapper or who you're supposed to be as a black man or who you're supposed to be as an entertainer, who you're supposed to be as a celebrity. I don't just follow those rules."

And he'd open up on his deeper issues too, such as his obsession over his public image. "I made so many mistakes the past year," he said, "I started swimming in wack juice I needed to get out of. I would read blogs and they would be like, 'His shoelaces are untied, he's a b—h'."

Though broadcast interviews would continue to allow Kanye a mouthpiece to deliver his sermons on the world, from this point on we would lose the insights into his personality that came with journalistic colour and questioning. When *Rolling Stone* joined him in London for three shows, it noted that he never wrote a set list but started tracks as the whim took him, stopping any song the minute he felt it wasn't getting the crowd going. He was also painted as verbose and easily distracted, coming up with lyrics mid-interview, making jokes and often digressing way off-topic. Here we'd learn about his surfing habits: "We're always moving around – we do about 200 shows every year – so the internet is the only way to be in contact with what's going on in the centre of the universe, which is New York. I look at party sites like What's Poppin'. I look at blogs. I look at porn, but I still only trust manual DVD porn purchases." And about his views on drugs such as pot, cocaine and ecstasy: "They seem like they might be OK. I don't know. A lot of people like those drugs. I don't do any of them... Contrary to the way I was acting for the past two years, I actually haven't tried coke. I've never even had the urge to. It scares me... Just because I live [in LA] doesn't mean I party there. I stay in Hollywood, and I see the flashing lights and the people dancing and drinkin', but I hardly ever see someone do coke. Like in *Boogie Nights*, or Eddie Murphy in *Dreamgirls*, I see people getting caught up in that whole thing and hanging out with fake-ass friends. Man, that shit could really be a real thing for me, but I won't allow it to be. My thing is making music and hanging out with my friends and doing the same regular shit I did before all of this. I don't go to a lot of parties in LA. That shit is wack, man. I don't like the scene there. I never got into it. I love LA, but fuck the parties. I don't want them to stop playing my music at those parties, though."

He'd claim to be a New York boy at heart, loving the familiarity of landing at JFK at 7am, tuning into Hot 97 and sinking into the city. "It's the greatest city in the world," he said, "next to Chicago, if I'm being politically correct. I fell in love with New York before I even went there, just from watching the old videos. And now when I'm in New York, people show me so much love, in a way where I can still get to where I need to go. That's what I love about New Yorkers. They also have somewhere to be." He'd explain the basis of his outbursts of unrefined honesty. "I like facing up to the realities – like black people being super homophobic... I'm not as brutally honest as I used to be. Sometimes honesty can be used improperly. You can use it to hurt somebody, which is wack. You have to have more tact and class than to blurt out honest statements. People can't handle the truth sometimes. I try my best not to lie to myself. I try to keep my finger on the pulse of pop culture. I feel the vibe of what's going on in the community, what's happening in the hood, what's people's temperament toward me as a celebrity, as entertainment, as a rapper, as a musician. When pop artists put a facade up and live in a fake-ass world, they don't deal with the reality… That's when you start falling off, when you make stuff that's less relevant to people."

And for the first time, he'd declare himself a Bono-style rock star. "I am a rock star," he stated, unequivocally. "Because rock stars don't need security, and I can go to dinner and chill. Rock stars can speak well, or hop on a plane to Paris if they feel like it. Rock stars can catch cabs, they don't need entourages and they don't have to pop out of limos all the time. Rock stars can wear the same clothes every day, they can get their shoes dirty and they don't need a fuckin' haircut. Rock stars can pull their dick out in public and then go rock 20,000 people. Rock stars have a wife and kids. Rock stars do the drugs that they want, and they can get over drugs, or they don't get over drugs and it fucks them up. Rock stars can give their fucking opinion without having to deal with . . . what's that thing I get dealt with every day of my life? Oh, yeah. Backlash."

"Every year I learn more," he said. "Times are still scary but I got to sit down with Daft Punk and Madonna, and with a lot of incredible individuals, and learn from them. I'm gonna keep making music so that 10, 20 years from now, I'll be able to be where Mick [Jagger] is, where Bono is."

For all his frustrations and ambitions, Kanye came across as a man largely content with the way his life was going, with the closeness and support of those around him and very happy to be settling down with the woman he loved rather than carrying on chasing girls the way he had throughout his single years. "When I say, 'How you stay faithful in a room full of hos?'," he said, "it's like when you first get money, you're going to go to the Gucci store, you go to the Louis store, you buy two of this, three of that. And now I've finally matured and I'm in a place where I can actually be faithful. I'll see a super-attractive girl and look and say, 'Wow, she looks nice' and just let it be that. It's not always that predator I-have-to-have-everything mentality that you can have in a sneaker store or in the music store… [I'm] maturing and being able to fight temptation. It's a similar type of impulse as overshopping. Being a shopaholic. Or when you're a little kid, you try and get as many phone numbers in the mall as you could… I'm just going to go and get married

– I'm not going to make a big deal out of it. It's not to prove anything to anyone – it's for me, for stability in my life, and I'm so happy that I found someone that I really love, that challenges me, that keeps my life interesting, that's just as crazy as I am... I think that both of us we're really special, and when you see those things combine it's something even greater."

Media backlash would be the last thing Kanye would be worrying about before too long. His world was about to flip upside down, and his music would flip with it.

CHAPTER TEN

808s & Heartbreak

He'd always tell his mother she was beautiful, that she looked just great the way she was. But some insecurities are too deeply felt for reassurances to brush away. And with money comes the chance, at last, to put them right.

On November 9, 2007, Donda West was released from hospital covered in bandages following five and a half hours of surgery for a tummy tuck and breast reduction, performed at her own insistence. Her release on the day of surgery was controversial; several doctors would later argue that she should have been kept in overnight for observation, or that her doctor should have insisted she have aftercare at the hospital. But then, some surgeons would have refused to operate on her at all without significant tests and reassurances. She was an overweight woman close to 60, and most surgeons wouldn't operate without medical clearance.

But Donda wouldn't take no for an answer. She'd had a fantastic year, after all. Having quit her role as chairwoman at the English Department at Chicago State to dedicate herself full time to managing Kanye and his West Brands LLC company as well as run the Kanye West Foundation, she'd also published a book about her experiences of bringing up a genius – *Raising Kanye: Life Lessons From The Mother Of A Hip-Hop Superstar*. Kanye wrote the foreword for the book, joking "I've known my mom since I was zero years old. She is quite dope", and the two had conducted book signing events together.

"He told me, 'There's no real acrimony between us, there's no controversy.' [So] he didn't think people would buy [the book]," she said. "But I felt there are a lot of things about Kanye and I that might be beneficial to other mothers and their children."

The publication had raised Donda's profile significantly. Several months before the surgery, she'd returned to Chicago State to deliver the keynote speech at a writing conference, and she was the star of her 40th high school reunion, where she talked cheerfully about the prospect of grandchildren and signed books for a fundraising auction.

Behind the scenes, though, she was busy talking her way into the operating theatre. She'd approached a surgeon called Andre Aboolian, who told her that at her age the procedure carried risks, and he wouldn't perform the surgery without medical clearance from another doctor. "I always insist on a medical clearance for women over 40," he said, "and in this instance it was particularly important because of a condition she had that I felt could have led to a heart attack."

When medical clearance wasn't granted, Aboolian refused to operate on Donda. But Donda didn't leave it there. Instead, she turned to Dr Jan Adams, a celebrity Beverly Hills surgeon she'd seen on numerous TV shows – *Plastic Surgery, Before And After* and Barbara Walters' *The View*. Adams had a book on the subject, *Everything Women Of Colour Should Know About Plastic Surgery*, which had been featured on Oprah. Little did Donda know that Adams had made a six-figure settlement over two malpractice suits filed against him back in 2001, or several charges for driving under the influence. Adams was on TV, and TV, we're programmed to believe, is infallible.

Adams took on the job, and discharged Donda on November 9 into the care of her nephew Stephan Scoggins, a registered nurse, despite strong advice that she should be seeking care in a medical facility. Donda took some Vicodin to help her sleep and woke the next day feeling fine. Reports claimed that Scoggins left her to attend a baby shower in the afternoon, ensuring there were friends downstairs in the house to take care of her while she rested upstairs.

In the evening of November 10, Donda felt a tightening in her chest and a sore throat. Suddenly she stopped breathing. One of the friends at the house, finding her collapsed, called 911; paramedics on the scene failed to revive her and Donda was pronounced dead at the hospital. An autopsy found she'd had a heart attack, the result of a coronary artery disease which might have been diagnosed during pre-surgery tests, but a coroner would conclude that she died from "multiple post-operative factors", effectively absolving Dr Jan Adams of any responsibility.

The tributes rolled in. Roc-A-Fella's website changed its home page to the legend 'In Loving Memory Of Dr Donda West' on a plain black background. Jay-Z asked for a moment's silence for her at the end of his NYC Hammersmith Ballroom show, saying "Let's get serious for a minute. This show is dedicated to Kanye West who had a death in the family. We got you, Kanye. Stay strong."

"I can definitely understand how that's a huge loss, and how that would be, and his relationship with his mom had a lot more depth to it than a lot of people's," said his erstwhile rival 50 Cent. "He was really close to his mom. I hope that he can work his way through it. If you're active, you'll find reasons to smile, reasons to be happy."

"This record alone just shows you the relationship he had with his mother," offered DJ Khaled, who'd had Kanye guesting on his 'Grammy Family' track in 2006. "There are always pictures of him and his mother. His mother is his life. And he had a close bond with her; they were best friends."

Jay and Beyoncé attended Donda's funeral alongside many of her colleagues and students as well as Anita Baker and John Legend, who performed one of her favourite songs, 'Summertime', during the service. For Kanye himself, it was a devastating period; his tributes to her would pour forth for some time to come. Just one week after her death he faced his first live appearance at Le Zenith in Paris. In front of 6,000 dumbstruck fans, he broke down in tears to the opening notes of 'Hey Mama'. And having finished a short run of European and UK arena shows, he lay low for several months over the Christmas period to grieve, emerging only to make peace with Evel Knievel. Approaching the end of his own life, Knievel saw Kanye in pain over the loss of his mother and invited him to his home to heal their rift. Kanye took the opportunity to explain to Knievel that the video was made in honour of Knievel's inspirational bravery and showmanship, and Knievel was impressed by his words. "I thought he was a wonderful guy and quite a gentleman," Evel said. "I know he's had some tough times the past few weeks and I hope things work out." Knievel, aged 69, died less than a week later.★

Kanye re-emerged on February 10, 2008, the word 'MAMA' shaved into his hair, to perform at the 50th Grammys ceremony at the Los Angeles Stapes Center. Amid flurries of fire and steam and before a technological temple with a neon pyramid at its centre – on which a computerised wire-frame Daft Punk would appear, pressing the chorus out of sampler pads – Kanye performed 'Stronger' in light-up jacket and shades as a string section played neon violins in the background, the first hints of the futuristic aesthetic he'd employ on the forthcoming 'Glow In The Dark' tour. But he really stole the show when he stripped away all of the production and sang from the heart. On an empty stage in mourning black he took to a lone spotlight to sing 'Hey Mama', its backing reduced to subtle bass notes and hints of strings and its introduction changed to a heartfelt new motif: "Last night I saw you in my dreams," Kanye sang, "now I can't wait to go to sleep… this life is all a dream, so my real life starts when I go to sleep."

It was a deeply moving moment, made all the more emotional as Kanye stepped up to collect the Grammy for Best Rap Album, matching Eminem's record for picking up Grammy awards with each of his first three rap albums. From his eight nominations that night, Kanye picked up four awards: Best Rap Album for *Graduation*, Best Rap Solo Performance for 'Stronger', Best Rap Performance By A Duo Or Group for his Common collaboration 'Southside' and Best Rap Song for 'Good Times'. "It definitely feels good to be home here at the Grammys," he said. "You know, we snuck in about four years ago, four or five years ago and now we basically made this our new place of residence. Working on a hip-hop album, and the state of the music

★ The settlement between Kanye and Knievel was never publically declared.

game – they say… you can't sell records. A lot of people said hip-hop was dead – not just Nas, but a lot of people just said the art form wasn't popping like that any more. I wanted to cross the genres and show people how we could still express ourselves with something fresh and new and that's what hip-hop's always been about, coming out with new sounds and stuff… You got to time the album better, you can't drop them the same year as me, this is my award."

The ceremony's background music began playing, a sign that the speaker should wrap up their speech. Kanye wasn't going to be cut off, though. "Come on, you going to play music on me?" he gasped, and kept talking. "For Mark Ronson and Amy Winehouse, if I don't get to get up here for album of the year, you deserve it just as much as me – I deserve it too… Just to say something about my mother; I appreciate all the support, I appreciate all the prayers. It would be in good taste to stop the music." The music respectfully stopped. "I appreciate everything, and I know you are really proud of me right now. And I know you wouldn't want me to stop, and you want me to be the number one artist in the world. And mama, all I'm gonna do is keep making you proud. We run this."

Kanye's tributes to his mother wouldn't end there. Some years later he'd launch a new project called DONDA, a creative design and content production company inspired by what Donda had taught him – the project would design clothes starting with footwear collaborations with Nike and Louis Vuitton, and eventually branch out to design record sleeves. "DONDA is a design company which will galvanise amazing thinkers and put them in a creative space to bounce their dreams and ideas," he tweeted on its launch, and expanded the concept in one of his few interviews. "The teachings and the confidence that was instilled by my grandfather into my mother, and from my mother into me," he said, "will create the best winter coat against doubters and dream-killers ever made," Kanye said.

He'd use his pain for his music, an essential part of the process of inspiration, he'd claim. "Creative output, you know, is just pain," he said. "I'm going to be cliché for a minute and say that great art comes from pain. But also I'd say a bigger statement than that is: great art comes from great artists. There's a bunch of people that are hurt that still couldn't have made the album that was super-polarising and redefined the sound of radio."

And before 2008 was much further along, he'd find all the more reason to create.

★ ★ ★

"It's always sad when things like this end, and we remain friends," Alexis Phifer told *People* magazine in April. "I wish him the best in his future and all of his endeavors. He's one of the most talented people I've ever met."

With his closest female relationship tragically cut short, his second wasn't far behind. Despite reports in the media that Kanye and Alexis Phifer were due to marry in mid-April to honour Donda's wish, Phifer was photographed on the red carpet of an Evenings In Vogue event in NYC, which featured her clothing line Ghita, without her engagement ring. "They'd been having problems," an unnamed friend of Kanye was quoted as saying. "Kanye is really focused on his show; he's putting everything into the show right now. Alexis is a nice girl, but Kanye has been going through a rough time. They hit a rough patch and for now they've split."

It was at this point that Kanye began to feel the downside of courting so much attention and publicity. The gossip columns went into overdrive, digging up any dirt they could find to find the reasons behind the split. *Touch Weekly* magazine ran an article quoting a "close friend" of Phifer's calling Kanye "an abuser" and telling a story about an argument the pair allegedly had at a Fourth of July party at their house. The source claimed that Alexis had come across Kanye looking at a nude picture of Kim Kardashian on his mobile phone.

A friend of Alexis Phifer and Paris Hilton, Kardashian was a socialite who'd shot to stardom in 2007 when a sex tape she made in 2003 with singer Ray J had leaked online. Following a $5 million settlement with the company that distributed the film, Kardashian was soon given her own reality TV show, *Keeping Up With The Kardashians*, a hit series on the E! entertainment channel. The show's success led to a naked shoot in *Playboy* and her first movie role in 2008, playing Lisa in *Disaster Movie*. Kanye, the story went on, denied having an affair with Kim, quoting him as saying he'd never be interested in "a whore with a fake ass". Then, according to the source, the row turned violent. "He said he couldn't control who sent him the photos. But then he started getting dramatic – huffing and puffing and making a big deal… They went outside, and Kanye pushed Alexis into some bushes with all his force. She was wearing a T-shirt and she got cuts and scratches everywhere and was bleeding. She was crying… He just left her there. He got in his car and drove away."

Kanye would refute the story in the lyrics of a later track, but an onstage rant in 2014 seemed to suggest he was already acquainted with Kardashian, and interested in her. "Seven years ago I met Kim and told her that I was going to marry her," he told a crowd of thousands.

Alexis herself would never make any such claims, telling the press that her relief in breaking with Kanye was more to do with wanting to shy away from the attention. "I think after experiencing being with somebody that is a celebrity, it's really nice to have your anonymity," she said. "I'm a mom so I would much rather be able to be out with my son and have nobody recognise me. I really think that's a cool thing as opposed to doing red carpets or something like that, but only if it's really pertaining to my [fashion] line because that's what I'm trying to sell… I'm not really trying to sell myself."

But whatever the root cause of the split, Kanye would turn to work to get him through the breakdown of his engagement and the long period of depression that followed. Rumours would suggest that his stringent rehearsals for his upcoming Glow In The Dark world tour had put extra strains on the relationship, a tour he would finance himself since the original sponsor Best Buy pulled out. The production was an elaborate attempt to push hip-hop into the arena rock league, a concept show based around the story of Kanye as the pilot of a spaceship hitting a meteor storm and crashing onto a rocky planet drenched in dry ice and overlooked by aliens in floating bubbles. Opening with a forlorn 'Good Morning' and taking in a stunning string of hits – 'Good Morning', 'I Wonder', 'Heard 'Em Say', 'Through The Wire', 'Champion', 'Get Em High',

'Diamonds From Sierra Leone', 'Can't Tell Me Nothing', 'Flashing Lights', 'Spaceship', 'All Falls Down', 'Gold Digger', 'Good Life', 'Jesus Walks', 'Hey Mama', 'Stronger', 'Homecoming' and 'Touch The Sky' – as Kanye dramatically attempted to make his way home, *Details* magazine would describe it as "Samuel Beckett meets Philip K Dick", a tale of desperate isolation in a seething sci-fi landscape, albeit one incongruously visited by large gold-painted women on a screen for 'Gold Digger'.

With support from Lupe Fiasco, N.E.R.D. and Rihanna, the Glow In The Dark spectacular would tour the world for the entire year, its first leg taking in over 50 arena and festival shows in the US, Canada and the UK between May 16 and August 7, including Kanye's own Madison Square Garden concert – and four subsequent legs stretched from Mexico to Australia via South America, the Far East and Europe from October 17 to December 7, with support in Europe coming from such acts as Mr Hudson & The Library, Consequence, Tony Williams and Kid Cudi, among others. It was a mammoth undertaking, and while its 61 dates in total would gross over $30 million and spawn on offshoot book featuring 400 photos of the tour by Nabil Elderkin, it would not be without its setbacks. Playing the Bonnaroo festival on June 14, the previous act, Pearl Jam, over-ran by 50 minutes, meaning that Kanye arrived on stage two hours later than advertised. By the time he took the stage at 4.23am the crowd were chanting "Kanye sucks!", but West soon silenced them with his grand parade of rap hits.

The "Kanye sucks!" chant would linger at the festival as funk musician Robert Randolph encouraged his audience to shout the phrase during his set. Upset, Kanye took to his online blog for one of the first of a series of legendary caps-lock rants. "I'm typing so fucking hard I might break my fucking Mac book Air!!!!!!!!," he wrote "Call me any name you want ... BUT NEVER SAY I DIDN'T GIVE MY ALL!... WE WERE OBVIOUSLY DEALING WITH FUCKING IDIOTS WHO DIDN'T REALLY HAVE THE CAPACITY TO REALLY PUT ON THIS SHOW PROPERLY. THEY TRIED 2 GIVE ME A TIME SLOT WHERE IT WAS STILL LIGHT OUTSIDE ... I HAVE A FUCKING LIGHT SHOW DUMB ASS, IT'S NOT CALLED GLOW IN THE DARK FOR NO REASON SQUID BRAINS!"

He'd come to see the event as the sociological opposite of Jay-Z headlining Glastonbury festival that same year and being accepted by the traditionally rock-based audience there. "I experienced racism in a way that I couldn't overcome at Bonnaroo festival this year," he said. "My set was sabotaged and my time slot moved. What was great about Jay-Z was that he overcame the racism and broke down more barriers, but we're fighting every day."

This wouldn't be his only online outburst of the year. When *Entertainment Weekly*'s Chris Wilson reviewed the Glow In The Dark tour and graded the show with a decent B+ score, Kanye took to his blog again. "What's a B+ mean?" he net-ranted. "I'm an extremist, its either pass or fail! A+ or F-! You know what, fuck you and the whole fucking staff!"

'Stronger' swiftly became a highlight of the tour, for Kanye and his fans. "I told people when I did 'Stronger' that it was my greatest beat to date," he said. "I could play just that beat and it got such a reaction out of people – even more than 'Jesus Walks'. Yet it's even better now in hindsight! We'd be doing shows in Asia and shit and after the show I'd be like, 'Man, I am really happy I have that song.' It embodies everything a Killers song, a U2 song, a N.E.R.D. song has. Everything you want in a song, it has. It's got crowd participation, it has the build-up, it has the longevity, it has the emotional chords, and it has the message."

In his days off the road, Kanye kept himself very busy. His business interests were expanding: he was planning to launch a chain of restaurants in Chicago called Fatburger and in May, West Brands LLC collaborated with a consultancy firm headed up by Neil Abrams to launch a new concept entitled Kanye Travel Ventures, a scheme which constructed high-end travel packages for his more salubrious fans. "While celebrity brand-driven travel programmes have been attempted in the past, none have demonstrated long-term viability," a press release for the project read, while stating this would be the first of its kind to take off. Kanye's business nous would also see him re-sign a commercial deal with Pepsi while simultaneously striking a multi-platform branding agreement with its biggest rival Coca-Cola. Then, on the charitable side of his dealings, in July he and MTV's Sway Calloway visited the homes of three veterans of the Iraq war who'd returned home to lives of debt and post-traumatic stress issues, his foundation and MTV providing them with money to help them keep hold of their homes and send their kids to college. "I know my music inspires people, but you can always do more," he told them. "You make me want to improve myself; we thought I'd come in and be an inspiration to you and lift your spirits, but actually you're inspirational to me because I'm going through a lot of losses."

He was also actively pursuing his fashion ambitions. Between shows in Europe, Kanye would be spotted in the front rows of Milan and Paris catwalk shows, or would dash off to parties where he'd meet with designers such as Raf Simons – chief designer for minimalist German fashion house Jil Sander – to keep his own oft-delayed dreams of a clothing line alive. "Every day is a struggle," he'd say of getting Pastelle off the ground. "I'm in the same position I was in with music before I got it together and finally managed to figure out what my style was. I used to have tracks that sounded like Timbaland and the next track would sound like DJ Premier… So, when I'm doing designs, I have one thing that looks like Ralph shit and the next thing is in BAPE area. It's really about figuring out how to embody all of these things I like but have my own voice. I have that opportunity to put my name on something and people will buy it, but I want to create something that has its own voice and other designers can look to and be inspired. I wasn't put on this earth to make money – I was put on this earth to make magic."

By July, Kanye was writing an irregular fashion column for *Complex* magazine and had signed up with Louis Vuitton to create what he'd call "salience" – a widespread awareness of the Kanye West brand. Rather than be a star turning up at a fashion house happy to put their name to whatever design is presented to them, however, Kanye set out to design his clothes properly, working his way up from the bottom. He took roles as an intern with Louis Vuitton's Marc Jacobs and with Raf Simons, learning the intricacies of designing every collar, studying how fabrics hang and spending days working on freehand sketches, eager to learn the trade. He read every design book he could, texted Simons daily and looked to move to Paris to master the craft, tired of being taken for a ride by designer labels every time he went for a meeting to discuss creating his own range of clothes.

"The big payback [is] I work with different designers and they'll see me coming, saying 'I wanna do this line,' and they're like, 'Cool, give me $150,000 for two weeks' work'!" he said. "It's like, 'This dude is so eager to get in – he's a millionaire who doesn't know his ass from his face, and we're gonna charge him up the fucking ass for a sketch, for an idea, for a sample.' Every time I did a sample line, it was over a quarter-million… [now] It's like pressing reset on my life. I moved from Chicago to New York and all I had was a bunch of ideas and a few DATs in my pocket and a relationship with an A&R guy at Roc-A-Fella. Now I'm moving to Paris and I have a relationship with Louis Vuitton, and it's like, 'Look how far I took that relationship to the biggest record label, and look where I took it in music…' Marc Jacobs is my fashion idol because of the way he merges all worlds, the way he's big in the hood and the head of the number one fashion house in the world. For me, Jay-Z's my big brother, but what he was to me in rap is what Marc Jacobs is to me in fashion – the feeling I get when I look at him is exactly what I got when I'd look at Jay-Z in the studio."

At home, his designer's eye remained keen. With a minimalist's sparsity, he installed solar blinds on the windows of his Manhattan apartment and decorated the place with a large white dining table, two brown leather couches, a 4ft limestone coffee table, a widescreen Bang & Olufsen TV and fascinating ornaments such as Solaris, a fibreglass bust of a female spaceship pilot by Colin Christian. With everything in the apartment controlled from one remote, it was the result of Kanye employing an apartment manager.

"Titles are very important," he'd explain. "I like to embody titles, y'know, or words that have negative connotations, and explain why that's good. Take the word gay – like, in hip-hop, that's a negative thing, right? But in the past two, three years, all the gay people I've encountered have been, like, really, really, extremely dope. Y'know, I haven't, like, gone to a gay bar, nor do I ever plan to. But where I would talk to a gay person – the conversation would be mostly around, like, art or design – it'd be really dope. From a design standpoint, kids'll say, 'Dude, those pants are gay.' But if it's, like, good, good, good fashion-level, design-level stuff, where it's on a higher level than the average commercial design stuff, it's, like, gay people that do that. I think that should be said as a compliment. Like, 'Dude, that's so good it's almost... gay.' 'Dude, you pay real attention to detail – that's almost, like, gay!' 'You had a whole conversation with that girl without bringing up sex? That was, like, gay!'"

And just as he was being inspired in fashion and design, the Glow In The Dark tour was becoming a huge inspiration for him musically. "I just had a bunch of ideas due to the tour," he said. "I mean, we went and did the tour and had to very quickly put together all the music from over three albums and make it sound like they went together. We remixed tracks like 'Touch The Sky' and 'Through The Wire' and made them sound as though they're part of one story. And in the process of doing that it inspired me to start making new music and try new instruments. Lots of monk choirs, timpani and 808 sounds… I made music with what I thought was the coolest instruments possible. And the coolest melodies possible. And the coolest subject matters!... I really like the way [Auto-Tune] sounds. I mean 'Jesus Walks' and 'Never Let Me Down' both had Auto-Tune on it. But even if I had never used it before, so what? I like it now. I'm an artist and at the end of the day sounds are like my paint. Basically no one can tell me what to paint with and that's the medium I chose to make these paintings. I just really want to tell anybody who wants to say anything about me for using Auto-Tune and they don't like it… Fuck 'em!"

The retro house sound of the Roland TR-808 drum machine – a piece of equipment used widely in the early days of hip-hop and beloved of the likes of Phil Collins, Boy George and Gary Numan★ – spoke to him too, of his Chicago roots and a new way of touching people. "I definitely loved house music," he said, "but even back then [growing up in Chicago], I might have liked hip-hop but when you go to a hip-

★ It had been Jon Brion's idea for Kanye to experiment with the instrument.

hop club everyone would just stand around and watch somebody break dancing or flexing in the middle. You might get a chance to break dance and kick a girl in the head! But go to a house club and you could actually dance up on a girl – so I said, "Man, I'll listen to hip-hop in the car but when I go to a club I want to go to a house club. At a house club I can feel on girls!"

These new inspirations, added to the traumas of losing his mother, watching his engagement crumble and his struggles with the ever-increasing media scrutiny that the celebrity he'd always dreamed of was now forcing upon him, resulted in his biggest ever burst of creative energy. His original plan to make a fourth college-themed album following the development of a young student's life was dropped in favour of a new genre he dubbed "pop art", considering it the musical equivalent of Warhol's sixties art vision. A therapeutic sort of music exploring how lonely it was at the top, and one that needed to be expressed in ways other than rapping.

"Melodies [were] in me," he said, "what was in me I couldn't stop."

★ ★ ★

The dialling code for Avex Studios, Kanye was amazed to discover, was 808. He knew he'd found his new home.

Five minutes away from the snorkelling hotspot of Hanauma Bay, 15 from the paradise of Waikiki, Avex Studios on the Hawaiian island of Honolulu seemed the perfect place for Kanye to work out his problems★. For just three weeks he worked, inviting a stripped down, but still relatively sizable, array of guests, producers and engineers including Plain Pat, Jeff Bhasker, No I.D. and Mr Hudson to help him make his fourth album. The sessions went quickly because Kanye had selected producers and engineers capable of taking his ideas and running with them even if he wasn't there. "There's a lot to be said for picking the right people," he said. "I had a really good engineer on this record, who was able to mix the album without me even being there. And you know

---

★ Aside from Avex, some sessions for *808s & Heartbreak* were conducted at Glenwood Studios in Burbank, California.

what? The album sounds good. There were songs produced over the phone where I was changing drums: 'Let's stop this here, mute that, put that snare there…' There are times when I tell my management, 'You just figure it out. What's your choice on this, what's your opinion? I'll trust you.' It's good to have people whose taste and judgement you trust maybe even more than your own… I like to find people who I can trust to just direct it well so I can use less of my brain sometimes. Because I think I use too much of my brain, and need to let some of it rest."

Between takes the team could surf, exercise, play ball, sunbathe or grab a beachside cocktail. But in the studio, they drenched themselves in darkness.

With the Roland TR-808 as his crutch and Auto-Tune as his shoulder to cry on, Kanye took a bold leap. He'd bare his fractured heart in a way that no rapper had ever done before. And, this time, he would sing.

Pitching the 808 to a distorted electronic sound akin to ancient arcade games backed by shadowy tribal beats – a sound he dubbed 'heartbreak' – he turned to T-Pain to help him master Auto-Tune, technology he'd used before, notably while remixing Lil Wayne's 'Lollipop' and 'Put On' by Young Jeezy. "His whole album is crazy," T-Pain would say, "and it's definitely a different kind of Kanye… He just had me in mind. *808s* is really all Kanye. I'm just here to keep it from [sounding] adult contemporary."

The fact that Auto-Tune was looked down upon by the hip-hop world frustrated Kanye – to him it was "the funnest thing to use" and a channel to help him rediscover the thrill of childhood by being utterly carefree in his music. It reminded him of being told that wearing pink was "gay" as a kid; it just made him want to embrace the technology to spite the narrow-minded naysayers. "Never lose your childhood," he'd tell the listening party.

Kanye's version of Auto-Tune, though, was unlike any his critics had heard before. *808s & Heartbreak* opened with a supernatural choir, a chiming piano, a reedy Pong electro beat and dense drums over which Kanye, as he explained in concert, sang an emotional ode to "an ex-girlfriend you call on Friday nights just to have sex… [she] says she'll come over but you wait all night and she still doesn't come knocking on your door."

This was the ominous and devastated 'Say You Will', a place where hip-hop and R&B merged with the gothic and dank electronic elements of the Cure and New Order, and it bore a far deeper emotional weight than he suggested. When Kanye sang "don't say you will unless you will" he was talking as much about Phifer's marriage promise as a booty call, and as he went on to describe his own emotional brutality in the relationship – "When I grab your neck, I touch your soul" – the song became one of his most lovelorn, honest and revealing to date. It built to a truly heartbroken note: "I wish this song really would come true," he sang, the chill in his automated voice barely suppressing the pain, "I admit I still fantasise about you".

'Welcome To The Heartbreak', produced alongside Jeff Bhasker and Plain Pat, delved deeper into his mental turmoil. "My head keeps spinning, I can't stop having these visions," Kid Cudi sang on the chorus of this portentous, cinematic pop throb reminiscent of a *Twilight* movie theme as Kanye stared his loneliness direct in the face, his fame and riches suddenly meaningless compared to the companionship, love and chance of a family life that he'd lost. When MTV's executive vice president Dave Sirulnick showed him photographs of his children, he recalled, all he could show him in return were pictures of his houses and cars; when his god-sister was getting married he had no-one to take as his guest, and felt so lonely and upset about his split that he had to leave early. "Chased the good life my whole life long," he lamented, "look back on my life and my life gone/Where did I go wrong?"

Less austere and more accusatory, 'Heartless' – the first of three tracks co-produced with No I.D. – was a bouncing concoction of pipe-based beats and sombre piano that veered the closest to rap so far on the record. Mirroring Stevie Wonder's 'Part Time Lover', the chorus tells of the voices Kanye hears in his head when he tries to sleep, constantly reminding him that he'd "lost his soul to a woman so heartless". The track was a one-way conversation between Kanye and his ex, a catalogue of disbeliefs as he tries to make sense of what the woman had done to him. "How could you be so cold as the winter wind?" he asked, "after all the things we've been through, I mean, after all the things we got into." Admitting that he'd done wrong by seeing other girls, he hit out at her for getting him back by parading her new boyfriend in front of him and for her mixed messages – she still calls him on the phone at 3am despite his insistence that they wouldn't speak any more and he's convinced she'll come back to him after finding solace in her friends for a few months. But ultimately the relationship is hopeless: "Baby let's just knock it off," he tells her, frustrated with her friends trying to drive them apart, "I got something new to see, and you just gonna keep hating me/And we just gonna be enemies". Whatever it was that forced the pair apart, the roots ran deep.

The best way Kanye could lift his spirits, of course, was to remind himself of what he'd achieved in his life. Enter 'Amazing', a tribal R&B brooder, with backing vocals from Mr Hudson and Tony Williams, built on clacking wooden drumbeats like spears against bark shields and a rousing piano refrain; a confident and stern backing over which Kanye could tell his ex, "I'm the reason everybody fired up this evening… no matter what, you'll never take that from me". His anguish has made him harder, he explains, turning him into a "monster… a problem that'll never be solved" as his ego balloons to keep him afloat through these rough waters. It was left to Young Jeezy to provide the link to Kanye's rap roots, providing a rapped final verse hinting at a drug dealing past borne of poverty.

The tribalism continued as he sank back into his melancholy despond for 'Love Lockdown', taiko drums lifting a minimalist ballad of subtle electronic beats and chiming piano into a propulsive and portentous chorus. The song was an intricate and conflicted exploration of his feelings towards his former partner; at times he felt he didn't love her enough, that "the vibe is wrong" and he needed to move on, at others he looked back at his decision to leave her with regret, admitting to his lingering feelings for her. The confusion he expressed made the emotion behind it that much more honest, reflecting the back-and-forth turmoil of a real-life break-up, exacerbated by public attention that means they have to "keep a secret code so everybody else don't know". Ultimately Kanye felt the victim of his own emotions, his tendency to keep his love on lockdown, and ended the song begging his partner to decide what they should do: "Gotta keep it going, keep the loving going/Keep it on the roll, only God knows/If I be with you, baby I'm confused/You choose".

"I usually just freestyle," Kanye said of writing the song. "There are tracks that I freestyle all the way from humming them to doing the drumbeat really quickly to going in the booth and singing. So a lot of stuff is freestyle. 'Love Lockdown' was a freestyle. I wrote the original song in one take – I just freestyled it all the way through. And I was like, 'I'm not loving you…' and by the end of it I was going, 'just keep your love locked down, your love locked down, keep your love locked down…' And then I went back and worked through it."

'Paranoid' delved further into the issues behind the split, with Kanye berating his girlfriend for being obsessed with the idea that he was cheating on her, going so far as to go through his phone messages looking for clues. Once again it was Kanye instigating the split, frustrated at the rows and sexless nights such prying leads to, telling his partner that, "A little time out might do you good, might do us good… you worry bout the wrong things" and that her distrustfulness will eventually lead to her never settling down for good. He suggested she hadn't been able to cope with the salacious rumours that fly around a celebrity like Kanye, or the nights she'd spend alone while he was on tour and would bring those bad feelings into the time that they did get to spend together. Musically, the track was relatively upbeat and dance-friendly; a modernist pop R&B banger adorned with sizzling blasts of Bond-theme synth and harmonious backing vocals from Mr Hudson and Kid Cudi on the chorus. A sign that, even in his darkest moments, Kanye's pop sensibility was still sharp.

As was his tongue. Keeping up the theme of distrust, come 'RoboCop' he was accusing his ex of being "a drama queen" who'd be "checking everything like I'm on parole" and turning his life into a horror story akin to Stephen King's *Misery*, in which a fan of a writer kidnaps and tortures him in her home, ostensibly out of admiration. By the chorus he was likening her compulsion to check up on him wherever he went to being in a relationship with the cyborg law-keeper RoboCop from

Paul Verhoeven's 1987 film of the same name and thinks she'll never get over her obsessive tendencies. The track even samples the movie, using RoboCop's catchphrase "drop it creep" at the end of the verses. The brooding futuristic Afrobeat track, bedecked with urgent strings, elegant orchestral sweeps and synthetic explosions sampled 'Kissing In The Rain' by Patrick Doyle, one of few samples used on the album. The female vocals are by singer-songwriter Esthero, who co-wrote three of the album's tracks, and it was originally intended to include a guest appearance by Herbie Hancock. It ended with a bitter coda in which Kanye called Phifer a "spoiled little LA girl" and mocked her habits – "You must be joking, or are you smoking?... Haha, that was a good one/Your first good one in a while". He'd later claim in a VH1 *Storytellers* show that he'd wanted to carry on the outro longer and tell more jokes, seeing himself as rap's Jack Black.

There were few laughs to be had in 'Street Lights', a reflective future soul ballad set to a phasing synth throb, menacing piano chords and atmospheric African drums in which Kanye considers that the street lights flitting by on a cab journey could symbolise the passing loves and moments of affection that fly by in his life on his way to his final destination of settled bliss. The tone and timbre of the track continued into the similarly Afro-orchestral pulse of 'Bad News', but here the tables turned. Kanye described discovering his partner has in fact been cheating on him, and could suddenly relate to the betrayal that his suspicious girlfriend had felt towards him. The gossip about her affair that he had to pretend he already knew, the resentment at being lied to and the realisation that he'd been wasting his life waiting for this person to fulfil "a dream that'll never come true". The bad news hit Kanye hard and deep; the story flipped to make him the cuckolded victim rather than the guy that needed to escape a cloying and untrusting relationship.

After this revelation, *808s & Heartbreak* took a vengeful turn. Having woken up to his fiancée's betrayal, 'See You In My Nightmares' was the most spiteful track yet, its military-style electronic pounding underpinning a chorus featuring an Auto-Tuned Lil Wayne snarling for Kanye: "I might see you in my nightmare/How'd you get there?/'Cause we were once a fairy tale/But this is farewell". On his verses Kanye declared he was leaving his partner for good and moving on with his life; he sounded angry but optimistic, his real anguish repressed for Lil Wayne to bark out on his furious final verse. "Girl we through," Weezy growled, "you think your shit don't stank but you are Mrs Pee-Yew", a reference to OutKast's track 'Roses'. This was *808s…* at its most vitriolic and distraught, a moving howl of hatred and despair.

After the disbelief and resentment, the next stage of Kanye's emotional roller coaster was grief. On a later tour he'd explain that 'Coldest Winter', an inventive amalgam of doomy gothic atmospherics and startling bursts of static sampled from Tears For Fears' 'Memories Fade', was about his mother, the one true love he'd ever known in his life: "Her love is a thousand miles away," he sang, passionately, "goodbye my friend, will I ever love again?" The desolation of losing Phifer had only exacerbated the loss of his mother too; Kanye had lost one false and one true love in the space of months and his desperation became truly harrowing on the album's final track, 'Pinocchio Story'.

A freestyle that Kanye had recorded at a show in Singapore, 'Pinnochio Story' made it onto the album at Beyoncé's insistence, since it was so raw and personal a diatribe. Over a maudlin piano and overwhelmed by the screams of his fans, Kanye looked deep into himself and his relationships with his mother and with Phifer to work out why "I got everything figured out/But for some reason I can never find what real life was about". Spiralling between downbeat melancholy and bawls of pure pain, he worked through his darkest thoughts. That he'd sacrificed real life and relationships in his relentless pursuit of fame. That, cutting through the all-your-heart-desires capitalist marketing fantasy of consumerism, his obsession with high fashion and ability to fly off on vacation at a moment's notice was a superficial sham when it came to helping him get through his current hardships: "There is no Gucci I can buy/There is no Louis Vuitton I can put on… to get my heart out of this hell and my mind out of this jail/There is no clothes that I could buy that could turn back in time". That after achieving all his dreams of fame and celebrity, he wished, like Pinocchio, to just be a normal person again, without all of the intrusion and demands on him. "I turn on the TV and see me and see nothing," he admitted, the polar opposite to the braggadocio of traditional rap, the definition of anti-ego, "What does it feel like to live real life, to be real/Not some façade on TV that no-one can really feel?"

Here was a brutally open portrayal of the unseen side of fame: Kanye sang of being constantly under scrutiny, always required to pose for fans' photos or sign autographs and never allowed to be seen to be unhappy with his charmed lot. A track that ended full of regret – for losing Alexis and his mother, for chasing the dream of rap stardom that led him to this low point, for losing himself in the extravagance of wealth. It was this ultra-honest and self-deprecating slant, along with its revolutionary minimalist sounds, that made *808s & Heartbreak* a real game-changer in hip-hop. Without it there would be no Drake, Frank Ocean or Childish Gambino, no legion of introspective and sensitive new rappers, no seismic shift in the ground rules of rap. And its influence would bleed into other genres too, be it the icy R&B of James Blake or the wintry folk of Bon Iver.

'Stronger' was the first dance-rap song that resonated to that level," Kanye would say of its impact, "and then *808s...* was the first album of that kind, you know? It was the first, like, black new wave album. I didn't realise I was new wave until this project. Thus my connection with [the graphic designer] Peter Saville, with Raf Simons, with high-end fashion, with minor chords. I hadn't heard new wave! But I am a black new wave artist."

Kanye had always strived to shatter the fundamentals of hip-hop and build the genre anew. And he did it by allowing himself to break, and offering up the pieces.

★ ★ ★

Virtually as soon as recording on *808s...* was completed, Kanye hit the road in Mexico, Brazil, Singapore, China and Europe, playing arenas across the UK and winding up the tour in Australia and New Zealand in December. Long before he'd finished promoting *Graduation* with that final leg of the Glow In The Dark Tour, Kanye was sharing *808s...* with the world. In a grey glen plaid suit adorned with a red pulsating broken-heart brooch, he passionately premiered the lead single 'Love Lockdown' at the MTV Video Music Awards on September 7 in front of a troupe of sinister masked drummers pounding out the tribal pulse, his fractured heartbeat.

The broadcast was the world's first exposure to his radical shift in style, and it understandably split the audience. Many were confused by the sudden change, the Auto-Tune singing, the downbeat lyrical theme. 50 Cent began mocking the song and West during his live shows. "I don't think the fans will forgive him for this," 50 Cent told MTV News. "I don't think it's cool… But I love him as an artist and I'd like to work with him in the future. It's a tough time for him. He's realising the pressure of being in competition with the best artist he can be in competition with – that's Kanye West. When [the fans] put you up against your best material, you really realise what it's like."

Kanye's chart momentum was unstoppable though. Despite the confusion, 'Love Lockdown' immediately hit number three on the *Billboard* chart on its September 18 release, selling 213,000 downloads in its first four days on its way to shifting three million copies. It came with a Simon Henwood-directed video, premiered on the Ellen DeGeneres show on October 7, featuring Kanye singing the song in an all-white apartment inspired by Patrick Bateman's place in the 2000 film *American Psycho*, which is invaded by hordes of African tribesmen beating djembe drums and wielding spears and shields.

On September 24 Kanye posted a blog revealing that the album was completed, and that he wanted it released before the originally scheduled December 16 date. "I changed my album to November something, 'cause I finished the album and I felt like it," he wrote, including a photo of himself and Young Jeezy at work in the studio. "I want y'all to hear it as soon as possible."

"I just woke up from a quick studio nap," he wrote later. "I've been workin' on *808s & Heartbreak* about 16 hours a day, and Superman passed out for a little bit. … I'm in Hawaii but I'm still on NY time, so I wake up mad early, do some business, blog, jog for an hour, play ball, eat and then hit the stu by noon. While approving the final cut for the 'Love Lockdown' vid, I marvel at the fact that it was written less than three weeks ago. I'm very excited about everything. … I guarantee this will be 50's favourite album of mine. This will be gangster's album of the year."

On October 14, West held a launch party for the record at Ace Gallery in LA entitled Kanye West Listening Party: Lights, Heartbreak, Nudity. The event was a collaboration with Italian visual artist Vanessa Beecroft whom Kanye admired and had contacted a month earlier, giving Beecroft a week to put together an installation piece to accompany the album's full playback. On the night, 700 guests including Jay-Z, will.i.am, Mos Def, Rick Ross, L.A. Reid, actor Jonah Hill, Sa-Ra's Taz Arnold, and director Chris Robinson were served Moët and Veuve Clicquot champagne before being led up into the art gallery loft, where 40 to 50 models stood naked in front of a blue light panel wearing only black stilettos, some with tangled wigs or woollen masks covering their faces. As the album played they posed, stretched and contorted in silhouette as multi-coloured lights bathed their skin. "I'm sure it's beautiful art, and many people can appreciate it on a much deeper level than I can," said TV host Jimmy Kimmel afterwards. "But I look out there and see a lot of good-looking naked girls and it makes me happy." The girls were reportedly discovered via open casting call and paid $1,000 each.

"When he contacted me a month ago, he caught me off-guard," Beecroft told the assembled onlookers after the performance. "But when I heard the album, I heard things that touched my own life." Kanye returned the compliment. "I've always been a fan of Vanessa's work and strong imagery," he said, praising her work on the "idea of nudity because society told us to wear clothes at a certain point." He also said, with no little bawdry humour, that he had been "touched" by the performance piece.

But his most heartfelt words, as usual, were saved for his music. He explained how he'd insisted to the heads of Def Jam that the album came out in 2008 and that he wanted the album filed under 'pop' on iTunes. "People think pop is bad, but Michael Jackson was pop and who can compare to him? These are pieces of real life that I'm putting out for people to judge," he insisted. "It's from my heart. I don't give a fuck if someone rates it 'hot' or 'not'. I'm here to bring positivity that cannot be judged. It's like judging a grandmother's love, and someone says 'Your grandmother gets two and a half mics.' Or, 'You grandmother didn't sell a million the first week.'" And referencing the fact that 'Coldest Winter' was about his mother's death, he opened up on the sadness that she died trying to conform to a cinematic ideal through cosmetic surgery. "The irony for me," he said, "someone who has talked about so many labels – Louis Vuitton this, Benz that, this girl look good, I'm not going out with you if you don't look good – the irony, for me to lose the most important person to Hollywood. And now it's time to deliver ideas in the most naked form possible."

After the listening, word spread that the entire record would be along the same emotional, Auto-Tuned lines as the single and the backlash grew. Feller rappers called him "sappy" and dismissed the music as a passing experiment – the widespread opinion was that the album would be a dud and, sales-wise, it'd flop like a dead fish off a high board. Some even went as far as to suggest that the record was tantamount to Kanye having a very public meltdown.

"It was just what was in my heart," Kanye said, defending the move. "The type of ideas that it was coming up with, the melodies that were in me – what was in me I couldn't stop. I think it's a path; it's a road that's been paved and given by God. There's so many signs, and I just have to follow the signs and the arrows of where he wants me to go and just be fearless about it. It's so crazy – hip-hop used to be about being fearless, and now it's, like, all about being afraid. It used to be about standing out, now it's all about fitting in... Now hip-hop is like a big high school or something. So that's why I respect people who just do whatever they want to do."

Others came out in support of his bravery. Common, whose *Electric Circus* album critics were beginning to liken Kanye's new direction to, said "I love it. I'mma tell you, as an artist, you wanna be free. I'mma do what I feel. You can't just cater to the audience. You gotta say, 'Hey, y'all, this is where I'm at.' For him to do an album called *808s & Heartbreak*, you know that's where he is at this moment. I heard some songs, and I think it's fresh. I think the people are ready for it."

"Do I love the music that's out right now?" said Lil Wayne. "I love it with a passion. I can sing your single word for word with you. Am I excited by it? Does it motivate me? Not one bit. That's because *808s & Heartbreak* hasn't come out."

"To be honest, even when 50 [sings], we have vulnerability," said P Diddy. "We are cats that always looked up to Mary J Blige or always looked up to Sam Cooke or R Kelly. We always wanted to sing, like singers wanted to rap. When we sing, we singing from the heart. It ain't about the key – you're getting exactly the rawness of how it feels. That's why people are digging it. Thank God for Auto-Tune and thank God for T-Pain."

"I think he's a great MC," added Pusha T. "When people tried to deny him in the past, he came with back-to-back-to-back great albums and songs to make you say, 'Damn, he's nice.' All the features and all of that, it just solidifies him. For him to come with *808s & Heartbreak,* I feel he's so proven in one lane. … He's a creative guy. He does what he wants. He's proven himself to me – not that he has to prove himself to me, but he does what he wants to. This *808s* album is hot. 'Heartless' is my shit."

And 'Heartless' was up next for release as a single, a second rapid-fire volley from *808s*… delivered upfront of the album, put out only weeks after the success of 'Love Lockdown'. After Kanye had first performed it in Denver and confirmed it would be his next single during a guest spot at a T.I. show at LA's Key Club, a snippet of the track leaked online on October 12 so Kanye posted an unmastered version on his official blog three days later and rushed the song onto iTunes for November 4. Hype Williams was once more called in for the video, an animated rendition of Kanye wandering heartbroken around the art deco neon and sleaze of Miami in tribute to Ralph Bakshi's film *American Pop.*★ Despite the leaks of 'Paranoid', 'Amazing', 'See You In My Nightmares', 'Say You Will', 'Street Lights', 'Welcome To The Heartbreak' and 'Bad News' online prior to the album's release too, 'Heartless' was another huge hit, entering the *Billboard* chart at number four and peaking at

---

★ The video used rotoscoped technology whereby Kanye and other actors were filmed and then the footage was drawn over. Several scenes take place in Kanye's own apartment, with the pictures of the Jetsons on the wall.

number two. Performing the song at the AMA Awards, where he won the award for Best Hip-Hop Album for *Graduation*, on November 23 Kanye attempted to recreate the video's concoction of bright and bleak, desperately bawling "How could you be so heartless?" on a stage set full of imposing neon signs, in a jacket emblazoned across the back with the word PASTELLE.

Out on the seemingly endless Glow In The Dark tour, tracks from *808s…* began to creep into the set lists. Initially 'Love Lockdown' appeared as the final encore during shows in the Far East, UK and Europe, and by the time it wound up in Australasia the set was opening with 'Welcome To The Heartbreak' and 'Paranoid' and closing with a raft of *808s…* songs as an encore. So by the time the album hit stores on November 24, not only had the shock of Kanye's drastic shift worn off but many of the songs were familiar to fans. Hence it debuted at number one in the *Billboard* chart (number 11 in the UK), selling 450,000 copies in its first week – half of *Graduation*'s first week sales but still impressive in an age when record sales were plummeting across the board due to online piracy and streaming – on course for platinum sales of 1.7 million in the US alone.

The reviews, though more mixed than on previous records, were generally favourable too. "This so should not work," wrote *The Sunday Times*' Dan Cairns, "yet *808s & Heartbreak* is a triumph, recklessly departing from the commercially copper-bottomed script and venturing far beyond West's comfort zone." "A dark mood settles over his usually sunny outlook as West weighs what he has lost in recent months (his mother's unexpected death, a broken engagement) against the dubious value of what he has gained (fame and fortune)," said *USA Today*'s Steve Jones. "He knows that no amount of conspicuous consumption is going to ease his inner turmoil. West deftly uses the 808 drum machine and Auto-Tune vocal effect to channel his feelings of hurt, anger and doubt through his well-crafted lyrics. And while some hip-hop fans may decry his decision to sing rather than rap (Lil Wayne and Young Jeezy provide what little rapping there is), he wisely brushes aside such creative limitations." "What makes *808s & Heartbreak* worthy of adulation and applause," gushed *Vibe*, "is that it's made by an artist who carries with him no other agenda but to make him and those who listen to him feel *something*."

"It's… his superstar-freakout album: his *Low*, his *Trans*, his *Kid A*," argued *Village Voice*'s Tom Breihan. "The one where he decides that frozen remoteness is the only thing that makes sense. The affably doofy Everydude rapper from *The College Dropout* has all but disappeared… *808s & Heartbreak* can be queasy and even morally indefensible sometimes. But that puerile sentiment also gives it its force. Intentionally or not, Kanye has tapped into a mood here that transcends whatever his personal troubles might be. With winter looming and economic futures looking scarier every day, the icy throb and barely contained rage capture the ambient dread bleeding into everyday life from all sides."

Some critics attacked Kanye's singing, *The New York Times*' Jon Caramanica writing "[it's] weakness for which this album will ultimately be remembered, some solid songs notwithstanding… At best, it is a rough sketch for a great album, with ideas he would have typically rendered with complexity, here distilled to a few words, a few synthesizer notes, a lean drumbeat. At worst, it's clumsy and underfed, a reminder that all of that ornamentation served a purpose."

Some called the record a "perverse detour", others "an information-age masterpiece", and over time the latter opinion prevailed. As it slunk into the end-of-year polls it also embedded itself into hip-hop's subconscious, deeply affecting the way rappers approached their music to this day. Sensitivity and vulnerability became en vogue; rap softened, refined itself, became more human.

Even through a tough year that had turned his life upside down and made him question everything, Kanye's self-belief remained steadfast. When his singing was called into question he admitted that some people had told him *808s…* sounded like a demo or a mix-tape and suggested he rapped more or even release the record under a pseudonym to distance himself from it, but he was unrepentant. "Don't matter. This game's pass or fail. There's no Bs, Cs, Ds. Either you bricked or you won, and this product's gonna be an A. Fans out there don't like it, 'cause of their own snobbery or instant rejection of Auto-Tune? But you can't reject the melody, you can't reject the story, you can't reject the subject.

That ['Heartbreaker'] hook is fucking Broadway, that hook is like . . . nineteen forties… Oh my God, I'm one of the greatest rappers in the world. I'll get on a track and completely ee-nihilate that track, I'll eat it and rip it in half. I wouldn't have to think of it."

"I think the fact that I can't sing that well is what makes *808s* so special," he'd say. "I love the fact that I'm bad at [things], you know what I'm saying? I'm forever the 35-year-old five-year-old. I'm forever the five-year-old of something."

Keeping his press profile relatively low compared to previous album campaigns, select interviews began appearing which featured Kanye often in a bullish mood, unwilling to probe too deeply into the pain that had inspired the album. "I'm not feeling that overly emotional Oprah stuff," he told *Details* magazine when it met him in his apartment for an article entitled *The Unravelling Of Kanye West.* "Dude, my life's actually better than it's ever been… Put this in the magazine: there's nothing more to be said about music. I'm the fucking end-all, be-all of music. I know what I'm doing. I did *808s* in three weeks. I got it. It's on cruise control… Man, we talked about music for God knows how long! Now let's talk about how my fucking sweater didn't come back right from Korea. That's what's interesting me."

On his statement that he was the voice of the generation, he was similarly adamant. "If not me, then who?" he asked. "Someone could be a better rapper, dance better. But culturally impacting? When you look back at these four and a half years, who's the icon at the end of the day? Who broke down colour barriers? What other black guy would a white person use as a fashion reference?"

He seemed happier discussing topics away from his album. He joked about a flight from LA he'd taken with Mos Def where the pair had freestyled the whole trip in first class. He recalled some of the lines – "Yo, I was fuckin' the game/You can call it statutory/But by the time I'm old/ You're building statues for me" – and admitted "I'm still catching up on sleep from that flight." He discussed his optimism at the recent election of Barack Obama as President. "When you heard he had won, all questions were answered at that point," he said. "It's a new face – open-minded, new thinking. The very concept that you can go from us being brought over as slaves to us becoming president… It restores all types of hope in the concept of democracy. It's a new face for America… When I saw that image of Barack on CNN, stood with his whole family on stage, I felt like I was in some futuristic movie. I was like, 'Damn, first we have iPods and now we have Barack – we really are in the future!'"

He praised the originality and style of OutKast, denied that he'd been lip-syncing on a snow-themed December edition of *Saturday Night Live* as many viewers had suspected and even opened up about his frustrations about G.O.O.D. Records – how he was too busy promoting his own albums to properly push his artists to radio, that he hadn't wanted the label when Sony first offered it to him and didn't have enough time to give over to calls about videos, recordings and wardrobe decisions. As a result his artists were beginning to feel adrift, out on their own, not getting the attention or hard push they should. The future of the label hung in the balance; Kanye was beginning to feel it was one of his biggest career mistakes.

Most revealing, however, were his thoughts on how his relationship split hadn't changed his desire to settle down. "What I feel like – 'cause I wanna be married, of course – I feel like the type of girl I would be with is a fellow superhero," he said. "So we get that 'already flying and now we're just flying together' thing."

There were dropped hints that he'd been enjoying the company of women after the shows on the Glow In The Dark tour, a smokescreen perhaps for the fact that by February 2009 he was dating Amber Rose, a one-time teenage stripper turned actress and model whom Kanye had first spotted in Ludacris' video for 'What Them Girls Like'. Rose was set to star as the poster girl for West's new line of sneakers for Louis Vuitton, due to be premiered at New York Fashion Week. Priced at $800-$1,140, the brightly coloured, high-top shoes were the first product in Kanye's long-awaited Pastelle range★ and to promote it Kanye even announced he was following Diddy's lead and changing his

★ The same year, Kanye would launch his footwear collaboration with Nike on the Air Yeezy.

name to Martin Louis The King Jr, an unexplained amalgam of Louis Vuitton and Martin Luther King Jr. The new name never caught on – far more successful in terms of publicity was Kanye and Amber's first public appearance together at New York Fashion Week, blowing the relationship wide open and instantly turning the pair into one of the glitziest and most photographed couples in the world.

"I'll pick out something and he'll be like 'Babe, just ... no.,'" Rose told *Elle* of the pair's sartorial connection. "I'm more electric pink and bright yellow. And Kanye's more like nude and bone." Kanye's aesthetic was becoming more futuristic with every appearance. In February he recorded a short set for VH1 *Storytellers* that saw him sing a handful of *808s...* songs and previous hits on a Devlin-designed set featuring a vast square hanging overhead like a canted mirror of the stage, visuals forming a thin strip between the two like a horizon or a spaceship's outer rim. The set helped enhance the sparseness of the songs.

The couple's fashion choices came under fire. Rose would show up to fashion events in shredded dresses or hooded dresses, and they raised many eyebrows when they began proclaiming their love of fur, long seen as a sign of callousness and cruelty in fashion circles. Nonetheless, Kanye turned up to Stella McCartney's Paris Fashion Week show, also attended by the president of PETA and noted vegetarian Sir Paul McCartney, and loudly argued that the clothes needed more fur on them. "Kanye West is the person pissing me off right now," pop star Pink told FHM Australia. "He just wouldn't shut up about how he loved fur. I mean, he's saying this to me, the PETA guy and Paul McCartney! I was just so grossed out by him. I'm like 'You're an idiot!'."

"There are so many people who I think are a waste of skin and he's up there," she continued. "I should wear him. Go on, donate yourself Kanye. People can wear your fur."

He'd arrive at other catwalk shows with Amber Rose both clad in full fur coats, and would also be spotted heading to NYC meetings in similar attire, to the disdain of PETA chiefs. "Kanye can't help making himself look like an idiot, whether at an awards show or a fashion show," said Vice President Dan Matthews. "He and his girlfriend look like pathetic creatures from a shabby roadside zoo."

If his tabloid presence was cantering out of his control thanks to his relationship and attacks on photographers, his online presence wasn't helping him stay under the radar. Interviewers during 2009 would note that Kanye was constantly posting to the internet, and in January, shortly after his MySpace and Gmail accounts were hacked into, he posted a wild caps-locked rant on his Kanye UniverseCity blog in a garish blue font. YOOOO WHY WON'T YOU LET ME BE GREAT!!!" it was titled, and continued, "I HAD THE TWO GREATEST DAYS OF MY LIFE AND WHEN I GET BACK FROM THE LOUIS SHOW I READ SOME SHIT CLAIMING I SAID I'M DOWN TO DO PORN AND SOME BISEXUAL PORN!!!! I CAN'T BELIEVE THE AVN WOULD POST FIRST PEOPLE BELIEVED THE TWITTER/STEPHEN COLBERT THING★, ROLLING STONE EVEN PRINTED IT!!!! NOW SOMEBODY HAS BEEN HACKING INTO MY MYSPACE AND SOMEBODY'S ACTUALLY HACKED INTO MY PERSONAL GMAIL ACCOUNT AND HAS BEEN EMAILING PEOPLE FROM IT... HEY WORLD I NO LONGER HAVE A GMAIL! I FOUND OUT I HAD TWELVE UNAUTHORIZED SKYPE ACCOUNTS UNDER MY NAME!!! THIS ALL IN THE PAST FOUR DAYS. WELCOME TO KANYE WEST WORLD! .... IT'S NOT OFFICIAL. I JUST GAVE THE PERFORMANCE OF MY LIFETIME FOR OUR NEW PRESIDENT ... THEN I FLEW TO PARIS AND THEY DEBUTED MY NEW SHOES THAT I DESIGNED WITH LOUIS VUITTON WHICH WAS A DREAM COME TRUE. PLEASE I BEG YOU, GIVE ME A BREAK!!!!! PL EEEEEEEEEEEEEASE!!!!!!!!!!!!!!!! LET ME BE GREAT!!! WHO HAVE I HURT SO BAD THAT THEY WANT TO DESTROY ME? WHO HAVE I EVER SPOKE ABOUT SO NEGATIVELY? I JUST WAS SPEAKING WITH OUR NEW PRESIDENT TWO

★ In 2008, in response to Kanye's comment that "I will go down as the voice of this generation, of this decade", comedy news reporter Stephen Colbert declared a sales war against Kanye in the vein of his battle with 50 Cent, pitting his own album *A Colbert Christmas: The Greatest Gift Of All* against Kanye's *808s*....

DAYS AGO... AND NOW THIS.... SIDEBAR... NEVER TAKE A PICTURE FROM MY OBAMA PERFORMANCE AND PUT IT NEXT TO A BS QUOTE LIKE THAT! THAT'S IN POOR TASTE! THAT UNDERMINES WHAT MY CONTRIBUTION TO THAT EVENT WAS AND SLAPS EVERYBODY WHO FELT UPLIFTED BY THAT PERFORMANCE IN THE FACE! A PICTURE SAYS A THOUSAND WORDS... LOOK HOW FRESH MY SUIT IS... NUFF SAID!"

The blog post was only one of Kanye's regular online rants that would become somewhat legendary amongst hip-hop commentators, adding to his reputation as a wild, unpredictable egotist prone to flying off the handle. An attitude bolstered by another online outburst in May when he realised that a fake Twitter account had been set up in his name. "I DON'T HAVE A FUCKING TWITTER," he blogged. "HEY TWITTER, TAKE THE SO CALLED KANYE WEST TWITTER DOWN NOW ... WHY? ... BECAUSE MY CAPS LOCK KEY IS LOUD!!!!!!!!!"

Kanye would also use the internet to connect more positively with his fans – in May 2009, for instance, he posted a photo of himself, actor and musician Jared Leto and the Killers' singer Brandon Flowers together, revealing that they were working on a track called 'Hurricane' together in Hawaii. And in June he put up a short film he'd made with Spike Jonze called *We Were Once A Fairytale*, in which he played himself, drunk in a nightclub, pathetically seeking out attention and sex until eventually ending up in the bathroom, where he vomits flower petals and cuts a tiny creature called Henry from his stomach with a Bowie knife and watches as the creature, in turn, kills itself with a miniature knife.

He'd use his website to connect with other artists too – having made a comment online about how Lloyd Banks was vastly underrated, Kanye was invited to guest on Banks' upcoming single 'Start It Up'. But it was his regular rants that would see Kanye parodied once more on national TV. Picking up on the idea that he believed the entire world revolved around him, the writers of *South Park* aired an episode on April 8 wherein its stand-up comedian character, Jimmy, writes a joke which the show's villain, Cartman, steals and passes off as his own: "Do you like fish sticks?", "Yes", "You like having fish sticks in your mouth?", "Yes", "What are you, a gay fish?". In the episode, the joke spreads nationwide, but when Kanye hears it he assumes it's a direct attack on himself and sets about hunting down the joke's originator before finally coming to terms with his inner gay fish. He goes to live in the sea, swimming and kissing the fish along to an Auto-Tuned parody of 'Heartless'.

Which can't have helped Kanye's mental state. Such online capital-letter bawl-outs were the result of seeing the public image he'd worked so hard to create exactly as he wanted it being stolen from his control, mimicked or mocked. The pressure was building from the media and the paparazzi, and he'd begun to crack – on March 18, 2009, he and his tour manager and bodyguard Don C appeared in court in LA charged with counts of misdemeanour vandalism, grand theft and battery following an incident at Los Angeles International Airport on September 11, 2008 when the two had broken the cameras of paparazzi following an altercation. Kanye had been heading to board a plane to Hawaii in the American Airlines terminal when he confronted a photographer taking his picture and threw the $10,000 camera to the ground. Spotting a TMZ film crew recording the incident, Don C demanded they hand over their camera too, and smashed it when they refused. Onlookers claimed that West rushed the TMZ videographer shouting "Give me that fucking tape!" and had to be restrained by police. West had also been arrested two months later in Gateshead in Newcastle, England, after getting into another scuffle with a photographer outside the Tup Tup Palace nightclub, but no charges were brought. For his irresponsible actions at LAX he could have been facing up to two and a half years in prison, but having paid for the camera to be replaced, injured no-one and voluntarily undergone 12 hours of anger management therapy, he and Don C were given 50 hours community service and the charges were dropped.

There was added pressure from his inner need to always be working on numerous projects at once – as well as playing some of the biggest shows of his life that summer, at festivals including Denmark's huge Roskilde and London's Wireless, Kanye was deeply involved in Jay-Z's latest smash album *The Blueprint 3* (in 2009, Kanye also produced or guested on tracks by Kid Cudi, Mr Hudson, Twista, Teriyaki Boyz and Malik Yusef), producing eight of the tracks and guesting on two, 'Hate' and 'Run This Town', the video for which reached number two on *Billboard* and was an ironic mocking of online rumours that Jay-Z was a member of the Illuminati, featuring Jay, Kanye and Rihanna conducting a secret masked torch-lit ceremony.

And ironically, the pressure bubble would pop during a moment of defending a friend against what he saw as the slight of the world.

A moment that would gain Kanye more notoriety than he'd ever thought possible.

★ ★ ★

Four little words. Four words that turned Kanye West from innovator to antihero, from champion to cheat. Four words that overturned the public sympathy ladled out upon *808s...*, upended his persona and very nearly buried his career. Four words that became his unwanted catchphrase, a schtick to beat him with for years to come.

Four words. "I'mma let you finish…"

It hard to tell who was the most shocked – the crowd, Beyoncé or Taylor Swift. Collecting the Best Female Video – the first MTV Video Music Award ever presented to a country artist in the ceremony's history – on September 13, 2009, the 19-year-old Swift seemed startled when her acceptance speech, the biggest moment of her young life, was interrupted by Kanye leaping onto the stage at the glitzed-up Radio City Music Hall in New York before a televised audience of millions and taking the microphone from her.

"Yo Taylor," he said, "I'm really happy for you, I'mma let you finish, but Beyoncé had one of the best videos of all time!" He pointed into the crowd where Beyoncé was filmed gasping. "One of the best videos of all time!" Kanye repeated and stood shrugging in the tirade of boos from the audience before handing the microphone back to a speechless Swift. She didn't finish.

"I think my overall thought process," Swift told ABC's *The View* show, "went something like 'Wow, I can't believe I won, this is awesome!

Don't trip and fall. I'm gonna get to thank the fans, this is cool. Oh, Kanye West is here! Cool haircut!... What are you doin there?' And then 'ouch', and then 'I guess I'm not gonna get to thank the fans'."

The backlash was instantaneous. The audience applauded Swift after he left the stage and Pink gave him a disgusted shake of the head as she passed him during an advert break and had to be escorted away by security. Rapper Wale later tried to back Kanye up – "You can't blame a man for speaking his mind" he said to further booing, then shrugged "Kanye, I tried". Swift herself was magnanimous in the event's press room, insisting she had "no hard feelings" for West, but it was Beyoncé herself who came out as the real hero of the night. Receiving her own award she declared, "I remember being 17 years old up for my first MTV Award with Destiny's Child and it was one of the most exciting moments in my life. So I'd like for Taylor to come out and have her moment." To a rapturous standing ovation, Swift returned to the stage with a noble "maybe we can try this again?" before thanking the director, actors and family members that had made her video possible. The controversy arguably turned Swift into an overnight crossover superstar.

And Kanye into a real-life monster. Twitter erupted into gushing slews of hatred towards him. Although unsubstantiated, website Gawker claimed to have unearthed a fairly convincing tape recording of Kanye continuing his diatribe against Taylor after the show. "I went back and rewrote my shit for two days," he was heard to rant, "I cancelled appointments to rewrite because I fucking care... Because I did that, Taylor Swift cannot win over Beyoncé! As long as I'm alive, and if I'm alive kill me then! Kill me then!... 'Cause there aint gonna be no more motherfuckin' Elvis with no James Browns. My mother died for this fame shit, I moved to fucking Hollywood chasing this shit. My mother died because of this shit. Fuck MTV. How the fuck Pink get to perform twice and I didn't even get asked to perform 'Heartless'? 'Heartless' is the biggest song of the year, it had the most spins of the first quarter. I don't know that Pink song, but I notice that she's pink."

"Did you look at my eyes?" he asked writer Noah Callahan-Bever in a phone conversation shortly after the event, explaining his frazzled and overworked psyche at the time of the incident. "I mean, really look in my eyes in the 'Run This Town' video? If you do, you can't tell me you're surprised by what happened. It was all there in my eyes."

It was one of those global media shocks that everybody had to have an opinion on. "Fuck you Kanye, it's like you stepped on a kitten," commented Katy Perry. Obama called him a "jackass", to which he responded, "I don't care if somebody the President or not. I care about thoughts, and how you helping people, and what you bring to the world. My music brings joy to people. What I create brings joy to people, and I'm about people." Some commentators even called his actions racist, which he found ironic since his actions were driven by frustrations from years of black artists being under-recognised.

"I just think that that's what he believed," Jay-Z said on the incident. "I thought it was rude, I thought it was inappropriate and I told him as much… [But] I don't think he was wrong… The way they're treating him… He's on the cover of every paper. He didn't kill anybody. No one got harmed. [He's just] a super passionate person."

"I knew his intentions and I knew he was standing up for art," Beyoncé said in an interview after she was presented with the *Billboard* Woman Of The Year award in October. He told me before when they said the nominees, 'You're gonna have this award' and when they didn't call my name he was completely shocked and when he walked on the stage I'm like 'no, no, no' and he spoke and I'm like 'no, no, no, no!' But in the end it ended up being a great night and Taylor Swift did get her moment and I didn't have to make an acceptance speech!"

In the days that followed his stage invasion, Mos Def came to visit his house, encouraging him to move out of America until the whole thing blew over. Instead, Kanye made several media appearances to try to explain himself. On Hot 97 he claimed the backlash was making him feel like "a modern day Emmett Till", the 14-year-old black child he'd mentioned in 'Through The Wire', murdered for supposedly whistling at a white woman. And he made an appearance on the *Jay Leno Show* looking extremely cowed and apologetic. "It's been extremely difficult just dealing with the fact that I hurt someone or took anything away from a talented artist, or from anyone," he confessed. "I only wanted to help people my entire life. I only wanted to give and do something that I felt was right and I immediately knew in this situation that it was wrong. It was someone's emotions that I stepped on and it was rude, period. I'd like to apologise to her in person." When did he know he'd done something wrong, Leno asked. Kanye looked down in shame. "As soon as I gave the mike back to her and she didn't keep going."

When asked what his mother would have thought, Kanye was silent for several sad seconds. "Obviously I deal with hurt and so many celebrities they never take the time off. I've never taken the time off – it's music after music and tour after tour after tour. It's a shame that my hurt caused someone else's hurt. My dream of what award shows are supposed to be caused… I don't try to justify it because I was in the wrong but I need to take some time off after this and analyse how I'm going to make it through the rest of this life, how I'm going to improve. I am a celebrity and that's something I have to deal with and if there's anything I can do to help Taylor in the future or help anyone, I wanna live this thing hard sometimes." At other times he'd not want to live at all – he'd admit some time later to contemplating suicide around this time.

"He has not personally reached out or anything," Swift told *The View*, "but if he wanted to say hi… I'm not gonna say that I wasn't rattled by it but I had to perform five minutes later so I had to get myself back to the place where I could perform… There were a lot of people around me backstage that were saying wonderful, incredible things and having my back and all the other artists that came and showed me love in the hours following it and all the people tweeting about it and all the fans, I just never imagined there were that many people out there looking out for me. It was wonderful to see there were that many people out there defending me so I didn't have to."

Kanye did eventually call to apologise in person to Taylor, but he'd later claim this was a mistake on his part, giving in to a nation's worth of peer pressure, a sign that he'd "faltered… as a human". He also, without explanation, cancelled a co-headline tour with Lady Gaga that had been planned to start late in 2009.

And then, seeing the sense in Mos Def's advice, he disappeared for a year.

First he fled to Japan to escape the paparazzi, holing up in the Tokyo Grand Hyatt Hotel, where the bar scene from *Lost In Translation* was famously filmed, for a month with his friend Virgil Abloh. Amber Rose no doubt joined him there too, as he'd later claim he dealt with the backlash with "God, sex and alcohol… I don't have an addictive personality, so that means that I can lean on what might be someone else's vice just enough to make it through to the next day. You know, just enough religion, a half-cup of alcohol with some ice in it and a nice chaser, and then … a lot of sex. And then I'd make it to the next week."

In November he moved base to Rome and lived there for several months, connecting with the classicism, a million miles away from the storms back home, not making any music at all for the first time since he could remember. He told friends he was through with music, even while playing them demos of tracks he'd made with Jay-Z and Jack White and talking about mingling 808 lines with Mobb Deep drums. Instead he was going to lose himself in fashion, in red and gold extravagances of leather and curlicue. While in Rome he interned at Fendi, learning more about the trade and suggesting his own designs such as a leather jogging pant though in the end Fendi rejected this idea. The break was essential to Kanye reassessing his life, getting his head around the idea of being globally derided. To consider his place in a world of art, culture and celebrity that he'd previously thought he'd always have the last word on.

"What was good about going away was it was the first time that I got to stop since my mom had passed," he told Ellen DeGeneres on his return. "I never stopped and I never tried to even soak in everything that had happened, It was the first time I'd stopped since I made it, since I started. It was time to take a break and develop more as a person, as a creative, focus more on my thoughts and my ideas and what I wanted to bring to the world. For your whole world to completely crash off of a moment of sincerity or alcohol or whatever it is… I feel like in some ways like I'm a soldier of culture and I realised that no-one wants that to be my job and I'll never go onstage again. I'll never sit in an award show again. But will I feel convicted about things that really meant stuff to culture that constantly get denied for years and years and years? I'm sorry, I will, I can't lie about it in order to sell records."

But he'd also admit in later interviews to the dark thoughts that had plagued his time away. "I know how it feels when the night demons come," he said. "Sometimes when it hurts so bad we have to just lie in the bed. Just lie in bed and don't move... Sometimes I turn the music up and drink and cry."

Over the years to come he'd have an attitudinal volte face on the subject. "It's only led me to complete awesomeness at all times," he'd say. "It's only led me to awesome truth and awesomeness. Beauty, truth, awesomeness. That's all it is... I don't have one regret... If anyone's reading this waiting for some type of full-on, flat apology for anything, they should just stop reading right now."

Back at the start of 2010 though, Kanye was still a repentant recluse. When he eventually returned to the US he didn't stay long in his often besieged homes, but fled to the furthest reaches of the empire to concoct his next grand opus.

The 808 was calling him once more.

The Louis Vuitton Don. MICK HUTSON/REDFERNS

The power trio: Jay-Z, Beyonce and Kanye at the 50th Annual GRAMMY Awards at the Staples Center in Los Angeles, February 10, 2008. LESTER COHEN/WIREIMAGE

Researching his craft at the Louis Vuitton fashion show for men in 2009. BERTRAND RINDOFF PETROFF/FRENCH SELECT/GETTY IMAGES

Kanye with Paul McCartney at the 2009 Grammys; when they collaborated together in 2015, many unwitting fans congratulated the 'unknown rising hopeful' McCartney on his good fortune in being 'discovered' by Kanye and thrust into fame and success.
KEVIN MAZUR/WIREIMAGE

Kanye and Amber Rose attend Alexandre Herchcovitch Fall 2009 during Mercedes-Benz Fashion Week at The Salon in Bryant Park in New York City, February 18, 2009. PAUL WARNER/WIREIMAGE

"Then I thought 'oh, Kanye West is here...'". KEVIN MAZUR/WIREIMAGE/GETTY IMAGES

Performing his apologetic 'Runaway' during the 2010 MTV Video Music Awards at NOKIA Theatre L.A. LIVE in Los Angeles, September 12, 2010. KEVIN WINTER/GETTY IMAGES

Chain Of The Gods: Kanye at Yankee Stadium, New York, September 15, 2010. KEVIN MAZUR/WIREIMAGE

Jay-Z and Kanye perform during the 2011 Victoria's Secret Fashion Show at the Lexington Avenue Armory in New York City, November 9, 2011. KEVIN KANE/FILMMAGIC

Kanye with his dad, Ray West, attend the Los Angeles Lakers vs Chicago Bulls game in Los Angeles, California, December 25, 2011. NOEL VASQUEZ/GETTY IMAGES

Kim Kardashian and Kanye West attend the Kanye West Ready-To-Wear Fall/Winter 2012 show as part of Paris Fashion Week at Halle Freyssinet in Paris, France, March 6, 2012. ERIC RYAN/GETTY IMAGES

Kimye – in a dress branded a 'disaster' by fashion critics – at the Costume Institute Gala for the "PUNK: Chaos to Couture" exhibition at the Metropolitan Museum of Art, New York, May 6, 2013. DIMITRIOS KAMBOURIS/GETTY IMAGES

Over the moon; Kanye atop the Yeezus tour mountain, Boardwalk Hall Atlantic city, New Jersey, February 2014. MARK O'DONNELL

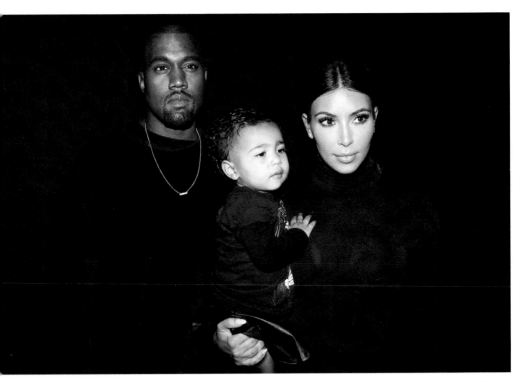

Kanye, Kim and their daughter North West attend the Balenciaga show as part of the Paris Fashion Week Womenswear Spring/Summer 2015 in Paris on September 24, 2014. BERTRAND RINDOFF PETROFF/FRENCH SELECT/GETTY IMAGES

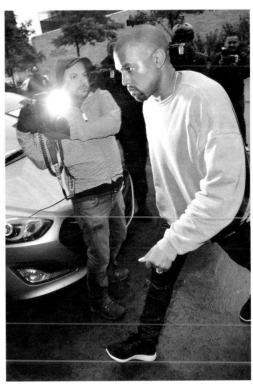

Kanye initiates his Spidey-sense to negotiate the stage at the Life Is Beautiful Festival in Las Vegas, Nevada, October 24, 2014.
JEFF KRAVITZ/FILMMAGIC

Extending his usual warmth to the paparazzi in Soho, New York, November 6, 2014. AALO CEBALLOS/GC IMAGES

Kanye accepts the Visionary Award, BET Honors, Washington D.C, January 24, 2015. OLIVIER DOULIERY/REX FEATURES

CHAPTER ELEVEN

My Beautiful Dark Twisted Fantasy

Kanye West's Hawaiian Rap Camp was a sun-blasted busman's holiday. Kid Cudi and Pusha T scribbled frantic rhymes in one studio; RZA prowled another in dragon tattoo T-shirts and pants, tapping Bobby Digital drum machines and being coaxed into recording hooks: "Champagne wishes and 30 white bitches/You know the shit is fuckin' ridic'lous". On one wall are posted Kanye's Commandments: 'No Tweeting', 'No Pictures', 'No Hipster Hats', 'Just Shut The Fuck Up Sometimes'.

For *808s…*, Kanye hired Avex Studios in Oahu for just three weeks. For its follow-up – initially titled *Good Ass Job* – he booked the whole place, all three studio rooms, indefinitely. Rap Camp would start every morning with breakfast held in Kanye's Diamondhead house for the crew: Cudi, Q-Tip, Pusha, No I.D., Consquence, RZA and anyone who was visiting. While his associates tucked into specially prepared flambéed banana and French toast from the team of on-site chefs, Kanye was often absent first thing. He rarely slept at the house, preferring to take 90-minute naps in the studio, in a chair or on a couch, during his all-night working sessions. In the studio, the desks were manned by engineers 24 hours a day so that Kanye could wander from one to another throughout the day or night; if he hit a creative wall on a track in one studio, he'd move on to the next to keep working.

Over breakfast the crew would discuss music – the newest Drake track, production techniques, the progress on the album and what it had to achieve before it could be considered finished. When Kanye would join them, racing over in his Porsche Panamera, he'd use the time to get communal opinions on parts of the record – asking each person what 'power' meant to them for a track of that name, or trying his latest rhymes out on them and welcoming their comments with a polite put-down of "That's really not at all a word I would ever say, but don't stop offering ideas, thanks!" or "Great – if my name was LL and I was making 'Mama Said Knock You Out Pt. II'." "It's always the same thing when we work together," said Cudi. "It happened on *808s*, too: 'Cudi, what are you thinking?' And I'll spit out something I think is good and hope he doesn't shoot it down… The process this time was a bit smoother; there was definitely an operation… We all have good ideas, and that's why the records usually come out the way they come out – everybody adds their flavour, and it ends up being a masterpiece."

After breakfast RZA would retire to the weight room, Cudi would get some sleep to escape any sporting activities and Kanye and the rest of his entourage would head out to play aggressive basketball with teams of locals at the Honolulu YMCA. Then work would start in earnest at 3pm, Cudi and other cohorts creating their ideas separately and presenting them to Kanye, while Kanye flitted around the building in a torrent of ideas or stuck to his laptop regularly updating his blog, surfing 15 fashion and art sites at a time for inspiration while shouting suggestions at engineers without looking up from the screen.

During a visit to the studio in March 2010, *Complex* magazine's Noah Callahan-Bever watched Kanye work for hours on the first verse of 'Power', which had existed as a free-form, wordless jumble for a month, and then head upstairs to see how Q-Tip was getting on with an a capella vocal he's laid down for 'My Momma's Boyfriend', before he eventually nodded off.

"Kanye West is the hardest working man in music," said Pusha T. "If it wasn't for deadlines, I don't know if anything would be finished. I've heard things that I thought were perfect, and I come back and they're more perfect – and they're still not done. The guy's the maestro. It's a totally unorthodox way – well, it's unorthodox to me, 'cause I've never seen anyone work in pieces like that. It was really on some Quincy Jones shit, man. We could easily be working on one song, thinking we're in a mode, and he'll hear a sound from someone like [producer] Jeff Bhasker and immediately turn his whole attention to that sound and go through his mental Rolodex to where that sound belongs on his album, and then it goes straight to that song, immediately. Now, mind you, his album is a collage of sounds. It has one consistent theme, but you really have to be some type of weirdo to be able to do that. It's like turning on the drop of a dime, in a car. A Maybach on a two-lane highway making a fucking U-turn. He's the most meticulous individual ever. I've never penned so many verses for one particular record."

His team saw his way of working as akin to the way that artists from Michelangelo to Andy Warhol or Damien Hirst would conceptualise and oversee artworks without necessarily touching the canvas themselves. "I'd never worked the way Kanye was working in Hawaii," Q-Tip said. "With Kanye, when he has his beats or his rhymes, he offers them to the committee and we're all invited to dissect, strip, or add on to what he's already started. By the end of the sessions, you see how he integrates and transforms everyone's contributions, so the whole is greater than the sum of its parts. He's a real wizard at it. What he does is alchemy, really… Everybody's opinions mattered and counted. You would walk in, and there's Consequence and Pusha T and everybody is sitting in there and he's playing music and everyone is weighing in. It was like music by committee. It was fresh that everybody cared like that. … If the delivery guy comes in the studio and Kanye likes him and they strike up a conversation, he'll go, 'Check this out, tell me what you think.' Which speaks volumes about who he is and how he sees and views people. Every person has a voice and an idea, so he's sincerely looking to hear what you have to say – good, bad, or whatever."

"We created those textures collectively," Kanye would explain, "I would be eating breakfast with Ross in the morning, and just come up with a line and stuff and we all go play ball and Nas would come out there and play ball with me and Common come up with another line... these are really great people that came together to make that... it's that communal process a lot of times."

For month after month, recording went on. No expense was spared – if Kanye wanted to work with someone on a whim, he'd fly them out. "The studio kind of reminded me of back in the days when I used to work on three or four projects at once, doing it all in the studio," said Pete Rock, who got the call to hit Honolulu via one of Kanye's bodyguards. "That's what he was doing – running back and forth from room to room to room to room. He had Kid Cudi upstairs, he was working on his album downstairs, then doing a mix on another record, and it straight reminded me of what I used to do back in the nineties... an important part of being creative is being able to be free in a good environment where you can make music and there's no interruptions or disturbance or anything. When I got there, Kanye was in the chair in the studio getting his hair cut.

When Nicki Minaj heard through Drake that Kanye wanted her on the album, she was on the first plane out, expecting a conscious rapper like Kanye not to like an overtly sexual artist like Minaj. "And I go to the studio and he has nothing but pictures of naked women on his computer that he'd invite me to look at," she said. "They were really artsy pictures, but you know he loves nudity, so it was a complete shock to me, 'cause I thought I had him all figured out, but I didn't. He was watching porn when we were in the studio – no shame in his game."

Minaj was a morning person, so shunned Kanye's invitations to breakfast to hit the studio, often arriving at 10.30am just as Kanye was leaving for the night. As a 6am riser, when she would try to stay for the late-night sessions she'd find herself falling asleep. "One time he caught me nodding off, and I thought maybe he would kick me out. I've never been so embarrassed in my life. You know how you're sitting up and you don't realise that you've just fallen asleep, but it feels like an eternity? When I picked up my head from sleeping, he was looking at me in the strangest way I've ever been looked at by a human being. He pulled his shades down and he looked and said, 'Oh, she's sleeping?' I wanted to crawl under a rock and die."

Still, Minaj felt Kanye brought out the best in her. "I remember a conversation I had with Kanye every time I sit down to write now. Every single time I sit down, I remember him asking, 'What is it that you wanna say? It's not about rhyming words, it's about what you really wanna say.' The fact that he wasn't even looking at me when he said it – he was on the computer looking at naked girls, I think – it was just a life-changing experience. Outside of Wayne, no one has ever spoken to me that way and caused me to better my craft. I credit him with bringing out something miraculous in me."

He was willing to travel too. When Kanye came across a minimalist Auto-Tuned track called 'Woods' by a soul-folk musician called Justin Vernon – taken from the cult classic *For Emma, Forever Ago* that Justin released under his Bon Iver moniker – and decided he wanted to sample it for a song called 'Lost In The World', he booked a flight to Vernon's hometown of Eau Claire, Wisconsin to record with Vernon at his home studio. Unfortunately the flight was grounded by a Wisconsin snowstorm, so Kanye convinced Vernon to fly out to Hawaii instead, where the pair got on so well that Vernon stayed a week, writing 10 songs with Kanye during 14-hour sessions he described as full of fun and creativity.

"I first got there a little jet-lagged from Minneapolis. Before I went to the studio, [Kanye] picked me up and we went to play hoops. He likes being in Hawaii – he doesn't get bothered by people bothering his shit. In the studio, he played the songs: 'Can you do something here?' We were going back and forth, listening to songs a couple times, just kind of going back and forth, me and [producer Jeff] Bhasker and Kanye and a couple of his friends… [It was] very spontaneous. Kanye slept like three hours a night, at the studio. He was the only one who didn't sleep at his own house. He'd work every day all day long and fall asleep in the middle of a sentence at four in the morning."

Bonding well with West creatively and enjoying the lengthy political discussions they'd have together, Vernon was brought out for two more week-long sessions and swiftly became an unusual addition to Kanye's core team. "After that first week he was like, 'I want you to come back'," Vernon recalled. "So I came back a few weeks later and it was the same kind of thing, throwing ideas around – there are a bunch of other songs I'd just throw down on, write a little hook, whatever. In the studio, he was referencing Trent Reznor, Al Green, the Roots – the fucking awesomest shit. It made total sense to me."

"I was surprised at how relaxed I was the whole time because he's a really cool guy, and really down to earth," Vernon said. "I'm just a fuckin' lumberjack dude from Wisconsin, I'm not going to go out there and try to be this awesome rap guy. I'm just doing my job. My favourite thing about Kanye is he just doesn't quit. He does not quit on a song… He's truly about approaching the song and finishing it and doing the coolest possible thing that he wants to express… He's a true artist in every sense. Every part of his expression, from his clothes to everything, is a part of how he lives his life, and I think that's why he's so successful. I would show him what I did and he would come back and be like, 'Oh, that's awesome.' Or, 'Oh, that's not cool.' And we would just work on it – there was no ego involved, it was just what's best for the song."

"I watched how they were willing to see so many ideas through and allow the weirdest things into songs," Vernon said. "Things that might not work initially, but that you could ultimately twist and contort into working. I watched them direct more than I watched them play."

"He's the executive, but he gives you room to explore yourself and to express whatever. Whatever's the best for the song, he'll get to that. By any means necessary, however it happens, he's down for it, and that means sometimes he's steering, and sometimes he's letting go."

Vernon was given his own little studio room to work in "because I'd do so much overdubbing to get my ideas out. So I ended up recording in this tiny back room, and then Kanye would come back and listen to what I came up with, and then we'd work on changing the lyrics. We'd just sit there and collaborate. It was fucking fun, man… some of the stuff I was doing with my voice was more weird and instrumental – basically building what would sound like a synth part with vocals. I felt very much like a session musician, and that was really cool, too."

"Rick Ross would just be sitting there a lot of the time while I was working on shit, on a piano bench right behind me, smoking blunt after blunt after blunt. In between takes, he'd inhale and then say real quiet, 'That was good, homie'. I'd be like, 'OK! I'll keep going!'?" I was literally in the back room rolling a spliff with Rick Ross talking about what to do on the next part of a song. It was astonishing. Kanye came back and was like, 'Look at you two guys. This is the craziest studio in the Western world right now!' There was one night where I was in the control room with the engineer and John Legend was in the sound booth singing along to something that I did. It was just like, 'Holy shit, man. There's John Legend in there singing like a motherfucker.'"

The rules of privacy were strictly enforced, yet still an unfinished mix of 'Power' managed to leak out in May 2010. "In the studio there would be sheets of paper that said, 'No tweeting, no talking, no emailing, no anything. Do not talk to anybody outside of this studio room'," said Pusha. "Then there happened to be a leak, and I remember Kanye ranting and raving, like, 'Fuck this! We're not going to ever work there again! We're going to work in hotel rooms!'"

And, for at least his next two albums, he'd stick to his vow. But the time the crew spent at Avex was, according to everyone involved, an environment that inspired a vaulting creativity. And the record that emerged was a whole world of dark, twisted and fantastical wonders.

★ ★ ★

It hit like a meteorite. A fiery angel falling to earth.

In the fake English accent of her Martha Zolanski alter-ego, one of her many different accents, Nicki Minaj laid out the central purpose of *My Beautiful Dark Twisted Fantasy*. Contorting Roald Dahl's poem *Cinderella* to her wicked means, she introduced the album like a fairy tale, promising to expose the real horrors behind the sanitised rap scene. "You might think you've peeped the scene," she said, "You haven't/ The real one's far too mean/The watered down one, the one you know/ Was made up centuries ago". The public face of rap, she claimed, was "all wack and corny... awful, blasted boring" and this album's version would be full of "twisted fictions, sick addictions, well gather round children, zip it, listen."

What the children heard was a glorious gospel choir hook sampled from Mike Oldfield's 'In High Places' and originally pieced together by RZA. "That actually started out as a *Blueprint 3* record," said No I.D. "It was going to be the intro for that album. Then Jay changed his mind, so we revamped the record and gave it to Drake. That record ended up going through a lot of phases. While I was in Hawaii, RZA came down and had a beat – but before that Pete Rock had given us a beat and then he ripped the drums and made it the rap part of it. The parts that me and 'Ye did was the chorus and the musical parts... Everything was done separately and a lot of different people contributed. Then Nicki did the intro and it went crazy. That's one of my favourite records, just because of all the emotions that came with it."

The hook was sung by Teyana Taylor, whom Kanye had met during the Glow In The Dark tour in 2007 and had bonded with over fashion. "At the time I was signed to Pharrell Williams and his Star Trak label," she explained. "Kanye used to always like my outfits. So from jump we became fashion friends and we'd talk about different clothes and designing different things. We'd email each other different garments that we liked. That's how we became friends and super close." Taylor was originally invited to Hawaii as a style advisor, helping Kanye look at Pierre Balmain clothes, but once in the studio she was determined to get onto the album. "Even though the invite really was to check out clothes, I had told myself I was going to get on that album – whether he knew or not... He started playing his album and I start humming and doing some little runs to what I'm hearing on the sly tip. I came in there humming! I knew what I was doing. So he hears me and is like, 'You can really sing. Yo, can you put some backgrounds on this song 'Hell Of A Life'?' He knew I was signed to Pharrell and all that, but I guess he didn't know what I could really do. Like I said, we were more fashion friends. He just knew I was fly.

"So then he tells me to do 'Dark Fantasy'. At the time it was pretty empty, just verses. He put me in another room by myself and said, 'Go.' I came back with a whole intro and chorus. I did all the scratches and the cuts myself with my voice. That's not a DJ thing when you hear my voice go like that. I was so nervous when I played it for Kanye. I hadn't been in the studio for so long. I was so excited to be trying out for that song. Rihanna was there… He loved it. He didn't add nothing or change anything. I ended up getting three placements on that album." Kanye also signed Taylor to G.O.O.D. Music. "Kanye always felt like I was the female version of him," Taylor said. "The way I believe in clothes. The visions and wanting to make more than just a great song. It's bigger than that. He's been where I've been, where people aren't believing in you."

Backed by Justin Vernon, Taylor helped bring Kanye back from exile at the very top of his game. "Can we get much higher?" she and an Auto-Tuned Vernon asked, a bold statement after the crash Kanye had taken in 2009. Unrepentant, Kanye's first verse, over a cinematic, brooding beat reminiscent of *Late Registration*, slipped straight back into the bragging tones of hedonism and extravagance that had characterised his pre-heartbreak *College Dropout* trilogy. "Mercy mercy me, that Murciélago," he rapped, referencing Marvin Gaye's classic soul track in honour of his flashy car, going on to boast about how he doesn't know the word for 'broke' in any language, his girlfriend – Amber Rose got a guest line in the verse – wears all the best clothes, his records are on every decent DJ's playlist and he was getting "so much head, I woke up in Sleepy Hollow".★

The second verse was more introspective, wondering how he could rebuild the buzz and standing he'd had before his hiatus and answer those that had copied him, despite still being the epitome of pop culture: "Sex is on fire, I'm the King of Leona Lewis," he argued, nodding to two of the biggest acts in the world in 2010. "Tell me, how do you respond to students?/And refresh the page and restart the memory?/Respark the soul and rebuild the enemy?" He also alluded to a drink problem he developed in the wake of his mother's death and which

★ *The Legend Of Sleepy Hollow* was a short story by Washington Irving later made into a film by Tim Burton, in which a headless horseman hunts for his missing head by night – here Kanye was suggesting he too had lost his 'head' from too much oral sex.

may have contributed to the Taylor Swift incident and his withdrawal from the public eye. "Sorry for the night demons still visit me/The plan was to drink until the pain was over/But what's worse? The pain or the hangover?"

Several lines from 'Dark Fantasy' had previously been aired on the G.O.O.D. Music Cypher at the 2010 BET Awards show, which featured a raft of the label's acts taking a verse. Kanye's was particularly revealing, as he followed lines about his drinking with more personal material that further admitted to his darker side: "I sold my soul to the devil, that's a crappy deal… 'cause they love you then they hate you then they love you again/Get away from me loneliness/Get away from me misery/Get away from me fake shit, I can't take the phoniness".

'Dark Fantasy' closed with a confessional that added to his belief that he'd made a pact with Satan by entering music with both eyes firmly on success. "I saw the devil in a Chrysler LeBaron," he intoned, "And the hell, it wouldn't spare us/And the fires did declare us/But after that, took pills, kissed an heiress/And woke up back in Paris★".

The recording of 'Dark Fantasy' was completed just three hours before the album was due to be delivered to Roc-A-Fella, but the scurry to perfect it would prove worthwhile. The track was a sensational opener to a revolutionary record, and it even reached number 60 in the *Billboard* chart on the album's release without ever being released as a single, epitomising the bold melodic and artistic leaps forward Kanye was making.

The temptor Beelzebub made another appearance in the next track, 'Gorgeous', a sketch of the issues facing young American black kids in 2010 – "penitentiary chances, the devil dances". Built around a classic bluesy guitar riff from the Turtles' 'You Showed Me', it opened with a hook that Kid Cudi had come up with after overhearing the beat in the studio. "I had the music already, and Kanye had the drums," said No I.D. "That's how we worked a lot of times, either he had the music and I had the drums or vice versa. I played the beat for him and he put it in the sampler and he did his little stutter step with it and it hit

★ Paris was Amber Rose's old stripper name.

immediately." "'Gorgeous' was one of those records that, as soon as I heard the beat, I was like, 'Man, this is the one. This is that 'This Can't Be Life' Kanye beat,'" said Cudi. "'This is that classic 'Ye beat. I want to be on this.' I came up to him, and I was like, 'Man, are you working on this record? Are you working on this beat?' He goes, 'Yeah... do you got an idea for it?' I was like, 'Yeah, I might.' I didn't. I was lying like a motherfucker. I was like, 'Yeah, man, I want to get on this joint'... Whatever Kanye tells me, I just try to put it in my little machine and make the perfect solution for it. That's always our collab formula, and that's just how 'Gorgeous' came about. He just kind of told me what he was trying to say, I threw out some words, we rearranged words, and we came out with a bunch of different options before we come up with the hook."

Cudi's hook, over a downbeat piano groove, portrayed the concerns Kanye had about his fame drifting away from him, and his awareness that this album was absolutely crucial in terms of his career post-Taylorgate: "No more chances, if you blow this, you bogus". But come his first verse, Kanye turned the spotlight on society's ills once more, highlighting the ghetto kids's fate – "All of them falling for the love of balling/Got caught with 30 rocks, the cop look like Alec Baldwin" – and arguing that such stereotypes of drug-dealing projects youths only came true because that's the behaviour that white America had expected of them; black crime was merely a self-fulfilling prophecy. He also pointed out the racist slant of drug convictions where a white kid called Brandon would get less jail time than a black kid called Jerome and the so-called random bag searches at airports always seemed to target Kanye rather than a white traveller. But he ultimately provided a ray of hope, insisting that his race would continue to rise: "I treat the cash the way the government treats AIDS/I won't be satisfied til all my niggas get it".

Come verse two, he cast hip-hop as their redemption, and the next step in a long line of styles of emancipation and protest music invented by African-Americans to exorcise their pain ("Is hip-hop just a euphemism for a new religion? The soul music of the slaves that the youth is missing?"). And in this context he cast himself as the leader and a God of the game "at the top of Mount Olympus", giving himself the alter-ego Malcolm West in reference to Malcolm X and claiming that he was assimilating himself into mainstream culture by dressing white because "they would try to crack me if they ever saw a black me".

Throwing a dig at *South Park*'s Trey Stone and Matt Parker by saying he'd "choke a *South Park* writer with a fish stick" and indulging in some Muhammad Ali-inspired ego-boosting, the latter half of the track suggested he'd finally overcome the problems that had plagued him on *808s...* ("If I ever wasn't the greatest nigga, I must have missed it!"). Hence he threw himself into verse three with a bullish demeanour, keen to return to his world of cocktails, sex and partying while looking back at his musical CV proudly and calling himself "the black Beatle", likening his talent to that of the best band of all time. From the social aspects of the earlier verses, Kanye had now descended into scrappy rap clichés – biting back at his critics for being unworthy to talk about him and dissing other acts, stating that his orchestral leanings will see him "play strings for the dramatic ending of that wack shit". "I'm coming after whoever, who has it?" he sneered. "You blowin' up? That's good, fantastic/That y'all, it's like that y'all/I don't really give a fuck about that at all".

"That was right around the time when Jay Electronica dropped 'Exhibit C'," No I.D. recalled, "and I remember I said 'Jay Electronica is the new guy, he's dope,' and 'Ye was real mad, like, 'What? I'm the guy, I'm the guy' and he went in and spazzed out on it."

Kanye was far happier to associate with the rap legends than the plucky challengers. Which is why the Wu Tang Clan's Raekwon ended up rapping the final verse on 'Gorgeous', having arrived in Hawaii purely to share insights into music with the group on the recommendation of his Wu Tang compadre RZA, and with no intention of collaborating with West at all. West, RZA told him, totally captured the experimental ideology of the Wu Tang collective, so he visited the studio and, seeing Kanye's talent at work up close, agreed to rap on the record. "[The] first thing I can tell you about Kanye West is that he's a hard worker," Raekwon said. "When you look at him, you can tell that he still has that whole hip-hop thing in his bones." Raekwon leapt on a classic slice of street balling – meticulous lines about smoking joints, high fashion, fast cars, the dangers of low-living and the redemptive promise of admiring hip-hop stars like himself and Kanye.

And as the third track, 'Power', proved, Kanye was a man with a work ethic worth admiring. "A song like 'Power' took 5,000 hours, like literally 5,000 man-hours to do this one record," he told the Power 105.1 radio station on its release as the album's first single on May 28. "That's the amount of time I was putting into every song on the album." The beat, originally meant for Rhymefest and largely created by rising producer Symbolyc One★ with assistance from Mike Dean, Jeff Bhasker, Kanye and Andrew Dawson, was pieced together from samples of King Crimson's late-sixties anti-Vietnam prog rock protest song '21ˢᵗ Century Schizoid Man', Continent Number 6's 'Afromerica' and 'It's Your Thing' by Cold Grits. The result was an urgent, psychedelic masterpiece merging the rock nous of *Graduation* with the tribalism of *808s…* and the essential catchiness of so many Kanye hits. Glitch-crazed, dark and apocalyptic, it was a bold return and a defining moment of *My Beautiful Dark Twisted Fantasy*, seen by many as a brilliant amalgamation of everything he'd done before, a conglomerate of 'Stronger', 'Jesus Walks' and 'Crack Music'.

With the hook line provided by guest singer Dwele and cackling laughter adding a demonic tone, Kanye took a trip through his schizoid, confused and twisted psyche. He went in full ego blazing. He was a superhero, he claimed, whose theme music was the boos and catcalls of his haters. He was a pivotal figure of the 21ˢᵗ century, defining the times and the decades to come. Again, he was the new Malcolm X, referencing a line from a policeman at the time, "no one man should have all that power". Kanye knew his power was fleeting and prone to corruption, and that rap pretenders would come to challenge him ("The clock's ticking, I just count the hours"), but in the face of a pessimistic society that keeps prisons open while closing schools – the latter naturally providing more need for the former – he opted for enjoying the power while he had it. "We ain't got nothing to lose, motherfucker

---

★ Kanye heard the beat and asked S1 to fly to Hawaii. When he arrived he found that Kanye had already produced several versions of his track.

we rollin'," he rapped, "with some white skinned girls and some Kelly Rowlands/In this white man world, we the ones chosen".

With his beef with MTV some years behind him, Kanye used the opening of verse two to launch one against another TV mainstay. "Fuck *SNL* and the whole cast," he barked, having been annoyed not just by the rumours that he'd lip-synced when last on the show but also the jibes that presenter Taylor Lautner, Swift's boyfriend at the time, had made about the Swift incident and a joke question he'd been asked on the show about his mother which he considered a low punch. Though he'd later perform the song on *Saturday Night Live*, changing the line, for now he was clearly furious: "Tell them Yeezy said they can kiss my whole ass". And having lashed out, he lashed himself inwardly; as the verse schizophrenically flipped from anger to introversion he admitted that the "childlike creativity" he'd always cherished was being crushed by "grown thoughts", and that the responsibility of the power he'd accumulated was killing the very thing that made him special. "Reality is catching up with me/Taking my inner child, I'm fighting for custody".

Then came the self-doubt. "Lost in translation with a whole fucking nation," he rapped of the way he'd been vilified after the VMAs "they say I was the abomination of Obama's nation". And while the end of the track saw a resurgence in confidence, as he declared "at the end of the day, goddamn it, I'm killing this shit... I don't need your pussy bitch, I'm on my own dick... I was drinking earlier, now I'm driving", it closed with Dwele expressing Kanye's most bleak message yet. Realising that the greatest power is in being able to surrender it willingly rather than allow it to be wrestled from them, he imagines the ultimate form of sacrifice, throwing himself from a high window in a "beautiful death".

Though morbid, Kanye intended the song to be inspirational and hopeful to listeners in recession-blighted America, and certainly marked a shift in his writing process. "I didn't write my raps down for my first four albums," he said, "like at all, I did it from the head straight to the booth. But on this last album, *My Beautiful Dark Twisted Fantasy*, I wrote it. I really put myself in the zone that my life was dependent on the success of this album. With that being the case, I said, 'You know what? No matter what anybody says about me, they won't – I can write something that can make someone that hates me the most have to really respect or love the song.' So even a song like 'Power', I spent 5,000 hours writing it, and it's really the psychology behind the lyrics; it's not just blatantly, 'I've got all the power' – 'No one man should have all that power.' It's worded in a really sensitive way that opens it up for everyone. Even if I use first person and say 'I, I, I,' it's always for everyone."

'Power' was premiered on June 27 at the BET Awards, his first onstage appearance since the VMAs. Standing in a red leather suit that would become a *Twisted Fantasy* trademark atop a volcano spewing steam with footage of mountain ranges and snowstorms creating a swirling vista behind him, he poured every ounce of self-belief into his performance, knowing he had everything to lose. It was a confident and eye-grabbing return, but the public still weren't completely won back over to the West way. The song reached a modest number 22 on the *Billboard* chart and in the UK it an even more modest 36.

The Marco Brambilla-directed video for the track turned out to be somewhat more of an event than the song itself. Covering only a minute and a half of the track itself, it was what Kanye would describe as a "moving painting", opening in close-up on Kanye's unmoving face and slowly drawing back to reveal more detail of the scene. He's standing in a corridor of elaborate black columns with a sword, representing the Sword Of Damocles, hanging over his head as more classical figures are revealed. In Roman myth the Sword Of Damocles, of course, represents the ever-present danger that comes with positions of great power. Nymphs with ibex horns stamp staffs, half-naked female courtiers writhe in Renaissance cloaks and two warriors fly in from either side of the screen, their blades scything for Kanye's head. Reflecting Greek mythology, classicist art and tarot imagery, it set Kanye amongst the most mysterious and revered forms of culture, and was hailed as an event akin to a Michael Jackson comeback.

And if it was events Kanye was creating, he rarely did better than on 'All Of The Lights'. Deciding he wanted all of the best singers on the planet on the track, he recruited no less than 14 guest vocalists over two years of trying to find 'the one' to sing on the song – Rihanna, Elly Jackson from La Roux, Drake, Cudi, Alicia Keys, John Legend, Elton John, The-Dream, Fergie, Ryan Leslie, Charlie Wilson, Tony Williams, Alvin Fields and Ken Lewis. Many of the voices were layered together into choral effects that made each indistinguishable, however. "He got me to layer up all these vocals with other people," Jackson recalled, "and he just basically wanted to use his favourite vocalists from around the world to create this really unique vocal texture on his record, but it's not the kind of thing where you can pick it out. I don't have a verse or anything. I can't actually hear my voice on it, but apparently it's there!"

"[Kanye] actually played his album to me, like, three months ago," said Rihanna, "and 'All Of The Lights', that was one of my favourite songs… So when he asked me to come up to the studio at two o'clock in the morning, I had to, because I loved it, I knew it was *that* song."

Introduced by a minute-long cello and piano interlude, with Elton playing the piano part, 'All Of The Lights' was another memorable pop moment from the album driven by fanfares of *Rocky* horns, intense treated drum'n'bass beats that sounded like exploding buckets and an infectious Rihanna hook revelling in the lights of high living – the paparazzi bulbs, the neon club signs, the arena spotlight. "Fast cars, shooting stars, until it's Vegas everywhere we are," sang Jackson, but the song soon took a darker turn. Throwing out a reference to Michael Jackson's death in 2009 – "MJ gone, our nigga dead" (and dedicating the album to Michael in its sleeve notes) – Kanye told the story of a man who'd domestically abused his girlfriend and been sent to prison, only to return to find she was with another man whom he then had to take to "Ghetto University", the original title of the song. He wasn't merely telling a story of regular ghetto life here – although it was a story familiar to millions of projects kids – but forging a metaphor for his own situation. He'd been exiled after abusing his fame at the VMAs, and now he was back having to fight for the love he'd become accustomed to before his fall from grace.

The second verse, in which the father is given a restraining order, shunned by his girlfriend's family and begs her to take him back for the sake of their daughter's need for a father figure, was less allegorical but still had hints of autobiography; the daughter representing the inner child he felt he was losing in 'Power' and his repentance was very real. And from there Kanye gives up control of the song, handing the final verse to Fergie from Black Eyed Peas to recount the coda in which the girlfriend tells of how she's unemployed, broke and tempted by a life of drugs. The closing line "K, we going all the way this time" could mean that she's agreeing to stay with him forever; again a familiar conceit amongst the many households where women succumb to abusive partners again and again.

Gradually, the album was morphing into the shadowy, fantastical take on Kanye's life that the title promised, and nowhere was he more devilish than on 'Monster', originally intended for Kanye's collaboration with Jay-Z, *Watch The Throne*. Dense and tribal as a jungle sacrifice, its ominous muffled beats – memorably described as a "hyperventilating death rattle" – backed some of the most vicious raps on a Kanye album yet. After Justin Vernon's breathless soul snarl asking us "are you willing to sacrifice your life?" a blood-curdling scream from Rick Ross unleashed a stream of vampiric lines: "Bitch, I'm a monster, no-good bloodsucker/Fat motherfucker". "I wasn't originally supposed to be on the record," Ross said, "I was next door working on another Kanye collaboration. I walked in, like, 'This is so big.' [Kanye] was like, 'Yeah.' He was playing the track, spitting his verse for me. That's before he even laid it. I'm like, 'That's dangerous.' At the same time, me being a hustler, I'm thinking of just an intro for the record. He told me the structure and the way he wanted it to go. I told him that was it. That's the way I would do it. He was on point with it. Me being the artist I am, I was sitting there talking to him and came up with an intro bridge. It wasn't a verse at all. It was just an intro or somewhat of a bridge to set the tone for 'Ye to come in."

On the slavering hook, Kanye too admitted that "everybody know I'm a motherfucking monster" from all of the gossip in the press, and used his bad reputation to his advantage in one of his most celebrated verses. Playing on his villain's image, he bragged about his rhyming skills – and there was an impressive example here, where he rhymed 'sarcophagus' with 'oesophagus' – technical ability, rap inventiveness and sexual allure with the style of a devilish seducer. It was as though, by admitting to his darker side, he could get away with blatant arrogance more freely.

Jay-Z contributed the second verse, likening himself to "sasquatch, Godzilla, King Kong, Loch Ness/Goblin, ghoul, a zombie with no conscience" and painting visions of hell from both the ghetto and the penthouse: "I still hear fiends screaming in my dreams/Murder, murder in black convertibles" he rapped of his early life on the Marcy streets, but even as a hugely successful icon he's still surrounded by "vampires and bloodsuckers… these fake fucks with no fangs trying to draw blood from my ice-cold veins". Here was a dark, artful take on Jay's familiar themes of street struggle and battling haters when all he wants is "love, I don't get enough of it".

But it was Minaj, overjoyed to be working on the same track as her childhood hero Jay-Z, who stole the show with her tour de force final verse. "It was a moment in history," said Rick Ross. "I knew then she's one of the greatest… I had the opportunity to sit in the studio while Nicki wrote her verse just off the record. That was when she earned my respect as a lyricist. She was a dope entertainer up until that day that I sat in the studio and watched her come up with what I feel is one of the dopest verses of the year." "I'd never heard Nicki" Vernon added, "then I got to watch her destroy that verse in the studio before I even knew who she was."

Shifting effortlessly from cutesy Barbie coo to barbarous growl over her 32 bars, Minaj built her personal beast from scratch, pulling up in a "monster automobile" and getting all of the most monstrous accoutrements – a Milan haircut, huge heels, gold teeth and fangs "because that's what a motherfuckin' monster do". And, once she'd taken on as monstrous a persona as possible, she bared her teeth at her haters – "Wait, I'm the rookie, but my features and my shows 10 times your pay?" A real Jekyll & Hyde of a performance, Minaj's wild and varied lines were the most dangerous and unhinged of the whole track.

After that modern-day 'Thriller' closed with a spooky final coda from Vernon, the next big-name posse cut shuffled into view. A track offered to Diddy and Jay-Z before Kanye decided he wanted it for himself,

'So Appalled' featured Jay-Z, RZA, Pusha, Swizz Beats and Cyhi The Prynce all taking sections of a plush orchestral drone epic with strong cinematic overtones, overlaid with industrial beats, distorted, mechanised yelps and a riff sampled from Manfred Mann's Earth Band's 'You Are – I Am'. Taking the common theme that life was "fuckin' ridiculous", a phrase introduced on Swizz Beats' opening bridge and expanded during a hook boasting of "champagne wishes, 30 white bitches... five-star dishes, different exotic fishes", they each took turns to point out what frustrated them most about the world. Kanye's first verse, written while he was in Rome working with the Fendi fashion house, attacked say-nothing pop rappers writing facile songs while "niggas is going through real shit", while Jay-Z laid into "fuckin beginners... little bitches too big for they britches" trying to drag him down, probably a reference to his beef with ex-protégé Beanie Sigel, and how staying in the game long enough will mean you're inevitably going to be abused by your youngers eventually, just for surviving so long at the top: "Dark Knight feeling, die and be a hero/Or live long enough to see yourself become a villain". In order to prove how he and his wealth were both here to stay, Jay also cast a few throwaway lines at the misfortune of MC Hammer, who famously lost the fortune he amassed with major hits in the eighties – "I lost 30 mill so I spent another 30," he rapped, "'cause unlike Hammer, 30 million can't hurt me". Hammer responded with a diss track called 'Better Run Run', in which he claimed "If I knocked on your door boy, I'll bust ya in the mouth".

Pusha's verse vented his frustration with his manager Anthony Gonzalez' 32-year prison sentence for leading a $10 million cocaine ring, as well as the lawmen that were still keeping him under surveillance for his drug dealing past, but the final verse by Cyhi The Prynce wasn't quite in keeping with the anger-spewing nature of the track, largely because it was never meant to be on the song at all. "I wasn't supposed to be on 'So Appalled'," he admitted. "People don't know that. I kinda cheated. [Kanye] said, 'Can you think of something to write on the hook?' I peeped he was kinda sleepy at the time. So he went to sleep, went to the room or something. I stayed in the studio and I said I'm not gonna just do no hook. I'm gonna do my verse. I did a verse and didn't tell him the verse was on there and I hid it. [Then] he was playing the album for some very important musicians and he played the song. He don't know my verse is gonna come on and everybody in the room goes bananas. He said, 'I gotta keep it.'"

'So Appalled' was yet another track that Kanye had to be convinced to keep on the record; this time he wanted to can the track after it had leaked online. "I had already raved over the record because it leaked," said Pusha. "I was like 'Listen, there is no way this can't be on your album, you'd have to be crazy'. He was like 'Really, you think so?' I was like 'C'mon man we got to stop treating rap like 'Oh it came out it's dead'. When it's good, we have to make people love it and digest it. We can't treat this like mix-tape throwaways like everybody else does. Everybody else does half-ass music."

In Cyhi's verse, he was cast as the outrageous one thanks to his money and sexual rapaciousness, and this tone carried over into the following track. 'Devil In A New Dress' was produced by Mike Dean and Bink!, who recalls Kanye's instant reaction to the work he'd done on a sample of Smokey Robinson singing Carole King's 'Will You Love Me Tomorrow', with added squealing guitar solo outro. "The reaction I got from him after I played the beat for the first time was real intense," he said. "I mean 'Ye just doesn't react to music if it's not genuine."

You can understand Kanye's love for the beat; its pitched-up soul sample would have tugged at his nostalgia strings, harking back to his own early work. He took the sultry romance of the track as an opportunity to paint a portrait of a relationship turning sour. "We love Jesus but you learned a lot from Satan," he rapped of a girl who'd made him do "a lot of waiting" for sex, his lust and frustration ultimately causing him to stray from the righteous religious path because "in that magic hour I seen good Christians make rash decisions". But once the pair had achieved their "consummation", things turned ugly. "How she gon' wake up and not love me any more?" Kanye asked as the girl turned on him, "I thought I was the asshole, I guess it's rubbing off." Out walking at sunset, Kanye would admire all of the sky's vivid colours while his partner was only concerned with money and jealous thoughts

– "You got green on your mind, I can see it in your eyes". When she threatens to leave him during a stormy row, he likens her to Mase retiring from rap at the top of his game to become a pastor: "Don't leave while you're hot, that's how Mase screwed up/Throwing shit around, the whole place screwed up… I hit the Jamaican spot, at the bar, take a seat/I ordered the jerk, she said 'You are what you eat'". The shallowness of the relationship is summed up in the verse's final line, a casual kiss-off. "You love me for me? Could you be more phoney?"

And on that sour note the romance, and the song, may well have ended, had Rick Ross not been invited back to the studio to record an epic final verse of classic baller rhymes about sex in limos, high class cars and irrelevant haters, delivered the day before the album's deadline. "I got a call, they wanted me to be a part of that record. [...] It was actually the last day before Kanye had to turn the record in, and I think that pressure just made it that much more special to me. So I just sat there, approached the record openly and as straightforward as I could. When I laid the verse 30 minutes later, I was extremely happy. I sent it to him, and he was too. I think it was one of the dopest verses I did this year."

Having called out a girlfriend for being phoney, the centerpiece of *My Beautiful Dark Twisted Fantasy* mercilessly turned the same accusations upon himself. 'Runaway' was a nine-minute epic of self-lacerating balladry in which Kanye threw up his hands and admitted to being a dreadful human being, particularly in the wake of his treatment of Taylor Swift. Since the song was recorded in March or April 2010, sufficient time had elapsed since the incident for Kanye to have developed some remorse for his actions. An accusatory piano note repeated mournfully, growing into an emotive riff around drums that Pete Rock found familiar. "He played 'Runaway'," Rock recalled, "and as soon as I heard the drums come in, I just started laughing. He used my drums from *Mecca And The Soul Brother*! I used these drums in an interlude before on this record called 'The Basement', and those drums come on before the song. I never heard anybody make a song the way he made it out of those drums. I thought that was genius."

To distorted, spectral Rick James roars of "who gotcha?", crunching trip-hop drums, gothic synths and chamber strings, Kanye built an emotive and stirring anthem of celebration for the world's shittiest individuals. "You've been putting up with my shit just way too long," he sang, addressing both a girl in the song and the world at large in an *808s*-style arena ballad, "So I think it's time for us to have a toast/Let's have a toast for the douchebags/Let's have a toast for the assholes/Let's have a toast for the scumbags". These were all insults hurled at him on Twitter following the VMAs, and now he was proudly acknowledging the truth in the slights, and calling together anyone else who'd ever done anything foolish they would come to regret.

As he went on to admit to all manner of dreadful behaviour, from sending pictures of his genitals to women via email★ to being addicted to "hoodrats", being incapable of intimacy, hurting his partner and never accepting responsibility for anything. "Run away from me baby, run away," he advised, yet later admitted "I don't know how I'mma manage if one day you just up and leave". It's unsurprising, perhaps, that Amber Rose turned down a role in Kanye's proposed video for the song, causing him to scrap the project for something a whole lot more ambitious.

Full of self-awareness, self-degradation and a heavy air of repentance, it was a track that would do his public image the world of good, taken as a musical apology for the wrongs he'd wrought upon poor Taylor Swift. But Kanye didn't want to be alone in admitting to his deepest, darkest faults. So he hyped Pusha up to join him in Club Asshole.

"'So Appalled'? That's a one-take verse," Pusha explained. "He was like, 'Go, please. I love this. Thank you, goodbye.' But I wrote 'Runaway' four times – and what he does not know to this day is that I was going through a relationship scandal in my life. So this man is asking me to write a song about a relationship and to say that I'm the biggest douchebag ever. He's telling me, 'Yo, you need to be more douchebag.

★ This line referred to a picture which emerged online in 2010 of Kanye with his penis exposed. "I only rap reality," he told Hot 97, "I'm looking at my Twitter, I just go to 'mentions' to see what people are talking about, they had the link, I went to it, you cannot imagine how disappointed I was that I got cut off... My email did go kinda crazy."

We need more douchebag!' I didn't want to say to him, 'Dog, I don't know if I even have douchebag in me right now.' I've been jammed up, and it's hard for me to even tap into that part, because I'm remorseful. And he's fucking beating me for fucking more. All I hear in my head is, 'More douchebag. More douchebag. More douchebag!' Finally, after a couple of days, I said, 'I'm going to go upstairs and get in total solitude and just do what I need to do.' And: '24/7/365, pussy stays on my mind.' It starts from there." So Pusha indulged his inner douche, playing up to being obsessed with sex, dismissive, unfaithful and condescending towards women and generally "young, rich and tasteless".

It was a verse that, ironically, pushed 'Runaway' to ever greater peaks of confessional nobility, and the track closed with four moving minutes wherein Kanye sang his self-hatred through a vocoder so distorted that his words were impossible to make out, as though he was so ashamed of himself he wanted to hide his own admissions in plain sight. There was no shame involved in the next track, 'Hell Of A Life', however. "I think I just fell in love with a porn star," Kanye yelled as a fuzzed, grimy and grotesque riff sampled from Black Sabbath's 'Iron Man' crashed in, the chorus of which Kanye would mimic via Auto-Tune for the song's hook. The riff lay over drums taken from Tony Joe White's 'Stud-Spider' and the Mojo Men's 'She's My Baby' was also sampled for 'Hell Of A Life'. As the foul-sounding rock writhe bled on through the song, Kanye lasciviously relates his relationship with the adult actress, based on his two-year affair with Amber Rose.

"No more drugs for me, pussy and religion is all I need," he sang, weaving odes to his lover's bedroom skills and making her his new addiction. Together they watch her work on film, discussing the price she's paid for various scenes and activities and the racism inherent in the idea that interracial sex was in some way kinky and degrading – "She said her price go down, he ever fuck a black guy, or do anal or do a gangbang/It's kinda crazy that's all considered the same thing". When they marry in the song and move into a mansion, they enjoy an open relationship ("nothing to hide, we both screwed the bridesmaids") with plenty of kinky sex involved, but Kanye is frustrated that his wife isn't respected because of her past, not allowed to rent a posh dress from Oscar de la Renta. The porn star life, and being associated with it, suddenly doesn't seem so glamorous, his twisted fantasy becoming darker by the minute. Come the outro he re-evaluates his dream of spending his life with a porno actress, instead deciding it's be a hell of a life just to have sex in a bathroom with her and get "divorced by the end of the night".

If 'Hell Of A Life' hinted that Kanye was disillusioned with the associations of Amber Rose's past, 'Blame Game' suggested everything was less than rosy in their relationship. Like 'Devil In A New Dress', it concerned the breakdown of an affair: "Let's play the blame game," sang a forlorn John Legend, with whom Kanye had collaborated on its writing, over remorseful piano, strings and drums sampled from Aphex Twin's 'Avril 14th', setting the context of the song slap bang in the middle of an argument, each of them calling the other cruel names but "at the end of it, you know we both were wrong". When Kanye took over for his first verse we found him in a bathroom taking a piss while flip-flopping over whether to stay with his girl or not; writing 'I'd rather argue with you than be with someone else' on the wall, then changing his mind, deciding to finish with her, then calls her at 2 a.m.

The array of different voices he adopted for his second verse – pitched up and down or distorted as to be unrecognisable as his voice – reflected the confused emotions of his inner monologue as he ran over the roots of their issues. "You weren't perfect but you made life worth it," he rapped, "stick around, some real feelings might surface", but swiftly admitted that their lust-filled sessions were far behind them now, and his girl was seeing someone else, a "local dude". There would be much speculation over who this other man might be. Some commentators would claim that Amber Rose cheated on Kanye with Fabolous, others that she was already seeing Wiz Khalifa, who was from Pennsylvania like Rose, and with whom she'd eventually settle down. There were even rumours that Rose had been giving Kanye's money to a secret boyfriend for the duration of their relationship.

Whoever the lines were referring to, Kanye was adamant he wouldn't be upset about being cheated on. "I hope you have a good time," he rhymed, "'cause I definitely be having mine/And you ain't gonna see a mogul get emotional every time I hear 'bout other niggas is stroking you". Even when his ex would "run my name through the mud" by claiming he'd been physically abusive to her, he'd try to keep calm, reminding her that she should be grateful he brought her to public attention by association.

Still, the issues stacked up. She'd be out late and not answering her phone. When he'd call her brother out of desperation, he was sure her brother was lying; she'd even been giving him Kanye's money to buy cocaine. And she'd always tell him that she wasn't right for him, that he needed a girl who could appreciate art in the same way he did, but, as Kanye admitted, "I was satisfied being in love with the lie". Ultimately, Kanye resigned himself to the end of the relationship, reciting a section of a poem by Chloe Mitchell like a prayer of letting go. "Things used to be, now they not," he read, "Anything but us is who we are/Disguising ourselves as secret lovers/We've become public enemies/We walk away like strangers in the street".

Unsurprisingly, Kanye and Amber would have split up by the time the album was released, although it would be January 2011 before the public first learnt of her new relationship with Wiz. But the painfully honest and personal final four minutes of 'Blame Game' would suggest they were together while she was still involved with Kanye. Setting the scene whereby he called her, failed to get through but then she accidentally pocket-dialled him back so that he could hear the conversation going on wherever she was. Here Chris Rock took the part of the "neighbourhood nigga" Rose was seeing, taping the entire scene over two hours of recording. He joked at length about how sexy and crazy she was in bed, asking her where she'd learnt incredible moves such as leaving her Jimmy Choos on during sex, talking dirty and working her "Cique du Soleil pussy". Her reply was always "Yeezy taught me", a phrase that would trend on Twitter when the album leaked. "I did that quicker than I read scripts that they offer me money to do," Rock said of his part on the track. "I thank [Kanye] so much it probably freaks him out. Especially at this late date, to get on something, the album of the moment, that stuff is priceless, you can't put a price tag on that. I felt invigorated by it."

Whether the event portrayed actually happened or not – and details such as a mention of the $30,000 watch that Kanye did indeed give to Amber and she then gave to Wiz suggest it wasn't entirely fictitious – the piece showed that Kanye had kept a relative good humour over the split, despite the heartbreak he expressed in the song. And he ended it with a reminder of how he had made her name: "Yeezy taught you well, Yeezy taught you well". Rose herself countered the allegations made in the song, claiming that the pair had split because Kanye had begun an affair with Kim Kardashian, which seemed to mirror the effect that Kardashian may have had on Kanye's relationship with Phifer several years earlier. "Kim is one of the main reasons why me and Kanye are not together," Rose told *Star* magazine. "She's a home wrecker. They were both cheating. They were both cheating on me and Reggie [Bush, NFL player] with each other… She was sending pictures, and I was like, 'Kim, just stop. Don't be that person.' I thought at least she'd be woman enough to respond to me. She never responded. It's very important that us women stick together and we don't fuck each other over like that."

The gossip columnists and websites leapt on this snippet, alleging that Kanye had become so enamoured with Kardashian's legendary sex tape that he'd watch it while having sex with other women to turn him on, and that he'd tried to convince her to leave her boyfriend, Reggie Bush, for him in 2009. The speculation only added to Rose's distress, and 'Blame Game' made things so unbearable for her that she broke down in tears during an MTV interview with Sway Calloway. "No one knows what I've been through and the things that I had to deal with when, you know, Kanye made his album, and he talked reckless about me on his album," she said. "And then, you know, I have people throwing things at me in the street, because they're fans of Kanye's. I'm just crying because I don't deserve to be bullied like that. I'm a nice girl, I don't bother anybody and I keep my mouth shut because I don't want any trouble. But to be bullied through music and stuff like that, it's not fair to me. I don't deserve that." It would be the last we'd hear of Rose's side of the story, however; rumours abounded that Kanye would give Rose $1 million to stay silent in the press about their relationship.

From the souring of the relationship as described in 'Devil In A New Dress' to this detailed and intimate portrayal of deeply personal events behind the scenes, the latter half of the album was becoming as autobiographical as *808s…*, tracing another affair as it disintegrated, Kanye's beautiful, dark, twisted fantasy of a fulfilled and happy life with a porn star falling apart. And the album continued the story; the opening of 'Lost In The World', sampled from 'Woods' from Vernon's *For Emma, Forever Ago* reflected the loneliness of the post-split terrain. Recorded by Vernon in his parents' log cabin in the winter woods after his own devastating break-up in 2007, the introductory sample consisted of Vernon's a cappella, Auto-Tuned voice describing the isolation of his self-imposed winter exile: "I'm up in the woods, I'm down on my mind/I'm building a still to slow down the time".

But Kanye, it turned out, was in no mood for moroseness. Instead, he wanted to celebrate his romantic emancipation – he wasn't feeling aimless and adrift without Rose but lost in a world of possibility and opportunity. Pumping industrial disco beats kicked in and the haunting track became a gothic-tinged party piece. "He plays me the track and it sounds exactly like how you want it to sound," Vernon said, "a forward moving, interesting, light-hearted, heavy-hearted, fucking incredible sounding jam. It was kind of bare so I added some choir-sounding stuff and then thickened out the samples with my voice… We were just eating breakfast and listening to the song on the speakers and he's like, 'Fuck, this is going to be the festival closer'. I was like, 'Yeah, cool'. It kind of freaked me out."

Suddenly, Kanye was back on the party scene – "I'm new in the city but I'm down for the night," he sang, before casting out a verse of devotion to a new woman in his life, some of his favourite lines of his career. "You're my devil, you're my angel/You're my heaven, you're my hell/You're my now, you're my forever/You're my freedom, you're my jail," he rapped exuberantly, the dichotomy of each line reflecting how he felt this new woman was both the best and worst thing for him. He'd later admit that he wrote the lines for Kardashian.

"I wanted to marry that girl from the first time I saw her and I had to wait through a bunch of relationships before I got my chance," he said. "It's just patience. With certain things it's like, 'This is what's right for me and this is what I should be doing' and you've got to be patient. You can express it in song. In 'Lost In The World' I wrote a poem for her. I knew I wanted a family and the very first time I saw a picture of Kim in Australia with Paris or one day she had come to the studio with somebody else, I don't remember where we first met, but I knew that that was my wife. I wrote [that verse], it was her as my muse and me as Shakespeare to write that for someone who inspired me to love, to create and to be an artist. She's my biggest inspiration and I was so happy that it worked on that song, 'Lost In The World'. We're not always in the position that we want to be at. We're constantly growing, we're constantly making mistakes, we're constantly trying to express ourselves and actualise our dreams. That song was the first step or second step or third step or twentieth step to the actualisation of the family that I have now."

While he waited for Kim, however, Kanye wasn't pining too hard. After splitting with Rose in July 2010, he was romantically linked with a string of women on the rebound. Beauty queen Angela Martini was rumoured to be hunting West down early in the year with an eye on the Kanye prize, while he allegedly hooked up with French model Virginie Maury in Cannes shortly after splitting with Rose and was linked to ex-Pussycat Doll Melody Thornton that autumn when they were snapped holding hands on several red carpets. He would also start a brief relationship with Selita Ebanks, a former Victoria's Secret Angel, after she appeared in the film he would make for 'Runaway'. No wonder he felt somewhat free and easy on 'Lost In The World'.

As the vital, distorted beat continued into the final track, *My Beautiful Dark Twisted Fantasy* closed by widening its viewfinder from the personal to the political. Truncating Gil-Scott Heron's 'Comment #1', an allegorical speech on the issues facing America and their troubled roots, 'Who Will Survive In America' described a godless, divided America "living as we do upside-down", where "the new word to have is revolution" and "people don't even want to hear the preacher spill or spiel… and America is now blood and tears instead of milk and honey". Heron traces the problem of suppression and racism towards African-

Americans – a "scandal… hosed down daily with a gagging perfume" – back to the origins of the country itself, claiming that America was "a bastard" country founded on lies of "democracy, liberty and justice" while slaves and their descendants were systematically denied basic human freedoms. That this rousing speech was met with only muted applause was a statement of how little attention is given, even today, to such a fundamental and glaring problem.

The iTunes version of the album had one bonus track attached, and a glittering one at that. Featuring Big Sean, Charlie Wilson and Beyoncé – who recorded her parts at 5 a.m. – 'See Me Now' was a cheerful radio pop-soul track adorned with frantic, crunching beats and upbeat, catchy choral backing vocals. It found the old Kanye re-emerging, full of his trademark arrogance – "This is an aristocracy," he said of the rap game, "I'm Socrates but my skin more chocolatey"★ – and regaling us about his golden beats, high-end shopping trips to Italian fashion designers and sports car showrooms, and sexy girlfriends. Throwing out some of his best puns yet – "If you fall on concrete, that's your ass' fault" ranked amongst his smartest – by the end of verse two he was likening his new brand of rap to a cross between pop and Christianity: "Like a mix between Fergie and Jesus/Imagine the direction of this immaculate conception". It was, in essence, his triumphant release from hip-hop jail song, returning from his Hawaiian exile with Beyoncé singing, "My niggas is home, I guess I got everything, everything I want", and references to ancient Gods and Greek mythology only served to enhance the new image he was portraying of himself as a classical deity in the video for 'Power' and his volcano-straddling live performance. Slowly, Kanye was inching towards declaring himself not just a monster, but a real-life God.

He also gave a shout-out to "Rosewood!" in reference to the Rosewood Movement, a set of stylistic rules by which his G.O.O.D. label signings must abide when seen together in public. When first unveiled with the tagline 'Rosewood Movement, suits all day' at such

★ Socrates famously spoke unpopular truths about society and politics in ancient Greece, and was persecuted by the government for his views.

events as a private show by Kanye and Legend on August 12, it seemed merely aesthetic – the rappers all wore matching Dior Homme suits, hard bottoms and shades. But when Kanye explained the ethos to Power 105.1, it was clearly more of an old-fashioned and gentlemanly way of life. "That's the Rosewood mentality," he said, "like affluence, like not cursing loud in public, pulling out chairs for your lady, opening up doors… calling your grandmother… taking care of your kids… That's where I'm at at 33 and it's ill 'cause I'm at this really good emotional, great place in my life, and they're always saying in hip-hop that you have to be in a dark place to make great hip-hop. I feel like I rap better than I've ever rapped at this point. I be writing raps and I don't even realise how positive they are. They just sound like regular good negative raps."

One Rosewood devotee was Big Sean, taking the final verse on the album claiming to be "the fastest in the world" as a result. And his associations with G.O.O.D. were seemingly improving his life beyond his wildest dreams, as he praised the team for being "like the new Miami Heat", beat on those who criticised Kanye for being a jerk ("How could you say that? He rode me and my mama around in his Maybach… if he a jerk, I bet you jerk him off") and revelled in his Rolex watches and Presidential suits. That song closed with a celebratory outro from Kanye: "I know what you thinking, 'This that Yeezy we all love"/I'm back baby!... Black excellence, baby, we the elite/We the greatest in the world".

The album he delivered to Roc-A-Fella was, he knew, a bold and revolutionary one. But he also knew there was a lot of work to be done before the world would give it a chance.

So, over the late summer and autumn of 2010, Kanye went on a charm rampage.

★ ★ ★

Silicon Valley sparked a thousand volts stronger the day Kanye West rolled up. Noses pressed against the office windows of Twitter and Facebook, legions of techies finally starting to realise just how powerful they were in the new media age. Powerful enough that Kanye was willing to turn up at their place of work and perform impromptu rap sets just to curry their favour.

Setting out to schmooze the tastemakers, Kanye visited the offices of major websites and music publications, to talk to them about the album and his mindset and throw out a few rhymes for the razzle-dazzle effect. "Everyone says all great art comes from pain," he told the *Rolling Stone* staff, decked out in his Dior Homme, "but I think my greatest art comes from excitement and joy. It's a completely different perspective, about being extremely excited about something that is only cool to me… It was important to find out a way to… not be limited by the art form of rap but to have rap bring it to another level. You'll notice there's times where is it rap or is it poetry? Is it spoken word or is it a speech?… There's people throughout history that their responsibility is to be conveyors of the truth onto next generations. I feel like I'm that type of person that has to carry on the truth and tell the story – not *his* story, to tell *the* story. It's like Raphael painting Jesus' wife knowing that the Pope would have his head but as an artist he said, 'I need to express this or I'll die inside, this is what I saw'. I feel like artists take their lives too seriously or not seriously enough. Who would really put their life on the line for what they really believe in? Who would make a sacrifice? People fall short of the greatness of rock'n'roll. They're all scared, everybody's a fucking pussy and everybody that could be a real rock star run away from popular culture."

The few journalists he did allow access to his world were given strict rules. Granting *Slate* magazine time with him, the journalist Jonah Weiner was told he could ask no questions at all, but was allowed to print what was said to him. Weiner revealed some insightful colour from his time inside Kanye's inner circle, spying on this cartoonishly arrogant character as he redesigned his Manhattan apartment in a maximal French emperor style. "Versailles is the shit… [I'm] turning the crib real Kingish," Kanye told him as he selected 13-foot projector TVs, floral-patterned gold goblets for water glasses and porcelain bowls with golden lion handles for cereal bowls. When considering whether to buy fur pillows he complained that he could never sleep on them, but bought them anyway, drawn to their lack of comfort. He admitted that, since he was always striving for greater artistic achievement, he found the life of luxury he'd always craved impossible to enjoy, so the discomfort of fur pillows served as a reminder that he was still unfulfilled. "I never feel like I'm not the underdog," he said. "I never felt completely comfortable."

The minutiae of his life was fascinating. He had a small private plane he called Babymama because it looked like the sort of gift he might buy a girlfriend. He hoped to buy a horse. His favourite fictional character was Ron Burgundy from *Anchorman*, whose line "I'm kind of a big deal" he'd quote regularly in half-parody of his own ego. He justified the Rosewood Movement style by claiming that "everything's the right backdrop for a suit" and even insisted his security wear Dior – he'd wear a suit everywhere but on his way to the gym because "I jog in Lanvin". He'd entertain Jay-Z and girls from Stockholm called Helena and Carolina with cocktails of Grey Goose vodka and grapefruit juice mixed in vintage Versace glasses.

When discussing his work he'd admit "I was off my head for the last two years on the drug called fame" and set himself up against the giants of classical culture in order to avoid being "limited by the art form of rap". "When I think of competition it's like I try to create against the past. I think about Michelangelo and Picasso, you know, the pyramids." And he laid out his thinking behind shunning the traditional forms of press promotion. "This is my problem with interviews, you know? What if you did music, and someone else could come in and change your words around and then release it to the radio? And you ain't even get a chance to listen to it before they dropped it to radio? That's how interviews are! You say what you say and then you get paraphrased. I wanna get approval over the shit."

He took this theory to its ultimate conclusion when he insisted on writing his own cover feature for *XXL* magazine. "There were times when I thought I was making the world better," he wrote, "or maybe I just wasn't thinking at all. I've been dealing with the MTV incident every day of my life since it happened. The single thing that hurt me the most is when I found out how much Taylor Swift wanted to work with me. It wasn't about black or white, it wasn't about wrong or right, it wasn't about real or fake. It was about humanity, and at no point in life can you think that you're such a god that you do not have to deal with humanity.

"My biggest goal is to be anchored in taste and beauty, and there are some things that I've done that are just blatantly distasteful. As I grow up, I want to be able to apply good taste at all times. Knowing the audience, knowing who you're talking to and how to be expressive and get your point across without being offensive is the key… Timing is everything. Good timing is a sign of good taste. I've heard people say, 'Kanye told the truth. Beyoncé should've won'. But that doesn't mean it was the right moment for me to express those feelings. There are certain people that know how to tell you things at the perfect time for you to be able to accept them properly. I wasn't that person then.

"I stress that the incident wasn't about Taylor personally. And it definitely wasn't about race. Where I messed up is, at the end of the day, it's your show, Taylor. It's your show, MTV… I wasn't expecting the reaction I got. When I did things like that or the 'George Bush doesn't care about black people' moment, it wasn't a matter of being selfish, from where I stood. It's more like I was being selfless – that I would risk everything to express what I felt was the truth. In this case, it was like I was driving a car and I needed to run this red light to make it to the airport, but by me running this red light, I ran someone over in the process, and that's what people saw from a distance. Now I'm the biggest jerk in the world. Good morning, Kanye West, this is your life.

"I knew I wasn't in a great spot publicly after the incident, but I would just block it out and work as hard as possible and let my work be my saving grace. In a way, I had thrown a Molotov cocktail at my own career, and it gave me an opportunity, for the first time, to go away and find out who I was. Because I felt very alone. The only person that came to visit me the night it happened was Mos Def. He came to my house right afterward and said, 'Move. You're not going to be able to make it out here. You can't make it in America right now. You have to move'. And that's what I did. I went to Japan for three weeks, then moved to Rome for the rest of the year. I worked as an intern at Fendi. On weekends, I would fly to Paris and sometimes take off four days just to be in Stockholm, Sweden, just to meet with Johnny who runs Acne, or the Fifth Avenue Shoe Repair, to find the perfect pair of jeans...

"I spent the last year improving every element of myself as a person. By default, my raps are way better now, because I'm at a point where I don't have to come up with lines – I just think of what I'm really doing and make it rhyme. January first of this year, I started back in the studio. I knew for a while I was going to start that day. I still had a lot of pain, and I needed to write that pain out, and it's on my new album. But toward the end is when the Kanye West music really came. Everything is a form of my music, but the style of *808s & Heartbreak* is better served by Drake and Kid Cudi than it is by me. I think they could both carry that sound better than I could, and also being that Cudi helped design that sound. That style of music is very nighttime, very streetlights. It's, like, 'streetlights glowing'... Drake was the first thing that actually scared me and put pressure on me, because it was the first thing that was blatantly from a similar perspective and lane. When I feel pressure, I step my game up. So I believe that Drake made great music for people to love and enjoy, but he also forced me to step my game up, because I have to be Kanye West."

The media was easily dazzled with a personal appearance and a flash of Kanye's wonky smile, but winning back the sympathies of the public would be a greater challenge. So he concocted a campaign of contrition and uncharacteristic personability. Signing up to an official Twitter account which swiftly gained over a million followers, he began tweeting incessantly, conducting Q&A sessions on the site. One exchange on the topic of Swift ran to 70 tweets on one day alone: "I wrote a song for Taylor Swift that's so beautiful and I want her to have it," he wrote. "If she won't take it then I'll perform it for her... I'm sorry, Taylor... She deserves my apology more than anyone. She had nothing to do with my issues with award shows. She had no idea what hit her. She just lil girl with dreams like the rest of us... Taylor loves rap music, I love country music... Some people's truth is Kanye is a racist... it's not my truth but I do believe it's my karma... Why are there so many tweets? Well, this isn't a simple subject. There are layers to this beyond me running on stage... These tweets have no manager, no publicist, no grammar checking...this is raw... With the help of strong will, a lack of [empathy], a lil alcohol and extremely distasteful & bad timing... I became George Bush overnight... How deep is the scar... I bled hard... cancelled tour with the number one pop star in the world... closed the doors of my clothing office."

He also used the internet to connect further with his fans via a real-time interview on UStream and on August 20, he launched G.O.O.D. Fridays to build up anticipation for the album's November release. Each week until the album came out, he would post a new track on his website for free and go online to connect with his fans. The series began with a remix of 'Power' that featured Jay-Z and Swizz Beatz, though Swizz's raps on the G.O.O.D. Friday releases would be mocked by many fans as noticeably poor, and was followed by 'Monster', uploaded only for a few days before being taken down and replaced with 'Runaway Love (Remix)' as the rabid response to it convinced Kanye to release it as a single later in the campaign. Early G.O.O.D. Friday releases included other tracks that would make it only to final album – a short version of 'Devil In A New Dress' and an unmastered 'So Appalled' – but most were teaser tracks that would end up on mix-tapes and compilation albums or as bonus tracks.

The quality of the beats and guests on these tracks was second to none, however. The warped psychedelic soul of 'Lord Lord Lord' found him waxing poetic about women and haters alongside Mos Def's musings on the universe and humanity's place within it – Mos announced he was signing to G.O.O.D. shortly after the song emerged – and Raekwon's dark drug dealing tales. The suave, chamber-orchestra posse cut 'Christian Dior Denim Flow' featured Legend, Cudi, Pusha, Lloyd Banks and Ryan Leslie accompanying a heavily fuzzed Kanye as he rapped about all of the high-class models he was hanging with or lusting after, from Noémie Lenoir to Arlenis Sosa and Anja Rubik, one of only five people Kanye followed on Twitter. And the strident, mechanical 'Don't Look Down' had vocoder-distorted effigies of Mos, Lupe Fiasco, Kanye and Big Sean weaving the kind of touching fairy tale that ran as a theme through the forthcoming album, this time about a woman leaving Sean devastated as she turns into a fiery phoenix and flies off into the heavens, a colourful, classical metaphor for losing a loved one. The same sort of phoenix that would feature, armless, in painted form on the cover of *My Beautiful Dark Twisted Fantasy* having sex with a grotesque depiction of Kanye in a painting by George Condo that would see the album banned by some retail stores. Condo later claimed that, when they met up to discuss his work and Condo painted eight or nine works for the album, West had specifically asked for cover artwork that would get the album banned, and Kanye would celebrate the controversy by designing a range of scarves with French designers M/M (Paris) based on the album's artwork.

The phoenix became a recurring motif in the *My Beautiful Dark Twisted Fantasy* campaign. Alongside releasing his G.O.O.D. Friday tracks, Kanye directed a 35-minute short film entitled *Runaway* as an accompaniment to the record, an extended music video for 'Runaway' inspired by Prince's 'Purple Rain', Michael Jackson's 'Thriller', Fellini, Kubrick and designer Karl Lagerfeld, full of fire and spectacle. Filmed over four days in Prague with Vanessa Beecroft as art director and working from a Hype Williams script, the film took in sections from nine of the album's songs as it told the story of a half-woman half-phoenix, played by Selita Ebanks, who crash-lands on Earth in the form of a meteorite, directly in front of West's sports car. To the strains of 'Dark Fantasy', Kanye – playing a character called Griffin – rescues the injured creature. In his apartment, told not to trust anything she sees on the news, she becomes accustomed to TVs and the wildlife in the garden and learns to dance to a remix of 'Power' that Kanye plays for her. As 'All Of The Lights' kicks in Kanye takes her to see a carnival parade of military drummers and a gigantic papier-mâché Michael Jackson head, with fireworks exploding above and spark-spewing acrobats tumbling all around. At a dinner party in a vast warehouse, however, the phoenix stands out for her appearance and mannerisms, the jibes of the other guests prompting Kanye to leave the table, walk to a nearby piano and tap out the opening notes of 'Runaway' as a troupe of black-clad ballet dancers scuttle in and writhe and pirouette along to the track. When a plump, feathered turkey on a silver platter is placed before the phoenix as part of the feast, its feathers the image of her own, she's upset by the idea of eating her brethren and lets out deafening screams, breaking up the party to West's embarrassment.

It's the beginning of the end; back at the apartment dark clouds darken the idyllic scene to the strains of 'Blame Game', and sitting outside at sunset, she tells Kanye that the statues of Earth are actually phoenix turned to stone and lays out the problem with his world. "Anything that is different, you try to change," she tells him, "you try to tear it down. You rip the wings off the phoenix and they turn to stone." She decides she needs to burn in order to go back to her world, but Kanye begs her to stay. After one last night of passion he wakes on his roof to find her gone, exploding in flame and taking off in a fireball to the sound of 'Lost In The World'. Premiered at VIP screenings in New York, LA, Paris, Chicago and London, as a taster and extended trailer for the album as a whole it was a cinematic tour de force.

The ballerinas would also become a motif. A key moment in his rehabilitation into the public's affections was his appearance at the VMAs on September 12, a major comeback slot on national TV, and performing the self-effacing 'Runaway' went down well, his toast to the douchebags, scumbags and jerk-offs widely regarded as an acknowledgement of his arrogant mistake at the previous year's award show and an unspoken apology to Swift. Here, clad in his red suit again, performing on a gigantic circular dais resembling the face of God's own Rolex and backed up by a Pusha T guest spot, he surrounded himself with ballerinas to add grace and import to the moving testimony of his own failings. For her part, Taylor Swift used her slot on the show to direct a calm and forgiving message to West – "Thirty-two and still growing up now," she gently sang, "who you are is not what you did, you're still an innocent."

America's heart thawed to him once more. When he attended the launch of the G.O.O.D. Friday track 'Good Friday' at the Mercer Hotel, he was mobbed by huge crowds waiting to see him, blocking entire streets in SoHo, and tweeted his appreciation of the love: "Just shut SoHo down... shit is crazy 2nt!!! This is the best night of my life uuuum so far... I know the city getting ready!" When he appeared on the *Ellen DeGeneres Show* and revealed that he'd had his entire bottom row of teeth replaced with diamonds because "diamonds were cooler... there's just certain things that rock stars are supposed to do", his sheer ridiculousness charmed the nation. When he was spotted on a Delta Airlines flight, he agreed to rap a verse of 'Gold Digger' over the PA system. And on its October 5 release, the same day its short film was premiered, 'Runaway' hit number 12 on the *Billboard* chart, 10 places higher than his comeback single 'Power' had peaked in May.

An October 23 release of 'Monster' fared less well, making number 18, but the reviews for *My Beautiful Dark Twisted Fantasy*, when they emerged throughout November, were like nothing Kanye had ever read before. Besides being hailed as the best record of his career, the album would also be crowned the best of the year by *Billboard, Time, Slant, Pitchfork, Spin, Vibe, Entertainment Weekly, The Telegraph* and *Rolling Stone*. Metacritic's rating out of 100, compiled from a wide variety of scores across the critical landscape, gave the album a huge 94, representing massive acclaim. The *Los Angeles Times* called it "the most critically acclaimed album of the year, a career-defining record" and the reviewers gushed like fountainheads. "*My Beautiful Dark Twisted Fantasy* is one of pop's gaudiest, most grandiose efforts of recent years, a no-holds-barred musical extravaganza in which any notion of good taste is abandoned at the door," wrote *The Independent*'s Andy Gill in a five-star review, while the *Los Angeles Times* also described it as "Picasso-like, fulfilling the Cubist mandate of rearranging form, texture, colour and space to suggest new ways of viewing things."

"Being crazy is this guy's job," wrote *Rolling Stone*'s Rob Sheffield, "and judging from the sound of his music, business is booming. *My Beautiful Dark Twisted Fantasy* is his most maniacally inspired music yet, coasting on heroic levels of dementia, pimping on top of Mount Olympus. Yeezy goes for the grandeur of stadium rock, the all-devouring sonics of hip-hop, the erotic gloss of disco, and he goes for *all* of it, all the time. Nobody halfway sane could have made this album...

On *Fantasy*, he gets ridiculously maximal, blowing past all the rules of hip-hop and pop, even though, for the past half-decade, he's been the one inventing the rules. There are hip-hop epics, R&B ballads, alien electronics, prog-rock samples, surprise guests from Bon Iver to Fergie to Chris Rock, even a freaking Elton John piano solo. It's his best album, but it's more than that – it's also a rock-star manifesto for a downsizing world. At a time when we all get hectored about lowering our expectations, surrendering our attention spans, settling for less, West wants us to demand *more*."

Despite referring to it as his revelatory "Luke, I am your father moment", later Kanye would actually look back on the album with a sense of disappointment. He'd explain that creating *My Beautiful Dark Twisted Fanta*sy was "a long, backhanded apology" to the public and the industry, and a way of proving to everyone that he still had great artistic worth, but was a little too eager to please and not what he was fully capable of. "It was like, all these raps, all these sonic acrobatics. I was like, 'Let me show you guys what I can do, and please accept me back. You want to have me on your shelves'," he'd say. "I don't have some type of romantic relationship with the public. I'm like, the anti-celebrity, and my music comes from a place of being anti. [*Twisted Fantasy*] was the album where I gave people what they wanted… I don't think that at that point, with my relationship with the public and with sceptical buyers, that I could've done 'Black Skinhead'… It's always going to be 80 percent, at least, what I want to give, and 20 percent fulfilling a perception…. Sometimes you don't even know when you're being compromised till after the fact, and that's what you regret. I don't want to come off dissing *Dark Fantasy*. It's me never being satisfied and then me coming and admitting and saying the truth. As much as I can air things out for other people, to air things out for myself, to say, 'I feel like this could've been stronger'."

Nonetheless, with anticipation for the album pumped by its glowing notices, it's no wonder the record leaked. On November 9, two weeks upfront of its planned release date of November 22, an edited, clean version was flying around the internet like a lightning bolt. In response, Kanye declared he was suspending the G.O.O.D.

Friday releases★. "Due to blogs leaking unfinished songs from my actual album I've decided to pass of Good Fridays this week," he tweeted. "It's messed up that one hacker can mess everything up for everyone… I love to take a year to finish my songs and deliver them to you guys in their most completed form… It would have seemed like since I give free music every week even the lowest form of human being would respect that enough not to leak unfinished songs from my real album…"

Despite the leak, Kanye stuck to the release plan. With the album hitting stores on November 22, he promoted it with several publicity events. First, he played a tiny, star-studded and vastly oversubscribed show at New York's Bowery Ballroom on November 23, where the likes of Spike Lee, Ivanka Trump, LA Reid and Questlove jostled in the guest list queue to cram inside and Justin Vernon made a surprise appearance for a nine-minute version of 'Lost In The World'. It was the scene of one of his earliest onstage rants too, a habit he'd become addicted to over the coming years.

"To come back and do 100k the first day, digital alone," he exuded, defending himself against the still-sore fallout from the VMA Awards 2009, "to be slated to do 600k first week, I don't talk about the numbers but what that number says is that the people want me to keep making music…but I ain't here to do no motherfuckin politics, I'm here to make music. I'm not here to talk in no interviews, nobody asking me no stupid ass questions. We had such a great win… If you're a child that's being abused by your parent, or you're a girl that's being abused by your man, the greatest win you can ever have, is for that person to hit you in public! You see? You see, I told you!…. There was no way for

---

★ There was one final G.O.O.D. Friday download released on December 17, the urban Christmas-themed 'Christmas In Harlem' featuring Cam'ron, Jim Jones, Pusha T, Vado, Musiq Soulchild, Big Sean, Cyhi The Prynce and Teyana Taylor. While sparing with the sleighbells, the track was as lush and festive as a rap Christmas song should be, Kanye rapping about the wonders of the season and receiving some hot sex for Christmas while his guests rhymed about their party plans, expensive presents and sending holiday wishes to their friends in the pen.

me to justify the way people judged me. When you do things like what happened last year it's disrespectful to everyone who's creative! It's a smack in the face of everyone who tries to do something real. If I wasn't drunk I woulda been on stage longer! Like, am I the only one who's not crazy here? Are you fucking kidding me? And then they run with it. And don't call me and tell me what I should do. I'm my own man!... Everyone wants to villainise people, even if you take the concept of George Bush. There's no leader in history that has been villainised in that way, and didn't get killed at war or commit suicide. So anyone that lives through it deserves one moment of redemption."

At this point a few crowd members started booing, but Kanye ranted on regardless, meandering from his point. "None are without flaw. The shit that people write on blogs is a reflection of what they feel about themselves... that they want to project through the people who are on TV! And now we are a mere surface of the energy that they are projecting on us! Everyone needs a villain, don't we? We need to blame someone. And for me to be considered a racist for stating a blatant truth, an obvious truth... but the nuances of my words, because I am very particular with my words, and the emotion that I felt at that time wasn't worded exactly right. But everybody came and said, 'Oh my God!' I'm talking about five years ago, I'm not talking about a year ago. I'm talking about Katrina. And everybody said, 'Oh my God, Kanye, I love you so much. I hated you until you said that. Now you're speaking for me. I always thought you were an asshole but now you said something that represents me'. And the whole time I'm thinking, that's not exactly what I wanted to say. I was emotional. That's not exactly how I wanted to word it. But I rode it, I rode it, just as Taylor never came to my defence in any interview, and rode the wave and rode it, and rode it. That's the way I rode the wave of the Bush comment. It's not about popular opinion, it's about when you look in your heart and know what's right and what's wrong..."

"Quit while you're ahead!" yelled a heckler, but Kanye wouldn't quit. "When you look in your heart, look at what the media did," he continued, talking about the recent interview in which Bush had called Kanye's Katrina outburst one of the lowest points in his Presidency.

"Look at how they exploited [Bush]. They said that he said it was his lowest moment. And America, we took that as a fact. When you look at that interview, he said it was *one* of his lowest moments. And he said it about 10 different things. But because of the popularity of me, they exploited that…to make you watch the interview, and make you feel that he was stupider than ever to think that a rapper comment could be his lowest moment. That's not what he fucking said! That's not what he said! He said it's *one* of his lowest moments. But it shows you the way they try to villain-ise! Everything would have been OK, if they didn't play the audio that day… none the wiser, none the wiser! They played the audio, they fucked up in front of everybody. They fucked up big time. If you a real artist, have no fear! Say what you want, do what you want, make what you want. If it's meant to be, the people will stand up, like they stood up for me, 600-thousand, after being the most hated person this time last year!"

Footage of the rant shot around the web almost as fast as the album had; though he looked pretty crazy, the publicity was gold. Two days later, on November 25, he made a more maximal public appearance at the Macy's Thanksgiving Day Parade through Manhattan, performing 'Lost In The World' atop a NYC-themed float featuring a 30-ft high Big Apple and miniature versions of the Statue Of Liberty and the Empire State. He wanted the world to know, he was back on top of the world.

His prickly nature garnered him a lot more attention later in the year, when an interview on the *Today* show ended badly. As host Matt Lauer questioned Kanye about his statements on President Bush in the Katrina telethon and Kanye related it to the Swift incident, the show's directors began playing footage of the VMA show in the background as Kanye spoke. Finding the sounds deeply distracting and feeling his emotions were being manipulated by the show to provoke a reaction, Kanye complained, "How am I supposed to talk with this running under?" and "I didn't need you guys to prompt my emotions. I don't need all the jazz." After the show he took to Twitter to express his anger.

"While I was trying to give the interview they started playing the 'MTV' under me with audio!!!!!!!" he wrote. "I don't mess with Matt Lauer or the *Today Show* … and that's a very nice way for me to put it! … HE TRIED TO FORCE MY ANSWERS. IT WAS VERY BRUTAL AND I CAME THERE WITH ONLY POSITIVE INTENT … I feel very alone very used very tortured very forced very misunderstood very hollow very very misused … I don't trust anyone but myself! Everyone has an agenda. I don't do press any more. I can't be everything to everybody any more … I can't be everybody's hero and villain saviour and sinner Christian and anti-Christ! … I can't take any more advice!!! I create, I'm creative, I have a good heart, everyone will see and understand one day."

Adding to his aggravation, Lauer announced on another show that Kanye would be returning to perform a "special live concert at the plaza" on the show a few weeks later. This, it appeared, was something of a surprise to Kanye, who continued his Twitterstorm from Dubai. "I'm not performing on the *Today* show for obvious reasons," he tapped. "I'm so happy the world got to see a small piece of 'the setup.' I blatantly said I'm not performing [on the show] on a tweet… and the next day they still announced a performance. Do you guys see what I'm saying now? This is just a small slice of the day-to-day bullshit that goes on that helps to precipitate the idea that I such an asshole. 'Cause when I don't perform, 'Oh nooow I'm the one that's crazy or a jerk'.

"I want you guys to look at that footage and start to put everything together now. It's very simple to call someone angry or spoiled or the one thousand names I've been called, but it's harder to try to take a look at what's really behind the curtain. I'm so happy that my real fans are not as 'basic' as the media makes them out to be. Did you see them try to justify playing the audio under my interview? Yo, sometimes you're just wrong and it ain't nothing you can say to justify it. Believe me, I know!… I'm not complaining. I'm tweeting because I'm so happy you guys got to see this shit really go down. I don't hate Matt Lauer… we don't promote hate. That's the whole point. I promote love and truth. You know what? We off that! They made a mistake. They thought they could pull it but they couldn't. That was just a small representation of a bigger media play that's been going on since the beginning of time. All positive energy… all smiles. Much love to Matt and the whole *Today* show. I accept ya'll future apology in advance." In the wake of the row, the person hired to give him media training to help control his public persona quit, after just three days on the job.

Amidst all this activity, 'All Of The Lights' was put out as the album's fourth single, peaking at number 18 in the US after the release of a Hype Williams video featuring Kanye, Kid Cudi and Rihanna drenched in multi-coloured strobe lighting that earned the clip a warning for potentially initiating epileptic fits. *My Beautiful Dark Twisted Fantasy*, released on November 22, hit the *Billboard* chart at number one, selling 496,000 copies in the first week and quickly reaching platinum status of over a million sold, and as of July 2013, it had sold 1.3 million copies. It was Kanye's fourth number one album in a row, and even though it would only chart at number 16 in the UK, West was dead on course to re-conquer the globe.

But to ensure his success, it was time to bond properly with big brother.

CHAPTER TWELVE

Watch The Throne

Precisely as planned, Kanye hit the hotels.

Initially *Watch The Throne*, an equal-footed collaboration between Kanye and Jay-Z, was going to be an EP. Five tracks, recorded on the hoof, wherever the two could get together. Their schedules didn't allow for much spare recording time, with Kanye still working on promoting *My Beautiful Dark Twisted Fantasy* and its remaining singles and Jay beginning work on the follow-up to his latest smash album *The Blueprint 3*. So inevitably, *Watch The Throne* came together in chunks. Starting in November 2010, whenever a gap came up in both of their diaries they'd fly to a convenient studio – Avex in Honolulu, Real World in Wiltshire, Electric Ladyland in New York – to work on tracks, or set up a portable studio in luxury hotel suites in Paris, Abu Dhabi, LA and the South of France. In Australia, when the pair convened for a lengthy period of time on the private Barford Estate in Sydney, Jay invited Russell Crowe to the studio to hear himself get name-dropped on a track, while Bruno Mars and Seal arrived to contribute to a number called 'Lift Off'.

It was to be a record made in first class, on a global holiday in some of the world's finest hotels with clusters of A-list celebrities on hand to bring the party glamour. These were quite possibly the most extravagant recording sessions ever held, and the choice of samples they were working on to make huge, bombastic songs were some of the costliest in music too – James Brown's most famous tunes, Otis Redding, Nina Simone and chunks of dialogue from Will Ferrell's *Blades Of Glory* movie pointing out just how expensive everything sounded. From the sound of it, Jay and Kanye had chosen the dream way to make a record. But, early on, things weren't exactly harmonious. Between sessions both Jay and Kanye were developing their own idea of what sort of record they should make together, so on the rare occasions they could come together these two gargantuan egos, both used to calling the shots, would quickly descend into heated arguments over the direction they should take, rows so horrendous that it would put Jay-Z off the idea of doing another collaboration for the foreseeable future. Jay would later claim the album went through "three iterations" as they scaled down their visions of the enormous, dramatic sound they wanted. And it would also quickly become clear that a five track EP would never encapsulate everything they wanted *Watch The Throne* to be. Sonically it was shrinking, but at the same time it grew into a full album.

The criticisms of those around them helped shape the record too. "Early on, I felt like Jay and Kanye were icons and I told them I didn't agree, as a fan, with the direction they were going," said No I.D. "Everybody's looking at me like, 'Who are you?' I'm like, 'I'm just me, but I want my feelings on the record that I want more from you guys. It's not even about who does it. I just want more from you icons. I want you guys to push it forward. You're going to sell, because you're already big. But you guys are important to push this forward. Push intelligence and decadence and all of the above forward in a creative manner'… I had been working with both of them a lot up to the point of making those statements, and then after I made those statements, I just kind of didn't come around much any more. They were like, 'Man, what's up?'

"I was like, 'I told you, that's not where I want to go, and I don't think y'all should go there'. And I was like, 'Yeah. I'll pass up the money and everything, and I'll go do something else, because I believe in what I believe in – right or wrong'. A lot of times with people like that, the people around them have opinions, but their security is being around them. They saw me say, 'I'll just go do Big Sean while you do that', and it was more credible at that point, even though we had known each other and worked together. It was like, 'Wow, you'll really just go work on that and make that really good? You know what, your points have been earned here'."

Hence, much of the material from these odd sessions around the globe would ultimately be scrapped for being too unwieldy and grandiose, eventually making up barely half of the finished album, though from the Real World Sessions they kept sections of 'Why I Love You', 'Illest Motherfucker Alive', 'H★A★M' and 'Murder To Excellence'; from Honolulu 'The Joy' and 'That's My Bitch' survived; from sessions at the five-star Le Meurice Hotel in Paris they kept parts of 'Niggas In Paris' and 'New Day'; and from the Sydney session 'Lift Off' made the cut. But one key track quickly made it into the public domain. 'H★A★M', an acronym for 'hard as a motherfucker', acted as a showcase for the operatic grandeur that Kanye and Jay had initially wanted for *Watch The Throne*: warbling opera singers, Wagnerian orchestras crashing like mighty waves and hip-hop's two biggest names spitting rhymes like avenging theatrical demons. Kanye introduced the project by claiming that it'll be so amazing it'll make rappers who were previously satisfied with their work want to kill themselves in shame, and boasted of his inter-racial sexual conquests while Jay-Z rapped about doing all of the things lesser rappers would die trying to achieve. "Watch the throne, don't step on our robe," Jay told the rap world; the bold bombast of 'H★A★M' acted as their self-coronation.

Released on January 11, 2011 as a digital download only, the song made number 23, instantly justifying the worth of the project. Suddenly they were married to the album, but knew that if it was ever going to be finished they'd have to take a different approach to recording. It would only be a cohesive record, Jay argued, if they set aside a fixed amount of time to make it rather than piecing it together bit by bit. "If we were gonna do it, we were gonna do it together," he told a small gathering of journalists at the first playback of the album that summer, "no mailing it in."

So, shortly after the release of 'H★A★M' in January, Kanye and Jay booked out a raft of hotel rooms at both the Mercer Hotel and Tribeca Grand in Manhattan, and turned the hotels into their own recording complex. They installed recording equipment, recruited their favourite beatmakers – Swizz, Mike Dean, Jeff Bhasker and others – and invited guests to come to deliver their rhymes in this salubrious impromptu studio, turning the hotels into buzzing hives of engineers, producers and artists. Since the hotels were so handy for a large number of New York rap notaries, unlike the Hawaii sessions *Watch The Throne* turned into an artistic and celebrity free-for-all, with all contributions welcomed. Kid Cudi, Mr Hudson, Frank Ocean and Beyoncé all paraded through the recording suites. Producer 88-Keys stopped by one day to catch up with Kanye – Kanye asked him if he happened to have any beats with him and Keys stayed and produced 'No Church In The Wild' within days. Givenchy's creative director Riccardo Tisci, the man recruited to design a very high-fashion sleeve for the album, popped in with fashion designer Phoebe Philo to experience the intense but always light-hearted recording. Both hotels shook with the heavy beat of creativity, music pumping from every room.

Between sessions, Kanye remained relentlessly busy. When he wasn't chasing women, being linked to model Kate Upton and allegedly getting his entourage to request the phone number of Victoria's Secret Angel Candice Swanepoel, he was wrapping up his various twisted fantasies. He was hard at work on two seasons of fashion shows in Paris, although the first, premiering his DW women's line – created in association with a team of 'ghost' designers, including the UK's Louise Golden – was a critical disaster. In the run-up to the show insiders claimed his plans were unworkable. "He was prone to changing his mind a lot," an anonymous source told Grazia Daily. "In fact the whole process was slightly excruciating as there were so many opinions that it took forever to get anything done… [It] will be extraordinarily expensive, some of it is virtually unproduceable." When the show arrived, watched by Jared Leto, Sky Ferreira and Lindsay Lohan, it was ridiculed by critics for being over-elaborate and featuring bottom-exposing hotpants, slashed bandage dresses, $6,000 shoes, fur collars in a spring collection and awkwardly placed zips. "Good thing Kanye has a day job," wrote the *Wall Street Journal*'s fashion blogger. "The only thing more painful than witnessing the dress was watching the model pitch down the runway in shoes so ill-fitting that her spike heels were bending at angles. One breastplate of a top – recalled the Flintstones... There were lots and lots of tight leather pants... Yet a vast quantity of luxury materials can't blind people to a lack of creative marksmanship." "Kanye West's fashion debut was like being subjected to an hour long MRI scan – but not as much fun," added *The Daily Telegraph*'s Lisa Armstrong.

"We don't know what the reviews will be," Kanye tweeted in the show's aftermath, "we don't know what they will say, but I got a chance to go to Italy and feel those fabrics... I took out motherfucking loans to get the best models, to get the best designers, to get the best venue. I gave you everything that I had.... This is my first collection. Please be easy. Please give me a chance to grow. This is not some celebrity shit. I don't fuck with celebrities. I fuck with the creatives in this room, the amazing people who spend every day of their life trying to make the world a more beautiful place. The amount of people that tried to get me a celebrity fucking deal. They said, 'You need to do boot-cut jeans, or you won't sell.' Shut the fuck up !... I can only grow from this point."

His second collection would go down better, but Kanye would close his personal line shortly afterwards, putting the criticism down to the fact that he wasn't an established designer who was "in a position to go crazy. I tried to come out of the gate going crazy. And it didn't work. So now I have to somehow put out something that says, 'I look sensible!'... The first collection was way better than the second. It was more artful. It was 30 collections in one. It just takes time for me to slow down and think like a normal person."

Over the spring and summer of 2011, Kanye also caused sensation on the festival circuit, with a grandiose production of classical spectacle and flouncing ballerinas. At the South By Southwest event in Austin on March 20, he brought out Bon Iver, Cudi, John Legend and Jay-Z to create the most talked-about set of the week; at Coachella he caused a stampede to the tent to see Justin Vernon hoisted high on a white cube pedestal in a white suit, swathed in pyrotechnics and surrounded by half-dressed feather-clad dancers as Kanye himself was lowered onstage from a crane. "Sunday night at Coachella with just the 80,000 people watching us," Vernon said. "That was pretty wild." He knows my scene. He knows I can't dance and shit. But I showed up and they were like 'Uh, you should probably put on some of these white clothes.' They gave me a bunch of white clothes and just said, 'Go up there'. It was surreal; it was cool to be a part of that big of a visual production but I'm not capable of constructing something like that for myself."

At Morocco's Mawazine Festival or Milwaukee's Summerfest, at Australia's Splendour In The Grass or the UK's Big Chill★, Denmark's Tivoli Gardens or Norway's Way Out West, it was Kanye they raced to see, mingling *My Beautiful Dark Twisted Fantasy* tracks into Jay-Z, Queen and Katy Perry covers and his own inimitable classics in his fresh red suit. He dotted his sets with eye-grabbing ideas – with 'H★A★M' as his introduction tape, the stage would fill with phoenix dancers scurrying wildly across the stage as the backdrop fell to reveal a classical portrait of Athena and Nike fighting Alkyoneus as Gaia rises as Kanye emerged on a white podium to hellfire operatic choirs. 'Hell Of A Life' was drenched in pyrotechnics and showers of sparks and, for the encore, the stage would fill with a billowing white sheet to the tune of Vangelis' 'Chariots Of Fire' before being pulled back to reveal classically dressed dancers and Kanye poised on a podium to play 'Runaway' surrounded by black-clad ballerinas jerking in freakish poses and slumping to the ground during the bridge. It was, without a doubt, one of the most theatrical and spectacular hip-hop festival shows in history. He'd learnt his U2 lesson well.

At the same time, in some quarters, Kanye was being demonised once more. Outfits such as a Zoolander-style leopardprint jacket and harem pants were mocked by the style press, and his attitude towards

---

★ The Big Chill was the scene of more controversy, as Kanye likened himself to Hitler onstage. "I walk through the hotel and I walk down the street, and people look at me like I'm fucking insane, like I'm Hitler," he said, having arrived onstage half an hour late due to vocal issues. "One day the light will shine through and one day people will understand everything I ever did."

women was called into question several times. Singer Lily Allen reacted angrily towards an ill-advised tweet from Kanye about abortion – 'An abortion can cost a ballin' nigga up to 50gs maybe a 100," he tweeted, "Gold diggin' bitches be getting pregnant on purpose. #STRAPUP my niggas!" And an unedited snippet of the video for 'Monster' was leaked in December 2010, and caused a stir amongst the feminist-leaning elements of the media. Inspired by classic gothic horror films, modern slasher hits such as *American Psycho* and *Saw* and a supposedly haunted 1972 painting by Bill Stoneham called *The Hands Resist Him*★, the video was set in a Frankenstein-style castle and featured models hanging by the neck from chains, decapitated or naked and unconscious – presumably dead – and being manipulated by Kanye in a bed. Though ghouls grasped at Kanye's naked flesh through an iron gate, zombies ate the innards of bodies and a vampiric Minaj tortured her own Barbie alter-ego, it was the depiction of passive, unconscious or dead women as being in some way erotic that met with the most objection. "What would have become of John Mayer, had he cut a video with dead black women strewn about and invoked black women throughout his lyrics in the manner Kanye does?" asked *The Atlantic*'s Ta-Nehisi Coates, labelling the video both sexist and racist, while Daphne Bramham of the *Vancouver Sun* asked "What's entertaining about women in lingerie hanging by their necks on chains? What's artful about images of drugged, unconscious women about to be sexually assaulted?" in an article titled 'Let's Label This Depravity For What It Is: Misogyny'. Activist Ann Simonton launched an online petition to get the video withdrawn from any sort of public broadcast, claiming that it glorified sexual violence against women. MTV banned it. When it finally emerged in June 2011, it came with a disclaimer attached: "The following content is in no

---

★ The painting of a young girl and boy standing in front of a dark glass door against which ghostly hands are pressed was purchased during its first exhibition in the early seventies – the owner of the gallery and the critic who reviewed the show all died soon after the exhibition. When the painting later appeared for sale on eBay the sellers claimed that the painting was cursed, and that they'd seen the figures in it move in the night, and even leave the painting altogether.

way to be interpreted as misogynistic or negative towards any groups of people," read a message at the start of the clip, making no apologies and insisting the viewer take Kanye's view of the piece. "It is an art piece and it shall be taken as such."

The world would take *Watch The Throne* as Kanye and Jay intended them to as well. On July 4 it was made available for pre-order on Jay's Life + Times lifestyle website in standard and deluxe editions, the Deluxe Editions including four extra tracks – 'H★A★M', 'The Illest Motherfucker Alive', 'Primetime' and 'The Joy' which included a sample of Curtis Mayfield's 'The Makings Of You'. The first two fans placing their order for the record were given prize spots at a press playback at the Mercer Hotel three days later: Jay-Z personally played journalists the entire album from his MacBook, in the very rooms where it was recorded.

Meanwhile, the second track from *Watch The Throne* to be released to the public was one of the best to emerge from the Mercer Hotel sessions, and a big favourite of the press at the playback. On Funkmaster Flex's radio show on July 19, ahead of its release as a digital download, a track called 'Otis' was aired, its title a dedication and tribute to Otis Redding whose instantly recognisable voice opened the song. "Sounds so soulful, don't you agree?" Jay said as Kanye looped Redding's seminal 'Try A Little Tenderness' into a passionate jive, a piece of hip-hop magic that came about from an on-the-spot challenge from No I.D., annoyed that Kanye and Jay were using too many co-producers and weren't hands-on enough with making their own music.

"I kinda didn't agree with the direction that *Watch The Throne* was going," said I.D. of the day he challenged Kanye to make a beat on his own, thereby creating Otis. "I felt like, 'Y'all were two of the best that did it as far as advancing, pushing the bar, the envelope of what hip-hop can do and is'. And I felt like some of the songs were copping out a little to me. I get the co-productions, but how you gon' do an album and you don't go to the machine and do one beat by yourself? We have always sparked this challenge in each other and it bled into the world, so I just wanted to hit him in the stomach real quick. This is what you got? He was like, 'No, that's cool. I'm 'bout to do something'. I remember even at the time at the label they was like, 'What the hell? No I.D. just came in and messed up our release schedule'. We all amongst ourselves really are battling each other each and every minute of life, but it's all in the spirit of advancement and the pursuit of dopeness, is what I call it."

"It was just conversation between me, Jay, Kanye, and a few other people," he continued, "I think Q-Tip was there. It just came out because they were like, 'What do you have for the album?' They played what they had, and I was like, 'I don't know if I have anything with this direction. It's just not what I do. If I do it I've got to really think it out and make it creative – and I don't have that right now. I don't even know if I *want* to have that right now'… It wasn't like I was better than this or that, or that what they were doing wasn't good. It was just that, at that moment, that wasn't a path that any of us had done musically, and I didn't understand why we were going there… I just felt like, 'That's not what I thought we were going to do'… There's a Kanye element that people want. We can't get a Kanye/Jay-Z album without that.

"Specifically 'Otis', that was the record. I was like, 'The sample record that Kanye does with no co-producer, where is that? The record that's not based on anything else that has that personality that he does?' We challenge each other, so I was like, 'You're just going to do an album, and you're not going to do one of those? What's up?' Kanye was like, 'OK. I got that', and they did it a couple days later."

It was a bold statement for both rappers; by placing themselves shamelessly alongside a major soul icon such as Otis – and later on the same track, James Brown's 'Don't Tell A Lie About Me And I Won't Tell The Truth About You', as well as 'Top Billin' by Audio Two – they were ramping up their own cultural significance to the status of modern legend, and their raps were just as brazen. Not only did Jay claim that he'd first invented the very concept of 'swag' that new acts such as Odd Future were now dotting through their rhymes, he set about a bout of extreme braggadocio to make *Watch The Throne* sound like the most extravagant rap album ever. He rapped about cruising Manhattan in his Maybach with his $200,000 watch on display, so rich that, were he to murder someone who criticised his partner Kanye, he could flee in a private jet and buy asylum in whatever country he ended up, so wealthy he was above the law. His final verse had more of a social conscience, stating that an underworld of heroic immigrants were becoming very rich from dealing drugs right underneath America's nose, proudly "driving Benzes with no benefits" and thereby smashing a crooked and repressive system. Kanye's lines, meanwhile, bragged of his luxurious tastes, travels and talents – "the Hermès of verses/ Sophisticated ignorance, write my curses in cursive". The sort of skills that were destroying the rest of rap's "lames".

Directed by promo legend Spike Jonze, the video for 'Otis' was suitably flagrant. In a frenzy of exuberant destruction, Jay and Kanye ripped apart a Maybach, pulling off doors, smashing out windows and skidding and speeding around an industrial lot in the wreckage, sparks and flames spewing from the wheels and models in every spare seat.* The clip encapsulated the fundamental tenets of fun, carefree creativity and extravagance that defined the *Watch The Throne* project, and the song screeched into the chart at number 12, sold 440,000 copies and earned a Grammy. Though the closest the track had to a hook was the Redding sample, critics raved, and anticipation for *Watch The Throne* went through the roof.

Everything about *Watch The Throne*, when it arrived, stank of money. The title spoke of power and riches. The Riccardo Tisci-designed sleeve was sheer, solid gold. The promotional T-shirts were designed by Givenchy and priced at $300 each. The price tag for the album came in at an estimated $2 million. Even the launch party swaggered; celebrities and industry were invited to a playback at the Earth And Space section of the American Museum Of Natural History on August 1, a reflection of the album's celestial brilliance. Released via Roc-A-Fella, Roc Nation and Def Jam, it was grand, opulent and so supremely ambitious that it's impossible to imagine how cataclysmic their original plans for the sound must have been, if this was the tamed-down version. The album thrived on the dynamics and dissonance of the two personalities that created it. Jay was the high-living, multi-millionaire elder statesman and family

---

* The car was eventually auctioned for the East African Drought Disaster charity.

man with the dark past, a street hustler who'd become a besuited hip-hop mogul and icon of business respectability, while Kanye played the loudmouth egotist and sexual predator with a taste for sonic demonics. Borrowing the deviant electro-tribalism and synthetic rock moods of Kanye's later albums, it threw Jay-Z into Kanye's dark, broiling rap volcano. And Jay found he was a born phoenix.

Akin to a stray tentacle that had been cleaved off of 'Monster' but still squirmed with life, opener 'No Church In The Wild' was a slab of Southern Gothic swamp rock seething with voodoo blues menace and laced with the yowls of James Brown, producer 88-Keys having sampled Brown's 'Don't Tell A Lie About Me And I Won't Tell The Truth About You' as well as 'K-Scope' by Phil Manzanera and 'Sunshine Help Me' by Spooky Tooth, and the drums of a woodland sacrifice. It steamed and slimed with the vibes of Tom Waits, Queens Of The Stone Age and Alabama 3, yet added a modernist hip-hop energy with its death-ray synths and ominous soul chorus from Frank Ocean. Ocean was a singer and member of rising controversial rap collective Odd Future that Jay had discovered from hearing his mix-tape *Nostalgia, Ultra* – and his introductory drawl set the quasi-religious atmosphere of 'No Church…'. "Human beings in a mob, what's a mob to a king?" he asked, "What's a king to a God? What's a God to a non-believer?" A study of the futility of power and ego, it asked the existential question of where faith, hope and survival lie in a Godless world full of leaders with only their own selfish interests at heart, where every position of influence is rendered irrelevant by each higher level of mindset. The implication was that power was worthless unless it was respected, but the atheist, with no power at all, who was in the most precarious position, out in the wild with no church for refuge. "Will he make it out alive?" Ocean asked.

Against this backdrop of humanity damned by its own self-interest, Jay and Kanye each laid out their own personal religion, steeped in Biblical, ancient Greek and Roman imagery. For Jay, up first, it was the hustler life and the ways in which it clashed with the church and the law. He found righteous reasons for the illegal acts he'd committed in his dealing days – if there was an all-knowing God, he argued, then

He would know that some acts deemed wrong by society aren't nearly so black-and-white. And there was hypocrisy throughout the system too: the religious figures who were damning him for his crimes were, he pointed out, liars and charlatans themselves, and Jay even explored Plato's Euthyphro dilemma – "Is Pious pious 'cause God loves pious?" – a reference to Socrates' philosophical question as to whether a person or deed is good within itself or if it's good because God loves it. As you'd expect from a rapper whose use of unconventional and cult-like symbolism had led to rumours of his involvement in some sort of shadowy Illuminati, ultimately he mocked religion by likening himself and Kanye to the Holy Ghost and Jesus respectively. Like the Beatles in '66, they were at least as big, if not bigger, than the Holy Trinity.

Kanye's verse, on the other hand, cast lust as his own true faith. Whether chopping out lines of cocaine on girls' skin, having threesomes or condoning all sorts of sexual proclivity – "No sins as long as there's permission/Deception is the only felony" – Kanye advocated a free-for-all approach to sex. He even came out in favour of polygamy as an unnatural human state: "Love is cursed by monogamy", he rapped. From the man behind 'Jesus Walks', this was a sign of a psyche reassessing his traditional religious morals in light of the ups and downs of life experience that had thrown him through the previous few years.

A lion's roar, a brief haunted carnival interlude and we had 'Lift Off'. An ornate, classically tinted piece based around a spacecraft ignition sequence – the song sampled actual audio from the Apollo 11 mission – it was the countdown for a record about to blast into the stratosphere – Beyoncé sassily declaring, "We're gonna take it to the moon, take it to the stars!" over celebratory synth fanfares and synthetic drums that resembled a welcoming parade to mark Jay and Kanye's arrival on this new rap planet. Although there was little in the way of a message to the track beyond what an intergalactically brilliant record they were making, Kanye did at least let slip some personal information on 'Lift Off', that he had tattoos on his arm of some of the pre-*College Dropout* songs he'd worked on that were the most important to him, specifically 'You Made Me', 'This Is My Life', 'So Ghetto', 'The Truth', 'This Can't Be Life', 'Nothing Like It', 'Izzo (The Anthem)', 'Hey Mama', 'Heart Of The

City' and 'Never Change'. The song would become the third of seven singles released from the album on August 23, dividing critics and making no significant dent on the charts, but it was a key hype song on *Watch The Throne* and gave way to a slowed-down sample of Baptist minister Reverend W.A. Donaldson's 1959 recording of 'Baptizing Scene', an introduction to the album's most memorable song of all.

'Niggas In Paris' was a church-like baller tune full of diamond-bright synths and dark tribal drums; a track that celebrated Jay and Kanye's incredible lifestyles as they spread their wealth across Europe, a toast to the fact that a one-time criminal like Jay was free and rich enough to live the highest life possible, partying for six days straight with models in $20,000-a-night suites at Le Meurice, drinking nothing but Armand de Brignac champagne and staggering out for A-list catwalk shows. "If you escaped what I escaped, you'd be in Paris getting fucked up too", he sniggered between jibes at the NBA who'd fined him $50,000 for visiting the locker room of the Kentucky Wildcats, as his position as a minority owner of the Nets team forbade him from mixing with college basketball players. Kanye, meanwhile, played on the album's royal theme by imagining himself in the place of Prince William, who'd married Kate Middleton that summer. "She said ''Ye, can we get married in the Mall?','" he rapped, picturing a high-class girl trying to pin him down, but explaining that if he had his pick of every woman in the world he'd personally go for more down-to-earth girls: "Prince William ain't do it right if you ask me/'Cause I was him, I would have married Kate and Ashley" (actress and fashion designer twins Mary-Kate and Ashley Olsen).

The track contained some of the most recognisable moments in modern rap, such as a final section of studio buzz, synthesized monks and bursts of static, and a section where Kanye's verse broke down at the line "got my niggas in Paris and they're going gorillas" to mock the incomprehensibility of some rap lyrics with some dialogue from *Blades Of Glory*. "I don't even know what that means!" said Jon Heder, to which Will Ferrell replies, "No-one knows what it means, but it's provocative. It gets the people going!" But probably the most lasting legacy of 'Niggas In Paris' was Kanye's phrase "that shit cray", which was taken up by a generation as a tongue-in-cheek statement of general appreciation and even caused a storm of Twitter debate over whether it was a reference to the Kray twins, famous London mobsters of the sixties.

On its September 13 release 'Niggas In Paris' was a huge smash, selling two million and reaching number five on the *Billboard* chart. On the subsequent tour, the song was so popular that the duo would perform it multiple times each night, getting a better and better reaction each time. At the first show in Atlanta on October 28 they played it three times; by the time the tour finished they were playing the song 11 times at every show.

Little could follow 'Niggas In Paris' live, but on record they trumped the track with a torrent of soul legends. First Otis, then James Brown, sampled by the Neptunes on the hook for the haunting, minimalist 'Gotta Have It', which also sampled three Brown songs: 'My Thang', 'Don't Tell A Lie About Me And I Won't Tell The Truth About You' and 'People Get Up And Drive Your Funky Soul'. Another single from the album that would be released on December 6, it was a fuzzy, experimental piece built around a spectral harpsichord, filthy synths and an airy female melody. Lyrically, the track tackled the African-American's natural desire for money and success, and the powers that kept them from it or wanted to away. Kanye's verse shifted from complaints about his character being assassinated over his Taylor Swift and Katrina outbursts – "Money matrimony, yeah they tryna break the marriage up" – to boasting of his private jets and huge club parties schmoozing radio executives in Miami, with Jay-Z interjecting more talk of million dollar watches. Jay's own verse was more gangsta, opening with a scene where he kidnaps a family to force a debtor to pay up before cruising the streets of New York and Chicago, a proud part of the rise of moneyed black men in Maybachs. Tense and dexterous, 'Gotta Have It' was one of the album's most accomplished pieces of interplay between the two stars, Kanye and Jay passing lines like championship basketball players.

Jay and Kanye had had very different opinions of Auto-Tune, Kanye utilising it to tremendous effect and Jay declaring it dead on 'The Death Of Auto-Tune' from 2009's *The Blueprint 3*. On the chilling 'New Day', Kanye won Jay over as guest producer RZA's backing track of maudlin piano and shuffling beat accompanied a sample of Nina Simone singing her classic 'Feeling Good' fed through the software. As the track progressed the sample was shifted from the highest setting of Auto-Tune down to the lowest, so that it became gradually more human, less computer. Over this increasingly moving and fleshed-out backing, Jay and Kanye recited open letters to their unborn sons, the unknowing heirs to the … *Throne*. Kanye hoped his son wouldn't be as egotistical, inconsiderate, racially insensitive and full of lust as he'd been, in order that he might not be as hated, judged or publically pilloried. He also took the time to regret his relationship choices, wishing he'd never left Sumeke or taken up with Amber Rose in the lines "I'll never let him leave his college girlfriend and get caught up with groupies in the whirlwind… I'll never let him ever hit a strip club/I learnt the hard way, that ain't the place to get love". Jay, who possibly already knew he was due to be a father, apologised to his child for the instant celebrity he felt would ruin their young life before it had even begun, but promised to fast-track them to the right path which he himself had taken so many years to find. And, so as not to repeat the sins of his own father, Jay said he'd never leave, "even if his mother tweaking". It was a touching track; on an album drenched in arrogant extravagance, 'New Day' oozed humility, selflessness and love.

The focus then turned to the women in their lives. 'That's My Bitch', a sister-piece to 'My Beautiful Dark Twisted Fantasy' as it too involved guest spots from La Roux's Ellie Jackson and Justin Vernon, showed little respect but actually felt like a dance-floor celebration of the female form, set to a propulsive electronic jungle pulse adorned with euphoric pop choruses, with beats sampled from another James Brown track, 'Get Up, Get Into It, Get Involved' as well as the Incredible Bongo Band's 'Apache'. On his verse, Kanye delved further into his relationship with Rose, telling of the attention she'd get at celebrity parties and how he'd taught her to become accustomed to the high life – the yachts, expensive art and front row seats at basketball games. There was a tinge of regret to these memories of a "twisted love story… Mary Magdalene from a pole dance", offset by Jay's verse, an all-out celebration of Beyoncé and other famous minority women. Halle Berry, Salma Hayek and Penélope Cruz, he argued, should be held up as paragons of beauty to rival the Mona Lisa – "Marilyn Monroe, she's quite nice/But why are all the pretty icons always all white?" And as for his own wife, not only was she "gangsta" and no gold-digger ("Told me keep my own money if we ever did split up"), but she was a work of art worthy of a place in the Museum Of Modern Art.

Having admired what he had, next he mourned what he'd lost. Kanye played only a small role in 'Welcome To The Jungle', an insistent synth rock beat from Swizz Beatz, joining Swizz himself on the hook and rapping a few lines about the pain of losing his mother between Jay's passionate verses that paid tribute to his fallen compadres. Biggie, Tupac, Pimp C (the UKG rapper and guest on 'Big Pimpin'' who died in his sleep in 2007) and Michael Jackson were all honoured as well as the family members he saw die and more metaphorical losses. He'd lost his childhood to selling crack and his faith from the struggles he'd endured. Becoming increasingly desperate and despairing as he raked over memories of internalising the pain of losing Biggie, turning to the shallow highs of champagne and dope to get him through and realizing that his celebrity and high connections don't help him in his darkest moments, this was one of the most revealing verses of Jay's career, a glimpse of the grief and torment behind the money, glitz and glamour. Here was proof that all the money in the world couldn't wipe clean every speck of life's grit.

From the personal, the record swung back to the political. Over an intense dubstep barrage of filth and fuzz sampled from Flux Pavilion's 'I Can't Stop', Kanye's distorted voice mutters "this is something like the Holocaust", sounding like he's rapping from the other end of a military radio. This was 'Who Gon Stop Me' and Kanye was referring to the "millions of our people lost" throughout America's history, victims of slavery, crime, poverty and disease. So, having escaped such a fate and become an inspirational figure to other black kids striving for success, Kanye was determined not to be stopped from living the most extravagant lifestyle possible. Weird sex, unconventional relationships, flagrant cash-flashing: Kanye was using the historical sublimation of his race to justify his showy and excessive life, suggesting that if generations had died to get him where he was, he and his culture had earned the right to flaunt it. With Jay's verse also honouring his own success – how he was such a born winner he could do it all again from scratch if necessary, 'Who Gon Stop Me' was a Top 50 US hit despite never being officially released as a single, on download figures alone.

After a plethora of songs obsessed with wealth and status, 'Who Gon Stop Me' was the start of a far more socially conscious closing section of *Watch The Throne*, and their next topic of discussion was gun crime. 'Murder To Excellence' was dedicated to Danroy Henry, an unarmed college student who was shot by police in 2010, and came in two distinct parts. The first – 'Murder' – was a strident slab of seditious bongo, rusted beats, doom-laden piano and acoustic strums put together by Swizz Beatz and topped off with a noble and spirited children's choir, sampled from Indiggo's 'La La La', and tackled the fact that the residue of centuries of poverty and slavery in America was an entire culture racked with desperation, violence and "black-on-black murder", and a police force ready to shoot first and ask questions later. In his opening verse, Jay begged the wannabe gangstas of the projects to stop shooting each other since "we on the same team" and there was already "too much enemy fire to catch a friendly". He posited himself as a figure of hope for them to rally behind, dreaming of inspiring a real unity amongst black youth: "What up blood? What up cuz? It's all black, I love us".

Kanye soon struck in with his own warning shots. "I'm from the murder capital where they murder for capital," he rapped – a line repurposed from Jay-Z's 'Lucifer' – later quoting the fact that there were more homicides in Chicago in 2008 than deaths of US soldiers in Iraq, earning the city the nickname Chiraq. Noting new murders in his hometown every day and that there were "41 souls murdered in 50 hours" in Chicago gang shootings between March 31 and April 2, 2010, he likened this wave of killing to a "genocide" and painted a disturbing picture of a family ripped apart by gang violence and the pain left behind: "I can still hear his mama cry/Know the family left traumatised/ Shots left holes in his face about piranha size". His point was that there's no achievement in the poor and downtrodden fighting amongst themselves, besides further ghettoisation and that "it's time for us to stop and redefine black power". He was preaching a shift in the black pride mentality away from the violent associations of the Black Panthers and towards a more instinctive pride in their race, entrepreneurism and its associated extravagances. This was rousing, inspirational and emotive stuff, out to redefine an entire culture.

To which end came 'Excellence', the second part of the track produced by S1 from a similar choir sped up until they sounded like poltergeists skipping along to menacing piano chords and, with samples from Quincy Jones' 'Celie Shaves Mr./Scarification Ceremony', the central crux of the entire album. Out to celebrate "black excellence" wherever they saw it, Kanye and Jay-Z redefined what it was to be young and black in America in 2011. They rapped of exclusive VIP clubs, boardrooms and reaching the highest levels of public influence, describing the "new black elite" they were both a part of alongside Obama, Oprah, Will Smith and others who'd broken into "the promised land of the OGs". This long-awaited change was proving slow in seeping through all levels of society though, they argued – "only spot a few blacks the higher up I go," Jay complained, looking around his Presidential functions, "that ain't enough, we gonna need a million more", while Kanye mused, "In the past if you picture events like a black tie/What's the last thing you expect to see? Black guys". Kanye rapped that this, and the fact that the average life expectancy of black men was only 21, were signs that the racist and genocidal American social system was working just as the white majority had designed it to. And *Watch The Throne*, with its metaphors of black ascendance and affections of royalty, was all about obliterating that tainted glass ceiling.

The album's gracefully electronic penultimate track, 'Made In America', was the inauguration speech of the new black elite. "I'm tryna lead a nation to leave to my little mans or my daughter," rapped Jay-Z over industrial pings and delicate piano tinkles resembling a synthesizer version of Bruce Springsteen's 'Philadelphia', "the scales was lopsided, I'm just restoring order". Frank Ocean's lush hook, thanking Martin Luther King and Malcolm X for paving the way for the rise of the likes of Jay and Kanye and praising the lord because "we made it in America" was similarly inspirational, and Kanye posed himself as a great success story on another verse ditching college for rap against his mother's advice and setting about building an empire of beats, fashion lines and hugely popular websites. Finally, in an artful closing verse Jay refashioned the Pledge Of Allegiance for this new leader state – suddenly 'Made In America' became the national anthem of an empire built on family, drugs and street honour.

A record as bombastic as *Watch The Throne* couldn't fade politely out though – it needed a climactic blaze of glory. Cue 'Why I Love You', a track released as a single on the same day as 'Niggas In Paris' and produced by Kanye around a sample from Cassius' 'I Love You So'. But his distorted, degraded and monstrous slab of *Graduation*-style synthetic arena rock, given an infectious pop twist by Mr Hudson's lusty sped-up bellow of a hook, was virtually Kaye's only contribution to the song. West took a back seat as Jay detailed the bitter break-up of Roc-A-Fella and his falling out with one-time protégé Beanie Sigel – after Sigel was jailed for a year on federal weapons charges and Jay wouldn't take responsibility for guaranteeing his whereabouts when a hearing came up to discuss his early release, and when he was released, Jay also kept him locked up in his contract with Def Jam when a better offer from G Unit came along. Cue a barrage of beef between the two, which Jay addressed in his passionate verses on 'Why I Love You'. Casting himself as a betrayed leader akin to Julius Caeser or Jesus, he rapped of burning thrones and crumbling empires, of Jay left tormented and alone in his corner office, hated and hounded by his most trusted associates. Yet the emotional root of the song was of a frustrated brotherly love that still beat strong, hence Hudson's hook, "I love you so, but why I love you I'll never know".

Watch The Throne was always intended to rule the world, and within seven days of its August 8 release it had conquered. Released on iTunes five days before the physical release to attempt to combat online leaks, it debuted at number one on the iTunes store in 23 countries and sold a record 290,000 units on iTunes alone, beating the record held by Coldplay, but Jay and Kanye's tenure would be short-lived as Lil Wayne would beat it by 10,000 sales less than a month later. And the physical sales weren't harmed by the move; the record was a *Billboard* number one hit from 436,000 first week sales. Publications from cult to mainstream roared its praises. "A beautifully decadent album by two of hip-hop's finest artists," wrote *Time*, "men with a lot of things to say and a lot of money to spend". "An audacious spectacle of vacuous pomposity as well as one of tremendous lyrical depth," wrote Allmusic. "They're hip-hop monarchs, and *Watch the Throne,* doesn't shrink from its own hype… This is an album that takes aim at the history books." claimed *Rolling Stone*.

There was a real sense with *Watch The Throne* that Jay and Kanye – and, indeed, rap itself – had reached the highest peaks of popular culture. They were outselling the rock'n'roll giants, and had broken through cultural barriers to become accepted and loved far beyond their niche beginnings. They were pop culture figures dictating fashion, music and even changes in racial and social attitudes. These were the monsters that really had become Gods.

And such an album needed a live spectacle to match. Stretching over 57 dates between October 28, 2011 in Atlanta and June 22, 2012 in Birmingham, England, the *Watch The Throne* joint arena tour broke all box-office records for a rap tour, with almost $50 million taken in the US and Canada leg alone. The performance raised the bar for hip-hop concert production, with Jay and Kanye emerging to 'H★A★M' on two identical rising hydraulic mini-stage cubes at either end of the arena, basking in eye-scorching bursts of laser and fireballs, each cube made up of screens showing footage of swimming sharks or snarling Rottweilers – designer Es Devlin put the show together under Kanye's direction of "Attenborough BBC wildlife content and lasers". Between them they tag-teamed up to 39 tracks every night, the biggest hits from each of their individual back catalogues plus every song from *Watch The Throne*. It's been described as the most spectacular rap show ever staged.

Though he'd put together monochrome behind-the-scenes short films towards the end of the tour and post them online as part of a short-lived series called VOYR, Kanye would claim that he was a dark presence on the tour; less comfortable with the touring life than Jay and not as at ease with spending so much time on his own, he'd often think he looked like the miserable one of the pair, as though he wasn't enjoying himself. But the tour was a great bonding exercise for the two, a chance for Kanye to connect with Jay like he never had before. During breaks in the *Watch The Throne* tour, Kanye even played his own shows, most notably a run of Australian festival dates in January 2012.

Watch The Throne had given him a real sense of accomplishment too, a belief that he could accomplish anything he set his mind to, even though it was snubbed come the 2012 Grammys. Though Kanye was the most nominated artist, up for seven awards and taking home four including Best Rap Album for *My Beautiful Dark Twisted Fantasy*, neither *Watch The Throne* nor *MBDTF* were nominated for Best Album, an eventuality he put down to having two albums out in such close proximity.

"I don't care about the Grammys," he said. "I just would like for the statistics to be more accurate… I don't want them to rewrite history right in front of us. At least, not on my clock." Having seen both Gnarls Barkley and Justin Timberlake snubbed for Album Of The Year when he was convinced either would have deserved it, Kanye had begun to believe the Grammys were a set up, and even offered to make one of his famed public declarations onstage in aid of Justin. "I was like, 'Do you want me to go onstage for you? You know, do you want me to fight?" he said. "I am so credible and so influential and so relevant that I will change things."

It was a night, and a philosophy, that would define Kanye's 2012. A G.O.O.D. year, pinched with paranoia.

CHAPTER THIRTEEN

Cruel Summer

"I'll admit, I had fell in love with Kim/Around the same time she had fell in love with him".

There can be few more romantic ways to tell your prospective partner you love them than via a hit song on radio. Kanye's wait was over: after just 72 days, Kim Kardashian's marriage to Nets basketball player Kris Humphries fell apart in late 2011. Kanye had kept himself firmly in the running throughout her short marriage, filming a *Star Wars*-insired skit with her for Comedy Central in 2011 and making a cameo in her new TV show *Kim & Kourtney Take New York*, and as soon as her split was announced, he coiled himself to pounce. The rapper was reportedly "all over" Kim at the LA after-show for his *Watch The Throne* show in December, where he'd stopped the show to greet Kim and her family from the stage, and Kim made a high-profile appearance at his second Paris Fashion Week show, wearing the $6,000 shoes he'd premiered in his debut collection the previous year. By April the pair were being strongly linked in the press, despite numerous sources claiming they were "just good friends".

Sensing his chance, Kanye was quick to get his feelings down on tape – with DJ Khaled and producer Hit-Boy, who'd worked on 'Niggas In Paris', he'd worked up a brand new track called 'Theraflu', named after the popular over-the-counter cold medicine, with no plan as to whether it would end up on Kanye's album, Khaled's or the G.O.O.D. Music compilation that Kanye was putting together. The rave-inflected, dance-hop modernist groove interpolated Mase and Puffy's 'Lookin' At Me' and sampled LL Cool J's 'Illegal Search', pressing home how serious Kanye was about his fashion ambitions – "I told you mahfuckers it was more than the music/In the projects one day, to Project Runway… six thousand dollar pair of shoes, we made it to the Paris news!/Don't talk about style 'cause I embarrass you" – and bit back at PETA's comments over his $100,000 fur coat. PETA's Senior Vice president Dan Matthews had responded to the song's lyric, "tell PETA my mink is dragging on the floor" with the following statement: "What's draggin' on the floor is Kanye's reputation as a man with no empathy for animals or human beings. He's a great musician but doesn't seem to have the fashion sense to design anything more than caveman costumes. We keep hoping that one day he'll find his heart and join evolved style icons – including Russell Simmons, Pink, and Natalie Portman – who have dropped animal skins."

But the song got the most attention for its personal revelations. "The whole industry want to fuck your old chick/Only nigga I got respect for is Wiz," Kanye rapped, acknowledging Wiz Khalifa for being upfront about his interest in Amber Rose to the extent of marrying her. And then came the killer lines, Kanye admitting that he'd been in love with Kardashian since before her marriage to Humphries, and that Kris was "lucky I ain't had Jay drop him from the team".★

The track, which would eventually be retitled 'Way Too Cold' and finally 'Cold' so as not to upset the makers of Theraflu, was premiered by DJ Flux on Hot 97 on April 4, and Kanye and Kim were in the studio together to hear it. Having shared that moment, they went off on what Kanye would describe as their first date, watching *The Hunger Games* and interactive theatre show *Sleep No More*, before drinks at the Manderley Bar and a nightcap at Kanye's TriBeCa apartment. "Kanye

---

★ Jay-Z only had a minority share in the Nets, so wouldn't have the authority to get Humphries sacked.

and I have been friends for years," she said on the *Today* show. "You never know what the future holds."

The media spotlight on the pair as their relationship developed was more intense than anything they'd experienced before. Kim was photographed on a 'walk of shame' from Kanye's apartment in the previous night's clothes. If she checked her phone during a laser hair removal session the papers wondered if it was a message from Kanye; if she had any blemish on her skin they called it a love bite. They were tracked as Kanye went to meet Kim's family, or arrived in hotels by separate doors. Every trip they took, be it swanning around London hand-in-hand when one of Kim's endorsement promotion jaunts coincided with the launch of the *Watch The Throne* tour's European leg with a massive five nights at the 20,000 capacity O2 Arena, stepping off A-list boat parties in Cannes, holding up Paris Haute Couture shows by running late or visiting children's hospitals, was meticulously documented. Telephoto lenses caught Kim's gold 'KW' earrings from a distance and fashion writers frothed every time they went out in coordinated outfits and gawped at every wardrobe malfunction. Their every glance and grin was recorded to the point where fans could argue they were living out the Kimye dream in real time.

Instantly, Kanye and Kim became one of the hottest celebrity couples on the planet. Kim's reality TV show *Keeping Up With The Kardashians* was already a huge hit and Kanye was undoubtedly the most avidly watched hip-hop star of the age, so together they were gossip column gold. From this point on there would have to be a story about Kimye – as they swiftly became known – in every celebrity-focused newspaper virtually every single day, no matter how mundane. Every time they bought something expensive, it would be catalogued and price-tagged in the media. Every time Kanye held up a plane by running late or sent champagne to a bride-to-be's table in a New Orleans club, it was gossip page news. When he hit his head on a street sign while walking hand-in-hand with Kim, film crews were there to capture his anger. When he made his uncharacteristically quiet debut appearance on Kim's show in July, allowing Kim to borrow his $500,000 Mercedes McLaren SLR Stirling Moss car and arriving at Kim's house to take her to a restaurant opening amid a barrage of are they/aren't they questions from her girlfriends and family, it was trailed as one of the biggest TV moments of the summer, and every time he made a rare cameo on the show the viewing public avidly sucked it up. Here was a chance to really see inside one of the world's biggest romances, and the insight rocketed Kimye's profile to unimaginable global heights.

The story of a smooth romantic ride wasn't as salacious as a rocky one of course, and so even a matter of weeks into their affair, the press were trying to throw spanners into the works. Articles emerged surmising that Kanye was leering at cheerleaders at a Knicks game while Kim was away in LA, and articles written any time Kanye looked slightly put out by Kim getting more attention than him on trips to restaurants, or skipped the red carpet at the Fifi fragrance awards where she was up for a prize for her perfume True Reflection. They even tracked down 'insider sources' on Kim's dissolving marriage to Kris: "When Kris found out about Kim going public with Kanye," said one, "he told his friends he wanted to tell West, 'Good luck dude, you are going to need it'… Kris knows for a fact that this dalliance between Kim and Kanye has been going on for at least the last two years. Kim kept in touch with Kanye after she married Kris and promised him that she would cut off communication with him, but she never did… Kris is suspicious of the timing of Kim deciding to go public with the relationship because the new season of *Keeping Up With The Kardashians* is premiering in May, and Kanye has released a new album."

One major early issue occurred when it emerged that, before their relationship began, Kanye had recorded a video of himself having sex with an unidentified woman described by some outlets as "a Kim Kardashian look-alike" in a hotel room, and there were threats that it would be leaked online. Kanye responded by considering releasing the tape himself, as several other celebrities had done to capitalise on the adverse publicity and quash any risk of blackmail. He decided against it, but didn't rule out the possibility of a future release. "For the most part, I'd rather people have one of those home videos than some of the paparazzi photos that get published," he said. "At least I recorded the shit myself. That tape couldn't have hurt me in any way if it came out – it could only have helped… Now, I just do exactly what I want to, whenever I want, how the fuck I want. 'Fuck you' is my message."

In Kanye's eyes, this incredible new level of fame and notoriety was a weapon he could turn to his own means, for cultural and social good. "We have relevance and what can we do with that to influence the world in a positive way?" he said. "That's the way I look at it. How can I make these photo shoots look better? And she'd be like, 'How can we go to this homeless shelter and give back to the community?' I'm an artist, my thing is visuals and aesthetics, I believe that's something I give to the world."

Kanye was doing his own bit for the good of culture and society of course – he was one of the first celebrities to visit the Occupy Wall Street protesters to lend his support and launched his design company DONDA in January 2012, announced during a two hour Twitter tirade that started at 5am: "I am assembling a team of architects, graphic designers, directors, musicians, producers, A&Rs, writers, publicists, social media experts, app guys, managers, car designers, clothing designers, DJs, video game designers, publishers, tech guys, lawyers, bankers, nutritionists, doctors, scientists, teachers… We want to help simplify and aesthetically improve everything we see hear, touch, taste and feel. …To dream of, create, advertise and produce products driven equally by emotional want and utilitarian need… To marry our wants and needs… We need as many amazing powerful smart talented wealthy people to be involved. Come get on board… don't just sit there… reach out. We can collectively affect the world through design…We need to pick up where Steve Jobs left off. We need to take what Michael Jackson felt and McQueen and Steve Jobs and we need make things better."

And while his life was being lived out in the glossy gossip pages, between the lines there was important work being done. Virtually every tabloid reported on the couple returning from Cannes in May and swiftly putting both of their LA homes up for sale to start looking for a gated mansion to move into together, but very few made any comment about why they were in Cannes in the first place. They, along with Jay-Z and Kid Cudi, were there to premiere a unique art installation that Kanye had put together, entitled *Cruel Summer*. In a parking lot alongside Palm Beach, the DONDA, OMA and 4X4 conceptual firms had erected a pyramidal tent designed to hold up to 200 people for the May 23 premiere, watching the film on seven screens; three at the front of the tent, two on either side and one each on the floor and ceiling. The film, shot on a custom-made camera rig which could shoot the same scene from multiple different angles simultaneously, a technique that has since become known as the Seven Screen Experience, was an extension of the cinematic work Kanye had done on 'Runaway', shot in Qatar and telling the story of a car thief played by Kid Cudi who falls in love with a blind Arabian princess whom he can only marry if he passes a series of three challenges set by her father.

Speaking after the screening, Kanye claimed the surreal 30-minute film, inspired by the *Watch The Throne* tour, was a "rough draft" and an attempt to "change entertainment experiences. Like if McQueen or Tarsem was to meet the entertainment value of Cirque du Soleil or Walt Disney... It related to a post-Steve Jobs, post-Windows era, where we're always on our BlackBerry in a ball game or at the movies ... I was very particular about having the screens separate, where your mind puts the screens back together, the way you put memories together. I'm not the best director in the world, but I had an idea that I thought would be amazing to inspire people, like a dream of one day this being the way people watch movies. You know, Tarantino doing a movie like this or a horror movie like this, animation, 3-D ... in this form that surrounds you. People want to go back and see it more and more because they missed something to their left or to their right, and it feels more like the experience of life... I can dream one day that this will be the way people will watch movies."

Critics were kind, the *Los Angeles Times* claiming the film "makes a 3-D Michael Bay effort feel like an iPad short", and *Rolling Stone* praising West's "great visual sense". Yet Kanye felt his innovation ws being ignored. "I shoot a film in Qatar with three camera crews, with Nate Brown, Virgil, Matt Williams, Nabil, all of these crew," he said later. "Three camera crews over five days, edited over 30 days... show it in Cannes, the night before amfAR on the beach, build it in a pyramid with Rem Koolhaas' agency, design the entire thing, put editors in it, blah blah blah, people give a standing ovation, I do an interview in *New York Times* the next year to say, 'Hey, I did this and I want to let you know I did it', right?... And then, it doesn't get mentioned in the interview and a week later they do an interview with George Lucas and Steven Spielberg and they're talking about what the next frontier of theatre will be and how it'll be higher priced tickets and it will be something that's surrounding you and blah blah blah, but maybe it's in the goggles, I said, 'Wait a second, I just only did the interview to tell people that I invented it. I made it'."

Kanye did come in for praise for the film's thumping, seat-shaking soundtrack, though, which was drawn from the film's accompanying album, also called *Cruel Summer*. Kanye's very own *The Dynasty: Roc La Familia*. If he'd seemed to lose faith in G.O.O.D. Music back in 2009, now Kanye was reviving his interest in the label. Envisioning a showcase for all of the great talent he'd acquired, he spent much of 2012, often in hotel rooms on the *Watch The Throne* tour, putting together an album featuring many of his signings. After the leak of *MBDTF*, Kanye was taking no chances this time – he refused to email any music anywhere, insisting the managers of his collaborators would have to fly to wherever he was in the world at that particular time to pick up the music for their acts to rap over. "'Ye would call me and be like, 'Yo, I've got this ill beat,'" Pusha T said. "I'd be like, 'All right, send it to me.' And he'd say, 'No, I'm not emailing it'. We get bogus emails from each other, from hackers. I don't even open my emails. If Don C. emails me something, before I touch it, I call Don and say, 'Don, did you email me?' So with that being said, I understand keeping things quiet."

Hence the record was a mystery, even to the rappers appearing on it. "I've done about 20 verses," Pusha said, "but the album's still a mystery to me because I don't know what's made it and what hasn't... It wouldn't be right if the element of surprise wasn't there for everybody involved except Kanye. That's his magic, man."

Besides the April release of 'Theraflu', now named 'Cold', Kanye had previewed the *Cruel Summer* album with a lead single called 'Mercy' on April 3. Originally titled *Lamborghini, Murci* and produced by new G.O.O.D. Music signing Lifted, the deep-bass track explored trap and dancehall music, new territories for Kanye, as Big Sean, Pusha, 2 Chainz and Kanye span rhymes celebrating copious ass-flesh, easy sex, euphoric drugs, fine rides and the pimp hustler life. And Kanye's stilted verse, rapped over a completely different beat based around 'Tony's Theme' from *Scarface*, settled him as the "fly to death" godfather of this wealth-laden, high-living crew, demanding "50 million or I'mma quit" from Def Jam and boasting of his luxury jets and tour buses, his effortless celebrity, his amazing drugs and that "my bitch make your bitch look like Precious".

Hudson Mohawke provided additional instrumentation on the track and Kanye added the dancehall vocals, sampled from Super Beagle's 'Dust A Soundboy', with the help of legendary Chicago producer The Twilight Tone. "I just thought, 'What could I do that would just be counter establishment? Or counter cliché, like what could I put on there?'" Tone said. "For some reason, I heard that dude… I had a vision. I heard that 'Well it's the weeping and the moaning' and I was like… 'Oh my God,' like I had chills… The next day he invited me to the studio, and he was there and a couple of his crew, and I played the sample and everybody froze, everybody paused. Like everybody. It's just that everybody was keyed to it. And 'Ye was like 'Oh snap,' and he started hitting the buttons on it. The rest is, as you would say, history or our story."

The song relaunched the GOOD Fridays initiative, and hit number 13 on the *Billboard* chart accompanied by a stylish, cinematic monochrome video featuring the G.O.O.D. Music crew dancing around an underground parking lot in fashionable gang leathers. It would go on to sell over two million copies in the US and *Complex* magazine would name it the best song of 2012.

Cold fared worse, reaching only 86 in the US despite a comical video featuring a small child rapping all of the parts on the streets of Manhattan alongside a fully-grown model escort while dancers in Donald Trump, George W Bush and Condoleezza Rice masks cavorted around them. And *Cruel Summer*'s third single, 'New God Flow', released on July 21, charted three places lower even though it was aired live at the 2012 BET Awards on a set dominated by a giant model of a Lamborghini

Murciélago, and performed at Jay-Z's high profile Made In America festival.

"'New God Flow' was about, in my view, something I read in a Birdman interview that I didn't like," said guest rapper Pusha T. "He said something like 'G.O.O.D. Music isn't nothing' and it had nothing to do with Wayne or Drake per se. That was Birdman saying whatever he wanted to say and that was the basis of where all of my lines came from. Everybody else was on their love of hip-hop shit."

'New God Flow' used several samples – the piano was taken from Marcos Valle's 'Bodas de Sangue', and the track also sampled Ghostface Killah's 'Mighty Healthy' and a sermon from Rev GI Townsel – and his lines on the menacing piano piece set out to justify his place amongst Kanye's G.O.O.D. Music posse, since he was a notorious large-scale drug dealer – "They say Pusha ain't fit with the umbrella/But I was good with the Yay as a wholesaler/I think it's good that 'Ye got a blow dealer/A hot temper matched with a cold killer" – and attack the label's unworthy critics who "claim they five stars but sell you dreams".*

Kanye's verse addressed the haters too, the people who'd accused him of selling his soul to get where he was without giving him credit for the hard work he'd put in and how he'd "made something from nothing" and risen from "the 312, where cops don't come through and dreams don't come true" and where there are "40 killings in a weekend, 40 killings in a week" due to police brutality and gang violence. He went on to posit himself as the preacher in a new G.O.O.D. Music church founded to enlighten the doubters, likening his shower of money in strip clubs to a Biblical flood and his dreams to those of Biggie Smalls, Martin Luther King and Rodney King in rap, influence and unity respectively.

Notably, in this verse he also mentioned his Air Yeezy 2 trainer which had just been launched by Nike to capitalise on the success of the first shoe. Kanye claimed his sneaker had "jumped over the Jumpman" by rivalling the Military Blue Air Jordan IV that came out on the same day and failed to sell as well as expected due to the competition from Kanye's line. Kanye's shoe was so hotly anticipated that one eBay

---

* Birdman has five red stars tattooed on his head and named his third album *5* Stunna*.

chancer put a pair up for auction before the June 9 launch date with a guide price of $89,000, and some fans slept on the streets outside stores for a week to buy the shoes at a 400 per cent markup. Yet, later, Kanye would be immensely frustrated that his ambitions in footwear would be held back in the aftermath. "Have you ever felt about a shoe, since the Jordans, the way you felt about the Yeezys?" he asked Jean Epstein on Hot 97. "The Yeezys was hip-hop. They gave us that feeling like we was back in fourth grade, like Jordan was winning again. But then Nike marginalised me, they only let me design two silhouettes. And thank you Nike for letting me design stuff, you also let Eminem design stuff, you let Pharrell do a dunk. But I designed the Yeezys and they didn't expect it to have that impact... As soon as it's too big, it's scary. It's like I was fine writing 'Find Your Love' with Drake on his first thing until he got too big, and that was the moment I had to adjust and deal with this new energy that was taking over the room. Nike was like 'No, we ain't gonna let you blow to the level that Drake, we're not gonna let it be a new brand, we already had that baby." He also claimed that wearing retro Jordans was a DONDA idea. "A lot of my ideas I put out in the world have been pilfered through by corporations... For me, it's a listening session to the world, the world is like my living room. I can do whatever I want, whatever I feel like, I can say whatever I want and I know that... I am going to be the greatest products human being of all time, because Tupac the greatest rapper."

After Ghostface Killah made an appearance on the album version of the track with a verse of classic gangsta balling, dealing and murdering, Kanye rounded out the track in the guise of a military drill sergeant rallying his G.O.O.D. Music troops with chants of "I don't know but I've been told/If you get fresh get all the hos... Who running shit today? G.O.O.D. Music!" And the fourth and final single released upfront of *Cruel Summer* backed up his belief. 'Clique', featuring West, Big Sean and Jay-Z, was a huge hit on its September 6 release, reaching number 12 in the US and number 22 in the UK. The song was a Hit-Boy production sampling James Brown's 'Funky President (People It's Bad)' but neither 'New God Flow' nor 'Clique' came accompanied by an official video. Its bold and brassy beat mingled M.I.A.-style Eastern electronica with trap and bashment flecks. With Roc Nation's James Fauntleroy providing the intro and Big Sean's★ hook giving a shout out to the label family – "Ain't nobody fresher than my muthafuckin' clique, clique, clique" he rapped, reflecting not just the unity of G.O.O.D. but the click of the camera shutters constantly trained on them all – the track became a celebration of brotherhood. Sean's verse found him passing his girls to his crew and Jay, an honorary member of the G.O.O.D. Music clique thanks to Big Brother, gave shout outs to his wealthy compadres Kanye, Rihanna, Beyoncé and Lebron James as well as his old drug-dealing partner Emory Jones, who spent a decade behind bars but never snitched on Jay.

Kanye's double-length verse on 'Clique' was more about self-aggrandisement, bragging about his exorbitant spending sprees at Louis Vuitton and Gucci, his sun-drenched vacations, how Kim became a superstar from her sex tape, the success of 'Niggas In Paris' that "got 'em hanging off the Eiffel" and he and Kim's standing as "un-American idols", hanging out with CIA chief George Tenet discussing their Maybachs. "There is some truth to that story," Tenet's spokesman Bill Harlow claimed, explaining that a few months earlier Tenet was leaving a business meeting just as Kanye arrived. "They bumped into each other... They chatted briefly. The next thing you know, it's recorded history. [But] there was no discussion of Maybachs, I think it's poetic licence. It's not his genre, he's more of a Bruce Springsteen guy."

Kanye's discussion of his riches – looking at houses next to Tom Cruise's mansion, flaunting black credit cards with no upper limit on them – had an undercurrent of reproach, knowing that his racial background made him more likely to flaunt his money than build on

---

★ Big Sean was convinced he wouldn't make the final cut of 'Clique' – "It's exciting to be a part of something like that, part of a family. Kanye really takes his time to try to help everybody out as much as he can and include people in the biggest opportunities they can be included in. By putting me on a song with him and Jay-Z, it was crazy. It was just me on the hook and I didn't think he liked it at first... but a month or two later I get a call like 'Yeah man, I love that shit', then later on I get a call from somebody else like 'Man, Jay on that song!'. So I thought 'They probably about to take me off, it'll just be him and Jay-Z'."

it in business terms: "I rather buy 80 gold chains and go ign'ant", but he still saw G.O.O.D. Music as his chance to build an empire to rival Rome and had aspirations to "design hotels and nail it", creating whole cities to his unique vision, a position granted him by a charmed life. "I been talking to God for so long," he rapped, "that if you look at my life I guess he's talking back."

There was certainly a charm to Kanye's *Cruel Summer*. Released a week after 'Clique' on September 14, it reached number two on the *Billboard* chart and sold 205,000 copies in its first week, a major achievement for a collaboration album that featured only sporadic Kanye appearances. On the sultry, ominous, Auto-Tuned 'Higher' he only received a producer credit as The-Dream, Pusha, Mase and Cocaine 80 took centre stage for verses of girls, dope, cars and designer labels. And there were three tracks on which Kanye was nowhere to be found. The dark synthetic throbs, hisses and pounds of 'Sin City' had John Legend, Travi$ Scott, Teyana Taylor, Cyhi The Prynce and spoken word artist Malik Yusef weaving tales from a fictional metropolis of racial suppression and hopelessness, representing America at its most foul. The gorgeously ethereal, fuzz-heavy tribal tongue-twister 'Creepers' was given over to a paranoid, drugged-up and insecure Kid Cudi. And the Hudson Mohawke production 'Bliss' was a glistening, glossy, plastic rock epic on which John Legend and Teyana Taylor showcased their impressive R&B stories of eloping together to a blissful life of jet-setting high life.

When Kanye did crop up, he made it perfectly clear who was in charge. On the skittering, bombastic album opener, 'To The World', he upstaged R Kelly's defiant hook and an uncredited Taylor with a suave, seductive verse about his successes in music, fashion and film as well as his ability to pull in the biggest names in R&B to open his album: "R Kelly and the God of rap shitting on you, holy crap". He compared himself to God again in his outro to 'The Morning', a crackling gangsta remake of 'Get Me To The Church On Time' that morphs into a traditional West Coast low-rider to which Raekwon, Common, Pusha, 2 Chainz and Cyhi reel out portraits of their backgrounds – be they hustling with their crew in the middle of gangland wars, growing up poor beside

Lake Michigan or "pushing karts at K-Mart" – and rubbishing rumours that the G.O.O.D. Music crew was in any way Illuminati-connected. Kanye's lines also suggest that he had been cheating on Amber Rose too: "If I knew she was cheating and still bought her more clothes/It's 'cause I was too busy with my Baltimore".

On stirring piano ballad 'The One', between descending tornados of crashing electronic drums, Kanye was upfront, proclaiming himself not just "at the helm" of G.O.O.D. Music and rap in general, but in a whole other stratosphere from his closest hip-hop rivals. "I'm the one baby," he stated, aligning himself with Jesus in much the same way he had done on the famous crown of thorns *Rolling Stone* cover, "Since God gave his only begotten son, baby/It's hard preachin' the gospel to the slums lately/So I had to put the church on the drums, baby... I been running on the sun, baby/We on a galaxy the haters cannot visit". Though Big Sean's verse about his rise from Detroit into the G.O.O.D. Music fold was impressively propulsive, Kanye owned 'The One', and he wasn't finished yet. Come the album's cataclysmic final track, 'I Don't Like', a remix of a track from Chief Keef's *Back From The Dead* mix-tape on which Kanye, Judakiss, Pusha, Big Sean and Keef laid out their pet hates, he was still comparing himself to Jesus as he rapped about how "The media crucify me like they did Christ/They want to find me not breathing like they found Mike", and stole the show with more revelations about his past relationships, pure gossip column gold. "A girl'll run her mouth only out of spite," he rhymed in narcotic slo-mo over an explosive cascade of booming gothic atmospherics, referencing the stories about him hitting Alexis Phifer, "but I never hit a woman, never in my life". As Pusha declared his hatred of fake rappers who've never lived the hustler's life they rap about, Keef laid into snitches and women who want more than sex from him, Big Sean took on the lowlifes crowding him and Judakiss bemoaned the times the drug supplies run dry, it was Kanye that shone brightest, from star value and raw honesty.

Perhaps due to less ambitious and adventurous production mentality than we'd seen on the last couple of Kanye albums – it was, after all, the first of his albums that didn't make a giant creative leap forward –

reviews of *Cruel Summer* were mixed, with some reviewers describing it as "a runway show of small, costly, uncomfortable missteps" and others "an unusually crowded solo album, but West's affiliates don't share his gift for fusing self-aggrandisement with soul-searching reflection". The album undoubtedly sat in Kanye's canon as an incongruous oddity, but almost every critic cited West's parts as the stand-outs, bolstering his position as a cultural giant of the 21st century. In *The Atlantic* magazine, David Samuels called him "the first true genius of the iPhone era, the Mozart of contemporary American music… a narcissistic monster."

Not that this was helping him fulfil all of his potential. When Kanye went for meetings with investors he hoped would get behind his most ambitious ideas for the future, ideas for amusement parks and grand schemes akin to his surround-sound movie experience and his second fashion show complete with go-karting circuits for attendees, he was stonewalled at every turn. "I went around and showed people what I'd done," he said, "and said, 'Hey, I made *Watch The Throne*, I made this amount of music for the past 10 years, I have this level of visuals, this level of communication, I can sell this many albums, and I also have these new inventions. Will anybody help me out?' I met with 30 billionaires, 30 companies, and basically everyone said, 'Fuck you'. I said, 'How could this happen? How could not one person want to invest in these different ideas?' I mean, if I grouped up with three guys in a basement and started a new tech company that was very similar to another tech company down the street, but it just so happened that I had a few more followers than the other guy, then I could get all the investment in the world and value my company at a certain amount. But then I have another idea and the entire world will say fuck you? Now, that is about money and power."

Instead, Kanye was chained to the gossip columns and the road. Throughout the summer the media lapped up every detail of the Kimye romance. She'd bought him a $400,000 Lamborghini Aventador for his 35th birthday, they whispered. She took charge when his $4 million Hollywood Hills house was struck by burglars in June, they hissed. Tabloids got hold of the private shots from estate agents charged with selling the house, and slavered over the kitsch décor of personally commissioned Jetsons artwork in the games room, Warhol paintings, a full-size Buzz Lightyear statue, an Antonio Citterio bed complete with red fox and chinchilla throws and a wardrobe holding 200 pairs of shoes. There were countless reports of their romantic nights out in Paris, where Kanye was thinking of recording his next album. On *Oprah*, Kardashian opened up about how the pair had bonded over losing a parent: "It's very comforting to have someone that knows everything about you, that respects you, understands, has gone through the similar things," she said. "I can really relate to his mother passing. He can really relate to my father passing. I mean, there's so many similarities in our life that ... I feel like I'm at a really happy, good space. 'I don't know why it took so long for us to get together, but I think I needed to go through all my experiences. I think we've always had an attraction to each other but we've always been in other relationships or it wasn't the right timing. And one day it just happened. It took me by surprise." She vehemently denied that the relationship was a publicity stunt. "It's your heart you're playing with. I couldn't sacrifice my heart for a publicity stunt," she said. "Having him in my life right now, in this way, says so much about us."

There was much rubbing of palms when a source close to Kris Humphries added fuel to the fire concerning the rumours that Kim had cheated on him with Kanye when they claimed he'd asked "If he was such a close family friend, why wasn't he invited to the wedding?" Kris later denied having said any such thing. And much sniggering when Kim started taking Kanye along to her beauty treatments, when pictures emerged of the two screaming their way around a roller-coaster ride at Six Flags Magic Mountain theme park and when Jay and Kanye stepped up to accept the Best Video award for 'Otis' at the 2012 BET Awards and Jay gestured for Kanye to speak, only to leap in and interrupt his speech with the words "Excuse me Kanye, I am going to let you continue..."

As early as July 2012, reports were emerging of Kanye working with designers on an engagement ring for Kim, using jewels from Donda's personal collection, while other outlets focused on more salacious stories. On July 4 much was made of Kanye appearing in a raunchy promotional video for Anja Rubik's *25* magazine, featuring surrealist, kaleidoscopic images of topless models and mystical symbolism. In August the *New York Daily News* reported that Kanye and Leonardo DiCaprio had joined a table packed with models at the exclusive PH-D Rooftop Lounge in NYC, where Kanye had taken to the decks to showcase some *Cruel Summer* tracks as well as a tune called 'Perfect Bitch', dedicated to Kim − "I'm honoured. I love it," she told TMZ. "I know he doesn't mean it in a negative way when he says the word 'bitch'. The song talks about how he was with so many other girls but could never find the right one until he met me." And the press leapt on a slight from 50 Cent towards the couple: "One man's trash is another man's treasure," he told *XXL*.

The couple were happy to play with their celebrity, regularly tweeting pictures from their private lives and appearing in a promo advert for the MTV VMAs with host Kevin Hart in which Kevin attempted to talk his way into the relationship, renaming it Kevyekim. Kim teased the tabloids with hints of wedding bells. "When this whole life is done, and it's just the two of us sitting somewhere when we're 80," she told *New York* magazine, "you want to have things to talk about that you have in common. I think that's something maybe I didn't value as highly as a quality I cared about in someone. If I have a design meeting, or he has one, we come back and talk about how our meetings went. It's cool, because you can definitely get more in-depth with someone who actually knows what you're talking about. So that's been a fun similarity we have. I think it's essential to have similarities."

"I definitely think anything I'd be in now is a permanent relationship," she said on *The View* TV show. "Kids is definitely something I want. I think I wanted that before." In *Tatler* she even posed in a wedding-style gown, saying, "It's so nice to have a best friend in this game who understands everything you're going through. Being with someone I've known for so many years is comforting. He's been there through so many different stages of my life and before I was famous, so this relationship is a different thing entirely. It's good to be aware that he definitely doesn't want anything from me too, because he understands the business. I can't even think about being with anyone else than the man I'm with."

Virtually every day, the stories rolled on. Kanye invited Kim to appear in a video for a mash-up of Khaled's 'I Wish You Would' and 'Cold', cuddling up to him at the end of the clip. He was in talks to become a judge on *American Idol*, and was insisting Kim eBay all of her clothes so he could give her a fashion make-over. This, at least, was true. "Nobody can tell my girl what to do," Kanye said the following year, claiming to have helped her attain a new structured, monochrome look inspired by Dries Van Noten. "She just needed to be given some platforms of information to work from… one beautiful thing is that as she discovers it, the world discovers it… For her to take that risk in front of the world, it just shows you how much she loves me. And how much she actually loves the opportunity to learn. You got, like, a million companies saying, 'This is impacting your brand! This is impacting your fans! And blah blah blah.' But she still sees this light of beauty". Kim was on a diet to reduce the size of her famous backside to fit into Kanye-designed clothes. They were hunting for a $10 million house in Miami together, where Kim was set to film her new TV series *Kourtney & Kim Take Miami* and Kanye allegedly flew into a rage when they dined in a restaurant close to one in which Kim's ex Reggie Bush was eating with his new girlfriend. He took her to Italy for her 32nd birthday, touring Rome, Florence and Venice with, according to Kim's TV producer Ryan Seacrest, a secret plan to propose on the big day (although since Kim was still going through her divorce with Kris, Kanye didn't propose in 2012). When she flew to London to launch a Dorothy Perkins range, he dropped everything to fly 4,000 miles to be by her side.

Kanye's 97-year-old grandfather Portland was quizzed on his opinion of her after Kanye had taken her to meet him in Oklahoma City. "She is beautiful," Portland said, "and she's just as sweet as she is beautiful – and that's what I liked about her! She was just down to earth, she's rich, and those kinds of people, they've got everything… Maybe they could have a successful marriage, but I'm not going to spend time worrying if they're going to make it or not… I don't do weddings. I don't like weddings… You spend a lot of money, then in a few weeks, you're separated!" Sadly, Portland would be robbed of the opportunity to attend Kim and Kanye's wedding; he died on August 10, 2013, a fortnight after his 98th birthday.

Meanwhile, reporters dug up an alleged reference to Kim in a 2009 verse Kanye had rapped on Keri Hilson's 'Knock You Down': "You was always the cheerleader of my dreams/Seem to only date the head of football teams/And I was the class clown that, always kept you laughin'/We, were never meant to be baby, we just happen... You should leave your boyfriend now". And Twitter lit up over Kanye's two-hour online rant about swearing in his records – "'I will admit that I sometimes go back and omit cursing from my records," he wrote. "I like to use profanity as a tool and not a crutch... Initially I was offended by anyone questioning anything in my music. I usually never tweet questions but I struggle with this so here goes... Is the word BITCH acceptable? Is it acceptable for a man to call a woman a bitch even if it's endearing?... If nigga is such a positive word, why do we feel so uncomfortable for white people to say it, even with a hall pass? Here's the age old question, would we refer to our mothers as bitches? Would we call our fathers niggers or better yet NIGGAS? Has hip-hop conditioned us to accept this word? Do we love this word as much as we love the word NIGGA in an endearing way? Stevie Wonder never had to use the word bitch to get his point across." As though learning his lesson, within weeks Kanye deleted all but one tweet from his entire page, leaving just the message for his eight million followers: "BE BACK SOON".

In September, Kanye pulled out of his planned appearance at the VMAs because Kim couldn't be there with him; he chose to keep his live unveiling of *Cruel Summer* a low-key affair. On October 24 he played an hour-long set including 'New God Flow', 'Mercy' and 'Clique' at the launch of the Samsung Galaxy II to a tiny crowd of just 1,000 invited guests at New York's Skylight at Moynihan Station, hitting the stage at 11.30pm. It launched a handful of dates to promote *Cruel Summer*, including a slot at the 12-12-12 Concert For Sandy Relief at Madison Square Garden alongside Paul McCartney, the Rolling Stones, the Who and Bruce Springsteen, and three shows at the Revel Ovation Hall in Atlantic City. In characteristically boundary-pushing style, Kanye constructed huge wraparound screens for these shows, engulfing the stage with stunning landscapes and snowstorms in a truly immersive live spectacle. Tidal waves crashed, flocks of birds swarmed, icebergs drifted and Kanye was lost in the middle of it all, his entire face covered with black or jewelled Margiela masks. The shows ended on December 30 with a happy announcement: "Stop the music," he demanded, before pointing out Kim in the crowd. "Make some noise for my babymama right here," he announced, and Kim blogged a confirmation the same day. "It's true!! Kanye and I are expecting a baby. We feel so blessed and lucky and wish that in addition to both of our families, his mom and my dad could be here to celebrate this special time with us."

The gossip pages went into overdrive. They mocked up pictures of what the baby would look like, speculated on its name and detailed every outfit that Kim wore to cover up her baby bump. A Twitter storm brewed over pictures from a New Year's Eve party in Vegas hosted by Kardashian for a reported fee of $300,000, with ill-reasoning commenters claiming that going to a nightclub made her unfit for motherhood.

Newspapers claimed there were $250,000 offers for Kim to document her pregnancy on the MyPregnancy.com website, and $3 million for the first baby snaps. The $11 million Bel Air mansion they bought to start their family in was photographed from the air while they were still refurbishing it in an Italianate style, installing a movie theatre, gym, make-up salon, bowling alley and basketball court. Papers began pitting Kim against the also-pregnant Kate Middleton, speculating on who would give birth first. The attention was becoming stifling, the spotlight scolding.

It was time, once more, for Kanye to escape.

CHAPTER FOURTEEN

Yeezus

Fresh from the Louvre, the chauffeur-driven Porche Panamera Turbo – the Batmobile of luxury cars – crawled the Parisian streets, past the high-end law and accountancy offices of the city's most exclusive neighbourhood, drawing up outside the 19th century No Name Hotel. Kanye had nicknamed his Paris hideaway thus to avoid unwanted attention from press and fans, but his activities were tough to ignore. By day he trawled the city's architectural and cultural highlights, absorbing its classical aura and modernist sheen. He was a regular at fashion shows, sometimes turning up in red ski masks, and he hit the Louvre five times, both on public and private visits, to admire a Le Corbusier lamp in the museum's furniture exhibit that he found particularly inspirational. He also visited several Corbusier homes alongside architect Oana Stanescu to soak in the style and talk to their owners about their thinking behind the minimalist designs he was trying to emulate in his new album. At the No Name Hotel deliveries of haute-minimalist furniture came and went to his self-contained loft apartment – rare Le Corbusier lamps, Pierre Jeanneret chairs, Frances Palmer cups – as Kanye decorated his suite in the style of the top end of Parisian architecture and design, and Kim visited wearing an ever-increasing array of jewellery that Kanye was buying her in Paris' classiest boutiques. By night, architects and designers such as Joseph Dirand, Alex Vervoordt and Kanye's new British design partner Katie Eary rubbed shoulders with Nas, the Weeknd, Daft Punk and a smattering of Kadashians at all-night hip-hop parties that drew complaints from other residents. For two months at the start of 2013, the No Name Hotel was the centre of the rap universe.

"In Paris, you're as far as possible from the land of pleasant smiles," Kanye said. "You can just trip on inspiration – there are so many people here who dedicate their lives to excellence."

With collaborators such as Evian Christ, Mike Dean and Daft Punk's Thomas Bangalter, who produced four songs on the album, describing the sessions as competitive, raw and very focused, Kanye went about creating the record from songs he'd started work on in mid-2012, but this time using a group therapy method. Each collaborator was given a song to work on and a strict set of rules – no dubstep bass was allowed and they were tasked with making music to "undermine the commercial". "We want to set ourselves apart from what is currently in rotation," said producer Anthony Kilhoffer, who'd been engineering for Kanye since *The College Dropout*. "A lot of times, Kanye sets parameters of sounds and styles that we can and can't use. For instance: you'll find there's no bass wobbles on this album. Dubstep is really big right now, but it's not something we could use in our production styles. He's always trying to not take the easy way out. So it's about achieving clubby, contemporary sounds while setting yourself apart from Skrillex or RedOne. We don't want to follow, we want to lead."

After being given their track to work on, they returned the following day to have the work they'd done discussed by West and his team. "We'll all sit around and critique it," recalled Kilhoffer. "It's kind of like an art class: 'This is what we did this afternoon, what do you think?'… We get to the studio at about two in the afternoon, and then work until maybe 11pm, go back to Kanye's house, play what we worked on, then maybe go back to the studio around midnight and work until three in the morning. A lot of people think, 'Oh, it's a Kanye project – spend a couple of days in the studio and then go out and party in Paris'. But it's serious work… To work well with Kanye, you've got to be able to take direction, and if you're told your idea's not good, you can't take it personally. Because it is art, a lot of people do get upset, but nothing goes through 100% without some comments or critiques."

"It's a room full of people who are working towards the same idea," said Evian Christ, a young UK producer who was new to Kanye's team, West having discovered him from his mix-tape *Kings And Them* during the *Cruel Summer* sessions. "You just know that when you hand something over to Kanye, it's gonna come back even better. That makes for a very easy working experience… Logic would seemingly state that an album with so many people working on it would sound disjointed, but what Kanye manages to do is get the best out of everyone working towards one sound. You can't really overstate how difficult it is to do that."

"Kanye's a world-famous star," said Justin Vernon, called in once more to work on the new album, "but it's just like working on music with friends. You're trying to do the coolest shit. Just being around motherfuckers who have been doing this for a long time and are getting better – like, there actually aren't that many of them in the world. There's no pedestrian fuckery on this album. People are working their asses off to make the best shit, and Kanye's leading the pack."

Once more, Kanye attempted to connect with his inner child while making the album, often closing his eyes and trying to think back to the age of three, "because we were all artists back then, [we] had the least barriers to our creativity… When you're three, you wake up one morning and say, I wanna ride a bike'. And then the next day, you wake up and say, 'I wanna draw'. I don't want to be in a situation where, because I was good enough at riding a bike one day, then that's all I can do for the rest of my life… I'm opening up my notebook and I'm saying everything in there out loud. A lot of people are very sacred with their ideas, and there is something to protecting yourself in that way, but there's also something to idea sharing, or being the person who makes the mistake in public so people can study that… all we have is today. You know, the past is gone, and tomorrow is not promised."

The recording environment shaped the sound of the record too. The living room space that Kanye had turned into his studio had dreadful acoustics – anything even slightly elaborate or bass-heavy would echo unbearably in the chasm of a room. So by necessity, Kanye had to strip the tracks back to their most basic minimalist elements, simplifying them and writing using just his voice and a drumbeat, a new way of working. With no operatic elements or what Kanye called his "snob heaven songs" included, he was going for the trap, drill and house influence of the eighties Chicago records he was listening to in Paris, his wild, minimalist rants making his new material resemble the likes of Run-DMC, KRS-One or J-Kwon's 'Tipsy', a record Kanye admired despite many considering it a dumbed-down form of rap.

Knowing that he had no way of matching the brilliance of *MBDTF*, Kanye instinctively felt he had to change his own rules. "*Dark Fantasy* was the first time you heard that collection of sonic paintings in that way. So I had to completely destroy the landscape and start with a new story… [This] was the beginning of me as a new kind of artist. Stepping forward with what I know about architecture, about classicism, about society, about texture, about synaesthesia – the ability to see sound – and the way everything is everything and all these things combine, and then starting from scratch… The risk for me would be in *not* taking one – that's the only thing that's really risky for me. I live inside, and I've learned how to swim through backlash, or maintain through the current of a negative public opinion and create from that and come through it and spring forth to completely surprise everyone – to satisfy all believers and annihilate all doubters. And at this point, it's just fun."

As a result of this stripped-back approach, the sessions went remarkably quickly. "I assumed that he was gonna do the maximalist thing again with this album, but it's more like 'Boom! We just made a song, and it bangs, so fuck you'," Vernon said. "It's such an awesome contrast."

Mike Dean estimated that he only spent 30 or 40 days in the studio for the new record, compared to 180 for *My Beautiful Dark Twisted Fantasy*. "It was probably the fastest record we ever made," said Kilhoffer. "And instead of doing 30 songs altogether, we only did 20. Still, we would explore all kinds of options: different tempos or drums, whether a song should be synth-based on real-instrument based. A lot of younger producers just get a beat, put a rap on it, and that's the song. There's no dissecting, or recreating, or considering the relevance in contemporary music."

Kanye found time for exploits outside the studio too, taking a vacation with Kim and Will Smith to Rio in February, attending the 2013 Grammys to accept three awards for 'Niggas In Paris' and 'No Church In The Wild' that made him the man with the most number of Grammys for anywhere near his age. In late February and early March he took time out to play a series of theatre gigs in London, Paris, Brussels and Amsterdam, where he garnered headlines for dissing Justin Timberlake during a performance of 'Clique': "I got love for Hov but I ain't fucking with that 'Suit & Tie'," he freestyled, referring to Jay-Z's latest single with Timberlake. Yet, despite such a brief recording span, when the sessions wrapped up in the spring and the album ran to 16 songs, it somehow hit three and a half hours of running time, over twice the length of *MBDTF*. Announcing the record's title as *Yeezus*, he played some tracks to journalists claiming the album was almost finished, but come April he'd realised the record was only a third complete, at best. It was Kanye's typical way of working – whenever a new beat showed him a glimpse of a new direction he hadn't tried before, he'd ditch half of an album to chase it.

On May 6, at the Metropolitan Museum Of Art's punk-themed costume gala, he premiered the first new track from the album, the provocatively-titled 'I Am A God', screaming and screeching the track while swathed in dense smoke⋆. The track was an instant attention-grabber, Kanye's arrogance expanding beyond anything even his harshest critics might have expected from him. To a subterranean electronic beat verging on horrorcore, horn-like house parps and cavernous industrial guitar clangs pieced together by Bangalter, West, Dean and Hudson Mohawke, he pompously espoused his deity status in defiance of all of the criticism he'd endured, demanding the instant massages, threesomes and valet service that a true God amongst men deserves. The track opened with a sample of Jamaican dancehall legend Capleton from 'Forward Inna Dem Clothes', and his main verse seemed to represent God reminding Kanye why he was heaven-sent; that he's the only rapper that could compare to Michael Jackson in influence, and that

⋆ Kanye also serenaded Kim at the show, declaring her "awesome".

he'd revolutionised rap from the very start, back when he was sporting his pink polos and backpacks. By the end of the song he was casually chatting with his near contemporary Jesus – "I know he the most high/ But I am a close high" – while stacking his money, a semi-comic satire on his own arrogance, but one he'd stand by.

"When I say 'I am a God', it's because I believe God is in all of us," he'd tell a crowd at a later live show, and when questioned on his preposterous statement, he'd refuse to back down. "When someone comes up and says something like 'I am a god', everybody says 'Who does he think he is?'" he said. "I just told you who I thought I was, a god! I just told you! That's who I think I am! Would it have been better if I had a song that said, 'I am a nigga'? Or if I had song that said 'I am a gangsta'? Or if I had song that said 'I am a pimp'? All those colours and patinas fit better on a person like me, right? But to say you are a god? Especially, when you got shipped over to the country that you're in, and your last name is a slave owner's. How could you say that? How could you have that mentality?"

The track, like much of *Yeezus*, was born of frustration. In the autumn of 2012, Kanye was invited to a Paris Fashion Week catwalk show by Yves Saint Laurent's Hedi Slimane, on the condition that he didn't appear at any other shows. "So the next day I went to the studio with Daft Punk, and I wrote 'I Am A God'," he recalled. "Cause it's like, yo! Nobody can tell me where I can and can't go. Man, I'm the number one living and breathing rock star. I am Axl Rose; I am Jim Morrison; I am Jimi Hendrix. You can't say that you love music and then say that Kanye West can't come to your show! To even think they could tell me where I could and couldn't go is just ludicrous. It's blasphemous – to rock 'n' roll, and to music… How can someone stop my opportunity to see something that he can teach me, that I can help teach the world?"

His rage came through in the recording of the track. "The very first time I heard Kanye say 'I am a God', we all were like, 'OK, that's where we're going - let's go all the way there'," said producer Noah Goldstein. "If you watch LeBron dunk in the middle of a game, you're gonna get up and freak out. And it was like that when Kanye spit the first verse of

'I Am A God'. It was really fucking early in the morning, and he just came downstairs, and was like, 'Yo, let's go'. It was the most emphatic performance. I was like, 'Holy shit!' I stopped and hit save really quick and thought, 'Fuck, I gotta back up the drive right now, man. That was crazy'."

"'I Am A God' was one of the first songs he had for the record," said Mohawke. "It was like the blueprint. The original version was even more directly in-your-face and aggressive than the final, but given the song's title, it didn't need this fucking apocalyptic, earth-shatteringly massive production to get its point across."

Aside from its arrogant subject matter, the song would become notable for including the most unintentionally hilarious line on the album – as the beat dropped out, Kanye barked "In a French-ass restaurant/ Hurry up with my damn croissants!" like the most demanding rap prima donna. "Sometimes I don't realise which lines are going to really resonate, but Kanye always does," said Goldstein. "Actually, 'Hurry up with my damn croissants' was one where I was like, 'Are you really sure you want to say that?' And he's like, 'Yes! That's staying in!' He literally has the best gut instincts of anybody I've ever worked with, as far as what music should be. So when he says a line has to stay in, I'm like, 'OK!' I will not argue with the god."

"One of my favourite things about Kanye is that there's always some personal flaws in his lyrics," Mohawke added. "He's honest. He's not trying to portray himself as some squeaky clean, perfect person. It takes him out of the realm of so many other mainstream rap artists who only focus on the bragging side of things; you don't necessarily feel like you have any personal connection with a lot of those artists, whereas Kanye puts so much of his own personality into his music."

During May Kanye made two more appearances, and further new tracks emerged. At the Roseland Ballroom in New York he played an Adult Swim party, projecting film onto a giant pyramid and indulging in a lengthy rant about how he was "a terrible, terrible celebrity… the worst kind of celebrity, because all I do is make real music… so I don't want nobody coming up to me with no cameras". And on *SNL*, performing deep in shadow before a backdrop of black KKK hoods, the three-headed devil hound Cerberus from Greek mythology and a flashing slogan reading NOT FOR SALE, he unveiled two ferocious new songs to the nation. Opening with snarls, howls and slaverings of a pack of angry dogs, computerised yelps and wickedly distorted house synth pulses, 'Black Skinhead' was a fiery tribalist glam stunner that stamped and shook with urban danger, derived from cut-offs from Daft Punk's *Random Access Memories* album. "The drums we had recorded earlier during the recording of our album, so we had those," said Bangalter of the beat that many *SNL* viewers would liken to Marilyn Manson tracks such as 'The Beautiful People' and 'Personal Jesus' or Gary Glitter's 'Rock N Roll Part II'. In Kanye's hands this strident and savage backing became the canvas for his most breathless and frenzied anti-racist rant yet: channelling the violent attitude of the British skinhead culture he attacked a society hell-bent on keeping the African-American community down. Casting himself as a Batman-meets-Malcolm X superhero come to save the day – "For my theme song/My leather black jeans on/My by-any-means on"*– he pointed to the lingering taboo of inter-racial dating – "They see a black man with a white woman/At the top floor, they gon' come to kill King Kong" – the intolerance of religious groups towards his music and the country's institutionalised racism. "Stop all that coon shit, early morning cartoon shit," he rapped, calling out the stereotypical portrayal of black people in old reruns of children's cartoons, "I'm aware I'm a king, back out the tomb, bitch".

"When 'Ye opened up that Maybach laptop and hit play on 'Black Skinhead', I jumped off the stairs onto the couch," said Travi$ Scott. "I was going HAM. That was when I heard the 'na na na na' part for the first time, I lost my fucking mind. That's some soccer anthem-type shit." "'Black Skinhead' almost got deaded because it was too much like a soccer song," added Mike Dean.

The *SNL* audience was in for more of Kanye's forthright politicking. He followed his intense and maniacal performance of 'Black Skinhead' with 'New Slaves', spitting his impassioned condemnations of

* Kanye had dressed up as Batman for a fancy dress party earlier in the year, with Kim as Catwoman, and had also been sporting leather trousers on a regular basis.

consumerist society while standing stock still and staring directly down the camera at the America he was accusing. The track's synth hooks began life as a tune by Ben Bronfman, over which Kanye's team layered the drums and rapped: "My momma was raised in an era when/Clean water was only served to the fairer skin," over sparse goth-house synth hooks that sounded like a rave in a graveyard, looking back to the days when blacks were forced to use the dirtier taps for their drinking water before highlighting more modern forms of racism. Now a black man starting his own fashion line, he argued, would always come under fire for having any help with his designs at all ("They wasn't satisfied unless I picked the cotton myself") and there were two types of racism in the clothing store; the "broke nigga racism" where they'd be asked to leave and the "rich nigga racism" where the stores assumed they would want to buy all of the most expensive items in the place because "all you blacks want all the same things". Thus he acknowledged that the chains of consumerism and financial greed were turning people of all races into "new slaves" – "Used to only be niggas, now everybody playin'/ Spending everything on Alexander Wang".

His second verse – which Kanye would tweet as "the best rap verse of all time" – was more pro-active. Declaring that "I'd rather be a dick than a swallower," he claimed he'll "throw these Maybach keys", and stood up to corporations who "can't control me", promising to refuse any restraining corporate deals which they assume "niggas can't read". "I see the blood on the leaves," he intoned, paying tribute to Nina Simone's anti-slavery classic 'Strange Fruit' and suggesting the image of slave blood on dollar bills, all tying in with his new slogan NOT FOR SALE. Then he turned his sights to other forms of enslavement, targeting the media that keep him hemmed in with lenses or conspiracy theories linking him to some Illuminati-style New World Order as a distraction from real issues, such as the run-for-profit prisons making money out of the huge number of blacks turned into "new slaves" by the prison system.

Ending with a distorted, Auto-Tuned orchestral outro from Frank Ocean and a snippet of 'Pearl Haired Girl' by Hungarian rock band Omega – a verse that translates as "One day the sun, too tired to shine/

Slept in the deep, green sombre lake/And in the darkness, the world did ail/Until she came, for all our sake" – 'New Slaves' was amongst Kanye's most direct and affecting conscious raps, and it was a message he was eager to get out to the world. Before he'd even finished recording it or writing the second verse, he was filming a video for the song, which he had projected onto 66 buildings across the world on May 17, including the W Hotel in LA, the Royal Ontario Museum, Prada stores and Wrigley Field in Chicago. The video, which consisted of Kanye's stoic face vehemently rapping the song, projected 50 ft high on these iconic buildings, caused chaos in Texas, where police shut down screenings scheduled for the Rothko Chapel and the Alamo.

The song, Kanye would explain, was a cry for recognition and emancipation. "[I want] the world to be better. That's why I said 'I throw these Maybach keys'. I would rather sit in a factory than sit in a Maybach. I want to tell people, 'I can create more for this world, and I've hit the glass ceiling'. If I don't scream, if I don't say something, then no one's going to say anything, you know? So I come to them and say, 'Dude, talk to me! Respect me!'… Respect my trendsetting abilities. Once that happens, everyone wins. The world wins; fresh kids win; creatives win; the company wins. I think what Kanye West is going to mean is something similar to what Steve Jobs means. I am undoubtedly, you know, Steve of internet, downtown, fashion, culture. Period. By a long jump. I honestly feel that because Steve has passed, you know, it's like when Biggie passed and Jay-Z was allowed to become Jay-Z. I've been connected to the most culturally important albums of the past four years, the most influential artists of the past 10 years. You have like, Steve Jobs, Walt Disney, Henry Ford, Howard Hughes, Nicolas Ghesquière, Anna Wintour, David Stern. I think that's a responsibility that I have, to push possibilities, to show people: 'This is the level that things could be at'. So when you get something that has the name Kanye West on it, it's supposed to be pushing the furthest possibilities. I will be the leader of a company that ends up being worth billions of dollars, because I got the answers. I understand culture. I am the nucleus."

"I'm 100 per cent a part of [consumerist culture]," he said. "I'm 100 per cent in it, and 100 per cent I want to overcome it. Sometimes I'm the communicator of it, sometimes I'm the maker of it, sometimes I'm the consumer of it, I'm in it, I'm in the game… It's funny; you drive in a Maybach past a homeless person and you ask, 'Who's more free?' You could be trapped to your possessions. You got to do this next deal because you got to do this with your house and you got to get this car and you got to keep up… And that's what it's like to be a celebrity a lot of times. Every rap is about how much money you make, how many cars you got, what house you get… Rappers and musicians trying to compete with ball players with way bigger contracts. Meanwhile, the music is the *Titanic* that's going down and everybody from the execs to the musicians are running around trying to see how they could still keep that certain house level, that certain car level that certain thing, up. And of course for me I'm blessed and I'm privileged because I made such a powerful impact that I can make a certain amount on tour. But also I'm blessed and cursed by my level of education, you know to be a visionary… We are constantly slaved, there is glass ceilings, there is glass fences, there is invisible walls… we want that clean water, I tasted and I see what it is like, we want to sing Louis Vuitton, we want to sing on a Gucci level… We want to be good. That's that thing that people are slaves to. That's that thing that I'm a slave to… That's that dreaming of a new pair of Jordans. That's the process of opening up a Nike box. That thing that Steve gave us when you open up your new iPhone and you got the iPhone 5… That's that Transformers in a box that you open up for Christmas or that new TurboGrafx16 or Sega Genesis or Amiga computer or a Nintendo… The process of the packaging, that's that porno mag that drug addict bought for you when you was 14 that was in that package and you figured out how to pay that drug dealer before there was internet – and you open up that and you know you are going to make five of those your girlfriend all weekend. That's why I'm on that runway, until I'm at the end of it."

The speed with which *Yeezus* was accelerating towards release, however, was perhaps a little dizzying this time. Outside of music Kanye was being sued for $150,000 over a sample he'd allegedly used in 'Gold Digger' by the copyright owners of a 1974 track called 'Bumpin Bus Stop', his first child was due in July – a daughter, they'd announced, amid stories that Kanye wanted to name the child North – and he was booked to make a cameo appearance as the head of an MTV news crew in *Anchorman 2: The Legend Of Ron Jeremy*. According to *Anchorman* star Will Ferrell, Kanye played his new tracks through the set's PA system for the rest of the cast to hear, but got annoyed when they had to turn it off in order to film the scenes. "He was like, 'Hey man, what's going on?' We didn't want Kanye to get upset, but at the same time, we kind of had to film… Then he started performing, and it gets to the point where he's screaming. He goes a full 100-miles-an-hour. Then he'd turn off and go, 'Anyway, thanks.' It was hilarious." He was also in the process of selling his $4.5 million NYC apartment as well as his house in LA, plus the world was suddenly starting to resemble the kids from his schooldays who'd call him gay for acting like his mother.

A story appeared in *In Touch* magazine on May 16 claiming that Kanye was homosexual and secretly dating designer Riccardo Tisci, the man behind the *Watch The Throne* artwork. The basis of these rumours came from fairly spurious sources – in January 2013 a fashion blogger called Bryan Boy tweeted, "Wait so Kanye West is gay? He and Riccardo Tisci were… lovers? And Kim Kardashian is a beard? Why am I the last to know?" and instantly the gossip hounds began digging for whatever evidence they could find. They pointed out that Kanye's Paris apartment was close to Tisci's and that Tisci had also bought a New York apartment close to Kanye's. They noted the leather skirts that Kanye had recently been sporting, and the large amount of time Kanye had spent away from Kim's LA base during her pregnancy, hanging out with Tisci more than his girlfriend and heading to Milan when Kim was in Paris. Kim's suggestion that she and Kanye lived "different lives" – she more open and he more private – was leapt upon and Perez Hilton dug out a comment that Tisci had made back in 2011, when asked about his best sexual encounters: "I have several but the one I think immediately is an experience I had with a man who is known. I never imagined that something could happen between us and it's still the hottest weekend of my life. Nobody really knows if this guy is straight or gay, it is a mystery. However, I was attracted to him, his way of speaking, thinking, walking, dressing. I love what he does as an artist. This weekend both, this intimate moment has only reinforced my attraction to him."

This was all very flimsy and unsubstantiated gossip, of course, and there was copious evidence to the contrary – numerous female lovers, plenty of girl-obsessed verses, a daughter on the way. Kanye would credit his relationship as helping him concentrate on his work. "Any woman that you're in love with or that loves you is going to command a certain amount of, you know, energy," he said. "It's actually easier to focus, in some ways… I'm the type of rock star that likes to have a girlfriend, you know? I'm the type of soul that likes to be in love and likes to be able to focus. And that inspires me."

So such dirt-raking can only have served to frustrate Kanye further at a time when *Yeezus* was struggling to come together as he wanted it to. In May the Def Jam top brass heard the album and described it as "dark", and just 15 days before the album was due to be delivered, Kanye turned to Rick Rubin for advice, and the record went through a swift and dramatic shake-up. "I'm still just a kid learning about minimalism, and he's a master of it," Kanye said. "It's just really such a blessing, to be able to work with him. I want to say that after working with Rick, it humbled me to realise why I hadn't – even though I produced *Watch The Throne*; even though I produced *Dark Fantasy* – why I hadn't won Album of the Year yet."

"It was good for me to go to the god, Rick Rubin, and play him my shit, ask him questions, and allow him to take this project to an entirely new level," Kanye said at the album's launch, "and he made a lot of great decisions at the end and pulled it to a whole new level."

"Kanye came over to play me what I assumed was going to be the finished album at three weeks before the last possible delivery date," Rubin said. "We ended up listening to three hours of partially finished pieces. The raw material was very strong but hadn't yet come into focus. Many of the vocals hadn't been recorded yet, and many of those still didn't have lyrics. From what he played me, it sounded like several months more work had to be done. I joined the project because after discussing what he had played for me, he asked if I would be open to taking all of the raw material on and help him finish it."

"I said, 'When are you thinking of finishing up?','" Rubin continued. "And he said, 'It's coming out in five weeks'. Like completely confident and fine… I said, 'I have a record coming out in November that's a lot further along than this'. He said, 'Really? What are you doing for the next five days?' I said I was going to go away. Then he said, 'Please help me. Would you be open to fixing it and shaping it and finishing it off?'… To me it seemed impossible what he was asking. I remember I wasn't feeling that well that day, and I was thinking, is the music making me sick? I don't feel good about this… I said, 'Maybe you should make it more concise. Maybe this is two albums. Maybe this is just the first half'. That was one of the first breakthroughs. Kanye was like, 'That's what I came here today to hear! It could be 10 songs!'"

So Kanye relocated to Shangri-La Studios in Malibu, near Zuma Beach at the end of May. Built by Bob Dylan and the Band in the seventies, the studio was bought by Rick Rubin in 2011; a plush complex of white houses and a backyard silver trailer, into which Kanye moved a variety of collaborators to completely rework the record, recording new vocals and verses and deconstructing the album until the raw bare bones remained.

"We ended up working probably 15 days, 16 days, long hours, no days off, 15 hours a day," said Rubin. "I was panicked the whole time. There was so much material we could really pick which direction it was going to go. The idea of making it edgy and minimal and hard was Kanye's. I'd say, "'This song is not so good. Should I start messing with it? Can I make it better?' And he'd say, 'Yes, but instead of adding stuff, try taking stuff away'. We talked a lot about minimalism. My house is basically an empty white box. When he walked in, he was like, 'My house is an empty white box, too!'."

"He wanted the music to take a stripped-down minimal direction," said Rubin. "A good example would be the song that became 'Bound'. When he first played it for me, it was a more middle of the road R&B song, done in an adult contemporary style. Kanye had the idea of combining that track with a cool sample he had found and liked – I removed all of the R&B elements leaving only a single note bass line in the hook which we processed to have a punk edge in the

Suicide tradition… He is a true artist who happens to make music under the wide umbrella of hip-hop. He is in no way beholden to hip-hop's typical messaging musical cliches. Hip-hop is a grander, more personal form because of his contributions, and hopefully his work will inspire others to push the boundaries of what's possible in hip-hop… He is pure in his art and in a form where so many choices artists make are often the result of business consideration. Kanye chooses to let his art lead. He didn't want a premeditated commercial [single] for his album as he looks at it as a body of work. I like it any time an artist follows his own vision of a project and doesn't use the cookie cutter template expected of most artists. Kanye proceeds on the road less travelled and I applaud him for it."

As with previous albums, work on *Yeezus* went right down to the wire. "We were working on a Sunday and the album was to be turned in two days later," said Rubin. "Kanye was planning to go to Milan that night. Five songs still needed vocals and two or three of them still needed lyrics. He said, 'Don't worry, I will score 40 points for you in the fourth quarter'. In the two hours before he had to run out to catch the plane, he did exactly that: finished all lyrics and performed them with gusto. A remarkable feat. He had total confidence in his ability to get the job done when push came to shove."

"He says, 'I have to go to this baby shower before I go to Milan. I'll be back at 4 p.m., and from four to six I'll do the vocals. Then I have to go'… Again it just seemed impossible, but that's basically what he did. He didn't come back until after four, and we probably didn't start until after five. He said, 'I have an hour and 10 minutes. Let's go'. And then it was full-on NBA finals. It probably ended up taking two hours. Five vocals. He wrote two lyrics on the spot."

The record they clawed together at the very last minute was referred to as "aspirational minimalism" by West and had Rubin exclaiming "it's unbelievable what's happening in there," as he staggered dumbfounded from the studio. Six songs were removed from the album to be held back for a follow-up: "There are a lot of amazing songs that were left off," Hudson Mohawke said, "stuff that you might consider to be more melodic or in line with Kanye's previous material – purely because they didn't necessarily fit this rough-edged, nineties-industrial-type vibe. A lot of the record is trying to avoid obviousness. Through the entire process of putting it together, there were tons of easy slam dunks, but rather than just going for the hits and having an album that nobody's going to give a fuck about in a month or two, he intentionally sidestepped the obvious route each time. I think that's what going to give it more longevity and put it in a category of records that you'll go back to in 10 years' time."

So *Yeezus* was clipped, stripped and reduced to a lean 40 minutes. And it was starting to sound mighty God-like…

★ ★ ★

Yeezus set out to unsettle. Originally it was due to open with the Nina Simone sample of 'Blood On The Leaves', a welcoming formula that Kanye had used several times on his records, not least on *MBDTF*. But at the last minute he changed his mind. He wanted the record to start with a shock of discomfort, a "Daft Punk sound… using postmodern creativity where you kind of lean on something that people are familiar with and comfortable with to get their attention." He wanted *Yeezus* to open with the sound of internet static, the tablecloth being pulled from underneath rap's wavering cutlery.

A flurry of futuristic phase. A cruel, minimalist beat and sizzling acid house bleeps and braps. An icy interlude of distant soul from out of nowhere was a snippet of 'He'll Give Us What We Really Need' by the Holy Name Of Mary Choral Family that had been re-recorded due to sample clearance issues. With 'On Sight', *Yeezus* was declaring itself another brave new swerve in West's ever-shifting evolution, this time into the dark Germanic basement dance floors.

"[Daft Punk] had a synthesizer the size of that wall right there," Kanye said. "This is just one session right here. This beat was originally like 14 minutes long, and that part in the beginning was something we completely just distorted, and I ended up making that the intro."

"'On Sight' sets a new bar," said Goldstein. "Nobody's doing that. There's no chance in hell that anybody's gonna put that on and be like,

'Oh, that's J. Cole'… There's only one person who can do that kind of shit." "'On Sight' puts a message across that this is a very different record," Mohawke added. "'On Sight' is my favourite song on the whole album, but I felt like people weren't gonna fucking know what they're listening to when that distorted acid instrumental comes in… But Kanye went ahead with it, and good on him for sticking to his guns, because that song really sets the tone."

"For people who didn't like *Yeezus* when it first came out," Kanye said, "it's a simple thing that I could've done to make them like it more, which I chose not to do. I coulda put 'Blood On The Leaves' at the beginning of the album, which I always do… it's a certain type of melody that I usually have. [But] I wanted to put that frustration."

"I wanted to take a more aggressive approach with music. You know, people go on a vacation and say, 'You got the drugs, you got the music, you got the wine?' ['Blood On The Leaves'] is in that territory. But I wanted to speak up and say… I'm gonna take music and I'm gonna try to make it three-dimensional, like – like – like on *Star Wars* and the hologram'll pop up out of R2D2. I'm gonna try to make something that jumps up and affects you, in a good or bad way. I'm going into a scream in the middle of the track because that's just the way I feel. But I'm not here to make easy listening, you know, easy programmable music… Taking one thousand meetings, attempting to get backing to do clothing and different things like that [and] getting no headway whatsoever. It was just that level of frustration. This is what frustration fucking sounds like."

Over this startling new style, Kanye poured out that frustration, a driving force for the album. He spat out his hatred of the gossip pages – "Fuck whatever y'all been hearing/Fuck whatever y'all been wearing/A monster about to come alive again" – and hit back at the trauma that Kris Humphries had been putting Kim through during their lengthy and tempestuous divorce proceedings. And he played up his old player image too, reeling off stories of easy sex in exclusive clubs as if to prove the old Kanye West still writhed proudly beneath this fresh alien sheen.

Having got an unexpected sonic punch in early, Kanye continued pummelling. 'Black Skinhead' followed, leading into 'I Am A God' and 'New Slaves', a powerful set of next generation industrial tech-rap that set *Yeezus*' tone to rabid and sepulchral, and 'Hold My Liquor' gave the first half of the record a more tender edge. A soft, somber throb of synthetic soul, it opened with Vernon and Chief Keef representing the intoxicating effects of alcohol and weed respectively, their slurred and Auto-Tuned vocal hooks taking on the roles of the angel and devil on Kanye's shoulder, the depressive and cocky sides of his personality wrestling for control. His drinking side admitted to being "dark and lonely" at times, and his smoking side admitted to being out of control, especially when he's had a sippy-sippy. This was brutally confessional stuff, and it appeared the reckless side of his psyche that Keef represented won out: as the beat rose and airhorn parps gave the track a sinister edge, Kanye launched into a verse of wanton hedonism and destruction. Waking up from an alcohol-induced coma from the night before, he found himself on the sofa of a girlfriend from five years ago, having smashed her car trying to park his Range Rover next to it while coming over in the hope that "One more hit and I can own ya/One more fuck and I can own ya". The sex had resembled transcendental meditation★, but a visiting aunt tells the girlfriend that Kanye's just "a loner/Late night organ-donor/After that he'll disown ya". The final line "Bitch I'm back out my coma" suggests the verse had been a dream, but commentators speculated that it was a dream exposing his regret over losing his relationship with Alexis Phifer, a dangerous dream to be expounding as fatherhood approached.

The sexual theme ran on into 'I'm In It', Kanye's most graphic celebration of the physical act in some time. A track that had started with a completely different melody and sample, had existed as a six-minute instrumental for some time and was finally stripped back to three minutes by Rick Rubin, its final version featuring a sample of

---

★ Kanye references author and proponent of transcendental meditation Deepak Chopra here, whom Kim had actually taken him to visit. He claimed that securing a deal with Adidas the same day was far more spiritually enlightening than his session with Chopra, and didn't go back for his second session.

'Lately' by Kenny Lattimore. It had an ominous, creepy Kanye rapping about interracial sex and all manner of experimental bedroom activity – "eye fuckin', eatin' ass… put my fist in her like a civil rights sign" – over what sounded like pitched down porn groans and crunching rock chords. Glorying in his unquenchable urge for excessive sex throughout his verses, the outro is full of self-reproach as Kanye realises that he's addicted to this wild, sexually rapacious lifestyle. "Go the kids-and-the-wife life/But can't wake up from the nightlife/I'm so scared of my demons". His mind racing "like a Tron bike", he was facing the realities of adulthood here, as well as his distrust of relationships, but found solace in his rap skills – "pop a wheelie on the Zeitgeist/I'm gonna start a new movement".

'I'm In It' was the album's most adventurous tune yet, shifting from those salacious, distorted MOR rock blasts to sections of pulsing house electronica and Jamaican reggae from Assassin to minimalist synth booms and sumptuous misty bridges featuring Vernon calling out this "star fucker", it was truly unclassifiable. "We're all trying to push things to be weirder," said Mike Dean. "I sometimes push for stuff to be more musical, and then Kanye pulls it back to hip-hop. 'I'm In It', for instance, had these crazy guitar parts and all this stadium stuff, and then Rick, Noah, and Kanye pulled it back. I wasn't very happy with that at first, but it came out really well." "That track is obviously very overtly sexual," Evian Christ added, "and the production mirrors that. When I first sent it, I had some breathy sex sounds laid on the snares, and by the time Kanye was rapping over it, it definitely went into overdrive as far as emphasising the sexuality. The first time I heard it with Kanye's vocals, I had to do a double-take on a couple of the lines. But if you're gonna do a song like that, you may as well go all the way; if you're gonna do a sex song, you may as well talk about fisting. To me, it was very definite – he absolutely knew what he wanted to do on that track."

"I don't even know what I'm singing on 'I'm In It'," Vernon admitted. "Kanye's talking about a bunch of really violently and stunningly visual sex shit in there, but it's not like he's saying stuff like that to his friends 24 hours a day. I mean, sitting around the studio, we all have intelligent conversations about the state of women in the world – I wouldn't say we had a conversation about feminism, necessarily, but we're sensitive to it. The imagery of the song is definitely intense, but so is *American Psycho*."

In stark contrast, 'Blood On The Leaves' was the album's emotional centrepiece. Opening with the subtle, stunning and instantly recognisable sample from Nina Simone's 'Strange Fruit', a moving and poetic portrayal of the bodies of lynching victims hanging from the trees, Kanye cut the sample to make the line "blood on the leaves" sound urgent and pleading as he delved, mildly Auto-Tuned, into his troubled thoughts on love over velveteen piano, bursting into doomy synthetic fanfares akin to a demonic *Rocky* theme as his verses billowed with emotion. Also sampling TNGHT's 'R U Ready', he bewailed the fact that he was hounded by the press and kiss-and-tell ex-girlfriends when all he really wanted was his lost mother's love, the one thing he couldn't buy, and then focused in on one particular ex that had betrayed him. "We could've been somebody/'Stead you had to tell somebody," he accused her, remembering her wild antics on Ecstasy, "running naked down the lobby, and you was screaming that you loved me" and the golden days "before the limelight stole ya… before they call lawyers/Before you tried to destroy us".

Since he'd never been through a divorce, these lines may well be flights of fancy. He told Big Boi at Power 106 that the song was a fictional story about a player who was first strung along and then blackmailed by a girlfriend. But the vitriol that broiled through them was unmistakably real, as he flung himself into a final verse attacking the groupies "trying to get a baby" from a rap star but not realising the star isn't interested in anything beyond sex, only to fall pregnant and ruin the rapper's marriage, finances and hedonistic lifestyle: "Now your driver say that new Benz, you can't afford that/All that cocaine on the table, you can't snort that/That goin' to that owin' money that the court got". Some claimed 'Blood On The Leaves' was a cathartic exercise, Kanye exorcising all of his fears over marriage and fatherhood before he took the plunge. But whatever the intention, the result is powerful work, and one which stunned viewers of the MTV VMAs in

2013 when Kanye performed it in front of director Steve McQueen's lynching tree backdrop.★

"'Blood On The Leaves' is a crazy-ass song, bro," said Travi$. "That's the Kanye West genius right there: only he would think that 'Strange Fruit' was missing a HudMo beat, and that the HudMo beat was missing 'Strange Fruit'. When I heard that, I was jumping on niggas' backs and shit." "I think Kanye had wanted to use that 'Strange Fruit' sample for a while," said Hudson, "but it was like, 'How in the hell are you going to get that to fit?' But it miraculously came together. Obviously, 'Strange Fruit' carries so much political weight, and 'Blood On The Leaves' is more about past relationships, but you can draw some parallels between the two. There's not an overtly political message in the final lyrics, but in some ways that would've been too easy."

'Blood On The Leaves' even impressed director David Lynch, who Kanye insisted should direct a video for it. "I think it's one of the most modern pieces and so minimal," he said, "so powerful but at the same time so beautiful. It's a great, great song. I feel I let [Kanye] down a little bit. 'Blood On The Leaves' is one of my favourite songs. I loved the song, and that's what brought us together, but I couldn't come up with ideas that thrilled either one of us."

'Guilt Trip' was originally planned for *Watch The Throne*, but made for a vital interlude on *Yeezus* with its shimmering ascending synth wash, atmospheric chords and devil-pitched hook sample from Popcaan's intro to Pusha T's 'Blocka'. Though somewhat unfocussed lyrically, it would certainly have perked up the ears of anyone looking for cracks in the Kimye front – "I need to call it off," went the intro, "another one, something gone... she lives her life/I'm living mine". Looking to the stars for guidance, he stated "she's into Leos and I was into trios", further suggesting his libido hadn't been tamed by his relationship, yet claimed "my heart got shot down" and turned to alcohol in order to dismiss the girl out of hand: "On to the next saga/Focus on the future

---

★ The VMA 2013 show was stolen, of course, by Miley Cyrus' notorious twerking performance with Robin Thicke, but Kanye cosied in on that action too, arranging to record a remix of 'Black Skinhead' with Cyrus in the wake of the controversy.

and let the crew knock her". Either Kanye was wallowing in his past mistakes here, or there was trouble in paradise.

"The vocal that I did on that song was a couple years old," said Kid Cudi of his emotive outro. "I forgot which session it was. Part of me was flattered, like, it's kind of cool that he thought of me. Then I started thinking about it more. It was like, why not call me and have me come in there and give it? Why underuse me? Why put four bars of vocals to coax my fans into thinking this is a legitimate Kid Cudi feature on this song and it isn't? I don't know how to feel but I would've much rather been off that song. I don't care to be on people's songs like that. Unless it came from a legitimate session where we're all vibing and have an idea."

For the penultimate track, 'Send It Up', Kanye turned to tech house kings Gesaffelstein and Brodinski after hearing the former's 'Viol', and hooked them up with Daft Punk to make a metallic, murderous hell-house whiner adorned with evil fuzz synths, which sampled Beenie Man's 'Memories'. "If a rapper had asked me to do a classic hip-hop beat, I would have said no," said Gesaffelstein, "[But] when I was with Kanye, he wasn't like, 'Do something hip-hop'. He was like, 'Do what you want'. For me, it's not hip-hop. I just want to mix ideas. I try to be open to the world of hip-hop now because I think we can change a lot of things in this music. I just want to work with people who want to change things. Now, it's always the same beats. *Yeezus* was something different. It's electro – and when I say electro, it's closer to the first wave from Detroit."

"In French rap," Brodinski added, "everybody just complains and talks about bad situations. I feel like there isn't so much of a story to tell. The American stuff, particularly out of the south, is what I enjoy and have even added those elements in my new album. There's substance behind the words. It tells the story of struggle and overcoming obstacles they've faced over the years. They celebrate their success by ballin' out. It's real and inventive, you know. When Kanye listened to our techno sound, he liked it a lot and asked us to produce something around those lines. He's a very smart individual and open to working with different ideas. It was one of the best experiences of my life."

Chicago drill rapper King Louis took the sonorous, narcotic opening verse of 'Send It Up', telling of Chicago gangland murders and schoolyard drug dealing, with a sliver of sex thrown in for good measure. And Kanye's verse was similarly throwaway, a classic tale of picking up a girl in a club for sex, given a nostalgic hue by the closing outro from Beenie Man's 'Memories': "Whether things are good or bad/It's just the memories that you have".

Yeezus wound up with another flashback, this time to Kanye's earlier, soulful style. Constructing a Jackson 5 style soul backing from Ponderosa Twins Plus One's 1971 track 'Bound' and the phrase "uh-huh honey, alright" from Brenda Lee's 'Sweet Nuthin's' from 1959, he created 'Bound 2', one of the album's most memorable and instant tracks, and concluded all of Kanye's soul-searching and emotional trawling with a sincere declaration that he was "bound to fall in love". Taking swipes at Kim's previous boyfriends in lines like "All them other niggas lame and you know it now/When a real nigga hold you down, you supposed to drown"*, his two verses portrayed the beginning and the happy ending of a romance, starting with cocky chat-up lines in a nightclub and ending with promises that "maybe we could still make it to the church steps" despite his continued interest in threesomes – the Celeb Dirty Laundry website claimed that Kanye had asked Kim for a threesome with a blonde model in 2012, but Kim had refused – and his colourful sexual history. The key Kanye lines here were "Close your eyes and let the word paint a thousand pictures/One good girl is worth a thousand bitches", undoubtedly a tribute to Kim, but the most memorable part of the track was the brilliantly incongruous interjection of an eighties arena rock style bridge sung by Charlie Wilson from the Gap Band, suggesting that life was one big party and no-one went home alone: "I know you're tired of loving, of loving with nobody to love… just grab somebody, no leaving this party with nobody to love". Tony Wilson

---

* Ray J, the ex-boyfriend with whom Kim had made her sex tape, released a diss track aimed at Kanye earlier in 2013 called 'I Hit It First'. Kanye was no doubt aiming these lines particularly at Ray.

originally wrote this bridge and he and John Legend both sang it before Charlie Wilson's version was selected for the final track.

Yeezus was a courageous, ground-breaking achievement, cementing Kanye's modus operandi as continual reinvention. And it arrived in a blaze of attention. "With this album, we ain't drop no single to radio," said Kanye. "We ain't got no NBA campaign, nothing like that. Shit, we ain't even got no cover. We just made some real music." Instead he premiered more new songs during his headline set at the Governor's Ball in NYC, where the audience sang Happy Birthday to him during 'Power', on June 9 in front of his *SNL* backdrop of black KKK masks and the ravenous Cerberus, and with a stage full of blinding lights dazzling the crowd. Between songs he explained his guerilla release strategy: "When I listen to radio, that ain't where I wanna be no more," he said. "Honestly, at this point, I could give a fuck about selling a million records as long as I put out an album this summer that y'all can rock to all motherfucking summer. And I don't give a fuck that the label's saying I can sell more records. And at this point, I don't really give a fuck about outside opinions. All I give a fuck about is my motherfucking clique." Kanye carried this attitude offstage that summer too; photographers wishing him happy birthday were cut down with a snarl of, "Don't ask me questions... don't ever talk!"

On June 14 the record leaked online in a tirade of Twitter excitement and confusion, some fans calling it musical and commercial suicide and live-blogging their confusion. "Kanye West's new album didn't leak online over the weekend," wrote the *Washington Post*. "It gushed out into the pop ecosystem like a million barrels of renegade crude – ominous, mesmerising and of great consequence."

"I really like the fact that people are loving this album or they're like, 'This is trash!'" said Noah Goldstein. "I don't really like up-the-middle music, because where's the opinion in that? I'd rather have people hate it than be in the middle... Part of my job is to be up on pop culture, but also keep track of what's going on in the depths of the music scene... I'm always thinking, 'Are we doing something that's already being done?' If so, we should stop. One of my friends said the album sounded like Death Grips, and I was like, 'I don't know what you're talking about, but OK.' I know of them, but I can definitely say that we did not listen to Death Grips once the entire time we were making this album."

Then, on June 18, the album officially dropped, clad in a minimalist, clear crystal jewel CD case with a red sticker holding it shut, and accompanied by a short promotional film based on *American Psycho*, in which Scott Disick mimicked Christian Bale's portrayal of Patrick Bateman, lecturing an associate on the brilliance of Kanye's work over drinks in his pure white apartment as he donned a white raincoat and picked up a large axe. "And then, there's a song 'I Am a God'," Disick ranted as he brought down the axe. "The title practically speaks for itself. But of course, the insecurities of the mainstream music press will never understand its true meaning because it's *ABOUT ME!*"

"I feel I was able to start making exactly what was in my mind again, not having to speak with the textures of the time," Kanye would say about the album. "Cause *Cruel Summer* is definitely Kanye West, and there's something weird and kind of off about 'Mercy'… It sounds like art still a little bit, even though it obviously was a radio smash. But when I get into the trap drums and things like that, certain songs that are blatant radio hits, it's like I'm speaking with today's textures. And that's – if you look at it 200 years from now, it's not going to stand out in the way that *808s* or *Yeezus* stands out, and can completely push or redefine or make people say, 'Hey, I completely hate that', or 'I completely love that', but let me just think differently. Because everybody is bound to 16 bars or eight bars – the radio thing. I was talking to Frank Ocean about this, and said, my mom got arrested for the sit-ins, and now we're more like the sit-outs. Like, sit off of radio, and say, 'Hey radio, come to us'. We need to find something new, because it's being controlled in a way, and manufactured in a way, that really awesome artists can make amazing music and not break as far past as, like, something that's very formulaic… I'm not trying to regurgitate myself. I showed – showed people that I understand how to make perfect. *Dark Fantasy* could be considered to be perfect. I know how to make perfect. But that's not what I'm here to do. I'm here to crack the pavement and make new grounds, you know, sonically and culturally."

A day later, on June 19, 'Black Skinhead' was released to radio as the album's first single, alongside a video that Kanye had been working on with photographer Nick Knight for five months, though Kanye was furious when an unfinished version of the video leaked online a week before release, tweeting "whoever leaked the video… fuck you". Utilising the same shadowy, aggressive aesthetic as his *SNL* performance, it featured a topless CGI Kanye in a bright gold chain rapping like a wolverine, but an interactive version of the clip released on West's website allowed the viewer to pitch down the speed of the video and take screen shots with a cursor that flipped the bird.

For all its rage and rapaciousness, 'Black Skinhead' was so startling and unexpected that it made little dent on the charts, reaching number 69 in the US and 34 in the UK. The public would take a while to acclimatise themselves to Kanye's latest form of minimalist industrial attack, but the critics were quicker off the mark. "[A] brilliant, obsessive-compulsive career auto-correct," wrote *Rolling Stone*'s Jon Dolan. "Every mad genius has to make a record like this at least once in his career – at its nastiest, his makes *Kid A* or *In Utero* or *Trans* all look like Bruno Mars." "Immediately stunning," concluded *USA Today*, "he created a polarising, multi-layered body of work that probably will be debated all summer." "The album is one long, efficient, inventive kick in the head," wrote the *New York Times*' Jon Parales. "Even by the standards of an artist who reinvents himself with each release, it's a drastic departure," attested The A.V. Club, "[his] loudest and most impulsive album."

Even legendary Velvet Underground founder Lou Reed, writing shortly before his death, added credence to Kanye's cultural standing by personally critiquing the album: "There are moments of supreme beauty and greatness on this record, and then some of it is the same old shit," he wrote. "But the guy really, really, *really* is talented. He's really trying to raise the bar. No one's near doing what he's doing, it's not even on the same planet… Actually, the whole album is like a movie, or a novel – each track segues into the next. This is not individual tracks sitting on their own island, all alone. Very often, he'll have this very monotonous section going and then, suddenly – *"BAP! BAP! BAP! BAP!"* – he disrupts the whole thing and we're on to something new that's absolutely incredible. That's architecture, that's structure – this guy is seriously smart. He keeps unbalancing you. He'll pile on all this sound and then suddenly pull it away, all the way to complete silence. And then there's a scream or a beautiful melody, right there in your face. That's what I call a sucker punch."

The album would go on to be voted the best album of the year by 18 publications, and appeared on 61 end of year lists, the most acclaimed record of 2013. Its sales figures didn't quite match its acclaim, however. It charted at number one in 31 counties including the US, UK, Canada, Australia and Germany, but because of the leak it only sold 327,000 copies in its first week, the lowest figures of any of his solo albums. Nonetheless, this represented the third best first-week sales of 2013 and *Yeezus* would go on to sell over one million copies. And Kanye's opinion of himself and his talents certainly wasn't diminished by the figures.

"People are going to look back 10 or 20 years from now and say, 'Man, I remember such and such was like this, but then Kanye got involved, and now it's like this'," he said in amongst the smattering of press interviews that emerged around the release – sometimes with major creative figures including author Bret Easton Ellis or director Steve McQueen, reflecting his elevated cultural standing. "On one end, I try to scale [my narcissism] back. Because I don't want to close any of the doors needed to create the best product possible. But my ego is my drug. My drug is, 'I'm better than all you other motherfuckers. Kiss my ass!'... [I'm] bubbling at the highest level of output."

He revealed that he was creative director on the new Jetsons movie and working on a new men's capsule line for APC which was set to include minimalist designs on hoodies, T-shirts and jeans, a collection that APC's founder and director Jean Touitou claimed took two long years of arguments and wrangles to create just three items for. "Kanye has strong obsessions and wants to go in so many different directions," Touitou said, "basically, he wants to redo the whole universe. When we finally finished this collection, I felt like, OK, if I made this happen, then I can achieve peace in the Middle East." But West told reporters that his ambitions were now reaching far beyond music, film and fashion. Showing signs of rampant megalomania, he dreamed of creating operas, movies, amusement parks, entire cities. Between making beats, he said, he was googling modern architects, and he likened himself to everyone from Picasso and Michelangelo to Steve Jobs, Le Corbusier, the Beatles, Brando, Tiger Woods, Azzedine Alaia and Kate Moss.

"Visiting my mind is like visiting the Hermès factory," he said. "Shit is real. You're not going to find a chink. It's 100,000 percent Jimi Hendrix... People say, 'Why do you want to destroy your name?' But I don't care about my name as much as I care about my ideas. I could do something completely wrong, and people could hate it, but then someone else could see it and do it completely right. And it's a push forward for civilization."

"I wanted to get into the cycle of an artist and the balance of commerciality and integrity," he told Hot 97. "My dream is every dream. I won't be limited to just one dream." Yet, despite his DONDA collaborator Virgil Abloh believing he was "one meeting away from being Walt Disney, he claimed his visions were still being compromised by the designers he was having meetings with – Renzo Rosso at Diesel, Bernard Arnault at LVMH and Francois-Henri Pinault at Kering. He was busy putting together teams of the best people to help him in his various projects and exploits, but in his mission to create high quality fashion that would make an emotional connection with people who otherwise couldn't afford it, he ran into directors who were wary of getting involved with him as he'd be impossible to control. "To have integrity, relevance and finances is like juggling on a tightrope. You gonna sacrifice one for the other. The world is set up so you've got to sacrifice one... Don't think that because I'm a celebrity I have true creative freedom. Celebrities are controlled by perception and finances, they are a new form of control slave."

"They try to distract you with celebrity income, meanwhile we're arguing about who got the most or the least, who got this car or this house, at the end of the day we're just playing in a bigger slave field. Meanwhile other people can really make product. It ain't too many celebrities with a boat on that barge out in Greece."

Such hold-backs, which he largely put down to his race, were particularly frustrating as he was convinced he was trying to create things for the good of humanity, "things that can make the world better. I'm not saying that I'm going to make a better world; I'm just saying that I will provide some things that will help." Declaring "[I want] the power to create what is in my mind… to have a thought or an idea and bring it into reality", he envisaged a future where he could walk into a gym, dictate Belgian designer Axel Vervoordt should redesign it, and it would happen on his whim. Or where movie directors organised school programmes involving wall-sized screens and lessons conducted via iPhone, pushing humanity forward in terms of technological interaction. Whether it was dreaming up a new product or concocting a unique way for movies to be watched, Kanye wanted a world that could be instantly Westified.

"The problem is that I like to be the inventor," he said. "I'm the person who works on the concept, who invents new thoughts, who brings new ideas into the universe. I'm not the guy who works on selling the idea – I'm not Vanna White for the new Hyundai. I am the guy who works on the concept for the car. So success, for me, is in having the ability to get my ideas out there… I just want to create more. I would be fine with making less money. I actually spend the majority of my money attempting to create more things. Not buying things or solidifying myself or trying to make my house bigger, or trying to show people how many Louis Vuitton bags I can get, or buying my way to a good seat at the table. My definition of success, again, is getting my ideas out there."

When quizzed on his music, he described his records as "sonic paintings", *Yeezus* as "a one-man gang bang" and explained how he was out to "break the glass ceilings, I'm frustrated". He name-checked those other famed Geminis Biggie, Prince and Tupac as his musical forebears and saw himself as part of Gil Scott Heron's activist lineage and Miles Davis' bloodline of stunning sonics. Acknowledging that he was no longer on the outside of mainstream music trying to beat his way in, now he felt he'd "uninvited myself" from a world he'd become disillusioned by, and he had no apologies to make about the arrogance of his album. "I made that song ['I Am A God'] because I am a god," he said, "I don't think there's much more explanation. I'm not going to sit here and defend shit."

"The biggest slavery that we have is our opinion of ourselves," said the man whose personality, his closest associates would reveal, flickered between "bombastic hotheadedness" and "vulnerability and clear-eyed self-awareness". "That's why my attitude is so shunned. It's not a matter of me believing in myself that's so scary to everyone, it's the idea of everyone else starting to believe in themselves just as much as I do that's scary… I'm like a broadcaster for futurism, for dreamers, for people who believe in themselves. We've been taught since day one to stop believing in our own dreams. We've had the confidence beaten out of us since day one, and then sold back to us through branding and diamond rings and songs and melodies – through these lines that we have to walk inside of so as to not break the uniform or look silly or be laughed at. So I hope that there are people out there laughing. Laugh loud, please. Laugh until your lungs give out because I will have the last laugh."

Kanye certainly seemed to be the only one laughing when scrapped footage from a failed 2008 HBO sitcom pilot emerged around this time, in which he appeared to be attempting to make his own version of Larry David's *Curb Your Enthusiasm*.

★ ★ ★

Amid allegations in the US magazine *Star* that in July 2012 Kanye had cheated on Kim with Canadian model Leyla Ghobadi, who claimed Kanye had slept with her after stating his relationship with Kim was "for publicity and nothing serious" – claims that were strenuously denied – another major release dropped.

Kim and Kanye's daughter, North 'Nori' – believed to derive from a combination of Kim's middle name, Noel, and Kanye's middle name, Omari – West was born weighing just under 5lbs on June 15, weeks earlier than expected. Reports in *US Weekly* suggested that Kim was suffering from the life-threatening condition pre-eclampsia ahead of the premature delivery and that the baby was in distress, and Kanye raced over from an album release party to be present throughout the birth. Thankfully all went smoothly; Beyoncé sent them the message "enjoy this beautiful moment together" via Tumblr and splashed out $5,000 on gifts for the young girl, Apple co-founder Steve Wozniak rushed over to meet the baby★ and Kim's famous relations brimmed with happiness at the new arrival. "She's doing great and she's beautiful!" Kim's mother, Kris Jenner, told HLN, "so very exciting!"

The clamour for the first photo of North was immense, so Kanye appeared on the season finale of Jenner's talk show on August 23 to show off a picture of the child for free. "To stop all the noise, I thought it'd be really cool, on her grandmother's season finale, to bring a picture of North," he said, and declaring of Kim, "I was in love with her before I ever even got to talk to her. I wanted to be with her so bad that I thought about picking up sports. I can have people saying that this is going to damage your credibility as an artist or a designer, and I say, 'I don't care, I love this woman'. She's my joy, and she brought my new joy into the world. There's no paparazzi and there's no blog comments that's going to take that joy from me." Becoming a dad, he told Jenner, had given him a new perspective on his actions towards Taylor Swift too. "The last thing I would want for my daughter," he admitted, "is some crazy, drunk black guy in a leather shirt to come up and cut her off at an award show... I was just a crazy rock star."

On the topic of fatherhood, he laughed, "I'm supposed to be this musical genius, but I can't work the car seat that well... After I lost my mother, there were times I felt I would put my life at risk. I felt like sometimes I didn't have something to live for. Now I have two really special people to live for, a whole family to live for, a whole world to live for." In interviews, Kanye promised to bring North up with the same values his mother had instilled into him but was still working out his thoughts on the matter, beyond feeling hugely protective towards his new family. "It's all brand new, how it feels to be a father," he said. "There are some things that I understand, certain things that I don't understand."

★ One of the first gifts Kim gave Kanye after the birth was a box containing two signed Apple mouses – one from Steve Jobs and the other from Wozniak.

According to *US Weekly*, sources close to the couple were claiming the arrival of North had made Kanye "a changed man", cutting short Greek promo trips to be with the baby, and even more determined to marry Kim in some lavish foreign ceremony than he ever had been.

For some time the pair had been preparing for North's arrival by stocking up on designer baby bags and $1,200 baby seats for a pair of new $1.2 million armoured vehicles to fend off kidnapping attempts as well as attacks from landmines and grenade launchers, and renovating their 9,000 sq ft mansion with the help of Romanian architect Oana Stanescu, adding a baby room to its French-style loft area and making every surface baby-proof. His demands were tough to meet, Stanescu suggested, as Kanye insisted on taking ideas from a variety of designers including Joseph Dirand and Tristan Auer. "It's uncomfortable for every single person," Stanescu said. "But it's supposed to be – that's what I think is the cool thing. Right now Kanye is just sponging things up, observing how these people work. He's going to take an idea from Joseph and one from Tristan and make it his own." Some reports claimed that the couple had spent more money refurbishing the house than it had originally cost, dropping $1 million on the security system and $750,000 on gold-plated toilets for the mansion. A level of opulence that even had President Obama bemoaning a change in popular culture towards extravagance and hopeless coveting: "There was not that window into the lifestyles of the rich and famous," he said of the good old days. "Kids weren't monitoring every day what Kim Kardashian was wearing, or where Kanye West was going on vacation, and thinking that somehow that was the mark of success."

Kanye's focus wasn't purely on himself and his family at this point, however. In July 2013 he launched a new Chicago school initiative called Got Bars through his non-profit organisation Donda's House; headed up by Rhymefest, the programme allowed students to record, release and perform their own music. "My mom spent her life as an educator and I am happy that Donda's House can pick up her torch and honour her life's mission," Kanye said in a statement on the programme.

On October 21, he set about making the family official. On Kim's 33rd birthday he blindfolded her and drove her to San Francisco's

AT&T Park where her family and friends sat silent and breathless in the stands. Pulling up before a torchlit 90-piece orchestra, he pulled off her blindfold to watch their performance and then, as pyrotechnics lit the sky and the baseball park's huge Jumbotron screen flashed the message "PLEEEASE MARRY MEEE!!!" he dropped to one knee and proposed with a 15-carat square diamond ring designed by Lorraine Schwartz. The proposal cost $200,000; the ring, we can only guess.

"I just thought it'd be dope," he later told Power 106. "I planned all that out. It was very much like a DONDA exercise. I'll sit with my team of creators and we'll say, 'What's the best version of this? OK, we want Lana Del Rey, oh she didn't show up'... She knew I was eventually gonna ask her to marry me, I just had to get that ring right. I worked with four different jewellers, three rings were made, only one actually hit the finger. The ring got changed the night before, that ring was less than four hours old by the time I gave it to her. I was nervous a little bit but it was more just everything happening on cue. They didn't have the lights exactly like I wanted it to be. I'm arguing with the guy who put it together for me, he's talking about 'It needs to be more romantic' and I'm like, 'It's a baseball field, what you talking about, if I wanted to be romantic I'd have gone to a small restaurant'. I gotta apologise to the race of males for turning it up so much." When asked about his plans for the wedding, rumoured to be being planned for the Palace Of Versailles in France with no upper budget limit, he was comically blunt. "Two words: 'fighter jets'."

He turned it up more come November. Working once more with 'Black Skinhead' director Nick Knight, he unveiled a video for *Yeezus'* second single, 'Bound 2', on his own VEVO channel, and caused an instant internet furore. Following cinematic scenes of horses galloping across canyon floors, Kanye appeared riding a motorbike in front of green-screened landscapes, only to be joined on the bike by a topless Kardashian, writhing suggestively as the bike bounced across the American desert. The concept was inspired by white trash T-shirt imagery, and Prince's *Purple Rain* movie, and would be widely parodied, from home-made recreations on the internet to a Christmas themed version on *SNL*.

"I think people are afraid of dreams," Kanye explained, later claiming that he'd wanted the video to feature more nudity than it did, "and that video is one of the closest things to the way that dreams look and feel, or the way joy looks and feels, with the colours. You know, I think there are rules to fashion, with the all-black everything, and rules to art, with white galleries. There are rules to how a lot of things are: the concrete jungle, stone pavement, brick walls. There are even rules to what a Brooklyn apartment looks like. But this video completely didn't respect any of those rules whatsoever. It's a dream, and I think the controversy comes from the fact that I don't think most people are comfortable with their own dreams, so it's hard for them to be comfortable with other people's dreams. I mean, look, it took some time for us to be comfortable with a walking, talking mouse, but that became an icon. So this stuff, what I'm doing now, is the beginning of me throwing out what it means to be a rapper – you know, with the gold chain."

Indeed, by then, out on the *Yeezus* tour, Kanye was upturning everything people expected a rapper to be.

★ ★ ★

July 2014, Finsbury Park, London. Kanye pressed his microphone to his faceless white cube mask as a waterfall cascaded over the huge screen behind him, and started speaking.

"Don't let nobody tell you what you can do, what you can believe, what you can achieve," he ranted. "People be looking at me like I got a problem or something. Like I'm uncontrollable or something. Like I don't do what I'm supposed to do. It's like they want to have everybody so brainwashed. They want to control everybody, rumours, lies, media, marketing. It's like they want to steal you from you, and sell you back to you after they stole it. They want to make you feel like you less than who you really are… The first thing they do is crush your dreams. Crush your dreams. Then add a couple drops of low self-esteem. And then I don't think everything is what it seems. And control you with lies. And control you with lies…"

For 10 full minutes, sometimes singing lines in Auto-Tune, with piano chords chiming away in the background, he went on; part motivational speech, part vocal freestyle. "How many people believe that what they dream about, what y'all want to do, whether you want to be a doctor or lawyer, a designer, a musician, video-game programmer, a lighting guy, a manager… how many people want to contribute something to the world? You see, I know you all might have seen some of my interviews and seen me on TV, but what I was saying the whole time is… they taking the idea of celebrity and trying to make me seem I was stupid or something. You know, when I take these meetings and shit, people they talk to you like you're stupid… I'm not gonna call no names out, I'm not going to mention Nike or nothing like that… But if you're a creative and you want to create, and you just want to create more, this is exactly what I've been fighting for. So if you hear me talking about Louis Vuitton or the Gucci Group or anything like that. I'm not dissing Louis Vuitton, I'm not dissing the Gucci Group and shit. I'm just saying, don't discriminate against me, because I'm a black man or because I'm a celebrity, and tell me that I can create, but not feel. 'Cause you know damn well there aren't no black guys or celebrities making no Louis Vuitton nothing. They let Pharrell make those glasses, and we liked them, right? They let me make those shoes, and we liked them right? And they say, 'No, no, no, nigger. Not no more. That's too much. That's too much. No, no, no, no, no, no, nigger not no more. That's way too much. That's way too much. Stay in your place. Sit in the front of that show and wear this jacket I made you. Stay in your place. Do what you get paid to do. Stay in your place. Don't embarrass yourself trying to chase your dreams. Save face. Save face.' That's why I got this fucking mask on, cuz I ain't worried about saving face. Fuck my face!… Now they finally got a headline. But fuck whatever my face is supposed to mean!… They try to control y'all and try to control me. And when I was in my negotiations, they told me, 'We don't negotiate with celebrities'. That's like a terrorist. They talk to you like it's fucking terrorist. You know, I just want to make something awesome. I just want to be awesome, and I want to hang around my awesome friends and change the fucking world, and that's exactly what I plan to do. And if you plan to do the same, put your hands in the air right now."

Throughout the *Yeezus* tour, the sermons came thick, fast and very, very long. Clad in his face-covering masks – some black, some white, some made from rainbow mirrors that refracted lasers around the arenas – and peering down from atop Mount Yeezus, he preached his passionate, rambling sermons. "The only difference between me and Lenny Kravitz is I turned up on these niggas, I don't give a fuck about looking cool or being cool," he told Madison Square Garden, paying respect to Kravitz, who was in the crowd, "There wouldn't be no song called 'Niggas In Paris' without Lenny Kravitz, because he was the first nigga in Paris. Lenny has the best taste and the dopest crib." "I hate business people," he told London's Hammersmith Ballroom, "I swear I'm a nice leader now. I swear I'll put the pink polo back on. I swear to you." "I'll crash the motherfucking internet when I feel like it!" he yelled at Las Vegas. At the Barclays Center in Brooklyn he raved at length about the genius of Nikola Tesla and director Alejandro Jodorowsky, in Tampa he stopped the show to bawl out his technical crew for "ruining my show" and likened himself to Thomas Edison, in Texas he ejected a fan for heckling him. "Fuck those nominations!" he said of his two latest Grammy nods from the stage in Phoenix. "It's only patronising. Don't patronise me. I would have rather had no nominations."

He'd be described as "part ego supernova, part prophet, part philosopher, part petulant child, part motivational speaker, and 'completely awesome at all times'" as he attacked Hedi Slimane, Bernard Arnault, Francois-Henri Pinault and Nike from the stage nightly, or invited Google chief Eric Schmidt to invest in DONDA mid-show. "When I compare myself to Steve Jobs, Walt Disney, Howard Hughes, or whoever, it's because I'm trying to give people a little bit of context to the possibilities that are in front of *me*, as opposed to putting me in the rap category that the Grammys has put me in," he'd explain. "In no way do I want to be the next any one of them. But I am the first me."

His speeches became a key part of the *Yeezus* show, another epic thematic spectacular based around the "Biblical redemption story" of the 1973 movie *The Holy Mountain* as well as Kanye's musings on the end of the world. Split into five segments – Fighting, Rising, Falling,

Searching and Finding – and featuring lots of Catholic symbolism such as statues of the Virgin Mary, the show took place on a 50ft high pyramidal grey mountain with a rising triangular catwalk at its foot, a set created by Es Devlin and Vanessa Beecroft. Here, masked dancers in nude body stockings formed a Greek chorus that carried him aloft or cavorted around him, spooky women scaled the peak and the mountain emitted volcanic eruptions of flame, lava and fireworks. At a climactic moment in the show, at the introduction to 'Jesus Walks', a rock wall cracked open and Jesus emerged to face him. "White Jesus, is that you?" Kanye said, "I've been looking for you my whole life, man!" "I didn't come to make bad people feel good," Jesus replied. "I came here to make dead people alive. To show people the light. That's all I need from you, to show people the light of truth in you." It's no wonder, perhaps, that an online community launched a new religion in the wake of the tour – Yeezianity.

Though sales in some key cities were double that of the *Watch The Throne* tour, Jesus wasn't necessarily walking with the tour itself, however. Opening in Seattle's Key Arena on October 19, 2013, this huge arena tour – Kanye's first solo tour in five years – made it through 29 dates until the last show of the year at Toronto's Air Canada Centre, racking up the second highest-grossing leg of any 2013 tour besides Paul McCartney's, despite a truck carrying the custom-made circular video screens being involved in a road accident on the way to Vancouver on October 30, destroying the equipment and forcing the *Yeezus* tour off the road for two weeks – three shows in Vancouver, Denver and Minneapolis were cancelled and gigs in Chicago and Detroit postponed until the screens could be re-engineered.

And Kanye was causing many a stir off the road too, and not just for allegedly asking the producers of *Later With Jools Holland* to iron his dressing room carpet. Back in July, after several months of surly barks at paparazzi while juggling the early days of fatherhood and tabloid scandal, Kanye had been drawn into another altercation with a pushy photographer at LAX. His temper getting the better of him as he'd just learnt that his grandfather was dying, he charged a snapper who was asking him relentless questions and tried to grab his camera, barking "I told you, don't talk to me, right. You're trying to get me in trouble so I step off and have to pay you like $250,000." The photographer, Daniel Ramos, allegedly ended up in hospital and had to walk with crutches for two weeks. In March 2014, having originally pleaded not guilty in November, Kanye would enter a no contest plea to a misdemeanour count of battery against Ramos and was sentenced to two years' probation, having to attend 24 anger management sessions and perform 250 hours of community service as well as paying restitution to the victim. "I was only doing my job, and he broke the law," Ramos said, insisting that West should serve a jail term. "I believe that if I did what he did to me, I would have been put behind bars… I simply asked him a question, and I didn't use any vulgar language. In fact, I gave him a compliment and told him that he was cool."

Kanye had also come under fire in September 2013 for accepting $3 million to perform at the wedding of the grandson of billionaire Khazakstan President Nazarbayev, a man accused of numerous human rights violations and political corruption, but his outspokenness in radio and TV interviews would gain him more publicity, both good and bad. In some of his most impassioned interviews ever, his self-belief blazed through. "I'm standing up and I'm telling you I am Warhol," he told Sway Galloway. "I am the number one most impactful artist of our generation. I am Shakespeare in the flesh. Walt Disney. Nike. Google." On San Fransisco's KMEL station he described he and Kim as "the most influential" couple in the world and on Hot 97 he explained why he'd recently ditched his Nike association and signed a lucrative deal with Adidas: "I took the Adidas deal because I have royalties and I have to provide for my family. Nike told me, 'We can't give you royalties because you're not a professional athlete'. I told them, 'I'll go to the Garden and play one-on-no-one'… Whatever is official, non-official, what y'all gonna see is I'm gonna be the Tupac of product. I'm gonna be the first hip-hop designer and because of that I'm gonna be bigger than Wal-Mart."

When Jimmy Kimmel spoofed him on his late-night comedy chat show, Kanye rang him directly, claiming to be "the most powerful voice in the media"… "He told me I had two choices," Kimmel said on his show that night, "apologise publicly… and that was really the only choice! The other choice he gave was that my life… 'Your life is going to be much better if you apologise'. Finally I'm in a rap feud. Right now we're at Def-Kanye Five: thanks, Kanye, appreciate it." Kimmel wasn't the only one to make fun of Kanye on TV; *South Park* featured him again in an episode called *The Hobbit*, in which a rumour starts at the school that Kim Kardashian is a hobbit. Taking things way too seriously again, he turns up in class to lecture the kids on why she isn't.

As for Kimmel, Kanye threw himself into a Twitter fury – "SHOULD I DO A SPOOF ABOUT YOUR FACE OR YOU FUCKING BEN AFFLECK?" Kanye tweeted, "YOU DON'T HAVE SCUM BAGS HOPPING OVER FENCES TO TRY TO TAKE PICTURES OF YOUR DAUGHTER". And finally, he went on Kimmel's show to face him down: "Don't try to antagonise me because you know what? It's not safe for you in this zoo," he told Kimmel after Jimmy had issued a grovelling apology. "Never think that I'm not for Chicago for one second and think you can walk up and disrespect me and my family constantly."

The spoof Kimmel had made was of Kanye's now-legendary interview with Radio One's Zane Lowe, which Kimmel had recreated with two child actors. And, to be fair, the Lowe interview was perhaps Kanye's crowning achievement of wild verbosity and rocketing ego. "We culture," Kanye declared. "Rap the new rock 'n' roll! We culture! Rap is the new rock 'n' roll! We the rock stars!... It's been like that for a minute… We the real rock stars, and I'm the biggest of all of 'em. I'm the number one rock star on the planet."

"They classify my motivational speeches as rants," he said, "like 'Why is he saying that? Why is he doing that?' Well I've reached a point in my life where my *Truman Show* boat has hit the painting. And I've got to a point that Michael Jackson did not break down. I have reached the glass ceiling – as a creative person, as a celebrity. When I say that it means I want to do product. I am a product person. Not just clothing but water bottle design, architecture, everything that you could think about. And I've been at it for 10 years, and I look around and I say,

'Hey wait a second – there's no one around here in this space that looks like me'. And if they are, they're quiet as fuck! So that means – wait a second – now we're seriously in a Civil Rights movement... For you to have done something to the level of the [Nike] Yeezys and not be able to create more and you cannot – you cannot create that on your own, with no support, with no backing... T-SHIRTS! That's the most we can make! T-shirts. We could have our best perspective on T-shirts. But if it's anything else, your *Truman Show* boat is hitting the wall... I've dedicated the past 10 years of my life to [fashion]. I spent 80 per cent of my time working on this, and 20 per cent of my time working on music. Why do you think this song 'Niggas In Paris' is called 'Niggas In Paris'? Because niggas was in Paris, because I had a office and a small courtyard across the street from Colette, where I couldn't even find a good pattern cutter. That's why we were in Paris. I put in the 10,000 hours. I've got a very particular, specific take on men's footwear. No one can say I cannot design or understand how to design, a guy's sneaker... People didn't love the Yeezy's the way they did for no reason. Picture this, for me to do the Yeezy's and not have a joint venture backing deal with Nike the next day would have been like if I made 'Jesus Walks' [and] I was never allowed to make an album... I eventually want to be the anchor and the force behind a billion dollar company and after I make that billion dollar step, then I can go in and say, 'Hey I've got an opinion on this and that could be a 10 billion dollar step', and I eventually want to be the anchor of the first trillion dollar company."

Declaring himself "a futurist, mentally", Kanye meandered from topic to topic, talking of his Yeezy brand making uniforms for a whole city and of the future of the internet – "You remember like, that you see future movies and everything was in the sky, like it moved to the sky? That's the internet. That's our sky. That's our future sky. We kind of thought we knew it was flying cars. We didn't get flying cars, but we can send movies like in two seconds". He stated, "If you're a Kanye West fan, you are not a fan of me. You're a fan of yourself. You will believe in yourself. I'm just the espresso. I'm just the shot in the morning to get you going, to make you believe that you could overcome that situation that you are dealing with all the time", and projected a new scheme for 'legalising' the paparazzi. "I'm changing things for my daughter. I'm going to tell my daughter, by the time she understands what it was, 'Man, me and your mother were in a completely different situation than you're in. At that time, paparazzi wasn't legal, people could take pictures, people could climb over your fence, people could do that you wouldn't even get paid for it. You see all these cheques that you're getting at age six, because people taking your picture? You don't have to worry about a thing ever again just because people want to take your picture, like I made that happen'. That's what I'm going to tell her."

He also astutely pinpointed major flaws with society in general. "We have to understand that we're not each other's enemy," he argued. "We have to stop discriminating against each other due to class and due to race and due to location or financial position. We have to say, 'Wow that is the best version, let's use it, let's bring it, let's bring it to light, let's move forward, lets push forward as a civilisation', because we are so jacked up on our own egos and so misguided by mainstream marketing, we don't know what the fuck is real, we would be out again to a fight, this quick, for the dumbest reason. We are pitted against each other, we are mentally not in a place to be accepting, to not be jealous and part of that jealousy and that frustration that goes across an entire globe is due to some of these other high corporation level limitations. Everybody is being served a nasty lunch food."

If the Zane Lowe interview caused much hilarity amongst commentators, an appearance on Power 105.1's *Breakfast Club* on November 26 caused much consternation. For much of the interview Kanye was firing great guns, comparing *Yeezus* to the rap *Born In The USA*, ordering every black Atlantan in town to boycott Louis Vuitton for the day, declaring that he loved the paparazzi and was "a performance athlete" of music and describing his onstage diatribes as "visionary streams of consciousness". But he ran into trouble over statements about politics. "Man, let me tell you about George Bush and oil money and Obama and no money," he said. "People want to say Obama can't make these moves or he's not executing. That's because he ain't got those connections. Black people don't have the same level of connections as Jewish people. Black people don't have the same connection as oil people."*

Coming just days after Kanye was criticised for featuring Confederate flags on some *Yeezus* tour T-shirts, his comments were taken as anti-Semitic by the Anti-Defamation League. "This is classic anti-Semitism," wrote ADL National Director Abraham H. Foxman in an online statement. "There it goes again, the age-old canard that Jews are all-powerful and control the levers of power in government. As a celebrity with a wide following, Kanye West should know better. We hope that he will take responsibility for his words, understand why they are so offensive, and apologise to those he has offended."

Kanye saw no need to apologise; this was his world and he continued to speak his own version of the truth within it.

And, with *Yeezus* having ascended on his huge gusts of hot air, it was time to wind himself down.

★ ★ ★

Besides holidaying with his family on the ski slopes of Utah or in the best restaurants in Paris, dealing with his LAX assault case, visiting China and the favela slums of Brazil, legally barring an online campaign to launch a rival to Bitcoin in his honour called Coinye West and announcing two further legs of the Yeezus tour – nine more US and Canada dates in February and seven Australian shows (which would eventually be rescheduled for September), with Kim and North in tow – and a smattering of summer festival dates in Sweden, Denmark, Ireland, the UK and the US, the start of 2014 was relatively quiet for Kanye, but began with more turmoil.

In January he let his anger fly again, as he was accused of assaulting a man in a Beverley Hills chiropractor's office when he went to accompany Kim to an appointment. Reports claimed that Kim arrived at the office and had to push her way to the door through a crowd including an 18-year-old man who'd approached her and said, "Fuck these faggot-ass

---

* The following year, on the same station, he'd return to the subject: "You can't effect change from inside the White House like that," he said. "You gotta have the money."

niggers". When Kim pulled him up on his racist language, he allegedly replied, "Fuck you, bitch, just trying to help you. Shut up, nigger lover, stupid slut" and then walked into the office for his own appointment. When Kanye arrived later, he chased down and repeatedly punched the guy, the fight broken up by the office massage therapist. Kanye later reached a civil settlement with the man for a reported $250,000 sum.

Settling into fatherhood and already well into the writing of a new album, he took most of the year out to work on the record with producers Rubin and Q-Tip, hoping to release it in mid-2014. He spent Grammys night partying in Malibu instead, did little promotion when his latest Nike shoe, the Air Yeezy II Red Octobers, launched in February (and immediately sold out) and quietly celebrated the tenth anniversary of *The College Dropout* with a cake decorated with the album sleeve. When honoured with an award for his contribution to hip-hop by the Tribeca Disruptive Innovation Awards, he sent a bizarre acceptance video which included footage of Laurel & Hardy dancing to his beats, CGI footage of a bear climbing some stairs and himself in discussion with Rick Rubin with their voices overdubbed in German. When he did step out to perform – recreating the *Watch The Throne* show at the SXSW conference in Austin alongside Jay-Z for a Samsung event in March, for instance – he was always the biggest thing in town.

As the winter turned to spring, Kanye's softer, romantic side bloomed. Kim received a thousand red roses for Valentine's Day, and he took to a remix of Jay-Z and Beyoncé's 'Drunk In Love' to shout out his adoration in hip-hop terms: "You a milf and I'm a muthafucker... as far as handling all that ass, I think you gon' needs some help... I know good pussy when I see it, I'm a visionary... I impregnated your mouth girl, that's when I knew you could be my spouse, girl". His verse on Future's 'I Won' was similarly triumphant: "You the number one trophy wife, so it's only right to live the trophy life," he rapped, "I wanna dip that ass in gold/I made it over NBA, NFL players, so every time I score it's like the Super Bowl".

During a rare TV interview on *Late Night With Seth Meyers* he said that his life had changed completely since becoming a father and discussed his plans to make more child-friendly music that his daughter could enjoy. Onstage in Connecticut he declared, "These past 10 years have been amazing. There's been some ups and downs. I made some mistakes and I've made some accomplishments. There's only one thing I regret. There's only one thing I wish I could change out of everything that's ever happened. I wish that my mother could've met my daughter."

He'd even earmarked a role for Kim in the script for a movie he was working on with Bret Easton Ellis, based on *Yeezus*, such was his love for the star. And as the wedding approached, details gradually emerged. According to the *Daily Star* – never the most reliable of news sources – Jay-Z had been asked to be best man, but had refused the role as he didn't want reality TV show cameras filming his family for the whole day, and Beyoncé wanted to avoid being on *Keeping Up With The Kardashians*. Instead, the couple threw Kanye an extravagant stag do at Jay's 40/40 sports club in NYC and paid $100,000 to hire a yacht for their honeymoon. There was a pre-nup which, should they divorce, granted Kim $1 million for every year they're married, up to 10 years, as well as the Bel Air house – at this point she was estimated to be worth $40 million, while Kanye was worth over $100 million. Reports claimed that guests were being asked to sign confidentiality agreements and would have their phones confiscated for the duration of the ceremony to avoid any press leaks.★ The two even appeared in wedding outfits on the cover of *Vogue*, another image that would be spoofed by everyone from James Franco and Seth Rogen to Kermit and Miss Piggy and even Kim's sisters Kylie and Kendall Jenner.

Their plans to marry in France were scuppered by regulations which insist couples have to be resident in the country for 40 days before the ceremony and the Palace of Versailles refused them permission to get married there, yet on May 23, 100 guests were invited to Paris and requested to don "cocktail" dress for a pre-wedding dinner, promised "details on arrival". The guests were given magnificent brunch at Chateau De Wildville, the home of designer Valentino Garavani, then granted a private guided tour of the Palace of Versailles in a flurry of flowers, high-

---

★ This followed the leak of footage of their engagement from YouTube co-founder Chad Hurley, whom they sued over the leak.

art and Musketeers. Beneath a grand statue in the hallway, Lana Del Rey performed 'Young And Beautiful', the song Kanye and Kim considered their special song, and the guests were treated to a pre-wedding dinner in the palace's Hall Of Mirrors as David Blaine performed magic tricks at their tables. "Kim's way more beautiful than I am talented," Kanye reportedly said as the couple greeted their party. Baroque music played by classically dressed musicians filled the halls, tables creaked beneath masses of fanciful French food and horse-drawn carriages arrived to whisk the guests away at the end of the evening. Versailles hadn't seen such opulence since the grandest days of Louis XIV.

The following day, 600 guests – actors, directors, fashion editors, designers, musicians and assorted friends – assembled at the 16th century Forte Belvedere castle in Florence, Italy, for the wedding of the year. At sunset, before a huge wall of white roses and peonies and a grand piano – with the Italian army watching on for added security and rented at a reported cost of $410,000 – Kim and Kanye married, both in Givenchy. Fireworks lit the sky and John Legend and Italian tenor Andrea Bocelli performed as the guests ate the wedding dinner of innovative Italian cuisine, Armand de Brignac champagne and a seven-tier wedding cake at 70-metre long marble tables. It was speculated the wedding cost around $12 million and, naturally, Kanye took the opportunity to give one of his lengthy motivational speeches. "We are warriors!" he reportedly told the guests. "There is not one person at this table that has not had to defend us at some point or another. At this table... the combination of powers... can make the world a better place. [These are] the most remarkable people of our time."

"I adore Florence," Kanye told Italy's *La Nazione* newspaper, "I love Italy and the Italian lifestyle. To tell you the truth, I already came to the banks of the Arno [river] with Kim last year, just the two of us, incognito. I think that our daughter, North, was conceived here among the Renaissance masterpieces. It was our first honeymoon. It is one of the most beautiful cities in the world – for me the most beautiful in Europe... I am composing a whole album, *Made In Florence*."

When the wedding screened on *Keeping Up With The Kardashians* it premiered another of Kanye's gifts to his new wife. A 50-second clip of 'Awesome' accompanied the scenes, an Auto-Tuned piano tribute to Kim which had Kanye crooning, "Why did you ever listen to people trying to hate on you?... 'Cause baby you're awesome... You look too good to be at work... I'd rather do nothing with you than something with somebody new". Naturally, he added a sly aside: "Also, I'm also awesome".

Donning matching 'Just Married' biker jackets before they left the party, the couple honeymooned in another castle in Cork, Ireland where they were reported to have left a four-figure tip at a local pub and boosted the Irish tourist trade by 11 per cent, and in Prague, winding down into a low-key post-wedding period. They holidayed in Mexico, organised a festival-themed first birthday for North called Kichella, oversaw a DONDA partnership deal with Roc Nation allowing Roc to manage all of its output and made a brave return to the Bonaroo festival, where Kanye memorably told the crowd "I ain't going after no one on the radio. I'm going after Shakespeare. I'm going after Walt Disney. I'm going after Howard Hughes. I'm going after David Stern. I'm going after Henry Ford. I'm going after Elon Musk."

In June, Kanye hit the Cannes Lions awards for creative and advertising professionals and held an open conversation with Steve Stout, Stephanie Ruhle and Ben Horowitz called Translation: Technology, Culture, and Consumer Adoption: Learning to Read the Cultural Landscape, in which he laid out his working philosophy. "Throughout my entire life because of the way my parents raised me, I was like 'I have to work with the number one'. I can't work with anyone but Jay Z because that's the number one. I can't represent any company but Louis Vuitton because that's the number one." He also put widespread public perception down to the power of advertising, referencing his 'Bound 2' video. "I still take a bashing for the 'Bound' video," he said. "I always say that if *Vogue* had come out before the 'Bound' video then everyone would have been like, 'Oh it's OK' and that's the endorsement. It took something established like *Vogue* to make everything OK and we had to wait."

His public speaking continued throughout the year; he spent time lecturing to LA fashion students as part of his community service, and raised boos from the crowd at the opening night of the Wireless

Festival in London on July 4 when he likened paparazzi intrusion to rape: "I don't care what you do in life," he said, "everybody needs a day off, everybody has the right to say, 'You know what, I need a minute to breathe'. I want to bring my family to the movies without 30 motherfuckers following me. Everybody here, they like sex right? Sex is great when you and your partner are like, 'Hey, this is what we both want to do'. But if one of those people don't want to do that, what is that called? That's called rape. That is called violation. So if I walk around and say, 'Look sir, I'm not feeling so good today, I need some space, can you please not fuck with me today? I need cut-off space, not violation'… I want my daughter to have that opportunity to decide whether she wants to be famous or not. I think to myself, 'What the fuck am I going to do, how can I change it and how can I give my daughter her childhood?'"

But Kanye also found time to hit the studio with Rihanna, head to Ibiza to perform at Riccardo Tisci's 40th birthday party alongside P Diddy, Justin Bieber, Naomi Campbell and Kate Moss, launch his military-style APC range on July 17★ and buy another LA mansion for $20 million in August, having decided to sell the Bel Air pad with the restoration barely completed. There were also rumours that he was working with Sir Paul McCartney, as he and McCartney became friendly backstage at the the Beatles legend's Dodgers Stadium show.

Even when he was rubbing shoulders with the musical Gods, though, the lightning bolts kept striking. At a show in Melbourne on the final Australian leg of the *Yeezus* tour on September 9, he insisted, "I can't go on with this song if there's people in here sitting down unless y'all sitting down because y'all handicapped," and then singled out a couple who'd remained seated, to boos from the crowd. "It reflects perhaps a lack of understanding of the difficulties people with disabilities face in everyday life," Matthew Wright, CEO of the Australian Federation of Disability Organisations, told *Daily Mail Australia*. "If there was a

---

★ Amid criticism from *America's Next Top Model* judge Kelly Cutrone, who said "I don't think there's one person who really works in the fashion industry who gives a flying fuck about Kanye West."

person in the audience with a disability that would have been very embarrassing for them."

And worse was to come; at the Syndey stop of the show Kanye went further, insisting that two fans who were in wheelchairs should stand up, only starting the next song when his bodyguard made his way to their seats to confirm they were indeed handicapped. At a show in Brisbane a few days later, he defended his actions: "At my concerts I make sure everybody has as good a time as possible," he said. "So all this demonising me, it ain't gonna work after a while. Pick a new target. Pick a new target!" Back home in Chicago, the disabled had the last laugh as a wheelchair-bound fan crowd-surfed towards the stage during Kanye's set at a benefit show appearance. Kanye saluted him as he went.

He was insisting on strict rules of privacy too. The next day, when Kanye was rushed to hospital in Melbourne for an MRI scan after complaining of severe head pains, other patients reported that the entire department was cleared out for him, even though his pains merely turned out to be a migraine. And at their Melbourne hotel it was claimed that the West family hired the entire 23rd floor at a cost of $10,000 per night for their entourage, and so that North could wander freely. Reports claimed that North, by now, had 200 items of clothing she'd never worn, a private chef in Paris and $50,000 diamond studs and her aunt Khloe referred to her as a "major fashionista". Kim, however, would claim that North will have to work for her living, although she hoped she would take over the family fashion firm. It was such flamboyant behaviour, perhaps, that earned Kimye boos when they turned up late to a Lanvin show at Paris Fashion Week in September, an event where they were known to be seen in somewhat regal dress and hired extensive security to help them get through the crushes of photographers at every red carpet.

Having whisked Kim to Hawaii and Vegas for her 34th birthday and performed a five-song set at a World AIDS Day concert in Times Square, the first hints of his new album began to emerge in December. On the 9th it emerged that he'd bumped into Seth Rogen in the lobby of a hotel in NYC, escorted him into a private limo and freestlyed the entire album for him. "Me and my wife had gotten some dessert and were in the lobby getting plates to bring back to our room," Rogen said, "And Kanye was like, 'What are you guys doing? Want to hear my new album?' So he takes us to this limo van and starts playing his album – except there's no lyrics only beats. So he raps the whole album and after each song, he stops it, like 'So what do you think?' We were in the van for two hours! Now I realise the next person he sees that he knows is getting pulled into that van. But I learned a lesson from it – which is that Kanye is seeking input at all times. Process-wise, it showed an openness and a fearlessness. We started screening our movies more and in rougher versions for our friends because of that."

For Christmas, Kanye reportedly spent $74,000 buying North a diamond tiara and an mini SUV and made plans to have a statue of Kim commissioned. And, as a gift to the rest of the world, on iTunes on New Year's Day he released the first track from his new album. 'Only One', the first song to emerge from Kanye's collaboration with Paul McCartney, was a lullaby dedicated to North, so sweet it made Kim cry every time she heard it. Lightly Auto-Tuned and accompanied only by McCartney's soft, soulful muted Rhodes organ and Ty Dolla $ign on backing vocals, the track was written as a message from Donda to Kanye, a form of channelling that Kanye believed was truly Heaven-sent. In a small LA bungalow where Kanye and Paul got together to write, Kanye freestyled stream-of consciousness lyrics as McCartney improvised on the keyboard; but when they listened back to the track, cradling North in his arms, Kanye couldn't remember singing the chorus line "hello, my only one". Realising that 'only one' was the original meaning of the name Kanye, he became convinced the words had come to him from a spiritual plane.

"My mom was singing to me, and through me to my daughter," he said. The song fell into place; it even resembled McCartney's own ode to his departed mother, 'Let It Be'.

Gradually, Kanye fashioned the lyric around this message he felt he'd received from the other side. "As I lay me down to sleep, I hear her talk to me," he sang, going on to imagine Donda talking to God and being told "he said he sent you an angel... you asked for one and you got two". Expressing her deep pride at "the man you always knew you could be", she offered him words of advice – "You're not perfect but you're not your mistakes… the good outweighs the bad even on your worst day" – and promised they'd meet again in the afterlife. It was, perhaps, the most moving lyric of Kanye's career.

As 2015 began, promising a new album and a tour⋆, Kanye really was the man he always knew he could be. He was writing with the most legendary artist on the planet, sitting on the most hotly anticipated album of the year and set to receive the Visionary Award at the BETs in February. The award panel described Kanye as "a multifaceted trailblazer and pioneer", exactly what West himself had been saying all along.

And – as the world was coming round to thinking – even at his most immodest, he was often right.

⋆ A VIP package of front row tickets for Kanye's 2015 North American tour was listed as a prize at Rihanna's Diamond Ball Auction.

Acknowledgements & Sources

Thanks, once more, to David Barraclough and Chris Charlesworth at Omnibus for their understanding and patience, to my agent, Isabel Atherton, at Creative Authors and to my wife, Jane, for her endless support.

Sources

New York Times, June 11, 2013, Jon Caramanica
Raising Kanye, Pocket Books, 2007, Donda West
Interview, February 2014, Steve McQueen
Sabotage Times, RedEye, 2004, Chris Campion
Chicago Tribune, 2004
Billboard, February 5, 2014, Erika Ramirez
Clash, 2008, Adam Park
Vibe, April 2004, Noah Callahan-Bever
Daily Telegraph, Chris Campion
Details, 2009, Ivan Solotaroff
MTV, Kanplicated, Shaheem Reid
The Oklahoman, CBS, February 2, 2013, George Lang
Themostaccess.com

Complex, February 6, 2012, Insanul Ahmed

Complex, May 14, 2013, Al Shipley

The Irish Times, November 2004

Complex, February 10, 2014, Insanul Ahmed

RedefineHipHop

Hot 97, June 12, 2013

Time, August 21, 2005, Josh Tyrangiel

MTV.com, All Eyes On Kanye West, August 18, 2005, Sway Calloway

Shaheem Reid, September 2, 2005

XXL , October 2009, Rob Markman

Planet Ill, Prodigy: An Infamous Walk Down Memory Lane, Ipopped Off, January 26, 2010

Chicago Tribune, February 11, 2004, Greg Kot

MTV, Kanye Recovering, 2004, Shaheem Reid

Live Wire, April 11, 2004, Billy Johnson Jr

Ebony, April 2006, Kimberley Davis

AXS Entertainment, January 31, 2012, Dee Windt

Jonathan Ross Show, January 12, 2013

XXL, March 2003

SOHH,com, November 28, 2005, Janee Bolden

MTV News, December 5, 2005, Corey Moss

PopMatters, March 5, 2004, Dave Heaton

Allmusic, 2004, Andy Kellman

The New York Times, February 9, 2004, Kelefa Sanneh

Vibe, October 16, 2003, Dan Frosch

Sabotage Times, November 29, 2013, Chris Campion

Vibe, April 2004, Noah Callahan-Bever

The A.V. Club, Nathan Rabin

The Village Voice, March 9, 2004

Entertainment Weekly, Michael Endelman

The Boombox, February 10, 2014, Sowmya Krishnamurthy

Details, Ivan Solotaroff

MTV, August 25, 2005, Shaheem Reid

PopMatters, March 5, 2004, Dave Heaton

Stylus, February 16, 2004, Josh Love

XXL, 2005

MTV.com, August 18, 2005, Sway Calloway

Complex, September 26, 2012, Benjamin Chesna

MTV2, The Making Of *Late Registration*, 2005

The Irish Times, November 2004

Entertainment Weekly, 2004

MTV News, All Eyes On Kanye West, August 18, 2005, Sway Calloway

MTV, October 20, 2005, Cory Moss

MTV, June 16, 2005, Abbey Goodman

MTV2, The Making Of *Late Registration*, 2005

MTV.com, December 8, 2005, Rodrigo Perez

Rolling Stone, August 20, 2007, Austin Scaggs

Abbey Goodman, June 16, 2005

MTV.com, December 8, 2005, Rodrigo Perez

Rolling Stone, 2004

Rolling Stone, September 8, 2005, Rob Sheffield

Entertainment Weekly, August 29, 2005, David Browne

Spin, August 30, 2005, Jon Caramanica

Sunday Mail, Australia, September 16, 2007, Nui Te Koha

Reuters, August 6 2007, Hillary Crosley

Playboy, August 30, 2005

Moviefone

Rolling Stone, December 15, 2005, Austin Scaggs

Australia Sunday Mail, September 16 2007, Nui Te Koha

Nightline, ABC News, September 24, 2007, Terry Moran

Baltimore Sun blogs, September 2007, Katy O'Donnell

The Today Show, Matt Lauer, 2010

Ebony, Kimberley Davis, April 2005

Blender, Sept 2005, Chris Norris

Time Out, September 14, 2005, Alex Raymer

MTV, Kanye West's Mother On Parenting And More, Sway Calloway

MTV News, December 6, 2005, Corey Moss

PopMatters, August 29, 2005, Jozen Cummings

The New York Times, December 18, 2005, Jon Caramanica

Teen Diaries, October 9, 2007, Aeshia DeVore

Popworld, July 8, 2007

Associated Press, December 12, 2006, Mitch Stacy

Rolling Stone, Austin Scaggs, September 20, 2007

MTV, September 10, 2007, James Montgomery

Associated Press Worldstream, Kanye West Says, August 21, 2007

Associated Press, November 3, 2006

Spin, January 2008, John McAlley

The Ellen DeGeneres Show, September 14, 2007

The Sydney Morning Herald, August 11, 2007, Eric Danton

RWD, August 15, 2007, Rajveer Kathwadia

MTV, Shaheem Reid, May 11 2007

Melbourne Herald Sun, August 3, 2008, Nui Te Koha

Concreteloop.com

MTV, Shaheem Reid, September 5 2007

MTV, Shaheem Reid, June 20 2007

Billboard, August 14, 2007, Jonathan Cohen

Baller Status, August 8, 2007

BBC News, August 11, 2007

MTV, July 23, 2007, Shaheem Reid

USA Today, September 9, 2007, Steve Jones

Nightline, ABC News, September 24, 2007

MTV, Mixtape Mondays, Shaheem Reid

Entertainment Weekly, September 28, 2007, Simon Vozick-Levinson

Complex, October 16, 2012, Ross Scarano

Popworld, July 8, 2007

Rapgenius.com

AllMusic, Andy Kellman

Stylus, Jayson Greene

Rolling Stone, Nathan Brackett

Time, June 12, 2007, Josh Tyrangiel

Los Angeles Times, Ann Powers

Slant, Eric Henderson

ABC Newsline, Home With Kanye West, September 24, 2007, Terry Moran

DJbooth.net, September 3, 2007

MTV, June 20, 2007, Shaheem Reid

Chicago Tribune, November 13, 2007

CNN statement

Associated Press Worldstream, November 21, 2007, Nekesa Mumbi Moody

Associated Press, November 28, 2007

People.com, April 21, 2008

MTV News, April 21, 2008

In Touch Weekly, April 2012

Vibe, June 7, 2010, Tracy Garraud

MTV.com, July 28, 2008, Jocelyn Vena

Rap-Up

Rolling Stone, October 15, 2008, Steve Appleford

MTV, November 21, 2008, Shaheem Reid

The Sunday Times, November 23, 2008, Dan Cairns

USA Today, November 25, 2008, Steve Jones

Village Voice, November 26, 2008, Tom Breihan

New York Times, November 25 2008, Jon Caramanica

Daily Mail, January 4, 2011

Daily Mail, January 23, 2010

ABC, The View, 2009

Complex, November 22, 2010, Noah Callahan-Bever

Daily Mail, September 23, 2009

Slate, July 2010, Johan Weiner

Vulture, November 24, 2010, Logan Hill

Pitchfork, August 13, 2010, Ryan Dombal

Pitchfork, June 13, 2011, Grayson Currin

Spin, June 29, 2011, David Bevan

Rolling Stone, August 7, 2012, David Peisner

Complex, December 23, 2011, Andrew Barber

Complex, March 18, 2012, Brad Wete

MTV, October 27, 2010, Steven Roberts

SOHH, August 1, 2010, Cyrus Langhorne

Power 105.1

MTV, November 22, 2010, Steven Roberts

MTV, October 11, 2010, James Montgomery
MTV, September 27, 2010, Shaheem Reid
RapRadar, October 20, 2010, Big Homie
PushaT.com, November 3, 2010, Joe Lay Pump
Vibe, September 15, 2010
MTV, November 10, 2010, Jayson Rodriguez
Complex, November 22, 2010, Noah Callahan-Bever
Star
92.3 Now
XXL, October 16, 2010, Kanye West
Los Angeles Times, November 30, 2011, Randall Roberts
The Independent, November 19, 2010, Andy Gill
Los Angeles Times, November 23, 2010, Ann Powers
Rolling Stone, November 25, 2010, Rob Sheffield
Grazia Daily, 2011
Daily Mail, October 5 2011
The Sun, June 2, 2011, Simon Cosyns
Esquire, July 2011
Dazed And Confused, July 28, 2011
The Atlantic, January 3, 2011, Ta-Nehisi Coates
Vancouver Sun, January 15, 2011, Daphne Bramham
Hiphop DX, February 9 2012, Sryon
Time, August 9 2011, Claire Suddath
Andy Kellman, August 18 2011
Rolling Stone, August 11 2011, Jody Rosen
Radar website
W, June 19, 2013, Christopher Bagley
Power 106, Big Boi
Los Angeles Times, May 24, 2012
Radio One, September 23, 2013, Zane Lowe
Hip-Hop Wired, September 27, 2012, Latifah Muhammad
Hip-Hop Wired, October 16, 2012, Kazeem Famuyide
Hot 97, Juan Epstein, 2013
Wired, September 20, 2012, Spencer Ackerman
Spin, September 17, 2012, Christopher Weingarten

The A.V. Club, September 25, 2012, Nathan Rabin
The Atlantic, 2012, David Samuels
Daily Mail, June 25, 2012
Daily Mail, August 12, 2012, Lizzie Smith
XXL, August 8, 2012, Mlelinwalla
New York, August 20, 2012
The View, 2012
Tatler, November 2012
New York Daily News, February 24, 2013, Hugo Daniel, Douglas Feiden
Pitchfork, June 24, 2013, Ryan Dombal
Rolling Stone, December 5, 2013
Fabulous, May 2013
Vogue Hommes International, 2011
The Wall Street Journal, June 14, 2013, John Jurgensen
Newsweek, June 27, 2013, Andrew Romano
Rolling Stone, April 30, 2014, Kory Grow
Complex, February 27, 2014, Joe La Puma
Pitchfork, February 4, 2014, Carrie Battan
Vibe, October 31, 2013, Rishabh Bhavnani
The Guardian, June 11, 2013, Sean Michaels
The Washington Post, June 17, 2013, Chris Richards
Rolling Stone, June 14, 2013, John Dolan
USA Today, June 14, 2013, Steve Jones
New York Times, June 16, 2013, Jon Parales
The A.V. Club, June 17, 2013, Evan Rytlewski
The Talkhouse.com
Hot 97, 2013, Juan Epstein
Daily Mail Online, June 12, 2013, Sarah Bull & Iona Kirkby
People, June 17, Maggie Coughlan
CBS News, August 23, 2013
Kindle Singles, 2013
Stereogum, December 11, 2013, Chris DeVille
CNN, March 17, 2014, Alan Duke
In The Morning, Sway Galloway
Hot 97, Angie Martinez

Jimmy Kimmel, October 9, 2013
Power 105.1, November 26, 2013
Daily Mail, June 19, 2014
Daily Mail, May 25, 2014, Georgia Hart
La Nazione, 2014
Daily Mail, June 17, 2014, Fay Strang
Daily Mail, August 11, 2014, Tamara Abraham
NME.com, December 9, 2014